InsidersChoice to MCP/MCSE Exam 70-293 Windows 2003 Server Certification:

Planning and Maintaining a Microsoft Windows Server 2003 Network Infrastructure

Second Edition

CD-ROM practice exam provided by BeachFront Quizzer, Inc.

Authors:

Patrick Simpson, MCT, MCSE
with the
TRP Author Certification Success Team

Published by

TotalRecall Publications, Inc.
1103 Middlecreek
Friendswood, TX 77546
281-992-3131

NOTE: THIS IS BOOK IS GUARANTEED:
See details at www.TotalRecallPress.com

TotalRecall Publications, Inc.

This Book is Sponsored by Beachfront Quizzer, Inc.

Printed in United States of America
Printed and bound by Data Duplicators of Houston Texas
Printed and bound by Lightning Source, Inc. in the USA and UK
Printed and bound by BookSurge, Inc in the USA and around the world

Paper Back
ISBN: 1-59095-044-5
UPC: 6-43977-04293-4

eBook
ISBN 1-59095-710-5
UPC 6-43977-64293-6

Worldwide eBook publication and distribution by:

The sponsoring editor is Bruce Moran and the production supervisor is Corby R. Tate.

This book is dedicated to my wife Joy, and my children Lucas, Bethany and Alexander, for their patience and support. Thanks also to Bruce for the encouragement and support. Lastly, but mostly, thanks be to God, from Whom all gifts proceed.

Patrick Simpson

InsidersChoice™ to MCP™/MCSE™ Exam 70-293 Windows 2003 Server Certification:

Planning and Maintaining a Microsoft® Windows Server 2003 Network Infrastructure

Second Edition

About the Author

Patrick Simpson

Patrick Simpson is an MCSE, MCT, MCNE, CNI, CCNA, among other things. He has taught and worked and written in the IT field for the past 12 years. He has been married for 20 years and has three children. In his spare time, he enjoys riding centuries with his wife Joy and playing his Martin guitar.

Pat is currently working in the technical consulting/education field and a contract Instructor in Green Bay, WI.

The TRP Author Certification Success Team

Alan Grayson

Alan Grayson has a Masters Degree in Systems Management, is a Microsoft Certified Trainer, a Microsoft Certified Systems Engineer and Microsoft Database Administrator and also holds a dozen other certifications.

David [Darkcat] Smith

David "Darkcat" Smith is a long time MCSE and trainer who has been working in the IT field for over 10 years. He specializes in directory services design and administration, though he also enjoys planning and implementing large scale rollouts.

Tom McCarty

Tom McCarty is currently an independent trainer, network engineer and consultant. He has worked in the computers and networking environment for 20 years as an administrator, end user support and instructor. Tom has the following certifications; MCSE on Windows NT 4.0, MCP+I, MCDBA, MCT on Windows 2000, and MCSA on Windows Server 2003. Along the way he has gained experience in Exchange 5.5 to 2000 upgrades, SMS 2.0 and NT to Active Directory migrations. In addition to Microsoft certification Ton holds CompTIA A+, Network+ and IT Project+ certifications. I always enjoy seeing the light come on in someone's face when they finally nail down something new.

Jada Brock-Soldavini

Jada Brock-Soldavini lives in suburban Atlanta and works for the State of Georgia as a Network Services Administrator. She has co-authored or contributed to other numerous works pertaining to Microsoft Windows technologies. She has an A.S. degree in Computer Information Systems and has been in the Information Technology industry for seven years. She is also married to Michael and the mother of three children Alyssa, Daniel and Christian. In her spare time she enjoys cooking, writing and reading anything that pertains to Network and Security technology.

Deborah and Patrick Timmons

Deborah Timmons is a Microsoft Certified Trainer and Microsoft Certified Systems Engineer. She came into the Microsoft technical field after six years in the adaptive technology field, providing technology and training for persons with disabilities. She is the President and co-owner of Integrator Systems Inc.

Patrick Timmons is a Microsoft Certified Systems Engineer + Internet. He has been working in the IT industry for approximately 15 years, specializing in network engineering and has recently completed his Bachelor of Science, Major in Computer Science. He is currently the CEO of Integrator Systems Inc., a company based in Charlottetown, Prince Edward Island, Canada.

Patrick and Deborah have four children--Lauren, Alexander, James and Katherine who take up a lot of their rare spare time.

About the Book

As an Microsoft Certified Trainer and practicing IT professional, I drew on my background to design this study guide specifically to help you *pass* the MCP/MCSE: Planning and Maintaining a Microsoft Windows Server 2003 Network Infrastructure Exam 70-293.

Part of the TotalRecall IT Certification Success System, this comprehensive study manual provides detailed information about each exam topic, includes numerous practical tips, and cites a wealth of useful websites, articles and other learning aids found in no other book. Since it also offers lots of real-world material, we know you will continue to reach for this handy reference when tackling challenges on the job.

Each chapter includes a pre- and post-assessment quiz to measure your comprehension of each exam topic. Chapter summaries reinforce key points. The large glossary at the end of the book provides a review of essential exam-related terms and concepts that will prove invaluable just before taking the exam. Helpful tips and time management techniques will alleviate pre-exam jitters and put you in control.

And we offer another exclusive—a copy of the popular BeachFront Quizzer CD with integrated eBook. The CD test engine includes practice exams drawn from a base of over 300 questions, along with detailed explanations linked to related chapters in an eBook version of this manual. Many explanations also link to additional resources, such as web sites, articles, etc. The adaptive nature of the BeachFront Quizzer software is that it keeps generating types of questions that you find difficult to answer until they are no longer hard for you. By focusing on your rough spots, we will get you certified fast—or get money back!

Introduction

Use this "Certification Success System" to pass the MCP/MCSE: Planning and Maintaining a Microsoft Windows Server 2003 Network Infrastructure Exam 70-293. This unbeatable package of comprehensive study manual and CD-ROM test engine with integrated eBook is literally guaranteed to help you pass the exam your first time or your money back! Two Microsoft Certified Trainers offer you a very readable combination of 300+ practice questions, "geekie" details, and serious research. Exclusive features include: comprehensive information about all core exam topics with a pre- and post-assessment quiz for each; figures, diagrams, and photos in abundance; chapter summaries to reinforce key concepts and procedures; helpful tips and time management techniques for test taking; lists of useful websites, articles and other learning aids; a glossary of 600 computer, IT, and telecommunications terms; and an exclusive BeachFront Quizzer Self-Help and Interactive Study Aid CD-ROM. This popular test engine generates randomized practice exams drawn from a base of 300+ questions, with answers conveniently linked to relevant chapters in an eBook version of this manual. Our BeachFront Quizzer software is adaptive—it keeps generating the types of questions you find difficult to answer until they become a snap. By focusing on your rough spots, we'll get you certified fast the first time—or get money back! See our web site www.totalrecallpress.com for details.

Patrick Simpson

A Quick overview of the book chapters:

Table of Contents

Chapter 3: Review Answers 183

Examination 70-293 Information

The Exam 70-293 went live August 28, 2003.

http://www.microsoft.com/traincert/exams/70-293.asp

Audience Profile

The Microsoft Certified Systems Engineer (MCSE) on Windows Server™ 2003 credential is intended for IT professionals who work in the typically complex computing environment of medium to large companies. An MCSE candidate should have 12 months of experience implementing and administering a network operating systems in environments that have the following characteristics:

- 250 to 5,000 or more users
- Three or more physical locations
- Three or more domain controllers
- Network services and resources such as messaging, database, file and print, proxy server, firewall, Internet, intranet, remote access, and client computer management
- Connectivity requirements such as connecting branch offices and individual users in remote locations to the corporate network and connecting corporate networks to the Internet
- Implementing and administering a desktop operating system
- Designing a network infrastructure

Credit Toward Certification

When you pass the Managing and Maintaining a Microsoft® Windows® Server 2003 Environment exam, you achieve Microsoft Certified Professional (MCP) status. You also earn credit toward the following certifications:

- **Core** credit toward Microsoft Certified Systems Engineer (MCSE) on Microsoft Windows Server 2003 certification
- **Elective** credit toward Microsoft Certified Database Administrator (MCDBA) on Microsoft SQL Server 2000 certification

Preparation Tools and Resources

We make a wealth of preparation tools and resources available to you, including courses, books, practice tests, and Microsoft Web sites. When you are ready to prepare for this exam, here's where you should start.

Instructor-led Courses for This Exam:

- Course 2278: Planning and Maintaining a Microsoft Windows Server 2003 Network Infrastructure

Microsoft Press Self-Paced Training Products

- MCSE Self-Paced Training Kit (Exam 70-293): Planning and Maintaining a Microsoft Windows Server 2003 Network Infrastructure
- MCSE Self-Paced Training Kit: Microsoft Windows Server 2003 Core Requirements, Exams 70-290, 70-291, 70-293, 70-294

TotalRecall Self-Paced Training Products

Examination 70-293

- **Planning and Maintaining a Microsoft Windows Server 2003 Network Infrastructure**

Microsoft Online Resources

- TechNet: Designed for IT professionals, this site includes How-tos, best practices, downloads, technical chats, and much more.
- MSDN: The Microsoft Developer Network (MSDN) is a reference for developers, featuring code samples, technical articles, newsgroups, chats, and more.
- Training & Certification Newsgroups: A newsgroup exists for every Microsoft certification. By participating in the ongoing dialogue, you take advantage of a unique opportunity to exchange ideas with and ask questions of others, including more than 750 Microsoft Most Valuable Professionals (MVPs) worldwide.

Skills Being Measured

This certification exam measures your ability to manage and maintain a Microsoft Windows Server 2003 environment. Before taking the exam, you should be proficient in the job skills listed in the chapters of this book. The skills shows which topics may help you reach competency in the skills being tested in the real exam.

Planning and Implementing Server Roles and Server Security

The objective of this chapter is to provide the reader with an understanding of the following:

Configure security for servers that are assigned specific roles.

Plan a secure baseline installation.

- **Plan a strategy to enforce system default security settings on new systems.**
- **Identify client operating system default security settings.**
- **Identify all server operating system default security settings.**

Plan security for servers that are assigned specific roles. Roles might include domain controllers, Web servers, database servers, and mail servers.

- **Deploy the security configuration for servers that are assigned specific roles.**
- **Create custom security templates based on server roles.**

Evaluate and select the operating system to install on computers in an enterprise.

- **Identify the minimum configuration to satisfy security requirements.**

Chapter 1: Server Roles & Server Security

Introduction:

Inevitably your server is being installed to play a role in the network, that is, to provide some particular service or services. From domain controller to file server, from application server to DNS to web server, the roles create different issues and call for different security measures. The initial tool used for configuration is the Configure Your Server Wizard, which we will look at first. Then we will look at the use of the Manage Your Server Wizard for on-going configuration and management, and the Security Configuration Manager tool for more detailed tuning and for automation of security settings throughout the Active Directory forest.

Our main focus in this chapter will be on the tools for configuring server settings, leaving the issues detailed in Microsoft's best practices for other discussions. This is not meant to suggest that the other issues are less important, they are simply not our focus at this point.

Getting Ready Questions

1. What is the primary tool used to configure a Windows 2003 server to a role such as file server or domain controller?

2. What are the incremental security settings provided by Microsoft in the form of .inf files called?

3. What Microsoft tool can be used to apply additional security settings to a group of computers through a linked GPO?

4. As the administrator of a company, you have a non-certified application that users are unable to run on Windows XP Professional computers. What can be done to allow them to run this application?

5. Where in a GPO can the security settings be found?

Getting Ready Answers

1. The primary tool for configuring a Windows 2003 server for a role is the Manage Your Server Wizard, which will allow the administrator to then launch the Configure Your Server Wizard to configure the server for a specific role.

2. Microsoft provides security templates, which are pre-defined groupings of security settings, in the form of .inf files for application to computers.

3. Security templates can be imported into GPOs using the Group Policy MMC.

4. Microsoft supplies a template called compatws.inf, which relaxes the local security settings on the client computer to allow them to run non-certified applications.

5. In a GPO, security settings are found under Computer Configuration|Windows Settings|Security Settings.

In the simplest sense, configuring a newly installed server begins after installation when the Manage Your Server Wizard starts automatically, asking you to choose the role this server will play in the network. Choosing Add or Remove a Role then launches the Configure Your Server Wizard to begin the configuration process.

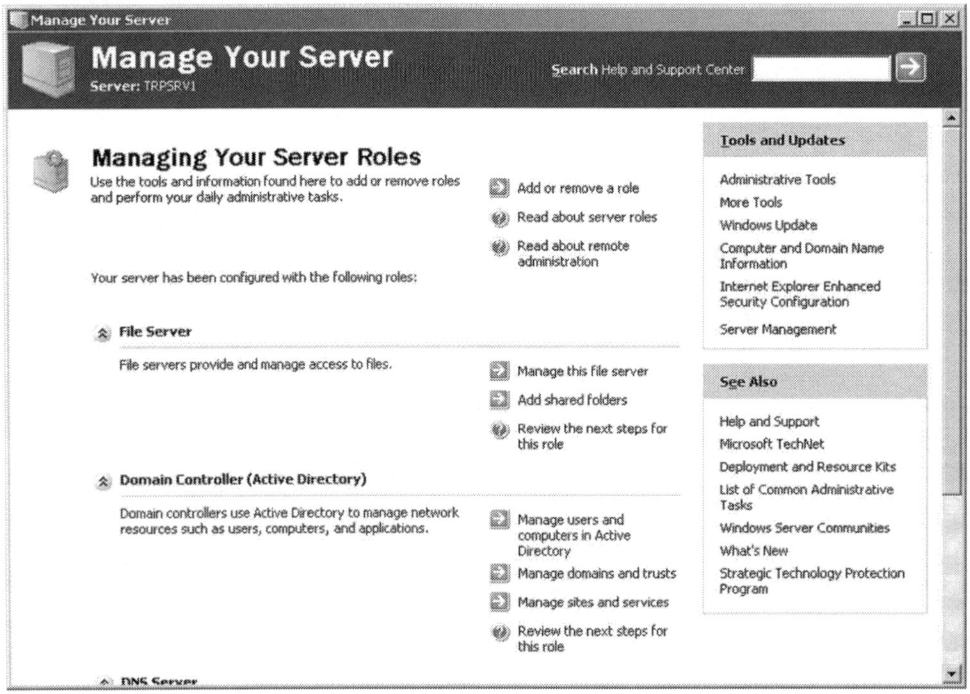

Figure 1—1: Manage Your Server Wizard

1.1 Configure security for servers that are assigned specific roles.

Microsoft recommends the use of the Configure Your Server Wizard to configure your server to fulfill a specific role. As a matter of fact, upon completion of the initial installation of Windows 2003, the Manage Your Server Wizard automatically launches and gives you the opportunity to begin the configuration process using the Configure Your Server Wizard. Whether your Windows 2003 server will be a domain controller, a DNS server, a DHCP server, or many of the other roles possible, all may be initially configured using this wizard.

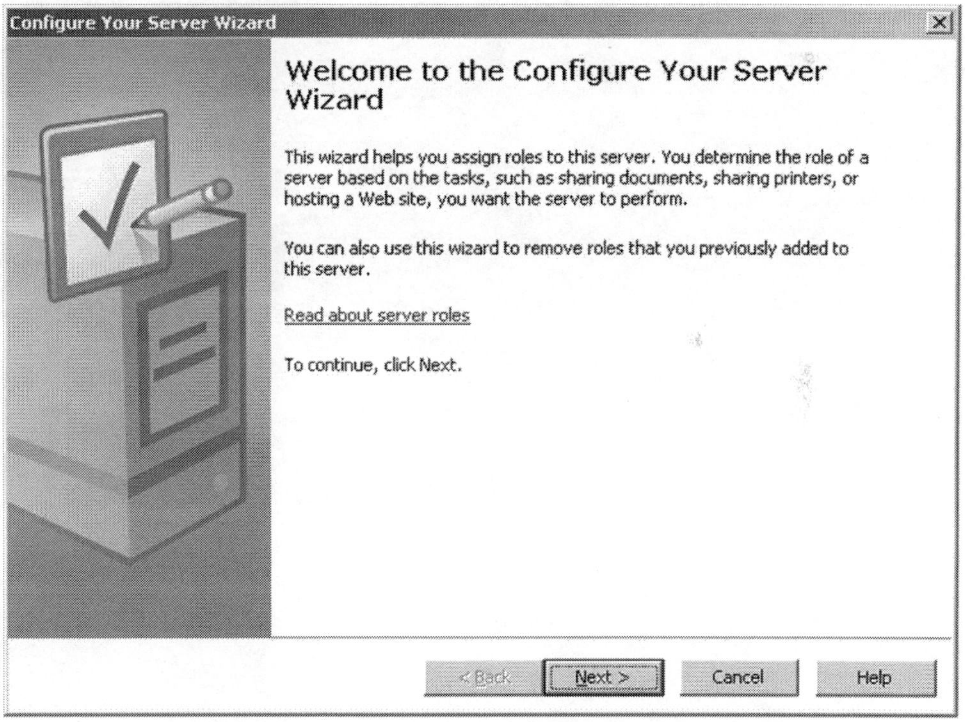

Figure 1—2: Configure Your Server Wizard

The wizard can be also launched from Administrative Tools, and begins by examining your server configuration. It will determine for which roles the server is already configured, and will also issue warnings about possible misconfiguration of the server. Upon examination, a list of server roles is shown, along with the current status of your server.

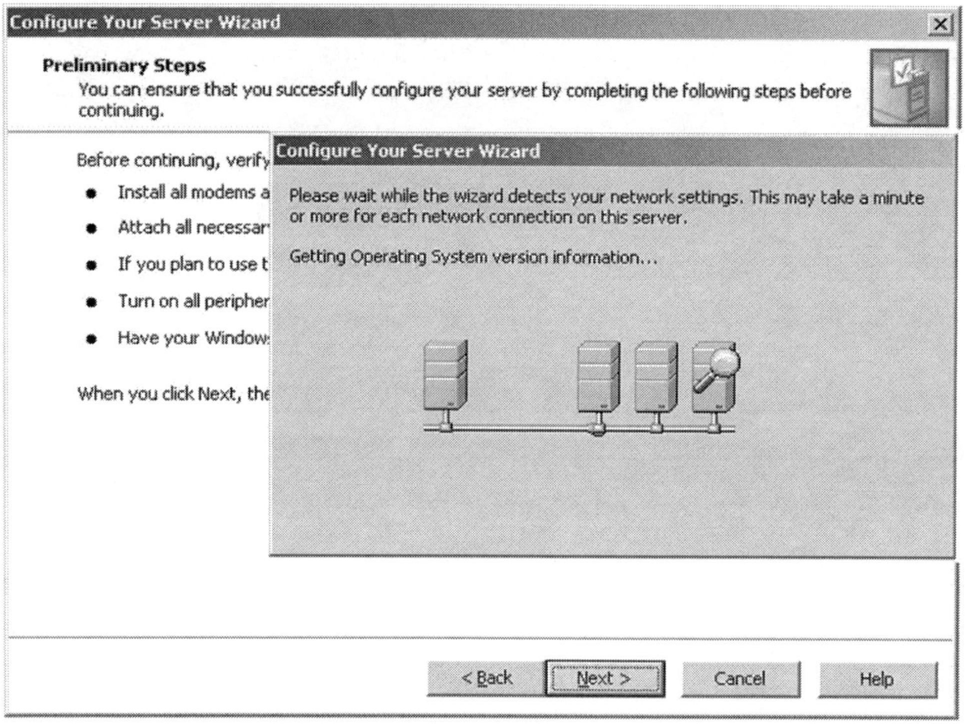

Figure 1—3: Role Detection in Configure Your Server Wizard

Once the detection process is done, a list of server roles is shown. The roles for which this server is configured are identified with a "Yes" next to the role. Additional roles can be added by simply selecting them from the window and choosing Next. Roles already configured can be removed by highlighting them in the window and choosing Next.

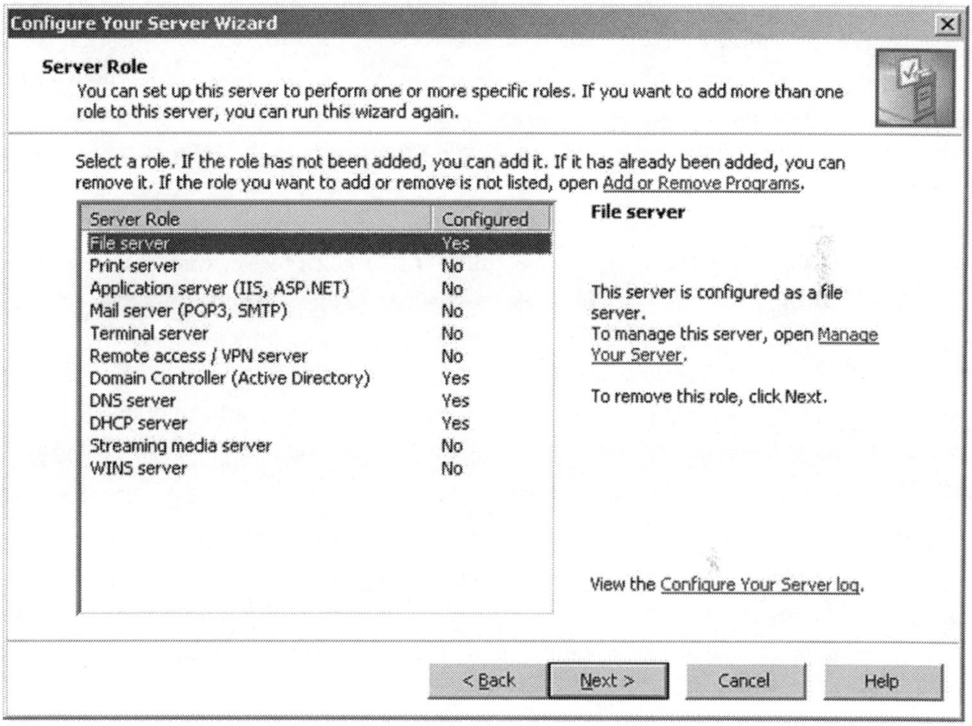

Figure 1—4: List of Roles in the Configure Your Server Wizard

Once a role is selected, the Configure Your Server Wizard will then walk you through the appropriate questions/decisions for the role that was chosen, and apply the security settings to your server necessary for that role based upon the answers given. Additional security configuration may be done later using the Manage Your Server Wizard.

1.2 Plan a secure baseline installation

Before configuring security on Windows 2003 servers or workstations, Microsoft recommends a checklist of activities that should be completed. The first step is to use Microsoft's security best practices, beginning with physically securing the server or servers (yes that means the old-fashioned, locked server room). Then the best practices detail several other steps, including identifying the various security groups both in the Active Directory and at the individual workstations. Particular focus is stressed on the rights for Domain Admin and Enterprise Admin groups, where they can install software, and who can link Group Policy objects in the forest. At the workstation the issue is whether users should have rights to install software, add drivers, etc. Best practices encompasses the use of NTFS and access control lists (ACL) for securing particular files, strong passwords and encryption of passwords using the utility syskey, and recommendations for the use of Software Update Services to ensure that all of the security patches in the network are up to date. Once a secure machine has been defined, then a strategy can be employed to ensure the secure settings will be applied. The main tools for this will be the Security Configuration Manager and Group Policy Objects in Active Directory.

Newly installed or upgraded Windows 2003 servers and workstations use the setup.inf security template to create the security settings for the installation. The settings can then be modified to increase the level of security for the computer. The most effective method for applying additional security settings once the installation has been completed is to link a Group Policy Object to the container in which the computer (or server) object resides, and have the settings applied through the GPO.

1.2.1 Plan a strategy to enforce system default security settings on new systems

All computers in a Windows 2003 network have Active Directory computer objects that can be used to further configure the computer settings. Planning the Active Directory structure, so that systems with like security settings needs have their respective computer objects in the same AD containers, facilitates the application of security settings through Group Policy Object configuration. Once the settings have been applied to the GPO, the computers will then have those settings applied to their Local Security Policy either upon restart or manually by running the gpupdate utility.

For example, all Active Directory domains have a Domain Controllers container within which all domain controllers computer objects are placed by default. Linked to this container is the Default Domain Controller Policy, through which the basic security settings for all domain controllers in the domain are set and applied. The Domain Controller Security Policy MMC in Administrative Tools provides a simple interface for configuring security settings in this manner.

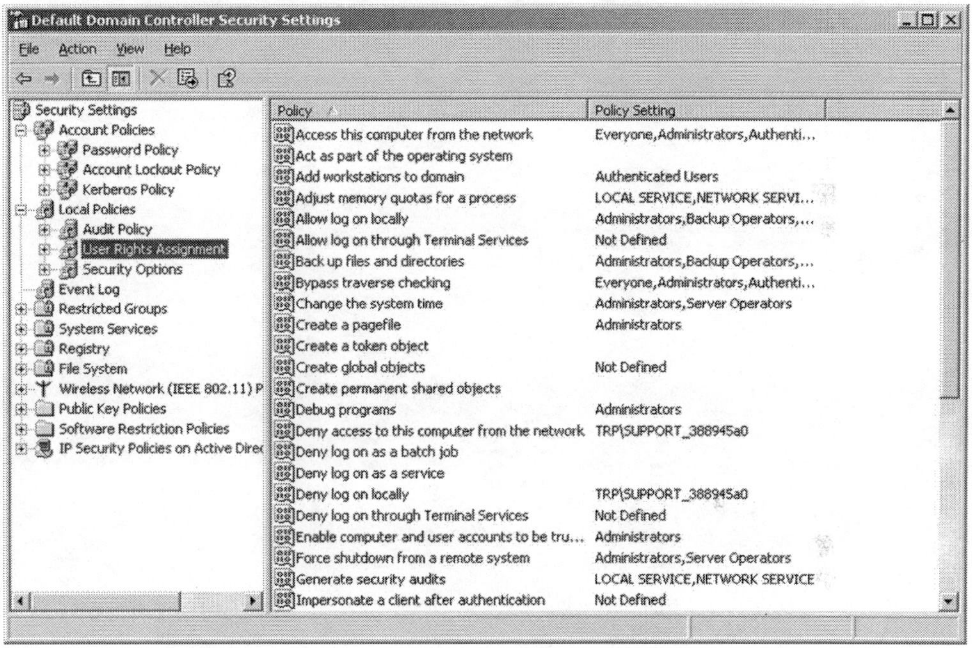

Figure 1—5: Default Domain Controller Security MMC

In a like manner, each GPO has under the Computer Configuration|Windows Settings, a Security Settings node. Right-clicking on the Security Settings node in the left-hand pane and choosing Import Policy opens a browse window into the default directory where the security templates are stored upon installation.

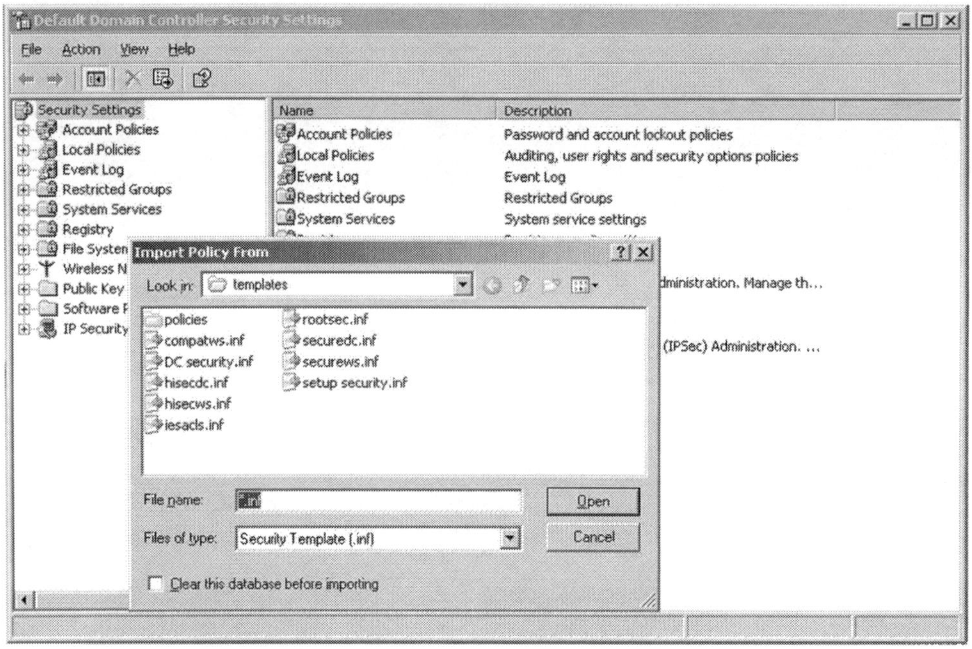

Figure 1—6: Import Policy within Security Settings in a GPO

Shown in the figure above are the default templates that ship and install with Windows 2003 server. Additional templates can be created using the Security Templates MMC snap-in, and saved in this directory for later import into the appropriate GPO. Once the settings have been imported into the GPO, a restart or running gpupdate will cause the settings to be applied. It is important to note that these templates incrementally modify security settings; that is, they are to be used after a server has been "promoted" to a certain role with the Configure Your Server wizard. They are not to be viewed as complete sets of security settings.

1.2.2 Identify client operating system default security settings

Within the security settings on client computers, the most significant area for configuration is the area of User Rights within Local Rights (see Figure 1.1 above). The following table summarizes the default User Rights settings for a Windows XP Professional client.

Policy	Local Setting	Effective Setting
Access this computer from the network	Everyone, Users, Power Users, Backup Operators, Administrators	Everyone, Users, Power Users, Backup Operators, Administrators
Act as part of the operating system		
Add workstations to domain		
Back up files and directories	Backup Operators, Administrators	Backup Operators, Administrators
Bypass traverse checking	Everyone, Users, Power Users, Backup Operators, Administrators	Everyone, Users, Power Users, Backup Operators, Administrators
Change the system time	Power Users, Administrators	Power Users, Administrators
Create a pagefile	Administrators	Administrators
Debug programs	Administrators	Administrators
Deny access to this computer from the network		
Deny logon as a batch job		
Deny logon as a service		
Deny logon locally		
Enable computer and user accounts to be trusted for delegation		
Force shutdown from a remote system	Administrators	Administrators

Policy	Local Setting	Effective Setting
Generate security audits		
Increase quotas	Administrators	Administrators
Increase scheduling priority	Administrators	Administrators
Load and unload device drivers	Administrators	Administrators
Log on as a batch job		
Log on as a service		
Log on locally	Administrators, Backup Operators, Power Users, Users,	Administrators, Backup Operators, Power Users, Users,
Manage auditing and security log	Administrators	Administrators
Modify firmware environment values	Administrators	Administrators
Profile single process	Power Users, Administrators	Power Users, Administrators
Profile system performance	Administrators	Administrators
Remove computer from docking station	Users, Power Users, Administrators	Users, Power Users, Administrators
Restore files and directories	Backup Operators, Administrators	Backup Operators, Administrators
Shut down the system	Users, Power Users, Backup Operators, Administrators	Users, Power Users, Backup Operators, Administrators
Take ownership of files or other objects	Administrators	Administrators

Table 1—1: Default User Rights in Windows XP Professional

1.2.3 Identify all server operating system default security settings.

Server operating system default security settings differ markedly. Of special note, the right to log on locally (which used to be called an interactive logon) is limited to members of the Administrators group. Users cannot log on to a Windows server locally.

Pop Quiz 1.1

Pop Quiz 1.1 Questions

1. Can the "Configure your server" wizard be used to define more than one server role at a time?

2. Is it possible to remove a role using the "Configure your server" wizard?

3. What is the recommended method for configuring security on a computer that is a member of a domain?

4. Will security settings in a GPO linked to the default domain controller's container be applied to all accounts in a domain?

5. Which built-in group has the right to take ownership of files and other objects by default?

Pop Quiz 1.1 Answers

1. No – you may only select one of the roles shown.

2. Absolutely! You may either add a role or remove a role using the "Configure your server" wizard.

3. In basic terms, use GPOs linked to OUs or other containers. How you configure the GPO is up to you, but it is good to start with one of the pre-defined security templates and make adjustments from there.

4. No, actually. GPOs affect the objects in the container where they are linked, and may be inherited by child objects in child containers as well. User accounts are not normally placed in the domain controller's container, so except in very unusual cases the security settings that apply to the domain controller's container will not affect user accounts in the domain.

5. Only the administrators group has this privilege. Remember, however, that having ownership does not itself confer any resource access permissions. It does, however, allow the owner to set those resource access permissions.

1.3 Plan security for servers that are assigned specific roles

As we will see, planning security for servers assigned the domain controller role is straightforward. Security is automatically applied when you promote a server to domain controller by the Configure Your Server Wizard and by the placement of the computer object in the Domain Controllers container in the domain, where security settings have already been applied to the Default Domain Controller Policy. Otherwise, servers can take on many different roles in the network, each of which has different security requirements. As discussed earlier, the settings are best applied by linking a GPO to a container in Active Directory and "pushing" the settings from the GPO to the Windows 2003 servers. This also presumes that Active Directory is organized in a manner that allows for the efficient use of GPOs for application of security settings; that is, containers that contain all of the domain controllers, containers that contain all of the DNS server, etc.

1.3.1 Roles might include:

Domain Controllers

As a Windows 2003 server runs the Active Directory Installation Wizard, the computer object that represents the server is removed from the container it was originally installed into and placed in the appropriate Domain Controllers container in the domain into which it is added. As mentioned above, the Default Domain Controller Policy then applies the default security settings for a domain controller. The domain controller security settings of special note are in the area of Account Policies and User Rights. Domain-wide logon policies are set here and cannot be changed elsewhere in the domain.

1.3.1.2 Web Servers

Windows 2003 servers run Internet Information Server (IIS) when they are deployed as web servers. These servers have different security requirements than almost all other roles. If they are deployed as intranet web servers, then they are not much more than file servers for http clients in the internal network. However, if they are exposed to external access, as in Internet web servers, or if they are deployed in a screened subnet and serve as web servers for Microsoft Exchange Outlook Web Access, then the potential for intrusion attempts is much higher. At a minimum, the latter deployment of web servers should only occur in screen subnets, that is, behind firewall architecture. Even then, these web servers should not also be domain controllers, because of the potential for exposure and compromise of the AD data.

1.3.1.3 Database Servers

Database servers will most often be running Microsoft SQL Server 2000. In most settings, these deployments occur within well-secured network environments, minimizing the risk of external threats. These servers could be "hardened" using the secure or insecure templates.

1.3.1.4 Mail Servers

Microsoft Exchange would be the typical application that you would use to turn your Windows 2003 server into a mail server. Exchange servers sometimes live in screened subnets, but most often can be found securely within a corporate network, behind solid perimeter firewall architecture. Generally speaking, Exchange servers should also not host Active Directory. That is, they should not also have the role of domain controller.

1.3.2 Deploy the security configuration for servers that are assigned specific roles

In most situations, default security settings are applied to Windows 2003 servers as they take on their different roles. In larger network environments, containers can be created for the different roles and Group Policy Object linked to the containers to apply specific security settings to those servers. For instance, a container could be created named Exchange Servers and all of the computer objects representing the Exchange servers placed in that container. Then a Group Policy Object can be created and linked to the Exchange Servers container. A security policy template can be created and the imported into the GPO, as shown earlier, to apply those settings to all of the Exchange servers.

1.3.3 Create custom security templates based on server roles

To create the security policy template noted in the previous section, you just need to run the Security Configuration and Analysis MMC on a server fulfilling a role, and save the security settings as a template, as shown in Figure 1-7 below. The template will be saved with the default templates as an .inf file and can then be imported into the appropriate GPO later for application.

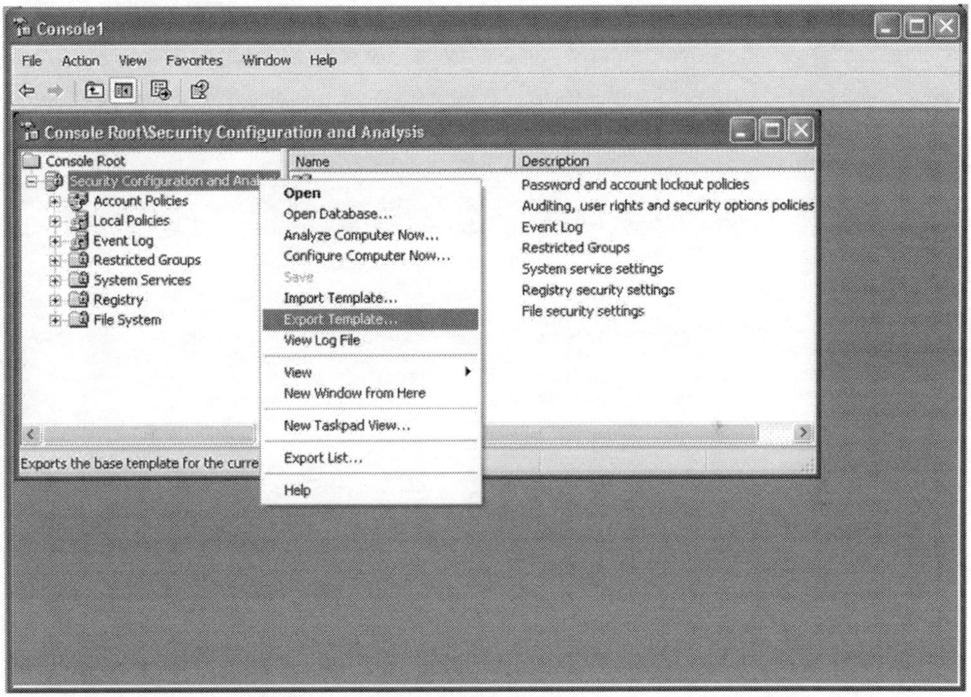

Figure 1—7: Exporting Security Settings

1.4 Evaluate and select the operating system to install on computers in an enterprise

1.4.4 Identify the minimum configuration to satisfy security requirements

The Security Configuration and Analysis MMC can be used to compare the security settings of a Windows computer with the settings in each of the default templates. The comparison process yields an output (see Figure 1-8) that notes differences between the settings on the Windows computer and the template by marking those settings with a red "X". Settings that will not change are shown with a green check mark. This allows you to easily identify the security settings differences and make the appropriate adjustments, based upon your security planning.

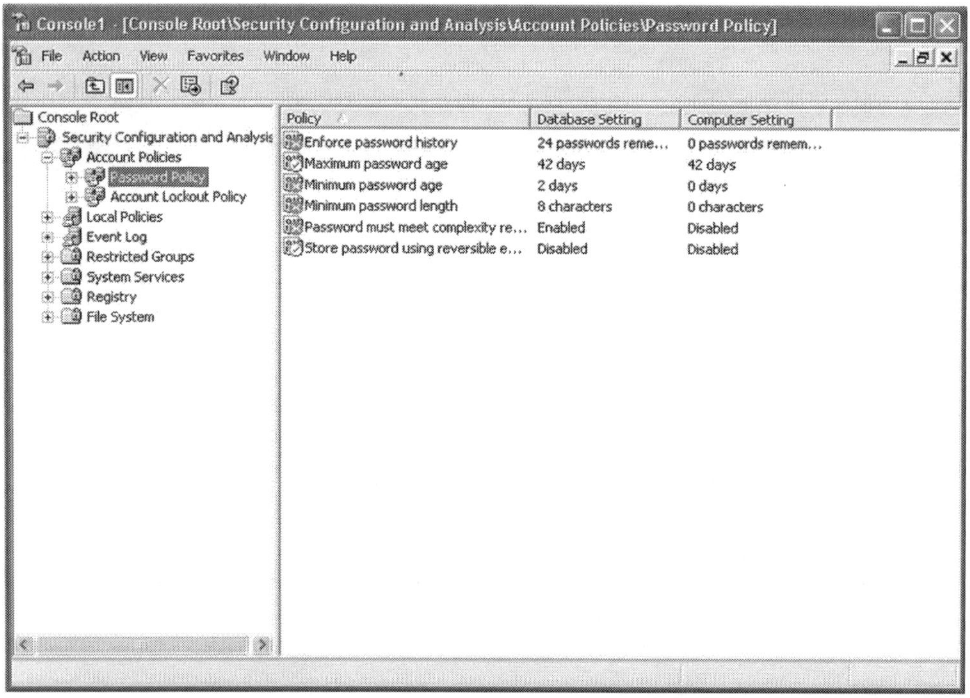

Figure 1—8: Comparing Security Settings Using Security Configuration and Analysis

Chapter 1: Review Questions

1. What would result from moving a GPO to the top of the list in a security template?
    A. It would be applied last
    B. It would not be overridden
    C. It would be applied first
    D. It would be overridden

---

2. You are the administrator of a Windows 2003 domain that contains Windows 2000 Professional computers. Which of the following security templates is used on Windows 2000 Professional computers and contains default settings for NTFS permissions, registry permissions, and default user rights?
    A. The Defltwk.inf security template
    B. The Basicwk.inf security template
    C. The Def.inf security template
    D. The Bas.inf security template

3. You have a Windows 2003 domain with OUs for your domain controllers (the DC OU), your other servers (the SRV OU), and workstations (the WS OU. The SRV OU contain child OUs for each specific server role in the domain. What should you do to apply a security template to the servers that aren't domain controllers with specific roles?

   A. Create a GPO and link it the SRV OU

   B. Import the security template to the GPO.

   C. Import the role specific security template to each role specific OU.

   D. Create a GPO and link it the domain

   E. Create a GPO and link it the DC OU

---

4. How can you make sure that the WWW publishing service on your web servers has an automatic startup type, and that the FTP service has a disabled startup type, allowing the Domain Admins to start or stop these services?

   A. Create a GPO and link it to the OU that contains the Web servers.

   B. Create and import a security template to comply with the startup specification listed by the policy. Ensure that Domain Admins are the only ones allowed to stop or start these services.

   C. Ensure that Domain Admins are the only ones allowed to stop or start these services.

   D. Create a GPO and link it to the domain.

5. If you are using the Securews.inf security template with a GPO, how can you prevent security configurations from causing client problems?

   A. Create a customized security template that reconfigures the appropriate security settings and add it to the GPO.

   B. Run the secedit /refreshpolicy machine_policy command on the clients

   C. Run the secedit /refreshpolicy user_policy command on the clients

   D. Run the secedit /refreshpolicy command on the clients

---

6. What steps would secure a SQL Server 2003 machine from use by unauthorized users on the Internet while allowing authorized users on an external web server to access the SQL Server through the internal firewall?

   A. Move any network adapter that directly connects the SQL Server to the Internet.

   B. Move the SQL Server to the company's intranet.

   C. Allow the users on the web server to access the SQL server through the Internet firewall.

   D. Leave any network adapter that directly connects the SQL Server to the Internet alone.

7. How can you ensure that only domain members can connect to a domain controller?

A. Use ESP and Kerberos for authentication

B. Use AH

C. Use ESP only

D. Enable the "Digitally sign client communications (always)" security policy to a linked GPO to the domain

E. Use AH and ESP only

---

8. You have two separate Windows 2003 forests with three domains in the first forest (Domain A, Domain B, and Domain C) and three domains in the second forest (Domain D, Domain E, and Domain F. You want users in the C domain to be able to access resources in the D and E domains. What trusts need to be set up?

A. A trust from Domain D to Domain C

B. A trust from Domain E to Domain C

C. A trust from Domain D to Domain B

D. A trust from Domain A to Domain B

E. A trust from Domain E to Domain A

9. Which of the following methods should you employ if you have users that have certificates or passwords who want to authenticate to a web site?
    A. Enable the Accept client certificate option
    B. Enable the Require client certificate option
    C. Disable anonymous access on the web site
    D. Enable anonymous access on the web site

---

10. You want your IIS and your ISA server, which are accessible from the Internet, to require L2TP/IPSec connections. You distribute the required certificates for the connections. You are using a RootCA and a PolicyCA, which are stand-alone and removed from the network. IssuingCA issues the IPSec certificates. When remote users attempt to connect the ISA server, they receive the error message, 'The client was unable to verify the identity of the server.' What should you do?
    A. Manually publish the CRL to the referenced CDP URLs at the IIS server
    B. Modify the CDP extension on RootCA and PolicyCA to include an HTTP URL that references the IIS server
    C. Modify the CDP extension on IssuingCA to include an HTTP URL that references the IIS server
    D. Renew the IssuingCA certificate

11. Which of the following would make an IIS server more resistant to Denial of Service attacks?
    A. Install URLScan on the server
    B. Uninstall the SMTP service on the server
    C. Uninstall the NNTP service on the server
    D. Uninstall the FTP service on the server

---

12. What steps can you take to make your IIS server less susceptible to Denial of Service attacks?
    A. Increase the SYN_ACK timeout on the IIS server's registry
    B. Decrease the SYN_ACK timeout on the IIS server's registry
    C. Install another IIS server and set up load balancing
    D. Block port 443

13. Which of the following security templates is the most restrictive?

A. An Account lockout duration of 60 minutes, an Account lockout threshold of 3 invalid logon attempts, and a Reset account lockout counter policy of 30 minutes.

B. An Account lockout duration of 45 minutes, an Account lockout threshold of 3 invalid logon attempts, and a Reset account lockout counter policy of 30 minutes.

C. An Account lockout duration of 30 minutes, an Account lockout threshold of 2 invalid logon attempts, and a Reset account lockout counter policy of 30 minutes.

D. An Account lockout duration of 30 minutes, an Account lockout threshold of 2 invalid logon attempts, and a Reset account lockout counter policy of 0 minutes.

---

14. Which of the following statements are true regarding Integrated Windows Authentication?

A. It won't prompt domain users for logon credentials

B. It will prompt domain users for logon credentials

C. It can be used whenever access to a Web server is confined to a Windows intranet

D. It helps track access

15. Which of the following actions are required when forcing users to authenticate through a newly created user account?
    A. Disable the FTP service
    B. Disable the NNTP service
    C. Disable the local default anonymous user account on the IIS server
    D. Disable the SMTP service

---

16. You have a Windows 2003 server that has the SQL service running on it. How can you prohibit the use of SQL Server login accounts on this server and stop any user from accessing the Windows 2003 server by using the SQL system administrator account?
    A. Configure the Windows 2003 server to use Windows authentication.
    B. Use the local Administrative account with MSSQL Server service.
    C. Configure the Windows 2003 server to use Mixed authentication.
    D. Use the local non-administrative accounts with MSSQL Server service.

Chapter 1: Review Answers

1. What would result from moving a GPO to the top of the list in a security template?

***A. It would be applied last**

***B. It would not be overridden**

C. It would be applied first
D. It would be overridden

Explanation: If you move a GPO to the top of the list in a security template, it would be applied last and it would not be overridden. It is given higher precedence.

---

2. You are the administrator of a Windows 2003 domain that contains Windows 2000 Professional computers. Which of the following security templates is used on Windows 2000 Professional computers and contains default settings for NTFS permissions, registry permissions, and default user rights?

***A. The Defltwk.inf security template**

B. The Basicwk.inf security template
C. The Def.inf security template
D. The Bas.inf security template

Explanation: The Defltwk.inf security template is used on Windows 2000 Professional computers and contains default settings for NTFS permissions, registry permissions, and default user rights. It sets everything as if it were an original installation.

3. You have a Windows 2003 domain with OUs for your domain controllers (the DC OU), your other servers (the SRV OU), and workstations (the WS OU. The SRV OU contain child OUs for each specific server role in the domain. What should you do to apply a security template to the servers that aren't domain controllers with specific roles?

***A. Create a GPO and link it the SRV OU**

***B. Import the security template to the GPO.**

***C. Import the role specific security template to each role specific OU.**

D. Create a GPO and link it the domain
E. Create a GPO and link it the DC OU

Explanation: You have a Windows 2003 domain with OUs for your domain controllers (the DC OU), your other servers (the SRV OU), and workstations (the WS OU. If you want to apply a security template to the servers that aren't domain controllers, create a GPO and link it the SRV OU. Then, import the security template to the GPO and import the role specific security template to each role specific OU.

---

4. How can you make sure that the WWW publishing service on your web servers has an automatic startup type, and that the FTP service has a disabled startup type, allowing the Domain Admins to start or stop these services?

***A. Create a GPO and link it to the OU that contains the Web servers.**

***B. Create and import a security template to comply with the startup specification listed by the policy. Ensure that Domain Admins are the only ones allowed to stop or start these services.**

***C. Ensure that Domain Admins are the only ones allowed to stop or start these services.**

D. Create a GPO and link it to the domain.

Explanation: You need to make sure that the WWW publishing service on your web servers has an automatic startup type and that the FTP service has a disabled startup type, allowing the Domain Admins to start or stop these services. Create a GPO and link it to the OU that contains the Web servers. Create and import a security template to comply with the startup specification listed by the policy.

5. If you are using the Securews.inf security template with a GPO, how can you prevent security configurations from causing client problems?

***A. Create a customized security template that reconfigures the appropriate security settings and add it to the GPO.**

B. Run the secedit /refreshpolicy machine_policy command on the clients
C. Run the secedit /refreshpolicy user_policy command on the clients
D. Run the secedit /refreshpolicy command on the clients

Explanation: If you are using the Securews.inf security template with an GPO, but the security configurations are causing the clients problems, create a customized security template that reconfigures the appropriate security settings and add it to the GPO.

---

6. What steps would secure a SQL Server 2003 machine from use by unauthorized users on the Internet while allowing authorized users on an external web server to access the SQL Server through the internal firewall?

***A. Move any network adapter that directly connects the SQL Server to the Internet.**

***B. Move the SQL Server to the company's intranet.**

***C. Allow the users on the web server to access the SQL server through the Internet firewall.**

D. Leave any network adapter that directly connects the SQL Server to the Internet alone.

Explanation: The following steps would secure a SQL Server 2003 machine from use by unauthorized users on the Internet while allowing authorized users on an external web server to access the SQL Server through the internal firewall. Move any network adapter that directly connects the SQL Server to the Internet. Move the SQL Server to the company's intranet. Allow the users on the web server to access the SQL server through the Internet firewall.

7. How can you ensure that only domain members can connect to a domain controller?

***A. Use ESP and Kerberos for authentication**

B. Use AH

C. Use ESP only

*D. Enable the Digitally sign client communications (always) security policy to a linked GPO to the domain

E. Use AH and ESP only

Explanation: If you want to ensure that only domain members can connect to a domain controller, use ESP and Kerberos for authentication. You can also accomplish this by enabling the Digitally sign client communications (always) security policy to a linked GPO to the domain.

---

8. You have two separate Windows 2003 forests with three domains in the first forest (Domain A, Domain B, and Domain C) and three domains in the second forest (Domain D, Domain E, and Domain F. You want users in the C domain to be able to access resources in the D and E domains. What trusts need to be set up?

***A. A trust from Domain D to Domain C**

***B. A trust from Domain E to Domain C**

C. A trust from Domain D to Domain B

D. A trust from Domain A to Domain B

E. A trust from Domain E to Domain A

Explanation: You have two separate Windows 2003 forests with three domains in the first forest (Domain A, Domain B, and Domain C) and three domains in the second forest (Domain D, Domain E, and Domain F. You want users in the C domain to be able to access resources in the D and E domains. A trust from Domain D to Domain C needs to be setup, as well as one from Domain E to Domain C.

9. Which of the following methods should you employ if you have users that have certificates or passwords who want to authenticate to a web site?

***A. Enable the Accept client certificate option**

B. Enable the Require client certificate option

***C. Disable anonymous access on the web site**

D. Enable anonymous access on the web site

Explanation: Disable anonymous access and enable the Accept client certificate option on the web site if you have users you want to authenticate to a web site that have certificates or passwords.

---

10. You want your IIS and your ISA server, which are accessible from the Internet, to require L2TP/IPSec connections. You distribute the required certificates for the connections. You are using a RootCA and a PolicyCA, which are stand-alone and removed from the network. IssuingCA issues the IPSec certificates. When remote users attempt to connect the ISA server, they receive the error message, 'The client was unable to verify the identity of the server.' What should you do?

***A. Manually publish the CRL to the referenced CDP URLs at the IIS server**

B. Modify the CDP extension on RootCA and PolicyCA to include an HTTP URL that references the IIS server

***C. Modify the CDP extension on IssuingCA to include an HTTP URL that references the IIS server**

***D. Renew the IssuingCA certificate**

Explanation: You want your IIS and your ISA server, which are accessible from the Internet, to require L2TP/IPSec connections. You distribute the required certificates for the connections. You are using a RootCA and a PolicyCA, which are stand-alone and removed from the network. IssuingCA issues the IPSec certificates. When remote users attempt to connect the ISA server, they receive the error message, 'The client was unable to verify the identity of the server.' Modify the CDP extension on IssuingCA to include an HTTP URL that references the IIS server, manually publish the CRL to the referenced CDP URLs at the IIS server, and renew the IssuingCA certificate.

11. Which of the following would make an IIS server more resistant to Denial of Service attacks?

***A. Install URLScan on the server**

B. Uninstall the SMTP service on the server
C. Uninstall the NNTP service on the server
D. Uninstall the FTP service on the server

Explanation: Installing URLScan on the server would make an IIS server more resistant to Denial of Service attacks.

---

12. What steps can you take to make your IIS server less susceptible to Denial of Service attacks?

***A. Increase the SYN_ACK timeout on the IIS server's registry**

B. Decrease the SYN_ACK timeout on the IIS server's registry
C. Install another IIS server and set up load balancing
D. Block port 443

Explanation: To harden your IIS server against Denial of Service attacks, increase the SYN_ACK timeout on the IIS server's registry.

13. Which of the following security templates is the most restrictive?

***A. An Account lockout duration of 60 minutes, an Account lockout threshold of 3 invalid logon attempts, and a Reset account lockout counter policy of 30 minutes.**

B. An Account lockout duration of 45 minutes, an Account lockout threshold of 3 invalid logon attempts, and a Reset account lockout counter policy of 30 minutes.

C. An Account lockout duration of 30 minutes, an Account lockout threshold of 2 invalid logon attempts, and a Reset account lockout counter policy of 30 minutes.

D. An Account lockout duration of 30 minutes, an Account lockout threshold of 2 invalid logon attempts, and a Reset account lockout counter policy of 0 minutes.

Explanation: The following security template is the most restrictive: An Account lockout duration of 60 minutes, an Account lockout threshold of 3 invalid logon attempts, and a Reset account lockout counter policy of 30 minutes.

---

14. Which of the following statements are true regarding Integrated Windows Authentication?

***A. It won't prompt domain users for logon credentials**

B. It will prompt domain users for logon credentials

***C. It can be used whenever access to a Web server is confined to a Windows intranet**

***D. It helps track access**

Explanation: Integrated Windows Authentication can be used whenever access to a Web server is confined to a Windows intranet. It won't prompt domain users for logon credentials and it helps to track access.

15. Which of the following actions are required when forcing users to authenticate through a newly created user account?
A. Disable the FTP service
B. Disable the NNTP service
***C. Disable the local default anonymous user account on the IIS server**
D. Disable the SMTP service

Explanation: Disabling the local default anonymous user account on the IIS server is required to force users to authenticate through a newly created user account.

---

16. You have a Windows 2003 server that has the SQL service running on it. How can you prohibit the use of SQL Server login accounts on this server and stop any user from accessing the Windows 2003 server by using the SQL system administrator account?
***A. Configure the Windows 2003 server to use Windows authentication.**
***B. Use the local Administrative account with MSSQL Server service.**
C. Configure the Windows 2003 server to use Mixed authentication.
D. Use the local non-administrative accounts with MSSQL Server service.

Explanation: You have a Windows 2003 that has SQL Server on it. You want to prohibit the use of SQL Server login accounts on this server and you want to stop any user from accessing the Windows 2003 server by using the SQL system administrator account. Configure the Windows 2003 server to use Windows authentication and use the local non-administrative accounts with MSSQL Server service.

Planning, Implementing, and Maintaining a Network Infrastructure

The objective of this chapter is to provide the reader with an understanding of the following:

Plan a TCP/IP network infrastructure strategy.

- Analyze IP addressing requirements.
- Plan an IP routing solution.
- Create an IP subnet scheme.

Plan and modify a network topology.

- Plan the physical placement of network resources.
- Identify network protocols to be used.

Plan an Internet connectivity strategy.

- Plan network traffic monitoring. Tools might include
- Network Monitor
- System Monitor.

Troubleshoot connectivity to the Internet.

- Diagnose and resolve issues related to Network Address Translation (NAT).
- Diagnose and resolve issues related to name resolution cache information.
- Diagnose and resolve issues related to client configuration.

Troubleshoot TCP/IP addressing.

- Diagnose and resolve issues related to client computer configuration.
- Diagnose and resolve issues related to DHCP server address assignment.

Plan a host name resolution strategy.

- Plan a DNS namespace design.
- Plan zone replication requirements.
- Plan a forwarding configuration.
- Plan for DNS security.
- Examine the interoperability of DNS with third-party DNS solutions.

Plan a NetBIOS name resolution strategy.

- Plan a WINS replication strategy.
- Plan NetBIOS name resolution by using the Lmhosts file.

Troubleshoot host name resolution.

- Diagnose and resolve issues related to DNS services.
- Diagnose and resolve issues related to client computer configuration.

Chapter 2: Managing Network Infrastructure

Introduction:

With the release of Windows Server 2003, Microsoft has enhanced network protocols to broaden capabilities of servers running the network operating system. The Windows Server 2003 family offers numerous improvements since the Windows NT 4.0 operating system was released. As well, additional features have been added since Windows 2000. Table 2.1 shows a short listing of some new and improved features and benefits.

Getting Ready Questions

1. Why use TCP/IP as a standard on a Windows Server 2003 network?
2. What is IPv6?
3. What are IP Address classes?
4. What is NAT?
5. What utilities can be used to troubleshoot Internet Connectivity?

Getting Ready Answers

1. TCP/IP is an industry standard, flexible and easy to implement.
2. IPv6 is the new 128-bit address range, which has improvements over IPv4.
3. IP address classes are ranges of IP Addresses used for networks.
4. NAT stands for Network Address Translation, which is used for private IP addressing
5. Some of the utilities used to troubleshoot internet connectivity include Ping, Nbtstat, Ipconfig, Netstat, and Tracert, to name just a few.

Feature	Benefits
Network Address Translation (NAT)	NAT is used to increase security within a private network. It works by translating private non-routable IP addresses such as 10.x.x.x or 172.16.x.x or 192.168.x.x to public routable IP addresses. This will hide the internal network infrastructure, which will increase network security.
Automatic Configuration for Multiple networks	This is a great coup d'état for Microsoft as well as the Support Helpdesk staff. This feature allows client machines to have settings used for two networks. Mobile clients can travel between home and the office without having to reconfigure the network settings each time they connect to the network.
Wireless networking	Supports the IEEE 802.11 standard. What is so great about this feature is that is has an automatic wireless network configuration feature. This feature allows clients to roam between different wireless networks regardless of the location. If you have a wireless setup in your home and you want to take your laptop with its wireless configuration to a coffee shop with wireless access and still have connectivity without reconfiguring the settings. Of course, this opens a completely new door for security issues and you need to configure security properly if you decide to implement a wireless network using Windows Server 2003.

Feature	Benefits
Web Distributed Authoring and Versioning (WebDAV)	The WebDAV protocol is supported by the WebDAV redirector. This allows clients to share files remotely over HTTP through firewalls
Internet Connection Sharing (ICS) available on Windows Server 2003 Standard and Enterprise Editions on x86 computers.	Using your broadband (DSL or Cable Modem) you can connect your small office or home network to the Internet. Once ICS is enabled on the machine that uses DSL you can use NAT to provide network services such as address translation and name resolution services.
Fibre Channel Support	Fibre Channel supports 1-gigabit-per-second data transfer rate on networks.

Table 2—1: Improvements made to Networking Protocols in Windows Server 2003.

TCP and UDP Contrasts

TCP and UDP are protocols used by TCP/IP. If you have ever configured Firewall Settings such as configuring a rule to allow traffic in or out on a TCP/IP network you would be faced with the task of choosing the delivery protocol for the traffic

You can think of TCP the same way you think of an Express Carrier Mail Service that you pay for because you have to have guaranteed delivery. The information is delivered as promised and on time. UDP on the other hand can be compared to good old-fashioned regular mail the delivery is not guaranteed but hopefully it will arrive at some point.

In general, differences in how UDP and TCP deliver data are similar to the differences between a telephone call and a postcard. TCP works like a telephone call by verifying that the destination is available and ready to communicate. UDP works like a postcard—messages are small and delivery is likely, but not always assured.

UDP is typically used by programs that transmit small amounts of data at one time or have real-time requirements. In these situations, the low overhead and multicasting capabilities of UDP (for example, one datagram, many recipients) are better suited than TCP.

The UDP protocol is a stark contrast regarding both services and features in relation to TCP. Table 2.2 compares differences in how TCP/IP communication is handled depending on whether UDP or TCP is used for transporting data.

UDP	**TCP**
Connectionless service. Hosts do not establish a session.	Connection-oriented service. Hosts always establish a session.
UDP does not guarantee delivery of a packet. It also does not send the data in a sequenced format or any type of acknowledgement that the data arrived at the destination.	TCP guarantees delivery by sending an acknowledgement and sending the data in a sequenced manner.
Programs that use UDP are responsible for providing any reliability needed to transport data.	Programs that use TCP are provided assurance of reliable data transport.
UDP is quick and it has low overhead. UDP can also support multipoint communications.	TCP is slower than UDP. The overhead for TCP is higher than UDP and it can only support point-to-point communication.

Table 2—2: Contrasts between UDP and TCP.

Both UDP and TCP use ports to identify communications for each TCP/IP program. Table 2.3 shows a very small and partial list of some well-known TCP server ports used by standard TCP-based programs.

TCP port number	**Description**
20	FTP server (data channel)
21	FTP server (control channel)
23	Telnet server
53	Domain Name System zone transfers
80	Web server (HTTP)
139	NetBIOS session service

Table 2—3: Brief list of TCP Ports with known service they support.

2.1 Plan a TCP/IP network infrastructure strategy

In order to run TCP/IP, you must have, at minimum, an IP address and a subnet mask. In order to communicate over a router, you must also have a default gateway address. The default gateway address is the address of the router than will route your packets out of your local subnetwork.

2.1.1 Analyze IP addressing requirements

When setting up your network infrastructure you need to know the following information so that the structure is setup properly and efficiently:

- Does this network need to connect to the internet?
- Will you need to have both Public and Private IP Addresses? Private Addressing schemes should be used according to IANA.
- If you need private IP Addresses, will a Firewall be in place to use for Network Address Translation?
- How many physically separate network segments are inside your current network structure?
- What is the number of hosts that will need to use the TCP/IP protocol on the segment?

Internet Assigned Numbers Authority (IANA) recommends that you use the private IP addresses shown in Table 2.4 below.

Private network ID	Subnet mask	Range of IP addresses
10.0.0.0	255.0.0.0	10.0.0.1 – 10.255.255.254
172.16.0.0	255.240.0.0	172.16.0.1 – 172.31.255.254
192.168.0.0	255.255.0.0	192.168.0.1 – 192.168.255.254

Table 2—4: Non-Routable IP addresses reserved by IANA.

Due to obvious security issues, only connect computers directly to the internet if they absolutely must be using a Public IP Address. If you use an ISP, they can typically give you IP addresses for your hosts that must have Public IP addresses. You can also contact IANA and apply for IP Addresses if your ISP cannot accommodate your needs.

2.1.1.1 Routing Table

Clients running TCP/IP make decisions on routing, which is controlled by the routing table. On a Windows XP or Windows Server 2003 with TCP/IP installed and configured, type the following command at the prompt (Figure 2.1).

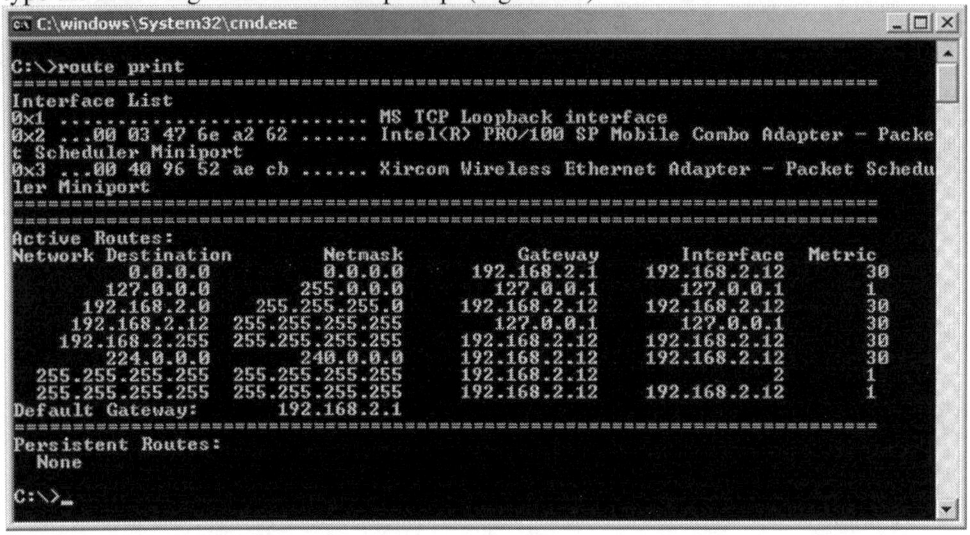

Figure 2—1: The Route Print command.

This table is automatically built automatically and is based on the TCP/IP configuration on the machine from which the command was run. If a host or network route is not found to be a match for the IP data packet then the machine will use a default route.

- Network Destination - The network destination is used with the destination IP address and netmask. The ranges can be between a default route 0.0.0.0 to 255.255.255.255 broadcast address. The broadcast address is used to communicate to all hosts on a network segment.
- Netmask –This is simply a subnet mask that is applied to a destination IP address.
- Gateway - Typically, the local machine gateway address is used for this route and it could be a local IP router on the local network.
- Interface - This is the local client's IP address.
- Metric - The metric is used to configure the cost of a route. The cost is measured in hops from the local host machine to the destination machine. A single subnet would be one hop. Each additional router would be considered an additional hop. Routes that have the lowest cost or hops will be selected to be used to send the network traffic.

2.1.1.2 Configuration Features

TCP/IP includes several features that simplify configuration on a single subnet and optimize TCP performance in high-bandwidth network environments.

These features include support for:

- Automatic and alternate private address configuration
- Large TCP windows
- Disabling NetBIOS over TCP/IP
- Better roundtrip time (RTT) estimation
- Selective acknowledgments
- ICMP router discovery
- DNS caching
- Automatic and alternate private address configuration

Host machines running on a Windows Server 2003 network will always try to contact a DHCP server first for IP addressing. If a DHCP Server is reached on the network then TCP/IP uses the information in the DHCP Server and connects to the network. If for any reason the host machine does not contact a DHCP Server then it will check to see if it has an alternate configuration. If the alternate configuration is available, the host machine will use that information to connect to the network. As a last resort in the event that the DHCP Server cannot be contacted and an Alternate TCP.IP configuration does not exist then the host machine will use APIPA to obtain its configuration parameters. If APIPA is used, Windows Server 2003 uses an address range between 169.254.0.1 through 169.254.255.254. This address is used as a temporary IP address configuration until a DHCP server is located. The subnet mask is set to 255.255.0.0. Therefore, if you happen to see a host on your network with an address range listed between the 169.254.0.1 and 169.254.255.254, you will know that the host machine could not reach a DHCP Server or use an Alternate configuration for its TCP/IP configuration.

The 169.254.x.x address on clients is caused by the DHCP server being unable to give the client IP address configuration information and because the alternate configuration on the client is not configured. If you do not want the 169.254.x.x address to ever be given to a client machine you can configure the Alternate Address information on XP clients under the TCP/IP properties and/or also disable automatic address configuration if your network policy allows it by editing the registry on the client machine. Always use caution before editing the registry of a computer. You can cause the computer to become corrupted and data can be lost. If possible, try this on a lab computer first. The registry can be edited as follows to disable APIPA:

Open the registry by clicking on Start then Run and type REGEDT32

Find the key

HKEY_LOCAL_MACHINE\SYSTEM\CurrentControlSet\Services\Tcpip\Parameters

Add the DWORD Value- IPAutoconfigurationEnabled: REG_DWORD with the value of 0 Close the registry editor and reboot the client machine. APIPA should now be disabled.

APIPA IP addresses are not used on the Internet. For Small Office or Home Office Networks SOHO APIPA can remove the need to configure IP Addresses on machines NOT connected to the internet. Just make sure the client machines have not had their registries edited to disable APIPA (which is not the default).

2.1.1.3 TCP windows

Window size reflects the maximum number of packets that can be sent without waiting for positive acknowledgment. Large TCP windows improve performance for TCP/IP if large amounts of data are being sent between the hosts. Usually the maximum TCP window size is usually fixed at the onset of connection and is 64 kilobytes. The TCP window size can be dynamically changed by using a TCP option as needed during longer sessions so that more data packets are being transmitted. Before you can use this option, you have to enable TCP1323Opts in the registry on the host computers. Once this is enabled, Windows Server 2003 can accept the host machines requests for the large TCP windows.

2.1.1.4 Roundtrip Time

Roundtrip time RTT is used to give an estimate of the time needed for roundtrip communication between a two host machines. This can improve performance and speed of TCP. This assists networks that use WANS over large areas such as continents, and networks that have satellite or wireless links.

2.1.1.5 ICMP router discovery

Internet Control Message Protocol (ICMP) router discovery uses ICMP messages to discover the default gateway on a network segment if it is not configured or given by the DHCP Server. ICMP router discovery uses two messages to discover the gateway.

- First Message – Host machine sends a router solicitation to find the gateway.
- Second Message – Router sends a router advertisement to respond to the host machine.

This is turned off by default on TCP/IP Windows Server 2003 machines and Windows XP clients. Install and use the Routing and Remote Access Service on the Windows Server 2003 to configure the ICMP router discovery option.

2.1.1.6 Disabling NetBIOS over TCP/IP

If you have host machines that do not use Microsoft Client Networking, DNS for name registration or File and Print Sharing you can disable NetBIOS over TCP/IP (NetBT). Computers that function in your environment as security hosts such as edge proxy servers or bastion hosts probably would be good candidates for disabling NetBT.

Use the WINS configuration option in the TCP/IP properties to turn off NetBIOS over TCP/IP

Test in a lab environment first before you disable NetBT. The host machine could be unable to browse the network and access files and shares on other machines with this disabled. NetBT is needed if the machine has to use the WINS service in the network environment.

2.1.1.7 TCPIP Database Files

The following Table 2.5 shows the database files that are stored in the systemroot\System32\Drivers\Etc folder on servers running Windows Server 2003 operating systems. Those of you familiar with UNIX will already recognize these file names. Table 2.5 is listed below.

File	Description
Hosts	Provides host name–to–IP address resolution.
LMHosts	Provides NetBIOS name–to–IP address resolution.
Networks	Provides network name–to–network ID resolution.
Protocols	Provides protocol name–to–protocol ID resolution.
Services	Provides service name–to–port ID resolution.

Table 2—5: TCP/IP Database Files.

To troubleshoot any of these files on a local computer, do the following:

- Always check for spelling errors and other typos.
- Check for invalid IP addresses and identifiers.

By default, the LMHosts file does not exist it is actually a sample file in the \System32\Drivers\Etc folder named LMhosts.sam. Creating an LMHOSTS file has to be done **exactly** right. Do. Think of your LMHOSTS file as a manual DNS listing. It is useful in the event you are having trust issues between domains. A freeware utility is available for download at the following link, which will assist you in creating the LMHOSTS file correctly:

http://www.freedownloadscenter.com/Network_and_Internet/Network_Management_Tools/LMHOSTS_Generator.html.

Windows Server 2003 servers use name resolution to translate numerical IP addresses. This is necessary for TCP/IP communications.

2.1.1.8 Host names

IP nodes are assigned host names up to 255 characters. The characters can be alpha, numeric, periods and hyphens and more than one host name can be given to a host. The Host names are used to identify TCP/IP host nodes and are used by programs that use the Windows Sockets programming interface. A good example of a Windows Socket programming interface is a FTP Program or utility or a Web Browser. Resolution for host names is simply mapping a host name to an IP Address. Host names can be either domain names or nicknames. The differences are:

- Domain Name – A name in the DNS namespace that is structured, such as www.google.com or www.microsoft.com. DNS is used to resolve these addresses.
- Nickname – IP Address alias assigned and resolved through the hosts file in the systemroot\system32\drivers\etc directory.

Network clients that need to resolve domain names have to have a DNS Server address configured in the TCP/IP properties of the network connection.

2.1.1.9 NetBIOS names

NetBIOS is used on networks that have services such as the Client for Microsoft Networks, File and Print Sharing for Microsoft Networks installed and running. Each time a computer starts up with the NetBIOS service it is registered with a 15-character name and an additional character 0x20, which completes the 16-byte NetBIOS name. If the computer name is not fifteen characters long then spaces will be added until the 15-character limit has been reached. There are different NetBIOS types and each of these types resolves NetBIOS names to IP Addresses differently. See Table 2.6 for a listing of the NetBIOS types and a description of how they resolve NetBIOS names to IP addresses.

If you have configured the WINS Server service on your Windows 2003 Machine then the NetBIOS types should look familiar to you.

NetBIOS Type	Description
B-node (broadcast)	This type of node is chatty. It sends broadcasts that disturb all nodes on a network. Routers typically do not forward these broadcasts, which mean that only NetBIOS names on the local network can be resolved.
P-node (peer-peer)	P-node uses a NetBIOS name server like the WINS server service to resolve NetBIOS names. Instead of using Broadcasts like the B-node the queries the name server directly.
M-node (mixed)	M-node works like a B-node as a default and will use P-node to resolve NetBIOS names if the B-node does not function.
H-node(hybrid)	H-node functions as a P-node by default and will broadcast using B-node if the P-node does not function properly.

Table 2—6: NetBIOS types and descriptions.

Windows Server 2003 machines are all B-node by default. Once you install and configure the WINS Server service on your machine then the Windows Server will become an H-node. WINS is necessary on networks using NetBIOS and should be configured on all Windows XP Professional clients and the Windows Server inside the network for proper resolution of NetBIOS names.

2.1.2 Plan an IP routing solution

IP Addresses are used to identify TCP/IP hosts and is unique for all machines on a network. You cannot have duplicate IP Addresses on client machines or networked peripherals. If you do happen to assign an IP address that is already being used to another host you will get an error that the IP Address is already in use. If you assign a server an address that is already showing in WINS and DNS being registered by another machine or server you will begin to have problems access information on the server or other machine with this IP Address. If you plan to assign an IP Address to a server or client, first use the PING command and ping the IP Address to see if it is being used. Also, check the WINS Server database and DNS to make certain that it is not registered as being in use.

IP address consists of a Network and Host ID.

- Network ID – This is the part of the IP Address that is common on all peripherals and computers on the network.
- Host ID – This is the part of the IP address that is unique to all peripherals and computers on the network.

Using the information above pertaining to the Network and Host ID the listing below shows the number of possible networks and hosts per network available for each class. Please memorize this table. The information in Table 2.7 is one that you will need to reference quite often and it will be on Microsoft Certification exams.

Class	**Network ID**	**Host ID**	**# of Networks**	**Hosts Per Network**
A 1-126	a	b.c.d	126	16,777,214
B 128-191	a.b	c.d	26.384	65,534
C 192-223	a.b.c	d	2,097,152	254
D	Reserved for multicasting	N/A	N/A	N/A
E	Reserved	N/A	N/A	N/A

Table 2—7: Network and Host ID listings.

The bullets below give more details regarding the IP Address classes. Listed below the last class list are three other IP Addresses that have different functions in a network. Pay close attention to the additional IP addresses because you can use them for troubleshooting and you will see these addresses on your network.

- **Class A –** This is used for very large networks. For Class A networks with 16,777,214 (2^{24} -2) possible hosts for 2,147,483,648 (2^{31}) unique IP addresses. Because they are so large, they take up half of all available IP Addresses in existence.
- **Class B –** Class B is used for medium-sized networks and universities or colleges. Users of the Class B IP addressing scheme can have 16,384 (2^{14}) Class B networks each with 65,534 (2^{16} -2) possible host addresses giving them 1,073,741,824 (2^{30}) unique IP addresses. These networks take one quarter of all IP Addresses in use.
- **Class C –** These addresses are used for smaller to mid-sized businesses and they make up one-eighth of all IP addresses in use today. There are 2,097,152 (2^{21}) Class C networks each with 254 (2^{8} -2) possible hosts for 536,870,912 (2^{29}) unique IP addresses.
- **Class D –** Class D is only used for multicast addressing and accounts for one-sixteenth of all IP addresses in use. Class D has 268,435,456 or 228 of the available IP addresses.
- **Class E –** Class E is available only for experimental uses and makes up 1/16th (268,435,456 or 228) of the all available IP addresses available (although not for use with public).
  - **Broadcast** – A broadcast address is used to send messages to all hosts on a network and it uses the IP Address of 255.255.255.255.
  - **Default Network** – A default network's IP address is always **0.0.0.0**.
  - **Loopback** – Loopback address is used by computer for troubleshooting purposes. It is used to send messages back to its own adapter. For example, you can ping your loopback address 127.0.0.1 if you are troubleshooting network connectivity on your machine. If you get a response back from your network card then you can know that your card is functioning. Although other problems could be occurring with the NIC this is a good starting point when troubleshooting.

The next step in implementing TCP/IP is to create an IP subnet scheme. Microsoft also has available a guide called Microsoft Systems Architecture at the following URL

http://www.microsoft.com/windowsserver2003/msa/overview.mspx.

This download is not just another document is has two parts and is geared for enterprise level environments. This guide will allow Administrators to design and implement technologies with lower and more controlled costs.

2.1.3 Create an IP subnet scheme

IP Addresses use subnet masks network IDs and host IDs within an IP address are distinguished by using a subnet mask. Each subnet mask is a 32-bit number that uses consecutive bit groups of all ones to identify the network ID and all zeroes (0) to identify the host ID portions of an IP address.

For example, the subnet mask normally used with the IP address 10.10.1.201 is the following 32-bit binary number:

00001010 00001010 00000001 11001001

This subnet mask number is 16 one-bits followed by 16 zero-bits, indicating that the network ID and host ID sections of this IP address are both 16 bits in length. Normally, this subnet mask is displayed in dotted decimal notation as 255.255.0.0. Table 2.8 displays subnet masks for the Internet address classes.

Address class	**Bits for subnet mask**	**Subnet mask**
Class A	11111111 00000000 00000000 00000000	255.0.0.0
Class B	11111111 11111111 00000000 00000000	255.255.0.0
Class C	11111111 11111111 11111111 00000000	255.255.255.0

Table 2—8: Address Classes and Subnet masks.

Typically, default subnet mask values (as shown in the previous table) are acceptable for most networks, provided the network has no special requirements and each IP network segment corresponds to a single physical network.

In some cases, you can use customized subnet masks to implement IP subnetting. With IP subnetting, you can subdivide the default host ID portion of an IP address to specify subnets, which are subdivisions of the original class-based network ID.

By customizing the subnet mask length, you can reduce the number of bits that are used by the actual host ID. To prevent addressing and routing problems, you should make sure all TCP/IP computers on any network segment use the same subnet mask.

2.1.3.1 IP Multicast Addressing

IP multicast addresses are reserved and assigned from within the Class D address range from 224.0.0.0 through 239.255.255.255. Table 2.9 is a partial list of well-known Class D addresses that are reserved for IP multicasting and registered with the Internet Assigned Numbers Authority (IANA).

IP Address Multicast Address	Description
224.0.0.0	Reserved Base Address
224.0.0.1	Used by the All Hosts multicast group. This contains all systems on identical network.
224.0.0.2	Used by All Routers multicast group. Contains all routers on identical network segment.
224.0.0.5	Used to send Open Shortest Path First (OPSF) routing information to other routers within a network.
224.0.0.6	Used to send Open Shortest Path First (OPSF) routing information designated OPSF routers within a network.
224.0.0.9	Sends RIP routing information to RIP v2 routers on network
224.0.1.124	Used by WINS for Replication to other WINS Servers and also Auto discovery of WINS Servers.

Table 2—9: IP Multicast Address and descriptions.

Multicast IP Addressing is commonly used with streaming online or distance learning, audio, video conferencing and other types of multimedia applications. If a server has IP multicasting configured it can send a replicated single data stream to many devices with very low overhead. IP Multicasting can be configured on a Windows Server by configuring the TCP/IP protocol and the Routing and Remote Access service.

2.2 Plan and modify a network topology

2.2.1 Plan the physical placement of network resources

Microsoft recommends you use three tiers to design the network layout. The three tiers are listed below:

- Access Tier- Made up of a large number of low to medium speed access ports. Clients connect to this tier and are able to access other areas of the network.
- Distribution Tier – This tier is responsible for distributing traffic between access layers. As well, it is where security (access control policies and network security) for the traffic should be implemented and subnets should be implemented. It also separates traffic based on where it is coming from and going to, such as local traffic or traffic going to other areas of the network.
- Core Tier – This tier is typically the high-speed backbone of the network and checks for efficient data transfers. This is where you may wish to implement redundancy when available between equipment.

Demilitarized Zones DMZ are also a consideration to implement when designing networks. These are used in conjunction with other security equipment such as firewalls, proxy servers' circuit gateways and application gateways to place boundaries between networks and internet connections. Make your applications that must be available 24/7 (database, e-mail, web-services) fault tolerant as well. The fail-over should be transparent to clients using the services.

2.2.1.1 Using Load Balancing

It is also a good idea to implement load balancing on your network. This is added redundancy that greatly enhances throughput on network cards. The traffic on the server is divided among the parallel connections. See Microsoft knowledge base article 323431 for information on setting up Network Load Balancing.

2.2.2 Identify network protocols to be used

The Windows Server 2003 edition you install and configure (some protocols are not supported on the 64-bit version of Windows Server 2003 such as OSPF, IPX/SPX used for Novell Networks) will affect which protocols you choose to install. As will, what other networks are connected or need to have connections to this network. If you have Novell Netware running, you may need to configure IPX/SPX.

The services needed for connection between a Novell Netware and Windows Server 2003 network (64-bit does not support IPX/SPX Protocol) are:

- NWLink Protocol
- Client service for Netware

Networks with Macintosh clients also have to make certain they configure the three services needed for supporting these clients on a Windows Server 2003 network. The services needed for Macintosh are:

- AppleTalk Protocol
- File Server for Macintosh
- Print Server for Macintosh

The 64-bit version of Windows Server 2003 does not support the Print Server service for Macintosh.

Windows Server 2003 also now supports new technologies such as:

- Support for Fibre Channel – Fibre Channel technologies run at a 1 gigabit per-second transfer rate and merges high-speed I/O such as Small Computer System Interface SCSI with IP.

- Web Distributed Authoring and Versioning redirector WebDAV – This allows for the remote sharing of documents over the internet without Firewall reconfiguration to a web server running HTTP.

- Simple Object Access Protocol SOAP – Used to exchange data in an environment that is not centralized based on XML and it runs on a multitude of protocols such as SMTP, HTTT, and FTP.

  You typically think of these protocols as being used by developers when new or existing applications are being written.

In addition to the features listed above Windows Server 2003 has improved Virtual Private Networking VPN technology. VPN technology is used create a secure tunnel which allows remote clients the ability to access the company network from the internet or dial-up. Windows Server 2003 supports two types of VPN technologies.

- Point to Point Tunneling Protocol (PPTP) – This protocol consists of two technologies the first is used for configuring authentication methods for the client and is called Point-to-Point Protocol (PPP). The second technology is used for data encryption and is called Microsoft Point-to-Point Encryption (MPPE).
    - Windows Server 2003 Standard and Web editions support the creation of 1,000 PPTP ports. Windows Server 2003 Standard allows for up to 1,000 incoming VPN connections and once the limit has been reached the clients will receive denied error messages until the number of connections is below 1,000. Windows Server 2003 Web edition only supports one incoming VPN connection.
- Layer Two Tunneling Protocol (L2TP) – This protocol consists of a PPP encryption method used by client machines and the Internet Protocol Security (IPSec). IPSec is used for data encryption, which is implemented with client certificates to implement enhanced security.
    - Windows Server 2003 Standard and Web editions support the creation of 1,000 L2TP ports. Windows Server 2003 Standard allows for up to 1,000 incoming VPN connections and once the limit has been reached the clients will receive denied error messages until the number of connections is below 1,000. Windows Server 2003 Web edition only supports one incoming VPN connection.

If you have used the Connection Manager Kit in the past to configure and rollout Internet Explorer to client machines you will be pleased to know that this feature has several new enhancements to reduce configuration overhead for client machines.

- A connection Manager Wizard is available to allow you to roll out configurations to client machines quickly and efficiently.
- Proxy Settings can now be set as automatically configured.
- The Connection Manager Favorites features will remove the repetitive task of configuring the Connection Manager as users move between dialing locations
- Administrators can also view client log files to assist with troubleshooting Connection Manager Connection problems.

With all of the enhancements to networking protocols in the Windows Server 2003 operating system, some older technologies were removed or are no longer supported on all versions of the Windows Server 2003 available for implementation. Support is no longer available for either NetBIOS Extended User Interface (NetBEUI) or the Data Link Control (DLC) protocol that was used with various printer types.

In addition, the Internetwork Packet Exchange/Sequenced Packet Exchange IPX/SPX network protocol used for communicating with Novell Network environments and the Open Shortest Path First (OSPF) protocol are not supported on 64-bit versions of Windows Server 2003. If you are planning to introduce Infrared Networking (IR), know that only Windows Server 2003 Standard supports this technology.

Since this chapter will deal specifically with one protocol in the Windows Server 2003 operating system, we will take a detailed look at the Transmission Control Protocol/Internet Protocol (TCP/IP). TCP/IP is a suite of standard protocols. It is used to build network infrastructure connectivity and allow client machines to connect to the network. Windows Server 2003 has an improved version of TCP/IP. The TCP/IP protocol consists of the following core protocols.

2.2.2.1 Internet Protocol v4

This core protocol is required by TCP/IP and is used to address and route packets between host machines. IPv4 was introduced in September of 1981 by RFC 791. The components of IPv4 have not significantly changed since its initial introduction. IPv4 addressing is built on binary mathematics (covered in detail later in this chapter) supporting either 8 or 16 addresses. When it was first introduced (before the Internet explosion and NAT) many address spaces were completely lost due to both inefficiencies of organizations to use the address space they were assigned and because of the limitation of the IPv4 binary algorithm. For example, an organization has a 16-bit address space and only has nine hosts. If you do the math, you will see that seven of the address spaces are "lost" because they are not being used. The numbers only get worse as the networking world grows exponentially after the internet explosion in the 90's.

Now, of course, just about everything from refrigerators to mobile devices can use IP address spaces. Address spaces are assigned and maintained by the Internet Corporation for Assigned Names and Numbers (ICANN). In addition to assigning address spaces for corporations ICANN coordinates the Domain Name System (DNS) to make certain that all IP addresses are different and that all addresses can be found by internet users. They also operate the InterNIC website to allow individuals and corporations the ability to register Internet Domain Name registrations. IP is used only to route data packets on the network. It is connectionless which means that before data is transmitted from a host to a host no session is established. This means that packets can be lost, delayed or dropped when using IP but the host would never get any acknowledgement of this occurring.

The IP datagram is made up of the IP header and the IP payload, which consists of the following information:

1. IP address of the source of the datagram.
2. IP address for destination IP datagram.
3. Time-to-live (TTL) – Tells the datagram how many IP segments that it can travel on before it is discarded. If an IP packet is forwarded by a router the TTL will always be reduced by 1 at minimum.

Before we move on to the other part of IP, we will address the newly introduced Internet Protocol v6.

2.2.2.2 Internet Protocol v6

IPv6 works with 128 bit address spaces. It was originally called IP-The Next Generation (IPng) and was introduced by the Internet Engineering Task Force (IETF) to add features not available with IPv4. Two of the added features are Quality of Service (QoS) and security for IP (IPv4 now uses Internet Security Protocol (IPSec) to secure data packets. IPv6 has three types of addresses shown in the bullets below:

- Unicast addresses - **Packets are sent** to one interface.
- Multicast addresses - Packets are delivered to numerous interfaces.
- Any cast addresses – Packets are sent to the closest routing interface.

IPv6 was also introduced to allow for easier configuration (instead of DHCP servers and manual configurations and to allows for additional address spaces since IPv4 addressing is growing and getting new addresses could be difficult for organizations to accomplish.

Teredo has been designed and is supported by Microsoft technologies as an IPv6 transition between IPv4 Internet hosts using NAT and IPv6. Host machines located behind NAT using the Windows Peer-to-Peer Networking technology use Teredo. Use the following URL to link to the Microsoft website for more information: http://www.microsoft.com/technet/prodtechnol/winxppro/maintain/teredo.asp

Instead of the IPv4, dotted decimal notation IPv6 uses 16-byte addresses in a colon-hexadecimal format. To be exact IPv6 uses eight 4-digit hexadecimal numbers with colons between each 4-digit numbers. IPv6 also suppresses leading zeros and compresses nearby all-zero 4-digit block with two colons (::)..

IP Address	IP Address using different suppression methods
IPv6 address	FEC0:0000:0000:0000:02AF:0AFF:FE3F:3F11
IPv6 address with leading zeros suppressed	FEC0:0:0:0:2AA:AFF:FE3F:3F11
IPv6 address with leading zeros suppressed with an all zero neighboring block compressed	FEC0::2AA:AFF:FE3F:2A1C

Table 2—10: IPv6 Addressing and suppression methods..

Instead of using a subnet mask to show the network ID, IPv6 uses prefix notation. IPv6 also does not support the use of broadcast messages.

- IPv6 is running on host
- Router Advertisements are not received by an IPv6 host on the network
- An IPv4 public IP address is configured on the host.

2.2.2.3 TCP

Unlike IP, Transmission Control Protocol (TCP) is reliable and connection oriented. It sends acknowledgements to host machine that the packet was received. TCP also can give a guarantee of packet delivery, which IP cannot do. This reliable protocol is the most preferred travel method for database and mail service programs. TCP functions by grouping bytes received by programs into segments. Once the segments are grouped, TCP numbers each segment for delivery. A three-way handshake is then performed by the host machines (the three-way handshake will process the sequence numbers and give the control information to the host computer). In a sequential manner, the data (which has also been encapsulated within IP datagrams) is transmitted and then acknowledged between each host.

2.2.2.4 Address Resolution Protocol

Address Resolution Protocol (ARP) is a required TCP/IP standard defined in RFC 826 it is used to addresses between TCP/IP based software and LAN hardware that uses media access control addresses. ARP also is used by local routers to forward IP datagrams to destinations outside the local network. ARP works by sending out a network broadcast that is looking for the media access control address for any hardware device that has an IP address. When the ARP request receives the answer to the network broadcast, the ARP sender and the ARP requester record each other's IP address a local ARP cache table. ARP will also forward datagrams to local routers for destinations outside the local network. ARP resolves MAC address of a router interface on the local network.

To view the ARP cache, type **arp –a** at a command prompt, as shown in Figure 2.2. To open a command prompt, click on **Start | Run** and then type **cmd.**

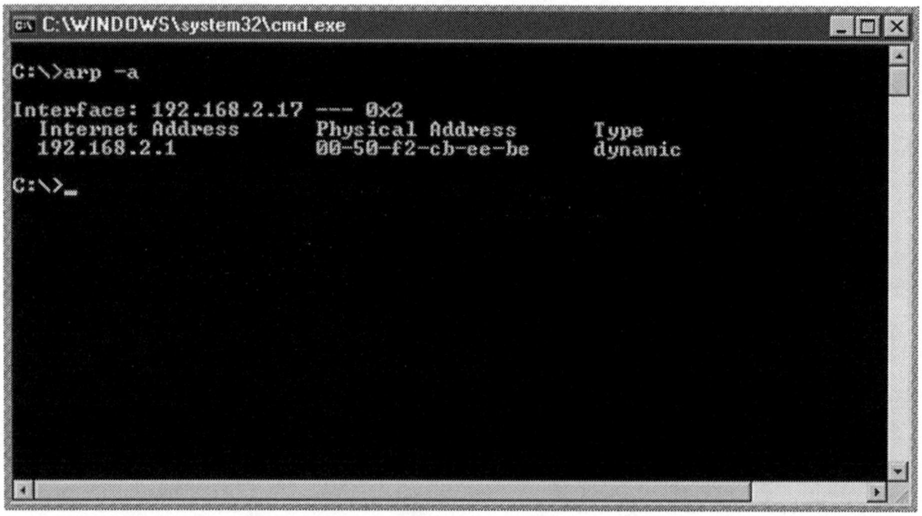

Figure 2—2: The Arp-a command.

Additional arp commands can be viewed by typing "**arp /?**" at the command prompt as shown in Figure 2 below. If the machine you use this command on has more than one network card then more than one ARP cache will be listed.

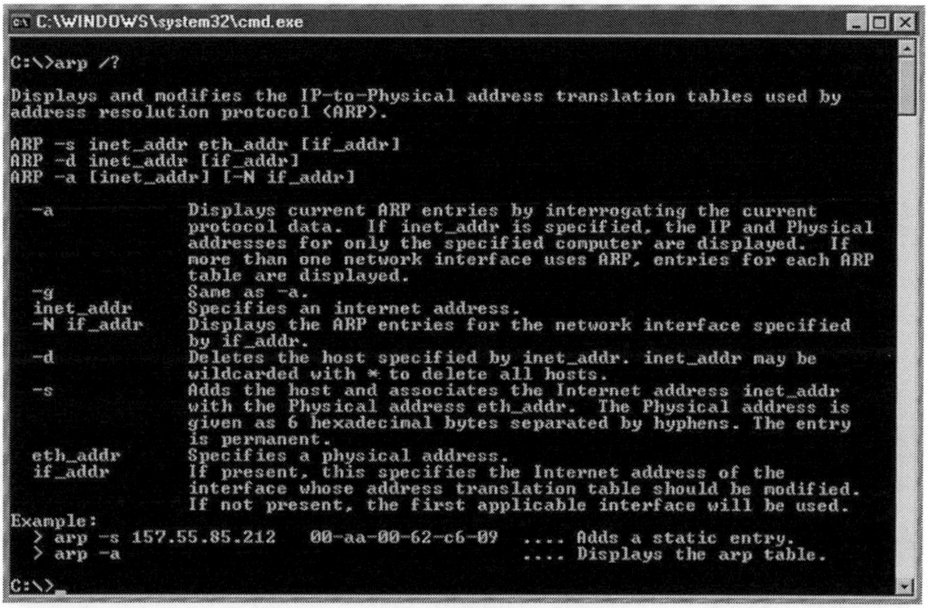

```
C:\WINDOWS\system32\cmd.exe

C:\>arp /?

Displays and modifies the IP-to-Physical address translation tables used by
address resolution protocol (ARP).

ARP -s inet_addr eth_addr [if_addr]
ARP -d inet_addr [if_addr]
ARP -a [inet_addr] [-N if_addr]

  -a            Displays current ARP entries by interrogating the current
                protocol data.  If inet_addr is specified, the IP and Physical
                addresses for only the specified computer are displayed.  If
                more than one network interface uses ARP, entries for each ARP
                table are displayed.
  -g            Same as -a.
  inet_addr     Specifies an internet address.
  -N if_addr    Displays the ARP entries for the network interface specified
                by if_addr.
  -d            Deletes the host specified by inet_addr. inet_addr may be
                wildcarded with * to delete all hosts.
  -s            Adds the host and associates the Internet address inet_addr
                with the Physical address eth_addr.  The Physical address is
                given as 6 hexadecimal bytes separated by hyphens. The entry
                is permanent.
  eth_addr      Specifies a physical address.
  if_addr       If present, this specifies the Internet address of the
                interface whose address translation table should be modified.
                If not present, the first applicable interface will be used.
Example:
  > arp -s 157.55.85.212   00-aa-00-62-c6-09  .... Adds a static entry.
  > arp -a                                    .... Displays the arp table.

C:\>_
```

Figure 2—3: The ARP command line options.

2.2.3 Internet Control Message Protocol (ICMP)

Defined in RFC 792 and a required TCP/IP standard Internet Control Message Protocol (ICMP) is used by IP based routers and hosts to report errors and give status information. For example, ICMP is used if any of the following are true:

- IP datagram does not get to its destination.
- A more favorable route is given to a sending host's data by an IP router.
- The transmissions rate of the datagram for whatever reason cannot be used by the IP router and therefore the datagram cannot be forwarded.

Various ICMP messages are identified in the ICMP header. Because ICMP messages are carried in IP datagrams, they are unreliable. Table 2.11 lists common ICMP error messages and descriptions.

ICMP Errors	Descriptions for error messages
Destination unreachable	The datagram cannot be delivered so the host will be informed by this error message.
Echo request	Checks to see if a router or host is on the network.
Echo reply	Gives a reply to ICMP echo requests
Redirect	Gives preferred route information to host
Source quench	Tells host that congestion is present and to lower rate that datagram are being sent.
Time Exceeded	TTL of the datagram has expired

Table 2—11: ICMP error messages and descriptions.

To send ICMP echo requests open the command prompt and use the ping command as shown below in Figure 3.

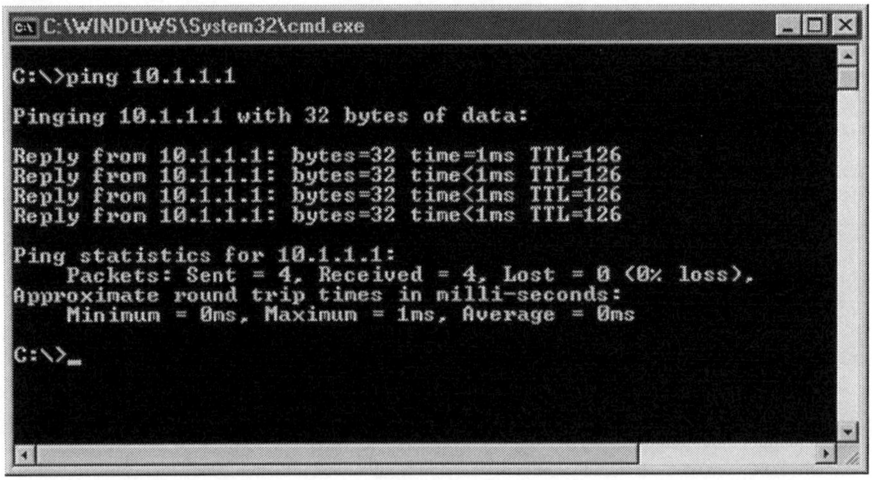

Figure 2—4: Using the ping command to send an ICMP echo request.

As you can see from the reply from the IP Address, the 32-byte packet was received in less than one millisecond and the TTL is 1236. The ping statistics are also shown below the reply information.

Figure 4 below shows a ping reply from hardware that does not reply to the echo request.

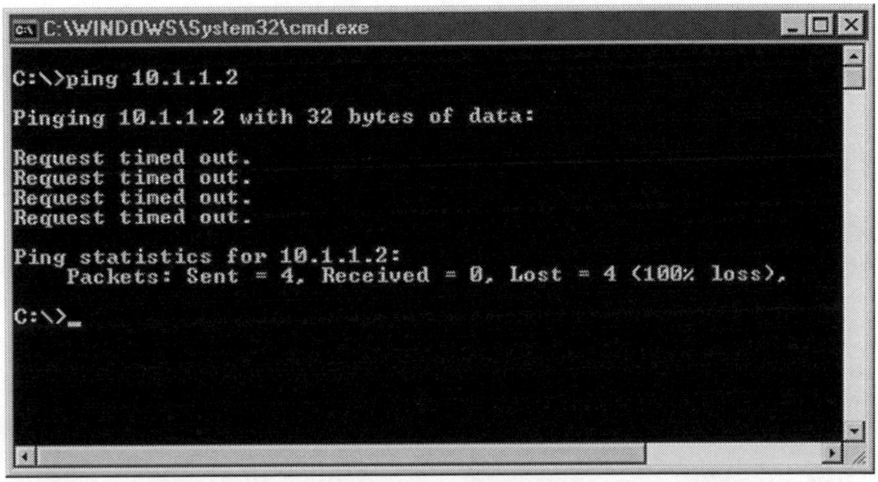

Figure 2—5: Ping reply from IP address that does not reply to echo request.

As you can see from the results the output is completely different that Figure 3. The echo request did not get an answer from the sender. The request will show as time out and the ping statistics show that four packets were sent and none was received. The Lost statistic shows also that all four packets were lost. To get a list of ping commands open the command prompt and type "ping /?" at the command prompt shown in Figure 5.

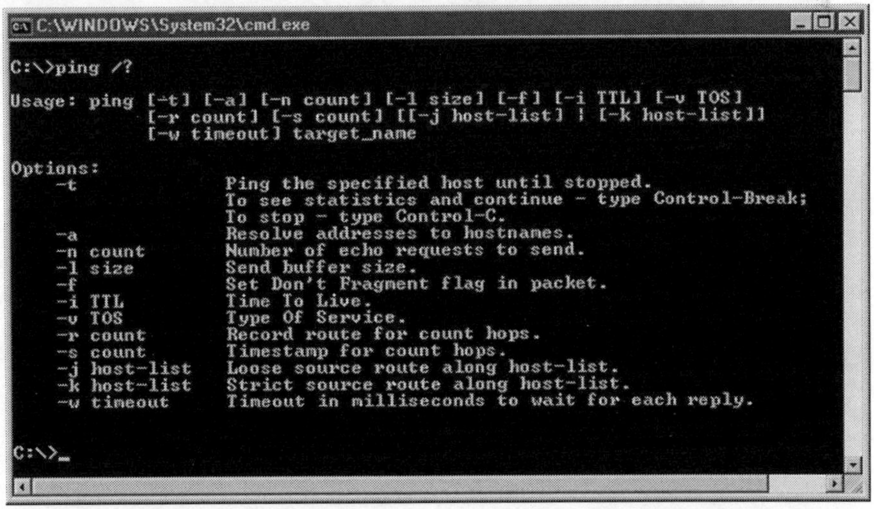

Figure 2—6: Listing of Ping commands.

The ping command is a simple and invaluable tool to use for troubleshooting network problems.

2.2.4 Internet Group Management Protocol (IGMP)

Internet Group Management Protocol (IGMP) is used by TCP/IP networks to allow computers to send its multicast group membership information to routers. Multicasting is frequently used with Streaming Audio and applications that which to broadcast update information. IGMP sends multicast IP traffic to just one IP address instead of many IP addresses. Host machines belonging to multicast groups act as subscribers to the multicast traffic. IP multicasting is similar to a newsletter subscription. When only subscribers receive the newsletter when it is published, only host computers that belong to the multicast group receive and process IP traffic sent to the group's reserved IP address. Multicast groups can be across networks and have no limitations such as size or member quotas.

Table 2.12 shows a listing of common IGMP explanation as well as their descriptions.

IGMP message	Explanation
Host membership report	A host sends this message to report that it has joined a multicast group.
Host membership query	A router that supports multicast traffic sends this message to query for new members.
Leave group	Host machines send this message to announce their departure from the multicast group.

Table 2—12: IGMP Messages and Explanations.

Before Multicasting can function properly, you need to make certain that the routers in your organization support the use of Multicasting. Before you try to setup multicasting, make certain you check with your hardware manufacturer to see if it is supported.

2.2.5 User Datagram Protocol UDP

UDP is fast and has low overhead and it delivers datagrams using a connectionless approach. The data is encapsulated and sent inside the IP data packets. UPD also uses ports as queues to send and receive messages. This queue allows UDP to receive more than one message at a time. IANA assigns UDP ports and it is not recommended that unassigned port numbers be used for UDP.

Ports numbers are broken into three categories:

- Well Known Ports are numbered between zero and 1023.
- Registered Ports are numbered between 1024 through 49151
- Dynamic and/or Private Ports are numbered between 49152 through 65535

Some common UDP ports are listed in Table 2.13.

Port	Service
23	Telnet
69	Trivial File Transfer Protocol (TFTP)
137	NetBIOS name service
138	NetBIOS datagram service
161	Simple Network Management Protocol (SNMP)
520	Routing Information Protocol (RIP)

Table 2—13: UDP Ports and Services associated with these ports.

For a complete and current listing of all UDP port numbers, you can visit the IANA website and view the port assignment numbers at the following URL:

http://www.iana.org/assignments/port-numbers.

Pop Quiz 2.1

Pop Quiz 2.1 Questions

1. What does ARP stand for and how is it used by IP?

2. What does 171.35.44.0/23 indicate?

3. What does a computer with an address of 169.254.0.3 indicate?

4. What node type will be automatically configured when a Windows XP or Windows Server 2003 computer is configured to use a WINS server?

5. On what network tier in the three-tier model would you expect to find a switch that provides access to end stations?

Pop Quiz 2.1 Answers

1. ARP stands for Address Resolution Protocol, and is used by IP to find the hardware address associated with an IP address.

2. 173.35.44.0/23 indicates a network address of 171.35.44.0 which uses a subnet mask of 255.255.254.0, That subnet mask uses 23 bits for the network ID space, hence the "/23" indicator.

3. That IP address indicates that the computer is configured to get its address from DHCP, that the DHCP server did not respond before the timeout period, and that there are at least 2 other computers in its broadcast domain.

4. H or Hybrid node is the node type automatically configured under those circumstances.

5. This one is somewhat tricky. The end stations (computers, printers) would be on the access tier, but the switch itself lives both on the access tier and on the distribution tier.

2.3 Plan an Internet connectivity strategy

When deciding on how to connect to the internet you need to ask yourself some questions such as how many clients will need a connection to the internet. Do any servers need internet connectivity? This may seem simplistic, but if you are in a small business, maybe only a few people need internet connectivity and not the entire office. Most large enterprises and mid-size businesses have connections that are T1 and above for internet connections. If you only have a handful of workers that need connections, you may choose to implement any of the following solutions for internet connectivity.

2.3.1 Small Office or Home Office

To connect a small office or home office (SOHO) network to the Internet, you can use one of two methods:

2.3.1.1 Routed connection

This is used by a Windows Server 2003 that has the Routing and Remote Access service installed and configured to behave as if it where a router. Packets are actually routed between Small Office or Home Office SOHO clients and the connection. This method takes a good understanding of IP addressing to implement.

2.3.1.2 Translated connection

This varies from the Routed Connection because the Routing and Remote Access service is used perform Network Address Translation. The packets are forwarded between SOHO hosts and Internet hosts. This is slightly less cumbersome to setup because of the simplified configuration process on the service. This method however may not allow all traffic to be translated between SOHO and Internet hosts. To configure a translated connection use either of the two methods detailed below:

- Use the Internet Connection Sharing ICS feature of Network Connections on Microsoft Windows XP, Windows Server 2003, Standard Edition, or Windows Server 2003, Enterprise Edition. It has a single check box configuration. The downside to this is that nothing else can be configured on ICS. Make sure you do not use this method on a server configured as a Virtual Private Network because the Network Translation Method explained below must be used.
- You can use the Network Address Translation (NAT) routing protocol provided with the Routing and Remote Access snap-in on servers running Windows Server 2003 and Routing and Remote Access.
- SOHO host machines receive name resolution, addressing and translation for NAT and Internet Connection

The NAT routing protocol component is designed to provide maximum flexibility in the configuration of the server running Routing and Remote Access to provide a translated connection to Internet. The NAT routing protocol component requires more configuration steps; however, each step of the configuration is customizable. Most of the configuration can be accomplished using the Routing and Remote Access Server Setup Wizard. The NAT routing protocol component allows for ranges of IP addresses from an ISP and the configuration of the range of IP addresses allocated to SOHO hosts.

The following table 2.14 summarizes the features and capabilities of Internet Connection Sharing and the NAT routing protocol component.

Internet Connection Sharing	Network address translation
Single check box configuration	Manual configuration
Single public IP address	Multiple public IP addresses
Fixed address range for SOHO hosts	Configurable address range for SOHO hosts
Single SOHO interface	Multiple SOHO interfaces

Table 2—14: Internet Connection Sharing and Network Address Translation features.

Internet Connection Sharing is a feature designed to connect SOHO networks to the Internet. The NAT routing protocol component is designed to connect small to medium business networks to the Internet. Neither Internet Connection Sharing nor the NAT routing protocol component is designed to:

- Directly connect SOHO networks.
- Connect networks within an intranet.
- Directly connect branch office networks to a corporate network.
- Connect branch office networks to a corporate network over the Internet.

Internet Connection Sharing (ICS) permits you to use Windows Server 2003 to connect a small office network or home network over the Internet. ICS provides Network Address Translation (NAT), IP addressing, and name resolution services for all the computers on a small network. This systematic procedure describes how to install ICS on a Windows Server 2003-based computer. The following hardware or software is required for this procedure: Installed TCP/IP on machines, cable modem connection or digital subscriber line DSL connected to an Internet service provider ICS cannot be used on a network that has the following installed and in use:

- DHCP Servers, Gateways or DNS
- Static IP addresses
- Has a Windows Server 2003 domain controller

Because ICS creates a static IP address for your network adapter and allocates IP addresses to other computers on your network, you will lose your connection to the rest of the network if other network computers already provide those services. If one or more of these conditions exist in your network, you must use Windows Server 2003 NAT instead of ICS.

Do not create a virtual private network (VPN) connection to a corporate network from the ICS computer. All traffic from the ICS host machine would be forwarded through the VPN connection to the corporate network. Your internet will not be accessible and data will be sent over the ICS machine.

2.3.2 NAT on a Server using Routing and Remote Access

This section will explain how to configure NAT on a Routing and Remote Access server. This example assumes you already have the Routing and Remote Access Service running. You have to be a member of the Domain Admins group or the computer account must be added to the RAS and IAS server group

On the Administrative Tools menu, click Routing and Remote Access. In the Routing and Remote Access MMC, click to expand the server you are configuring and then expand IP Routing in the left pane. Right-click General, and then select New Routing Protocol. Choose the NAT/Basic Firewall check box then click OK. Right-click NAT/Basic Firewall in the left pane and select New Interface. Click on the interface that represents the inside network interface and click OK. From the Network Address Translation properties choose Private interface connected to private network and then click OK. Right-click NAT/Basic Firewall in the left pane and then click New Interface. Click the interface that is the outside network interface and click OK. In Network Address Translation properties, choose the Public interface connected to the Internet **option and c**lick to select the Enable NAT on this interface check box. Next, choose OK. The NAT server can automatically assign IP addresses to internal network clients. You may want to use this functionality if you do not have a DHCP server that is already assigning addressing information to clients on the internal network.

2.3.3 Configuring Internet Connection Sharing on a Computer

Log in as Administrator and you can configure the network connection on the ICS host computer. Before you begin to configure the adapter, make certain you have Firewall Software and any other Internet Sharing Software uninstalled or turned off.

Open **Network connections** by clicking on **Control Panel.** Select the Adapter that was just installed and **Right-click** then rename it to **Internet Connection** (or anything you select as long as you will know what it is used for on the host). Select **Properties** and choose **General** and make certain than the **Client for Microsoft Networks and TCP/IP** are listed. Choose the **Advanced** option and **click** to enable the **Internet Connection Sharing for this Connection** option. Choose the **Advanced** tab, select Enable Internet Connection Sharing for this connection box, and select OK to return to the desktop.

2.3.3.1 Windows Client configuration for ICS

Log on as a member of the Administrators group to set up the Windows clients that will share the Internet connection. Select **Start** then click **Control Panel** and double-click **Network Connections.** Right-click **Local Area Connection** and then choose **Properties**. Select the **General** tab and make certain that **Client for Microsoft Networks and Internet Protocol (TCP/IP)** is chosen. Select Internet Protocol (TCP/IP) and choose **Properties.** Click on the **General** tab and choose the Obtain **an IP address automatically** option and then select the **Obtain DNS server address automatically.** Choose **Advanced.** Check to be certain that the IP Settings such as DNS and WINS are all empty, because they will be provided by ICS. Return to the desktop by clicking **OK**.

It is not recommended that you use Dial-up networking to connect to the internet when using ICS. The bandwidth available for the connection is very low.

2.3.3.2 Troubleshooting ICS

- If you connect your Broadband (cable modem or DSL) to a hub, make sure you have turned off File and Print Sharing. Otherwise, you may find that users who need to access these devices may not be able to use them. Additionally, having File and Print Sharing enabled makes your network susceptible to major security problems. Verify that firewall software or other Internet sharing software from third-party manufacturers has been removed. Make sure that only the ICS-enabled computer is providing IP addresses, forwarding DNS names, or acting as a default gateway. If not, ICS may not work or you may experience unexpected behavior.
- Remove the slow NetBEUI protocol.
- Make sure the ICS computer is always available for other host machines use. It is used to provide addressing and forward DNS information to machines using this feature.
- Remember that ICS cannot be configured at all. If you need to configure IP Addresses that machines are using then use NAT instead.

ICS is not a solution for everyone of course but it is a great resource for small offices and home networks needing to have multiple internet connections on a small budget.XXXXX

2.4 Plan network traffic monitoring.

Why would one plan for monitoring? There is a simple reason – monitoring the impact of implementing new technologies (IPSec, for example) or removing services from the network allows you to plan for the "cost" of these decisions.

2.4.1 Network Monitor

By creating a monitoring plan, you are able to delineate the strategy that will be used to test the proposed solution, before you put it into place. Some of the things you want to include in a monitoring plan are:

- What specific area are you monitoring
- What is the criteria for success
- What resources, both computers and persons, are required for testing

An administrator may want to set up a staging area, or test environment, that emulates your actual network infrastructure, so that you can gain data on a solution prior to its implementation. There are two key plans to remember when considering a staging environment to monitor:

- The test environment should be kept separate from the actual working environment.
- The test environments must accurately represent the actual working environment, including the constraints

One key element in the monitoring process is establishing environmental baselines. The current network infrastructure will be an "unknown" without baseline documentation, and the risk to implement new technologies will be far greater.

Windows Server 2003 comes complete with a substantial collection of networking client tools to help an administrator handle and sustain network performance. These tools can be used to settle everyday network configuration and interoperability challenges. The following table lists the technology and the tools used to manage and maintain the network.

Technology	Tools	Definition
DHCP	Network Monitor	to detect and troubleshoot networking problems by capturing and viewing the frames (or packets) that a computer receives or broadcasts on a local area network
	Sysmon	measures the performance of local or remote computers on a network as well as collects and allows viewing of extensive data about hardware resource usage and system services activity
	Ipconfig	Displays all current TCP/IP network configuration values and refreshes DHCP and DNS settings. Used without parameters, ipconfig displays IPv6 addresses or the IPv4 address, subnet mask, and default gateway for all adapters.
	Audit logs	Includes several logging features and server parameters that supplies advanced auditing capabilities. The following features can be specified: The directory path in which the DHCP server stores audit log files. A maximum size restriction (in megabytes) for the total amount of disk space available for all audit log files created and stored by the DHCP service. An interval for disk checking that is used to determine how many times the DHCP server writes audit log events to the log file before checking for available disk space on the server. A minimum size requirement (in megabytes) for server disk space that is used during disk checking to determine if sufficient space exists for the server to continue audit logging.

Technology	Tools	Definition
DNS	Dnscmd	A command-line tool for managing DNS servers. This tool can be used to script batch files, to help automate the management and update of existing DNS server configurations, or to perform set up and configuration of DNS servers.
	Registry Editor	An advanced tool for viewing and changing settings in the system registry, which contains information about how that computer runs.
	DNSLint	An add-on Microsoft Windows utility that helps to diagnose common DNS name resolution issues. Available for download from the Microsoft site.
	Nslookup	Displays information that can be used to diagnose DNS infrastructure.
IPSec	IPSec monitor	Provides information about which IPSec policy is active and whether a secure channel between computers is established.
	IPSec policy snap-in	Manages IPSec policies for secure communication with other computers.
	Active Directory Users and Computers	Tool used to perform day-to-day Active Directory administration tasks. The tasks that can be performed with this tool include creating, deleting, modifying, moving, and setting permissions on objects stored in the directory.
	Group Policy	Enables directory-based change and configuration management of user and computer settings, including security and user data.
	Event Viewer	Used to view and manage event logs, gather information about hardware and software problems, and monitor security events. Event Viewer maintains logs about program, security, and system events.
	Resultant Set of Policy (RSoP)	A feature that simplifies Group Policy implementation and troubleshooting by using WMI to determine how policy settings are applied to users and computers.

Technology	Tools	Definition
Network access	Event Viewer	as above
	Remote access diagnostics	Used to collect detailed logs and information about a remote access connection. Diagnostics can be set from the Diagnostics tab of the properties of the connection in the Network Connection folder, or run specific diagnostics by typing the **netsh ras** diagnostics command at the command line.
	Network Monitor	as above
	Netdom	a tool that allows management of Windows domains and trust relationships from the command line
	Kerbtray	Used to display ticket information for a given computer running the Kerberos protocol. The Kerbtray icon is located in the system tray (on the right side of the taskbar) and can be used to view and purge the ticket cache.
Routing	Hostname	displays the host name portion of the full computer name of the computer
	Ipconfig	as above
	Netstat	displays active TCP connections, ports on which the computer is listening, Ethernet statistics, the IP routing table, IPv4 statistics (for the IP, ICMP, TCP, and UDP protocols), and IPv6 statistics (for the IPv6, ICMPv6, TCP over IPv6, and UDP over IPv6 protocols). Used without parameters, netstat displays active TCP connections.
	Nbtstat	Displays NetBIOS over TCP/IP (NetBT) protocol statistics, NetBIOS name tables for both the local computer and remote computers, and the NetBIOS name cache. Nbtstat allows a refresh of the NetBIOS name cache and the names registered with Windows Internet Name Service (WINS).

Technology	Tools	Definition
	Address Resolution Protocol (ARP)	Displays and modifies entries in the Address Resolution Protocol (ARP) cache, which contains one or more tables that are used to store IP addresses and their resolved Ethernet or Token Ring physical addresses. There is a separate table for each Ethernet or Token Ring network adapter installed on your computer.
	Netdiag	Used to display information about IPSec policies and statistics, report network configuration, and test basic networking capabilities and domain-based functionality.
	Tracert	Determines the path taken to a destination by sending ICMP Echo Request or ICMPv6 messages to the destination with incrementally increasing TTL field values. The path displayed is the list of nearside router interfaces of the routers in the path between a source host and a destination.
	Ping	Verifies IP-level connectivity to another TCP/IP computer by sending ICMP Echo Request messages. The receipt of corresponding Echo Reply messages are displayed, along with round-trip times. Ping is the primary TCP/IP command used to troubleshoot connectivity, reachability, and name resolution.

Technology	Tools	Definition
	Pathping	Provides information about network latency and network loss at intermediate hops between a source and destination. Pathping sends multiple Echo Request messages to each router between a source and destination over a period and then computes results based on the packets returned from each router. Because pathping displays the degree of packet loss at any given router or link, it can be determined which routers or subnets might be having network problems. Pathping performs the equivalent of the tracert command by identifying which routers are on the path. It then sends pings periodically to all of the routers over a specified time period and computes statistics based on the number returned from each.

Table 2—15: Windows Server 2003 Monitoring Tools

2.5 Troubleshoot connectivity to the Internet.

TCP/IP has many utilities that can be used to troubleshoot network connectivity. The command line is used by these utilities and can be accessed by clicking on **Start** then Run and then typing **CMD.** Table 2.16 below lists some of these utilities.

Utility	Description
Arp	Address Resolution Protocol (ARP) cache that holds software-to-hardware address mappings that are used for sending data on the local network. This command displays the information. Type arp /? For a viewing of all the switches available with this command.
Hostname	Shows the host name of the computer.
Ipconfig	Used to show current TCP/IP configuration information. This command has helpful switches that can be used to release and renew IP configuration information. Use the /? Switch with the command to see a listing of all switches available.
Nbtstat	If you are using NetBIOS over TCP/IP then this command checks for connections and updates the LMHosts cache.
Netsh	Shows the TCP/IP settings on either the local computer or a remote computer.
Netstat	Shows statistics for protocols as well as current TCP/IP connection information.
Nslookup	Queries DNS Server and checks records, domain host aliases, services, and operating system information.
Ping	Used to check to see if TCP/IP working by sending packets to other machines.
Route	Shows local IP routing table for viewing and editing as needed.
Tracert	Shows the network route taken by a packet until it reaches its destination.
Pathping	This is used to traces the route a packet takes to its destination and it then shows information on packet loss (if any) for each router in the destination path.

Table 2—16: Internet Connection Sharing and Network Address Translation features.

The table above shows a few utilities you can use to troubleshoot TCP/IP connectivity. Please review the Microsoft Resource kit for additional TCP/IP utilities. Another tool called netdiag.exe can be installed from the Windows Server 2003 CD under the \support\tools folder. It can also be used to troubleshoot TCP/IP configuration problems.

2.5.1 Diagnose and resolve issues related to Network Address Translation (NAT)

Network Address Translation troubleshooting can be done using the following simple steps on a Windows Server. Most of these troubleshooting techniques are common sense things to check. Table 2.17: gives some examples of NAT troubleshooting.

Problem	Possible Solution
Port Translation problems	Check the Public Interface properties to make certain the **Translate TCP/IP headers** in the **General** tab. This is if more private hosts than public hosts are available.
Public Addresses are not correct	Check the **Address Pool** tab on the public interface for errors.
NAT interfaces do not function properly.	Check to see if both the public (outside – internet connection) and the private (inside SOHO connection) are added to the NAT routing protocol.
Internal machines are not receiving IP address configurations	Make sure that NAT name resolution has been enabled on the internal (SOHO) interface.

Table 2—17: NAT troubleshooting issues and resolutions.

You can always check out the Microsoft Knowledge base for issues regarding NAT troubleshooting. It can also be a good idea to review the most common issues before you begin to install and configure NAT. Often caveats will be listed and you can be informed before you begin and the knowledge can save you valuable time when implementing this technology.

2.5.2 Diagnose and resolve issues related to name resolution cache information

Microsoft has specific utilities you can use for troubleshooting name resolution problems. Depending on the type of error you are receiving, select the utility to begin the troubleshooting on the machine. This is of course after you have verified that the other machine is powered up and available for use.

Again, many times it could be an issue as simple as the other machine being powered down that could keep you from accessing information on that machine Use Table 2.18 below for a list of problem descriptions, things you can check before the utility is used for troubleshooting name resolution issues.

Issue	**Things to check**	**Utility to use:**
Cannot resolve name of machine to its IP address	Are the DNS Servers configured properly on host machine? Also, review the configuration of the machine you are using as well.	Use the ping command to see if you can send a packet to the host machine. From the server you can also use the nbtstat –n command to view a listing of all machines connected to that server. If you see the machine listed then you need to check the WINS address of the other machine.
Cannot resolve name of a computer using LMHosts.	Check the hosts file or DNS Server to see if the host name is listed with the proper IP Address and Hostname.	Try to Ping the machine. Use Nslookup at the command prompt. This sends DNS name queries to the primary DNS Server listed on your machine. Check the IP Address entry in the LMHosts file for accuracy. Check the spelling in the LMHosts file on machine. Make sure the mapping information (computer name to IP address) was entered in the LMHosts files and not the hosts file in the etc directory. Type the hostname command at the prompt to get the fully qualified domain name of the machine.

Table 2—18: Diagnostic utilities you can use to troubleshoot Name Resolution problems.

2.5.3 Diagnose and resolve issues related to client configuration

If it is just your machine experiencing difficulty and you do not have any other means in which to check connectivity with other client machines, always start troubleshooting TCP/IP by checking your local machine. You would not believe how many times it is something related to a configuration issue or possible CAT5 connection issue with a cable. Once you are convinced your server or machine is not the problem, you can use some basic commands to resolve client related configuration issues. IPCONFIG can show you details of your computer or server connection. See Figure 7 for an example of this command.

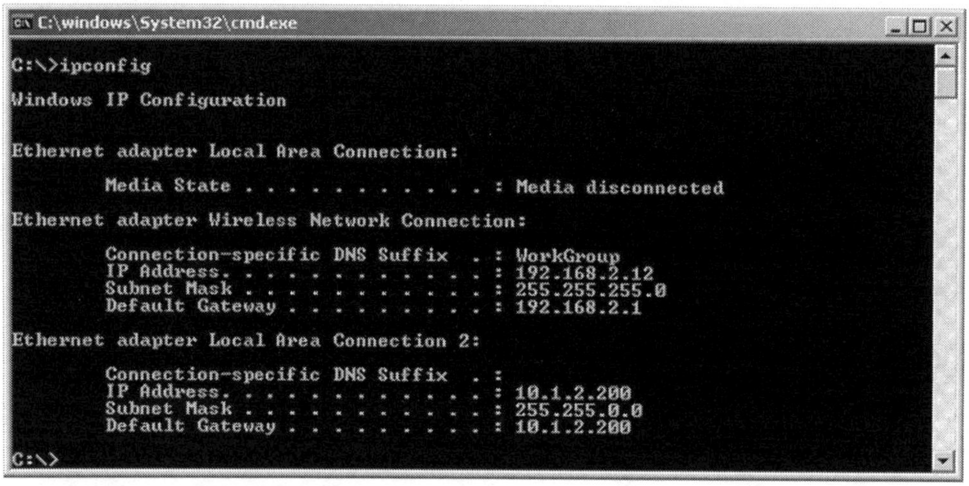

Figure 2—7: The IPCONFIG /all command.

As you can see from the output this command shows the Ethernet adapter (which happens to be wireless) and the IP Address, Subnet and Gateway information. If more than one adapter is installed as shown here it also shows the Secondary IP Adapter information.

For older clients using the Windows 95, Windows 98, and Windows Millennium Edition operating systems have to use the **winipcfg** command. The **ipconfig** command will not work on these client machines.

Of course, IPCONFIG has many command line switches that will give you more information and allow you to perform other functions. The IPCONFIG /all command will show a more detailed report than the IPCONFIG command. Figure 8 shows the IPCONFIG /ALL command in use.

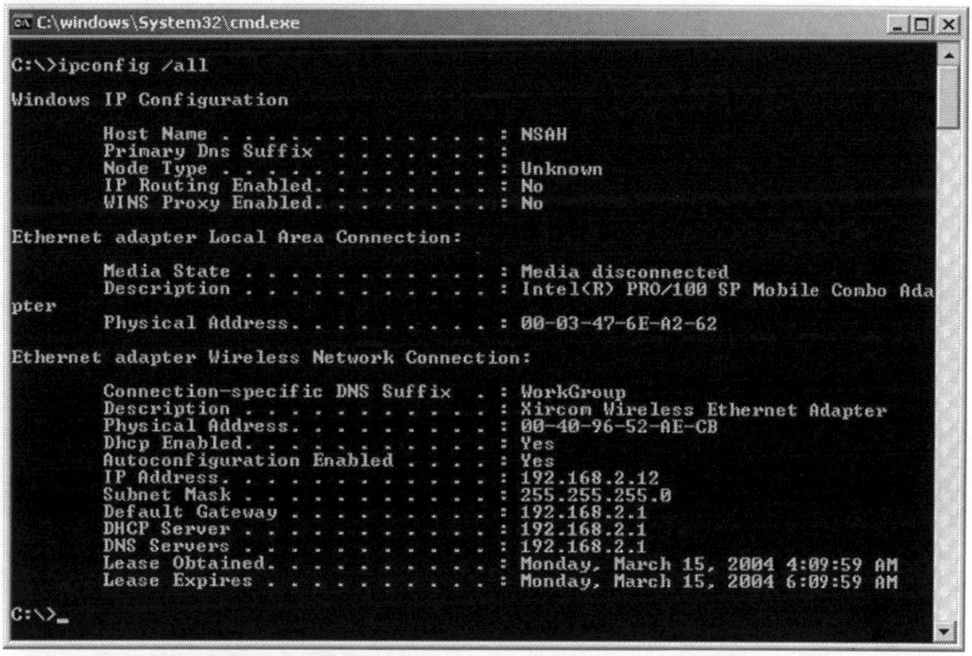

Figure 2—8: The IPCONFIG /all command.

When you use the **ipconfig** command with the **/all** option, a detailed configuration report is produced for all interfaces, including any configured serial ports. With **ipconfig /all**, you can redirect command output to a file and paste the output into other documents. You can also use this output to confirm the TCP/IP configuration of each computer on the network or to further investigate TCP/IP network problems. If a computer is configured with an IP address that is a duplicate of an existing IP address, the subnet mask appears as 0.0.0.0. You can also release the IP configuration of a machine by typing ipconfig /release at the prompt as shown below in Figure 9.

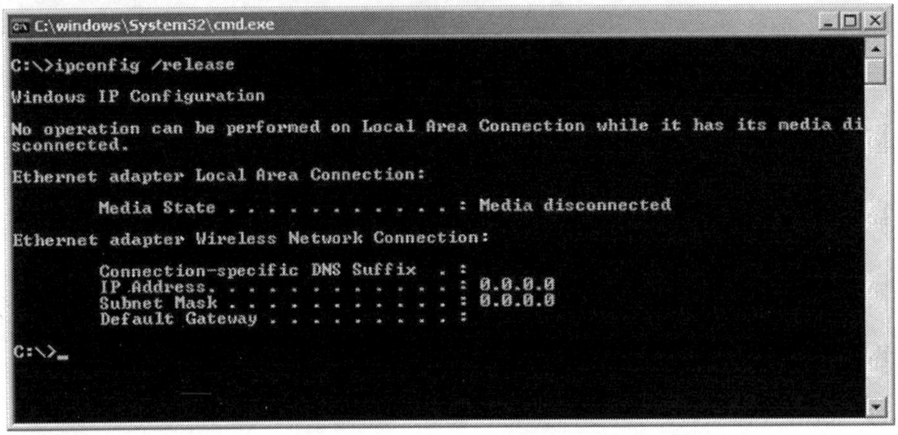

Figure 2—9: Releasing the IP configuration information of a machine.

Once you have used this command you will either need to perform an Ipconfig /renew of reboot the machine to have the IP information reissued to the machine. If it does not have any IP configuration information then it will not function on the network. Figure 10: shows the ipconfig /renew command.

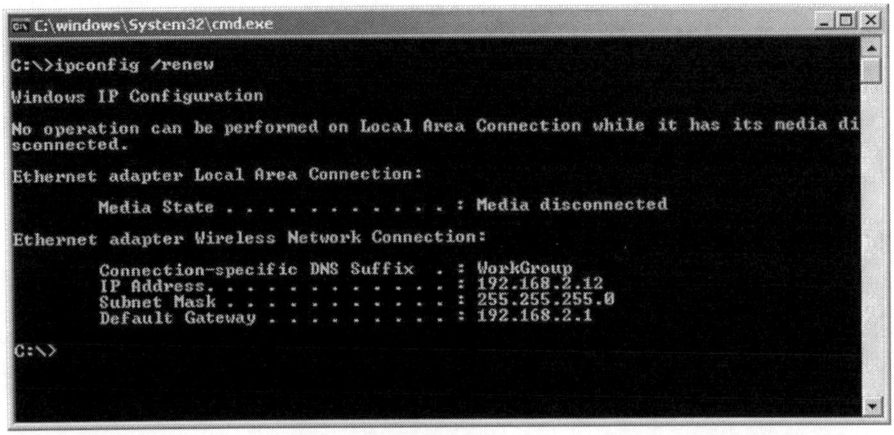

Figure 2—10: The ipconfig /renew command.

The machine should renew its IP configuration information as shown above. If the machine could not reconnect then you need to check the CAT5 cable, LAN Adapter hardware properties and driver information to rule out any problems with these components. As well, verify that other machines able to connect to the network.

Microsoft also has a Technical Reference guide that also will give added insight for troubleshooting TCP/IP it can be found at the following URL: `http://www.microsoft.com/resources/documentation/WindowsServ/2003/all/techref/en-us/default.asp` at the time of this writing.

Pop Quiz 2.2

Pop Quiz 2.2 Questions

1. What are the differences between a routed and a translated connection to the Internet?
2. What is the difference between ICS and NAT?
3. What are the client configuration requirements when using ICS?
4. Should you perform network monitoring on a local computer or from a remote computer?
5. Which IPCONFIG command can have its output redirected to a text file?

Pop Quiz 2.2 Answers

1. A routed connection indicates that the internal network uses public IP addresses with a basic router, while a translated connection uses a form of NAT and private internal addresses.

2. Several, actually. One is that NAT is a server service, while ICS can be enabled on either a server or desktop operating system. Another, and more important from a planning perspective, is that ICS supports a single internal subnet while NAT can work with many. Finally, ICS is very simple to configure, while NAT is less so.

3. Simply ensure that the client is configured to use DHCP or Server Supplied for its IP address.

4. Unlike system monitoring, where the monitor itself will skew the results when run locally, network monitoring should be done locally because there will be no additional network traffic associated with the monitoring.

5. IPCONFIG /ALL |file.txt (use the pipe character to redirect).

2.6 Troubleshoot TCP/IP addressing

2.6.1 Diagnose and resolve issues related to client computer configuration.

In order to run TCP/IP, you must have, at minimum, an IP address and a subnet mask. To be able to communicate over a router, you must also have a default gateway address. The default gateway address is the address of the router than will route your packets out of your local subnetwork.

Your IP address uniquely identifies you on your network. If two computers have identical IP addresses, then communication will fail. While Windows Server 2003 does support IPv6, for the most part, networks are still using IPv4, which is an IP address entered in decimal format in four parts (i.e.: 10.10.72.100). We will deal with this addressing issue in this section.

Each part is called an octet, because they are actually binary numbers of eight characters each. Which part of the IP address is the network address and which part is the host address primarily depends on the Class of the IP address. This is determined by the value of the first four bits of the first octet.

So why do you need a subnet mask? The subnet mask is a binary number designed to separate the network ID from the host ID on an IP address.

> **NOTE:** Two Ways of Showing Subnet Masks – You will note that, on occasion, an IP address will appear along the lines of 192.168.0.0/24. The term /x simply means x bits from the left side of the mask; so /24 would mean a subnet mask of 255.255.255.0.

A Class A address has a decimal address range in the first octet of 1-126 (127 is reserved for loopback purposes). The network identifier is the first octet only, and the remaining three octets are used for unique host addresses. The default subnet mask is 255.0.0.0.255 is 11111111 in binary, and that provides the mask for the network address.

A Class B address has a decimal range in the first octet of 128-191.The network identifier is the first two octets of the IP address, and the unique host addresses are provided from the last two octets. The default subnet mask is 255.255.0.0.

> **NOTE:** Automatic Private IP Addressing (APIPA) automates address configuration for hosts on a single-subnet network uses 169.254.0.0/16, which is reserved by the Internet Assigned Numbers Authority (IANA).

A Class C address has a decimal value range in the first octet of 192-223, with a default subnet mask of 255.255.255.0.The first three octets provide the network ID, and the last octet provides the network address.

TCP/IP decides whether an address is local (remains within the subnetwork) or remote (sends it to the default gateway for further routing) by using the subnet mask on the computer sending the information, and applying it to both the computer sending the information and the computer receiving the information.

Let's say that Computer A has an IP address of 192.168.0.22, and Computer B has an IP address of 192.168.32.11.Computer A wants to send data to Computer B. Because the IP address begins with 192, it is a Class C address. Presuming that the default subnet mask is used, IP will ascertain that the network address for Computer A is 192.168.0.x and the network address for Computer B is 192.168.32.x. The addresses are not the same so the data will be sent to the router (default gateway). If Computer B had an IP address of 192.168.0.112, the subnet mask will be applied to both IP addresses, and the result will be the same – both computers have a network address of 192.168.0.x. IP knows that the address is local and will send it out to Computer B.

There is a set routine to troubleshoot communications with TCP/IP. You use two utilities, IPCONFIG and PING. Both these utilities are part of a standard TCP/IP suite and are used at the command prompt. Let's say you are having trouble reaching a host on a different network than you. Follow these steps to troubleshoot TCP/IP:

1. Run IPCONFIG at the command prompt. What should appear is your computer's IP address, subnet mask and default gateway. If the IP address comes back 0.0.0.0, your computer does not have an active IP address, so cannot communicate on the network. If your computer is set for automatic configuration, the problem may lie either with you or with your DHCP server. Make sure that your network card is configured correctly and that the cable is securely connected at the back of the network card. If you have a valid IP address, write down the IP address, subnet mask and default gateway for further troubleshooting purposes.
2. At the command prompt, ping your loopback address (Syntax: PING 127.0.0.1). This will check to see if the network card is responding. If successful, move on to Step 3.
3. At the command prompt, ping yourself by IP address. This will actually send a test packet out to the network and back. If successful, move on to step 4.
4. At the command prompt, ping the near side of the router – your default gateway. This will test to see that you can reach your gateway. If you cannot reach your gateway, then the problem may lie with your subnet mask, or with the router itself. If you can reach your gateway, then the problem lies with the router, with the client on the other side, or with network traffic. Move on to Step 5.
5. At the command prompt, ping the far side of the router, or a different address that is not in your subnetwork. If you receive an answer, the problem is not with your system.

Sometimes the problem lies with name resolution, rather than TCP/IP configuration. If you can ping the IP address of a remote host, but you cannot ping the computer by hostname, then name resolution is the problem, not the protocol itself. Check to see if you have a DNS server configured. Try pinging another computer by hostname.

Connections that fail to resolve by name can still be made by IP address by typing \\IPADDRESS at the Run Command box.

2.6.2 Diagnose and resolve TCP/IP addressing issues related to DHCP server address assignment

There is a definite order to diagnosing and resolving issues related to DHCP. The first step is to determine if it is a client problem, a server problem, or a problem within the infrastructure. Once you have been able to determine where the challenge lies, you will be able to select the tools that will help you solve the problem.

Only one client is affected (client-side issue)

- Is the client properly connected to the network?
- Is a lease being received?
- Where is the lease originating?

These questions outline some of the most common problems associated with the client. As client-side problems tend to be more common that server-side, we will look at the solutions for these challenges first. Most of the time, ipconfig is all you will need to determine the problem.

The client is not properly connected to the network:

Make sure that the hardware is connecting properly to the network. If is amazing how often these problems are solved simply by making sure that the cable is plugged "into the back" or that the wireless network card is actually connecting to the router. You should, at least, have a link layer connection.

The client is not receiving a lease:

Quite often, it will appear that the client has an IP address, but the address will be something in the 169.254.0.0 range. That indicates that the client is using an APIPA address, as mentioned in the previous section. In XP, for example, if a DHCP server is not reached after approximately 60 seconds or leased configuration fails, the client uses the setting on the Alternate Configuration tab to determine whether to use APIPA for automatic TCP/IP addressing. You might need to disable the APIPA to troubleshoot this problem. You should be able to use **ipconfig/release** and **ipconfig/renew** to further investigate the problem.

The server is not reachable from the client network.

If you have another computer that does have a proper address, you can try to ping the address of the DHCP server. If you cannot successfully ping the DHCP server address, you will have to investigate that problem first.

2.6.2.1 Many clients are affected

When a significant number of your clients are affected, the problem probably lies either in the infrastructure or with the DHCP Server.

- Infrastructure issue*:*
  - Are the relay agents and routers property configured?
  - Are packets routing between subnets?
- Server-side issue:
  - Is the service operating properly?
  - Are scopes properly configured?
  - Are there any leases available?

In order to determine if the problem is related to the server-side infrastructure, you should examine the relay agent and routers and make sure that they are properly configured. This is the most common relay agent problem and may prevent DHCP messages from being forwarded to the DHCP Server. **Network Monitor** can help in checking for this issue.

As well, if you have subnets, you should verify that the packets are routing correctly between them. You can use **ping**, **pathping**, and **tracert** (among others) to help ascertain if the problem that is occurring is related to the infrastructure.

You should also determine if the problem is occurring on the server-side. You can do this by examining the logs to see if the DHCP service is running, verify that the scopes are properly configured (and not overlapping) and that leases are available in the proper scopes as well as ensuring that the server has been authorized. If a router is improperly configured, or if a name server option is inaccurate, it will seem as if the client cannot connect to resources. Verify that the options are configured correctly.

2.6.2.2 DHCP Audit Logs

By default, the DHCP service will record startup events, shutdown events and critical errors in the System Log file. However, you can more closely monitor the activity of the DHCP service by enabling detailed event logging. This audit log is saved, by default, in the DHCP database directory (*systemroot*/System32\Dhcp), and is named DhcpSrvLog*day* (where *day* is the first three letters of the day of the week).

All errors encountered by the DHCP service will be recorded in this log. As well, you can specify the following details:

- You can change the "save" location of the audit log file from the default location to a different folder on the server.
- You can specify a maximum size restriction for the total amount of disk space (in MB) that the DHCP logs can use.
- You can specify how often the DHCP server can write audit log events to the file before checking for available disk space. This is called the "interval".
- Finally, you can specify a minimum size requirement, in MB, for server disk space that is used during disk checking, in order to ascertain that sufficient space is available for the server to continue logging.

Steps for Troubleshooting DHCP

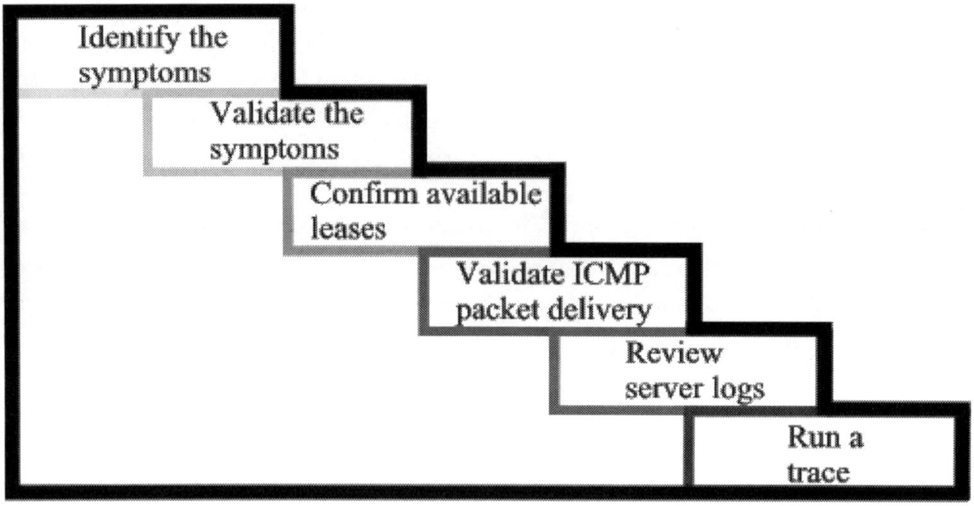

Figure 2—11: Troubleshooting Steps

As shown in Figure 2-1, there are six steps you can take while troubleshooting DHCP.

- **Identify the symptoms** - Gather as much detail as possible on what is happening from the user who is having the problem. It is easier to narrow down what the problem might be when you have all the information available.
- **Validate the symptoms** – Validate what the user is experiencing. Check for yourself what the symptoms are. Use **ipconfig /all** to check the TCP/IP configuration of the workstation. Do not decide on a solution until you are certain exactly what the problem is.
- **Confirm available leases –** Once you have ascertained that the problem is not client-side, verify that the server actually has leases available for the client to use. If there is no scope available, or the scope has used all its available addresses, the addressing problem is explained, and you can come up with a solution.
- **Validate ICMP packet delivery** – Verify that the DHCP server can be reached from the client's subnetwork. Use another machine in the same subnet, if necessary, to ping the DHCP server, or use **ipconfig /release** and **ipconfig /renew.** It is a good idea to supply the client with a temporary, static, currently unused IP address while troubleshooting.

- **Review server logs –** If there is a problem with the service itself, the event and audit logs may provide information to help you carry on troubleshooting. In Figure 3-xx, the DHCP server could not be authorized on startup, and was stopped.
- **Run a trace** – If you have not been able to identify the problem by this point, you may be able to gain some insight by capturing and examining DHCP packets on the network. If is recommended that you capture packets from more than one of the broadcast domains, so that you can examine and analyze all of the transactions between the client, relay agent(s) and server.

```
ID Date,Time,Description,IP Address,Host Name,MAC
Address
00,04/19/99,12:43:06,Started,,,
60,04/19/99,12:43:21,No DC is DS Enabled,,MYDOMAIN,
63,04/19/99,12:43:28,Restarting rogue detection,,,
01,04/19/99,13:11:13,Stopped,,,
00,04/19/99,12:43:06,Started,,,
55,04/19/99,12:43:54,Authorized(servicing),,MYDOMAIN,
```

Figure 2—12: DHCP Audit Log Example

2.7 Plan a host name resolution strategy

2.7.1 Plan a DNS name space design

Of the three options available, the first option mentioned is the least advantageous. If you choose to go with the same namespace for both internal and external use, it will require very careful and precise planning, and a split DNS infrastructure, to guarantee that the internal namespace is not reachable from the Internet.

Because of the challenges involved, and the potential security issues that could arise, using the identical internal and external namespaces is never the recommended solution. In most situations, the result is that clients are unable to locate the resources they need, because their computers are receiving incorrect IP address resolution from DNS. It is made even more challenging when NAT is involved and the external IP address is unreachable for the internal clients.

Whenever possible, one should try to follow the recognized "best practices" when planning to implement namespaces. These methods include:

- The use of distinguished names;
- Separation of internal and external namespaces; and
- The creation of namespaces that are compatible with Active Directory.

Making use of these practices, as guidelines will assist you in lowering the administrative "price tag" for supporting the namespace after implementation.

Using a set of distinguished names that do NOT overlap as the basis for your internal and external DNS use is considered a "best practice". Let's say, for example, that the existing registered namespace for your organization is ***enterprise2k3.com***.You now have a couple of options:

- Make the internal namespace both separate and discontiguous with the external namespace. Use ***enterprise2k3.local***, for example, if you never plan to make the internal resources available externally.
- Make the internal namespace separate but contiguous with the external namespace by using a subdomain for the internal domain. Using ***corp.enterprise2k3.com*** would be an example of using this option.

Note: ***local*** is not a recognized namespace on the Internet and can be used for internal use only.

Ensuring that your internal and external namespaces are separate will make it simpler to maintain and lower the administrative cost after implementation.

Another factor to consider when planning your namespace is whether your organization is going to implement Active Directory. If an implementation of Active Directory is planned now or in the future, make sure that the namespace you select is compatible with Active Directory.

Central to Windows 2003 Server operation is name resolution using DNS. Without proper name resolution, your users will not be able to locate resources on the network. If is critical that you create your DNS namespace with Active Directory in mind and that the external namespace does not conflict with your internal namespace. Take into account the following strategies when planning your namespace:

- Verify the domain name that your organization has registered for use on the Internet (in this section we have been using ***enterprise2k3.com***). If a domain name is not yet registered, you might want to arrange to have a name registered for Internet use. Whether or not you choose to have a domain name registered, the name you choose for internal use should be unique. You can identify domain names already in use by going to Internic (http://www.internic.com).
- If you already have an existing external namespace, the delegated namespace (subdomain) structure may be the ideal choice. To make administration easier, give different locations or organizations different subdomains such as ***canada.corp.enterprise2k3.com*** or ***sales.corp.enterprise2k3.com***, then use the DNS subdomain (***corp.enterprise2k3.com***) as the organization for the root of Active Directory. This gives isolation to all of the AD data in the domain or domain tree.
- Only the names that you want accessible from the Internet should be included on external servers. Internal servers should have only the names that have internal access. The internal DNS servers can be set to forward any requests they cannot resolve to the external servers for resolution.
- Ensure that you have not unintentionally created root servers. When running the Active Directory Installation Wizard (DCPromo.exe), root servers can inadvertently be created, which might interfere with internal clients' name resolution at upper levels. An example of this would be internal clients' being unable to reach external sites or parent domains. If this problem occurs, check to see if the '.' zone exists and remove it, unless you intend the server to be the root server.

2.7.2 Plan zone replication requirements

DNS zones provide both fault tolerance and reliable DNS availability for clients. Because of this essential service, they should be available from more than one network DNS Server. The method in which these zones are updated and kept uniform depends on which implementation of DNS you have chosen to implement:

- **Zone transfer** occurs in a standard (traditional) DNS zone
- **Zone replication** occurs in an AD-integrated zone

Zone transfers always commence at the secondary server in the zone. They are sent to whichever master server is configured to be the zone's source. Upon receipt of the request, the master server will respond, allowing the secondary server to pull either a partial or a full transfer of the zone database.

NOTE: A zone master server can be any other DNS server that loads the source. It does not need to be the primary server for the zone.

The current implementations of DNS no longer require that a zone transfer request be filled with a full transfer of the entire zone database, as was the case in earlier implementations. Instead, an incremental transfer allows the secondary server to pull only the changes needed, a more efficient process for propagating zone updates and changes. This helps reduce network traffic and increases the speed in which the transfers are completed.

Zone replications, the method of propagation in an Active Directory-integrated zone, adds a new level of efficiency to the replication process. This new process, called ***multimaster replication***, allows all domain controllers for the domain that are also DNS servers to modify/update the zone and then replicate the changes to other domain controller/DNS servers, rather than allowing only the primary server for the zone to make updates or modify the zone.

This replication processing is performed on a "per-property" basis, which is more effective than a full zone transfer. It also differs from the standard incremental zone transfer, because only the **result** of all changes to a record is sent, rather than all the changes made since the last transfer.

NOTE: DNS zones used to support an Active Directory domain are stored in the domain or application directory partitions of Active Directory.

2.7.3 Plan a forwarding configuration

Because you may have a number of servers in your DNS configuration set up in several ways in order to perform specific functions within your corporate environment, you must verify the functionality provided by each one when designing the plan for your server implementation. This section will discuss the different DNS server roles that you may wish to consider.

2.7.3.1 Caching-Only Server

Caching-only servers perform name resolution on behalf of clients and then store (cache) the results. They are not designed to be authoritative for zones so do not store either standard primary or standard secondary zones. The only thing stored in the cache is the most frequently requested names and associated IP addresses to answer subsequent client queries. Caching-only servers help to reduce traffic across a WAN in the following manner:

- A caching-only server first attempts to locate the requested information in its cache for client resolution. Only if the requested information is not available will it perform a query to locate the required information. At the same time, it will update its cache. The more information that is stored in cache, the less likely it is that the server will need to perform a query. In this way, WAN traffic is reduced.
- As mentioned, a caching-only server does not maintain primary or secondary zone files, so it does not generate zone transfer traffic.

This becomes particularly important in a situation where a remote office has a limited amount of available bandwidth for connecting to the corporate office. By using a caching-only server and configuring it to send recursive queries to the DNS server at the corporate office, the corporate server must assume the full workload and responsibility for providing a complete answer to the query. This is a viable solution because the corporate server should have a greater amount of available bandwidth for connecting to the Internet or an intranet.

2.7.3.2 Non-Recursive Server

A non-recursive server is a DNS server on which recursion has been disabled. In other words, this prevents the server from using recursion to resolve names on behalf of clients. As well, the server is unable to forward requests, so if it is unable to resolve the name directly, it will return a negative response.

This type of server should be used when your DNS servers are authoritative for one zone or more AND are Internet facing. This is critical because, while the server can resolve names internally for your clients, computers on the Internet cannot use your DNS server to resolve other domain names on the Internet. This set up also allows you to restrict your clients to resolving names internal to your organization, if that is the corporate preference.

2.7.3.3 Forward-Only DNS Server

When a DNS server, configured to use forwarders, cannot resolve a query either locally or by using its forwarders, it will try to do so using standard recursion. There may be times when you do not want this to happen. It is good to know that you can also configure a DNS server to not perform recursion after the forwarders fail. In this arrangement, the server will not attempt any additional recursive queries to resolve the name; rather, it fails the query. This configuration is called a forward-only DNS server. Unlike a non-recursive DNS server, a forward-only DNS server builds up a cache relating to the domain name and uses this cache to attempt to resolve host names.

Configure your network firewall to allow only one DNS server to communicate with the Internet. Then use forwarders to manage the DNS traffic between your network and the Internet.

A conditional forwarder is a DNS server that forwards DNS queries consistent with the DNS domain name stated in the query.

The DNS server setting for a conditional forwarder contains the following elements:

- For which domain names the DNS server will forward queries.
- At least one DNS server IP addresses for each domain name specified.

A DNS server that is configured to use a forwarder has a unique method of resolving queries. It will first attempt to resolve the query using its cache, and the primary and secondary zones that it hosts. If it is unsuccessful, it will send a recursive query to the forwarder. The server will then wait briefly for a response from the forwarder before attempting to contact the DNS servers in its root hints.

> NOTE: When a DNS server forwards a query to a forwarder, it sends a recursive query to the forwarder, rather than the normal iterative query sent during standard name resolution.

There may be instances when you want DNS clients in discrete networks to resolve each others' names, but not query DNS servers on the Internet. In those cases, configure the DNS servers in each network to forward queries for names in the other network to a specific DNS server. Each specifically named DNS server will build up a large cache of data, reducing the need for recursion.

2.7.4 Plan for DNS security

There are three levels of DNS security. You need to determine the appropriate security level for your network based on your organization's needs. The following three levels of DNS security will help you understand your current DNS configuration and enable you to increase your organization's DNS security.

Low-level security is a standard DNS deployment without any security precautions configured. You deploy this level of DNS security only in network environments in which there is no concern for the integrity of your DNS data or in a private network in which there is no threat of external connectivity.

When you implement low-level security:

- Your organization's DNS infrastructure is fully exposed to the Internet.
- Standard DNS resolution is performed by all DNS servers in your network.
- All DNS servers are configured with root hints pointing to the root servers for the Internet.
- All DNS servers permit zone transfers to any server.
- All DNS servers are configured to listen on all of their IP addresses.
- Cache pollution prevention is disabled on all DNS servers.
- Dynamic updating is allowed for all DNS zones.
- UDP and TCP/IP port 53 is open on your network firewall for both source and destination addresses.

Medium-level security uses the DNS security features that are available without running DNS servers on domain controllers and storing DNS zones in Active Directory. When you implement medium-level security:

- Your organization's DNS infrastructure has limited exposure to the Internet.
- All DNS servers are configured to use forwarders to point to a specific list of internal DNS servers when they cannot resolve names locally.
- All DNS servers limit zone transfers to servers listed in the name server (NS) resource records in their zones.
- DNS servers are configured to listen on specified IP addresses.
- Cache pollution prevention is enabled on all DNS servers.
- Dynamic updating is not allowed for any DNS zones.

- Internal DNS servers communicate with external DNS servers through the firewall, allowing only a limited list of source and destination addresses.
- External DNS servers in front of your firewall are configured with root hints pointing to the root servers for the Internet.
- All Internet name resolution is performed by using proxy servers and gateways.

High-level security uses the same configuration as medium-level security, in addition to the security features that are available when the DNS server services running on a domain controller and DNS zones are stored in Active Directory. In addition, high-level security eliminates DNS communication with the Internet. This is not a typical configuration, but it is recommended whenever Internet connectivity is not required.

When you implement high-level security:

- Your organization's DNS infrastructure allows no Internet communication with internal DNS servers.
- Your network uses an internal DNS root and namespace where all authority for DNS zones is internal.
- DNS servers that are configured with forwarders use internal DNS server IP addresses only.
- All DNS servers limit zone transfers to specified IP addresses.
- DNS servers are configured to listen on specified IP addresses.
- Cache pollution prevention is enabled on all DNS servers.
- Internal DNS servers are configured with root hints pointing to the internal DNS servers hosting the root zone for your internal namespace.
- All DNS servers are running on domain controllers. A discretionary access control list (DACL) is configured on the DNS Server service to allow only specific individuals to perform administrative tasks on the DNS server.
- All DNS zones are stored in Active Directory. A DACL is configured to allow only specific individuals to create, delete, or modify DNS zones.
- DACLs are configured on DNS resource records to allow only specific individuals to create, delete, or modify DNS data.
- Secure dynamic updating is configured for DNS zones, except the top-level and root zones, which do not allow dynamic updates at all.

2.7.4.1 Securing zones

After you have identified the replication process that you will use, you must secure the zone transfers. You can secure your zone transfers in several different ways. By default, the Windows Server 2003 DNS Server service only allows zone information to be transferred to servers listed in a zone's NS resource records. Although this is a secure configuration, for increased security you should change this setting to allow zone transfers to specified IP addresses.

Your network security specialists still need to protect your network against IP spoofing, in case an attacker attempts to impersonate one of your specified IP addresses. Be aware that changing this setting to allow zone transfers to any server might expose your DNS data to an attacker who is attempting to footprint your network.

With the increasing use of virtual private networks (VPNs), DNS zone replication can occur across public networks, such as the Internet. It is important to protect the names and IP addresses replicated over these public networks against unauthorized access. You can protect the replication data by using IP Security (IPSec), VPN tunnels, or Active Directory.

For your security, you need to encrypt all replication traffic that is sent over public networks. If you encrypt replication traffic by using IPSec or VPN tunnels, you should consider using:

- The strongest level of encryption and VPN tunnel authentication.
- Routing found in the Routing and Remote Access feature of Windows 2000 to provide the IPSec or VPN tunnels.

2.7.4.2 Planning a DNS Strategy

You can protect replication traffic by using Active Directory–integrated zones. Because these zones are stored in Active Directory, they provide inherent security by:

- Exclusively replicating between DNS servers that have Active Directory integrated zones.
- Requiring all DNS servers that have Active Directory–integrated zones to be registered with Active Directory.
- Encrypting all replication traffic between DNS servers.

You can reduce the impact of DNS replication traffic on overused network segments to improve data transmission rates for other network traffic.

To improve the performance of replication traffic, consider:

- Using fast zone transfers to compress the zone replication data in a standard DNS infrastructure. Note that older versions of BIND do not support fast zone transfers.
- Modifying the replication schedule of secondary zones to replicate during non-peak hours of operation.
- Performing incremental zone replication instead of complete zone replication when possible.

Incremental zone replication requires BIND version 8.2.1 and later. The Windows NT 4.0 DNS service performs only complete zone transfers.

2.7.5 Examine the interoperability of DNS with third-party DNS solutions

DNS servers running Windows Server 2003 are compliant with most of the Request for Comments (RFC) related to DNS.

The primary benefits for interoperability in these environments include:

- Full interoperability with other DNS server implementations that implement RFC-compliant behavior for DNS name service.
- Use of Windows DNS servers to provide DNS service on the Internet.

Request for Comments (RFC)
An official document of the Internet Engineering Task Force (IETF) that specifies the details for protocols included in the TCP/IP family specifications used to define the DNS protocol. This provides clear benefits for operating DNS servers in mixed or heterogeneous environments. For more information about RFCs, see DNS RFCs.

For interoperability testing, the Windows Server 2003 DNS development team has tested Windows Server 2003 DNS Server and Client services with the following versions of the Berkeley Internet Name Domain (BIND) DNS server implementation:

- BIND 4.9.7
- BIND 8.1.2
- BIND 8.2
- BIND 9.1.0

Interoperability and configuration issues related to using Windows Server 2003 DNS with other various environments, or when using DNS servers on the Internet, are covered in the following sections.

2.7.5.1 DNS considerations for Active Directory

In order to locate Active Directory domain controllers, DNS is required. The administrator has the option to set up the DNS Server service as part of the installation of Active Directory.

NOTE: When you install Active Directory on a server, the server is promoted to the role of a domain controller.

During the Active Directory installation processes, the wizard provides you with the option to automatically install the DNS Server service and add new zones locally. These zones will be created based upon the DNS name you specify to the wizard.

It is a good plan to allow for fault tolerance, which can be done by having two domain controllers each running the DNS server service and hosting AD-integrated zones.

DNS is required for network resources to locate Active Directory domain controllers. You can elect to set up the DNS Server service as part of the installation of Active Directory using the Active Directory Installation Wizard. When you install Active Directory on a server, the server is promoted to the role of a domain controller.

When you install Active Directory on a server, the Active Directory Installation Wizard provides the option to automatically install the DNS Server service and add new zones locally. When you select the option to install and configure a DNS server using the Active Directory Installation Wizard, zones are created based on the DNS name you have specified in the wizard.

A simple method of redundancy and fault tolerance planning is to have a DNS server running on each domain controller. For each subdomain, have at least two domain controllers running the DNS Server service and hosting Active Directory-integrated zones.

2.7.5.2 Zone transfer with BIND and other DNS server implementations

As discussed earlier in this chapter, two Windows DNS servers will always use a compressed fast transfer method for a zone transfer, which includes multiple resource records (RRs) in each communication sent to finish the transfer of the zone between servers. In Windows 2003 DNS, this is the default method when initiating a transfer to other DNS server implementations. However, when necessary (such as when transferring to BIND servers prior to version 4.9.4), Windows 2003 DNS Servers can be configured to perform the zone transfers using the slower, uncompressed method.

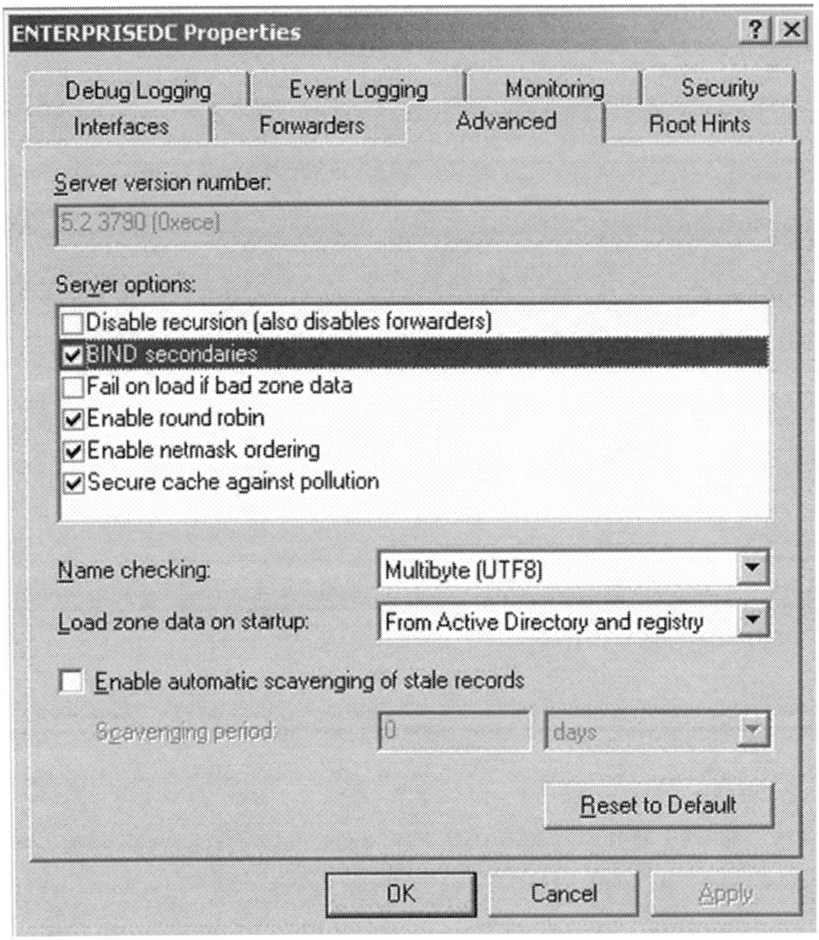

Figure 2—13: Preventing Fast Transfers

When you select the **Bind Secondaries** check box in advanced server properties, no fast transfers are made. By default, the check box is cleared to enable fast transfers. When transferring a zone between two Windows DNS servers, the DNS Server service always uses a fast transfer method that uses compression. This method includes multiple resource records (RRs) in each message sent to complete the transfer of the zone between servers. For DNS servers running Windows Server 2003, this is the default method used when initiating transfer with other DNS server implementations.

If necessary, DNS servers running Windows Server 2003 can be configured to transfer a zone using the slower uncompressed transfer format. This enables successful zone transfers to be made with DNS servers that do not support the faster transfer method, such as BIND servers prior to version 4.9.4.

2.7.5.3 Supporting Active Directory with other DNS server implementations

As an administrator, when deploying Active Directory, you may find that DNS has already been implemented using some other solution – for example, UNIX BIND DNS. You may discover that these DNS servers are running legacy versions of BIND DNS and, therefore, are not able to support the requirements for Active Directory. There are a couple of solutions to this issue:

- Upgrade any BIND DNS servers to version 8.1.2 or later of the BIND
- Migrate any of your current DNS zones to Server 2003, in order to use the DNS Server service provided.

It is always preferred that you run the DNS Server service provided with Windows Server 2003. However, you can use other implementations of DNS, provided they support these standard specifications:

- The SRV resource record [as outlined in the Internet draft, "*A DNS RR for specifying the location of services (DNS SRV).*"]
- Dynamic updates in DNS [RFC 2136] (recommended, but not essential)

While dynamic update support is only recommended, not necessary, the SRV resource record support is mandatory because it is required by Active Directory to provide basic DNS support. You must keep in mind, however, that there will be additional manual support of SRV resource records for Active Directory to function properly if the DNS Server does not support dynamic updates.

Note: A good example of a DNS implementation that supports SRV records, but does not support dynamic update, would be the DNS Server service with Windows NT 4.0, provided it has had Service Pack 4 or greater applied. (SRV resource record support was added with SP4).

In many large organizations, DNS is already implemented using other solutions, such as UNIX DNS servers that run legacy versions of BIND software. In some cases, these DNS servers are not equipped to support the DNS requirements for deploying Active Directory. This issue can be addressed in one of two ways:

Upgrade any BIND DNS servers to version 8.1.2 or later of the BIND software to meet the DNS requirements for Active Directory support.

Use the DNS Server service provided with Windows Server 2003 family, migrating, if possible, any of your current DNS zones to DNS servers running Windows Server 2003.

Although the DNS Server service is recommended to support Active Directory, you can use other DNS server implementations for this purpose. These other implementations, however, should support the following standard specifications:

The service location (SRV) resource record, as described in the Internet draft, "A DNS RR for specifying the location of services (DNS SRV)."

Dynamic updates in DNS, as described in RFC 2136.

Support for dynamic updates is recommended but not essential. Support for the SRV resource record is mandatory because it is required to provide basic DNS support to Active Directory. For example, a DNS server that does not support dynamic updates, like that provided with Windows NT Server 4.0 (updated to Service Pack 4 or later) supports the DNS requirements of Active Directory because SRV resource record support was added with Service Pack 4.

Additional manual administration of SRV resource records is needed for DNS configuration support of Active Directory to function properly on a DNS server that does not support dynamic updates. For more information, see Service location (SRV) resource records.

2.7.5.4 Interoperating Windows DNS servers with other DNS server implementations

You may decide not to migrate your entire solution to Windows Server 2003. Another option is to use the Windows DNS Server service and manage it in a split DNS configuration in which you will not upgrade or migrate the existing DNS servers for the root zones. The Server 2003 DNS will provide the management of any DNS domain names required to register, update and support for use with Active Directory.

In that instance, you can adjust your DNS namespace design strategy in one of two ways:

- You may create a single new subdomain in your current DNS domain namespace in which to place your initial Active Directory domain. Referring back to our example of ***enterprise2k3.com*** as the active registered domain name, a single subdomain such as ***corp.enterprise2k3.com*** could be created in which to place your initial DNS namespace used by Active Directory. Before you create the zone for this new subdomain, you should have these subdomains delegated away at the primary zone.

- You can also create multiple subdomains, based on your DNS second-level domain, simply to support registration of DNS names related to Active Directory. While more complex to implement, this method allows for less change to the current, non-Windows-based DNS implementation. In this case, the domain name ***enterprise2k3.com*** is both the root DNS and the root Active Directory domain name.

If you decide to use the Windows DNS Server service, you can manage it with a split DNS configuration in which existing DNS servers for root zones are not to be upgraded or migrated to other DNS solutions. Windows Server 2003 DNS is to be deployed and is to provide management of any DNS domain names required to register, update, and support for use with Active Directory.

You can modify your DNS namespace design plans in either of the following ways:

- Create a single new subdomain in your current DNS domain namespace to root your first Active Directory domain.

  For example, if your organization has registered and is using a second-level domain name, such as microsoft.com, you can create a single subdomain such as example.microsoft.com and use this domain to root the DNS domain namespace used by Active Directory. The DNS Server service is automatically configured to support Active Directory when you install the first domain controller.

  Before you have created a zone for the new subdomain at a computer running the DNS Server service, you can delegate these subdomains away at the primary zone for your second-level domain, such as "microsoft.com." In some cases, you might only need to notify another DNS or UNIX system administrator in your organization to make the delegation for you. For more information, see Delegating zones.

- Create multiple subdomains based on your DNS second-level domain to support registration of Active Directory in DNS.

  For example, if your organization has a registered second-level DNS domain name already in use (such as microsoft.com), you can create additional subdomains that are delegated to Windows DNS servers and used only for registering DNS names related to Active Directory.

  This method is more complex to implement, but enables less change to your currently deployed DNS infrastructure that is not Windows-based. With this namespace design, you create only those additional subdomains and appropriate zones needed to support your Active Directory deployment.

For example, if your organization has a registered second-level DNS domain name already in use (such as microsoft.com), you can create additional subdomains that are delegated to Windows DNS servers and used only for registering DNS names related to Active Directory.

This method is more complex to implement, but enables less change to your currently deployed DNS infrastructure that is not Windows-based. With this namespace design, you create only those additional subdomains and appropriate zones needed to support your Active Directory deployment. For example, in this configuration, the domain name microsoft.com is both the root DNS and the root Active Directory domain name for your organization.

For this configuration, you first need to create zones for the following subdomains using the DNS Microsoft Management Console (MMC) console on a DNS server running Windows Server 2003:

- child1.trpress.com
- child2.trpress.com

Before these zones are created, you can delegate these subdomains away at the primary zone for your parent or second-level domain name or notify another DNS administrator who manages these zones for your organization to do so. For more information, see Delegating zones.

2.7.5.5 Using DNS on the Internet

To establish a presence on the Internet, an individual or business must first apply for and register a second-level domain name with an authorized DNS domain name registration authority. Your Internet service provider (ISP) can often perform this function and obtain a name on your behalf, usually for an additional fee.

To register your domain name, there are several required tasks, including

1. Selecting and researching a second-level domain name that is not currently registered or in use.

This can easily be done if you have Internet access by using a WHOIS query engine provided at the Web site for your applicable Internet DNS domain name registrar. Be prepared to select an alternate name if your WHOIS query indicates that your preferred selection is already registered and in use.

2. Registering and obtaining at least one IP address valid for use on the Internet.

This address is needed for the DNS server on the Internet that you want to establish as the host for the primary copy of the zone based on your second-level domain name.

In many cases, if you are using an ISP to register a domain name on your behalf, they can specify the IP addresses for one or two of their servers as primary and secondary for the Internet.

As part of the registration process, an applicant must provide at least two currently active DNS servers that are used on the Internet as the primary and secondary servers designated for the new domain. This requirement is necessary to ensure proper Internet root server configuration and referral for others that query for your registered DNS domain name on the Internet.

After one IP address has been obtained, you can sometimes arrange (or your ISP can do so on your behalf) to use another company or ISP's DNS server as a secondary server for the zone. If you still need to obtain an IP address directly for use in the United States, a valid IP address can be obtained through the American Registry for Internet Numbers (ARIN). In other countries or regions, you might contact your local Internet service or telephony provider to find out how to register and acquire an IP address if one is needed.

Complete the registration application form and submit it with your registration fee to the appropriate Internet DNS domain name registration authority. Registrations are typically in force for a finite period and must be periodically renewed. For more information about selecting and registering your Internet DNS name, see the VeriSign Global Registry Services Web site.

2.7.5.6 Interoperability planning: Configuring related services

Windows Server 2003 DNS provides several interoperability options with other TCP/IP services. The following options can be used to reduce the amount of time you need to spend administering your DNS infrastructure:

2.7.5.7 WINS forward and reverse lookups

The DNS Server service provides for the use of WINS lookup. This feature enables configured DNS zones to refer queries not answered from current zone information to a WINS server for further resolution. With this added search of the WINS namespace, both DNS and WINS are used to complete a full search of registered names for a matched response.

WINS lookup is supported for both forward and reverse lookup zones and can be enabled on a per-zone basis or configured for selected zones. This feature should also be configured to prevent replication or zone transfer of WINS resource records to servers with other DNS implementations that do not recognize the WINS resource records.

2.7.5.8 Dynamic integration with DHCP servers

For Windows Server 2003 DNS, the DHCP service provides default support to register and update information for legacy DHCP clients in DNS zones. Legacy clients typically include other Microsoft TCP/IP client computers that were released prior to Windows 2000. The Windows Server 2003 DNS-DHCP integration enables a DHCP client (that is unable to dynamically update DNS resource records directly) to have this information updated in DNS forward and reverse lookup zones by the DHCP server.

2.7.5.9 Configuring Related Services in a Mixed DNS Environment

Server 2003 DNS offers many interoperability choices with other TCP/IP services. Verifying the following selections will help you reduce the amount of time you need to spend administrating your DNS:

WINS forward and reverse lookups: The DNS Server service allows the configuration and use of WINS lookup to refer unanswered queries to a WINS server for further resolution. WINS lookup is supported for both the forward and reverse lookup zones, and should be enabled on a "per-zone" basis. As well, this feature should be configured to prevent replication or transfer of WINS resource records to DNS implementations that do not recognize WINS.

Dynamic integration with DHCP servers: DHCP provides support for the registration and updating of information for legacy DHCP clients in DNS zones. (In this instance, a legacy client refers to TCP/IP clients running operating systems prior to Windows 2000.) Server 2003 DNS/DHCP integration allows a DHCP client to have their information updated in the DNS forward and reverse lookup zones by the DHCP server when they would normally be unable to dynamically update DNS resource records.

Pop Quiz 2.3

Pop Quiz 2.3 Questions

1. What are the five steps recommended for troubleshooting TCP/IP connectivity?
2. What does it mean if a DHCP client with a valid address cannot ping its DHCP server?
3. Which name resolution method is required when using Active Directory?
4. What does the term "zone replication" indicate?
5. Why is an Active Directory Integrated zone considered inherently secure?

Pop Quiz 2.3 Answers

1. IPCONFIG; ping loopback (ping 127.0.0.1, ping loopback); ping computer's IP address (as shown in IPCONFIG); ping computer's default gateway; ping an address not in the computer's broadcast domain (far side of the router).

2. This could be one of two things, actually. Either the DHCP server is down, or the network infrastructure between the client and the DHCP server is down.

3. For Active Directory, DNS is required, and that DNS must support SRV (service location) resource records. Support for DUP (dynamic update protocol) is not a requirement for Active Directory, however.

4. Zone replication is used when a DNS zone is configured as Active Directory Integrated, making zone information part of Active Directory replication to domain controllers.

5. Because replication will only occur as part of Active Directory replication, which means that it will only be replicated to other domain controllers for that domain.

2.8 Plan a NetBIOS name resolution strategy

2.8.1 Plan a WINS replication strategy

You should implement automatic name resolution using WINS when:

- You have a large organization with multiple broadcast domains that would make the administrative overhead of an LMHOSTS file unmanageable.
- You have a dynamic IP environment; that is, a DHCP environment in which IP addresses are configured automatically and may change frequently.
- You have applications and servers with NetBIOS requirements.

If you are unsure whether you have NetBIOS applications, either you can use Network Monitor to capture name resolution traffic, or you can contact the application developer. If you have a NetBIOS application, you will have a NetBIOS application server.

2.8.2 WINS is the preferred solution in a multi-broadcast environment

If you plan to use more than one WINS Server for fault-tolerance or redundancy, you will need to have a plan in place for replication. Deciding on whether a WINS Server is to be a push or a pull partner depends on different factors, including the configuration of your WINS Servers, your network infrastructure and the speed in which changes need to be distributed throughout the entire network.

If your WINS solution consists of more than one WINS server, you need to plan for replication. You must also plan for replication if you have an availability requirement. Your decision to configure another WINS server as either a push partner or pull partner depends on several considerations including the specific configuration of servers at your site, whether or not the partner is located across a WAN, and the importance to distribute changes throughout the network.

You can increase availability by planning a WINS solution that uses multiple servers configured with replication. Your placement of the servers depends on:

2.8.2.1 Network Infrastructure

When planning a WINS solution, you must examine the various connections in your network infrastructure. WAN connections can sometimes cause availability and congestion problems. Determine if connections are congested by testing the WAN link; if they are, assuage the problem by placing a WINS server at the remote site.

What you do have to remember, however, is when you place the WINS server at the remote site, you are swapping client registration/resolution traffic with WINS replication traffic. The benefit to this, of course, is that you can determine when the replication traffic occurs, by setting parameters, which, of course, you cannot do with registration and name resolution traffic.

The network infrastructure includes the various connections. WAN connections can cause problems with availability and congestion. You can determine if connections are congested by testing the WAN link. If they are, you can alleviate the problem by placing a WINS server at the remote site. However, if you place an additional WINS server at a remote site, you trade client registration and resolution traffic for replication traffic. The advantage is that you can set parameters to determine when replication traffic occurs, which you would not be able to do with registration and resolution traffic.

2.8.2.1 Service Availability

If you have only one WINS Server, you may find you have service availability issues. If the resources are available, you can consider placing your WINS Server on a server cluster. By doing this, you are providing immediate failover and restart in the event of hardware or service failure, as well as faster restoration of failed servers, because database resynchronization is not required.

While server clusters provide a higher level of service availability for WINS (and other) servers, most of the time they require more computing resources than would multiple WINS servers using replication. As well, Server 2003–based servers that belong to the same server cluster require persistent, high-speed connections among all the servers in the cluster.

You can also use a Windows server cluster solution to increase the availability of an individual WINS server. By placing the WINS server on a server cluster, you are able to provide immediate recovery in the event of hardware or service failure.

Windows server clusters provide a higher level of availability for individual servers. However, this solution generally requires more computing resources than multiple WINS servers that use replication. Windows server clusters provide a solution that is appropriate for solving availability issues associated with a single WINS server. Windows Server 2003–based servers that belong to the same server cluster require persistent, high-speed connections among all the servers in the cluster.

By configuring WINS in a server cluster, you can:

- Provide immediate failover and restart in the event of a failure.
- Restore failed servers sooner because database resynchronization is not required.

2.8.2.2 Location Constraints

As mentioned earlier, adding a WINS server to a remote location will provides redundancy and fault-tolerance in case a server or router fails. However, when planning positioning and replication for WINS servers, you must decide on an acceptable convergence time for your network.

NOTE: *Convergence time* is the period it takes for a new entry in a WINS database to be replicated from the WINS server of origin to all other WINS server partners.

You will want to minimize replication paths and convergence times. You can do this by selecting both push and pull (push/pull configuration) when planning replication partners when possible, using push-only or pull-only partnerships only when required by slow WAN links. Let's say, for example, you have a branch office. It is not necessary that the local names from the branch office be propagated into the central servers, situated in the central hub. In this case, you would want to configure the WINS servers in the branch office as pull partners and the central WINS server as a push partner so that the local NetBIOS names are not pulled across the WAN link, and bandwidth is saved.

As well, you want to select persistent connections between WINS partners. Doing this will improve replication performance, especially in high-bandwidth networks.

A **hub-and-spoke** WINS replication model will allow for the shortest convergence time. An example of this sort of configuration would be one WINS server designated as the central server, and all other WINS servers as both push partners and pull partners of this central server. By doing this, you ensure that the WINS database on each server contains addresses for every node on the WAN.

A WINS **chain** replication model is when each server is a push-pull partner of a nearby WINS server. In this model, the two servers at the ends of the chain would be push and pull partners with each other.

NOTE: Only one WINS proxy should be installed on each subnet. Configuring more than one WINS proxy per subnet can overload the WINS servers on the same subnet.

Adding WINS servers to remote locations provides name service redundancy in case a server or router fails. *Convergence time* is the time it takes for a new entry in a WINS database to be replicated from the originating WINS server to all other partner WINS servers. When planning placement and replication for WINS servers, you must decide on an acceptable convergence time for your network.

2.8.2.3 To minimize replication paths and convergence times:

Select push/pull when planning replication partners.

Avoid the use of limited replication partnerships (push only or pull only) between WINS servers, unless this is required for slow WAN links. For example, assume that you have a remote office where propagation of local names into the centralized servers (located in the central hub) is not desired. In this example, the branch office WINS servers would be configured as pull partners, and the centralized WINS server would be configured as a push partner. This saves bandwidth because local NetBIOS names are not pulled across the WAN link into the WINS servers.

- Select persistent connections between partners to improve replication performance in high-bandwidth networks.
- Plan for a hub-and-spoke model for WINS replication. This provides the shortest convergence times.

Only one computer configured as a WINS proxy should be installed on each subnet. Configuring more than one WINS proxy per subnet can overload the WINS servers on the same subnet.

In one possible configuration, you can designate one WINS server as the central server and configure all of the other WINS servers as both push partners and pull partners of this central server. Such a configuration ensures that the WINS database on each server contains addresses for every node on the WAN. Another option is to set up a chain of WINS servers, where each server is both the push partner and pull partner of a nearby WINS server. In such a configuration, the two servers at the ends of the chain would be push and pull partners with each other. You can establish other replication partners for your site's needs.

2.8.3 Plan NetBIOS name resolution by using the LMHosts file

This section briefly discusses the use of an LMHosts file for NetBIOS name resolution for TCP/IP networks (NetBT). There are a few ways to resolve NetBIOS (computer) names to IP addresses:

- IP Subnet Broadcast
- NetBIOS Name Server (WINS)
- LMHosts file
- NetBIOS name cache

NetBT is defined by RFCs 1001 and 1002, which look at the different configurations that allow a computer to resolve NetBIOS names to IP addresses. These methods are b-node, p-node, m-node, and h-node.

- **B-node** (or broadcast node) uses broadcasts to resolve names.
- **P-node** (or peer-to-peer node) uses point-to-point communications (directed name queries) with a NetBIOS server (such as a WINS server) to resolve names.
- **M-node** (or mixed node) uses broadcasts first (b-node), then uses directed name queries (p-node) if broadcasts are not successful.
- **H-node** (or hybrid node) uses name queries first (p-node), and then uses broadcasts (b-node) if the name server is unavailable or if the name is not registered in the WINS database.

As well, a fifth node type is a Windows implementation of NetBIOS name resolution:

- **Microsoft-enhanced** which uses the local LMHosts file plus Windows Sockets gethostbyname( ) calls (using standard DNS and/or local Hosts files) in addition to standard node types.

What is LMHosts?

An LMHosts file is, essentially, a local "phone book" – a text file, stored locally, that lists IP addresses and NetBIOS names. It is the NetBIOS equivalent of the HOSTS file used in hostname/IP address resolution. It must be created, and modified, manually. A sample of an LMHosts file is stored in *systemroot*\System32\Drivers\Etc\LMHosts.sam.

The following rules should be followed when creating or modifying the entries in an LMHosts file:

- Each entry MUST be on a separate line. The final entry in the file MUST be followed by a carriage return.
- Enter the IP address in the first column, followed by the corresponding computer (NetBIOS) name.
- The address and the computer name must be separated by AT LEAST one space or tab.
- NetBIOS names can contain uppercase and lowercase characters as well as special characters. To ensure that a name is used accurately, place it between double quotation marks.
- Every NetBIOS name is 16 characters long. The portion of the name that is defined by the user is the first 15 characters; the16th character is reserved to identify the network client service (resource type) that registered the name. For example, ***computername*[00h]** indicates that the name was registered by the workstation service, while ***computername*[21h]** indicates that the name was registered by the RAS Client Service, when started on a RAS Client.

- Entries in the LMHosts file can represent any Windows-based computer running TCP/IP. There is no need to distinguish between different platforms in LMHosts.
- The number sign (#) character is usually used to mark the start of a comment. However, it can also designate special keywords.

The following table lists keywords that can be used in the LMHosts file:

Keyword	Description
\0xnn	Support for nonprinting characters in NetBIOS names. Place the NetBIOS name in double quotation marks ("*computername*") and use **\0xnn** notation to specify a hexadecimal value for the character. *Note that Microsoft LAN Manager TCP/IP does not recognize the hexadecimal format.* *Note that the hexadecimal notation applies only to the sixteenth character in the name. Use blanks to pad the name so that the special character is last in the string.*
BEGIN_ALTERNATE	Used to group multiple INCLUDE statements. A sole successful INCLUDE statement triggers the group to succeed.
END_ALTERNATE	Used to mark the end of an INCLUDE statement grouping.
DOM: *domain*	Part of the computer name-to-IP address mapping entry. This indicates that the IP address is a domain controller in the domain specified by *domain*. This keyword affects how the Browser and Logon services behave in routed TCP/IP environments. *Note: To preload a DOM entry, you must first add the PRE keyword to the line. DOM groups are limited to 25 members.*
INCLUDE *filename*	Forces the system to seek the specified filename and parse it as if it were local. Specifying a UNC filename allows you to use a centralized LMHosts file on a server. *Note: If the specified filename resides on a server outside of the local broadcast subnet, you must add a preloaded entry for the server.*

MH	Part of the computer name-to-IP-address-mapping entry. This defines the entry as a unique name that can have more than one address (multihomed). *Note: The maximum number of addresses that can be assigned to a unique name is 25.* *Note: The number of entries is equal to the number of network adapters in a multihomed computer.*
PRE	Part of the computer name-to-IP address mapping entry. By default, entries are not preloaded into the name cache but are parsed only after WINS and name query broadcasts fail to resolve a name. This causes that entry to be preloaded into the name cache. *Note: The PRE keyword must be appended for entries that also appear in INCLUDE statements; otherwise, the entry in the INCLUDE statement is ignored.*
SG *name*	Part of the computer name-to-IP address mapping entry. This connects that entry with a user-defined special (Internet) group specified by name. *Note: The SG keyword defines Internet groups by using a NetBIOS name that has [0x20] in the 16th byte. A special group is limited to 25 members.*

Table 2—19: LMHosts File Keywords

The following example shows how all of these keywords are used:

```
192.168.1.102     "uniqueapp       \0x14"            #special
app server

192.168.1.103     filesrv      #PRE                  #file
server

192.168.1.21      localsrv     #PRE

192.168.1.2       main         #PRE    #DOM:mydomain   #main
for mydomain



#BEGIN_ALTERNATE

#INCLUDE \\localsrv\public\lmhosts          #adds LMHosts
from this server

#INCLUDE \\main\public\lmhosts              #adds LMHosts
from this server

#END_ALTERNATE
```

Figure 2—14: Example of Keywords

The servers named **filesrv**, **localsrv**, and **main** are defined, by the **#PRE** keyword, as entries to be preloaded into the NetBIOS cache at system startup.

The servers named **localsrv** and **main** are defined as preloaded and identified in the **#INCLUDE** statements as the location of the centrally maintained LMHosts file.

Note that the server named "**appname \0x14**" contains a special character after the first 15 characters in its name (including the blanks) and so its name is enclosed in double quotation marks.

The number sign, when not used with a keyword, designates the start of a comment.

While most organizations now choose to use WINS Service for NetBIOS name resolution, there are some times when using an LMHosts file is appropriate:

- You have a small organization with a small number of clients, or an organization that is running as a peer-to-peer network.
- You have a static IP environment (non-DHCP) in which IP addresses are configured manually.
- Clients and servers are on different broadcast domains because there is a router between them.
- You need to reduce broadcasts on your network it is consuming too much network bandwidth.

NOTE: You should not add an LMOSTS entry for a computer DHCP client computer, because its IP address can change dynamically. To avoid name resolution problems, make sure that the clients entered in the LMHosts file are configured with static IP addresses.

NetBIOS name resolution can occur in three ways. You can perform name resolution by using broadcasts, or, for more efficiency, you can perform name resolution either automatically or by implementing an LMHOSTS file.

Implementing an LMHOSTS file for name resolution is most appropriate when:

- You have a small organization with a small number of hosts: for example, an organization that has only 20 computers.
- You need to reduce broadcasts on your network because broadcast traffic is consuming too much network bandwidth.
- You have a static Internet Protocol (IP) environment; that is, a non-DHCP environment in which IP addresses are configured manually.
- Clients and servers are on different broadcast domains because a router has been placed between them.

The LMHOSTS file requires considerable administrative overhead when changes need to be made, because those changes must be made on all computers that use an LMHOSTS file.

2.9 Troubleshoot host name resolution

2.9.1 Diagnose issues related to DNS services

2.9.1.1 DNSLint

The most frequently used tool to troubleshoot delegation issues is the Nslookup tool. The downside to this tool is that it is quite time-consuming and performed manually. Using the new tool, DNSLint, you can automate the task.

DNSLint is a command line utility. The syntax for using this command is:

```
DNSLINT /D DOMAIN_NAME | /AD [LDAP_IP_ADDRESS] | /QL
INPUT_FILE
[/C [SMTP,POP,IMAP]] [/NO_OPEN] [/R REPORT_NAME]
[/T] [/TEST_TCP] [/S DNS_IP_ADDRESS] [/V] [/Y]
```

There are three main switches. At least one of them must be specified when you want to run DNSLint. These switches validate DNS records and produce an HTML statement. The three switches are:

2.9.1.2 DNSLint /d (domain)

This switch is used to request a test on a particular DNS domain name and helps identify potential triggers of "lame delegation" and related DNS issues. You must specify a domain name to test, and it must be a name that is registered for use on the Internet or one that is used in a private namespace. For domain names used in a private name space or registered Internet domain names that are more than two levels deep, used the /s option must be to bypass an InterNIC "whois" lookup

You cannot use the /d switch with the /ad switch.

2.9.1.3 DNLSint /ql (query list test)

This switch verifies a user-defined set of DNS records, by means of testing, on multiple DNS servers. Using the /ql switch allows you to test the DNS records specified in a text input file, done by specifying the full path and name of this file immediately after the switch.

In order to have the correct syntax for the text input file, run dnslint /ql autocreate. This will create a sample text input file called In-dnslint.txt, which contains a sample template for the input text files. You can then use this sample file as a template to create your files.

The /ql switch supports A, PTR, CNAME, SRV and MX record queries.

2.9.1.4 DNSLint /ad (Active Directory)

This switch is used specifically to test the DNS records responsible for Active Directory forest replication. Specify the IP address of the LDAP server you are using for the text immediately after the /ad switch (usually an Active Directory domain controller). If you have installed DNSLint on the domain controller, you do not need to specify an IP address, as the default value of the switch is the loopback address (127.0.0.1).

> **Note:** You must use the IP address, not the FQDN, of the domain controller. Names are not accepted by the /ad switch.

You must use the /ad switch with the /s option. /s specifies the IP address of the DNS server authoritative for the _msdcs zone in the AD forest root (typically, the subdomain where DNS records used for Active Directory forest replication are registered). You can use the switch **/s localhost** to ascertain whether the local system can resolve records that are found in the AD tests. Specifying the IP address (or localhost) will bypass an InterNIC "whois" lookup.

> **Note:** The /d, /ql and /ad switches cannot be used at the same time, or in any combination. Each of these switches must be used individually, or in combination with optional switches, as noted.

The other switches listed in the syntax above are optional. They are:

The **/v (verbose)** switch turns "verbose mode" on. When activated, DNSLint will output to the screen each step it takes to collect data. Using this in combination with the **/r (report)** switch allows you to specify the name and location of the generated report file. If no name or location is specified, the default name is Dnslint.htm and the default location is the current directory. The ".htm" is automatically appended to the filename because the report is generated in HTML. The HTML format is mandatory; there is no way to designate an alternate format.

However, you can use **/t** to request output to a text file as well as to the HTML file. The generated text file will share the same name as the HTML file, with a ".txt" file extension. It will be created in the same directory as the HTML report file.

DNSLint, by default, will open the HTML report file immediately after it generates it, typically using the default browser software (probably Internet Explorer). If you do not wish to have the report opened after generation, make sure to use the **/no open** switch, especially helpful when you are doing DNSLint testing using scripts.

To specify the location to where you would like the report file written, you must specify the full path as well as the name of the desired report file. Both local drives and UNC paths are recognized.

By default, when DNSLint creates a report that, by name, already exists in the location you specified, it will ask you whether you want to overwrite the existing file. By using the **/y** switch, you can have DNSLint automatically overwrite any existing file by the same name. This switch works for both HTML and text files. Again, this is helpful when you are automating your reporting process using scripts.

Only UDP Port 53 is tested by DNSLint by default. These days, however, many DNS servers do not accept DNS queries on TCP Port 53, because of potential attacks on that port. If you wish to verify whether a response is received by the TCP Port 53, use the **/test tcp** switch to request that it be tested along with the UDP port.

You can use the **/test_tcp** option with **/d** and **/ad**. However, you cannot use the **/test_tcp** option with **/ql** or the **/ad /s localhost** combination, simply because with the **/ql** function, TCP port 53 can be tested directly from the input file and the **/ad /s localhost** function tests whether the local DNS server can resolve the Active Directory Forest replication records. Instead, in this case, you can test the connectivity by using **/ad /s *ip_addr***, ***ip_addr*** being the IP address of a DNS server that is authoritative for the _msdcs zone in the root of the Active Directory domain.

The **/c (connectivity test)** switch tests the well-known e-mail ports on all of the e-mail servers it finds while in the process of inspecting DNS servers for the domain name specified. SMPT, POP3 and IMAP4 are all supported. When the **/c** switch is specified, by default DNSLint will attempt to connect to all three ports on each e-mail server that it discovers -- TCP 25 (SMTP), TCP 110 (POP3), and TCP 143 (IMAP4).

One of three responses will be reported by DNSLint -- **Listening**, **Not Listening**, or **No Response**. In addition, if the response is **Listening**, DNSLint will also return the response from the port (if any).

It is important to note that before indicating a **No Response**, DNSLint will retry the connection three times, standard behavior for any TCP client. This process can slow down the completion of the report.

In order to optimize the report operation of DNSLint, you may wish to specify which email ports you wish to have checked, rather than using the default behavior of DNSLint – checking all three ports each time. This is done by using a comma-delimited list -- /c smtp,pop,imap (or any combination of the three).

You can use the **/s (server)** switch with the **/d** switch as well as the **/ad** switch. The **/s** switch has several functions, but it only accepts one type of data, a valid IP address of a DNS server (with one exception, localhost). As mentioned earlier, the **/s** switch will bypass the InterNIC "whois" lookup, useful for private networks, domain names deeper than second-level domains, or domain names not supported by InterNIC.

2.9.2 How to Troubleshoot Host Name Resolution

When troubleshooting host name resolution issues, you can focus on several specific areas. Adopting a generic troubleshooting process will help you to scope any host name resolution issue. The following is a systematic troubleshooting procedure for troubleshooting host name resolution.

1. Determine the scope of the problem

You need to determine if only one host cannot resolve names, or multiple hosts; if multiple hosts cannot resolve names, the problem is probably with the server and not the client(s). In addition, you should determine if only one name cannot be resolved or several names. This will help you to identify if it is a client observer problem.

2. Identify if it is a client or server problem

If your scope determination indicates that the problem might be with the client, you should check to make sure that client configuration settings are correct. If your scope determination indicates that the problem might be with the server or the network infrastructure, you need to investigate the server settings and the infrastructure for possible failure.

3. Verify that client settings are correct

If you have determined that the problem is with the client(s), you need to verify that the client settings are correct including the IP addresses of the DNS server, client domain name, connection suffix, suffix names to append to queries, ands on. If the client settings are incorrect, you have discovered the source of the problem.

4. Verify that network traffic can reach the server

If you have ruled out a client problem, you need to make sure that network traffic can reach the server. You can use ping, pathping, and so on to perform this function. You also need to make sure that any intermediate devices are not filtering DNS traffic.

2.9.3 Optimizing and Troubleshooting DNS

To ensure that the server records are correct, you should:

- Verify that the server is running and the DNS service is operational.
- Make sure that the server is listening on the proper interface.
- Check the zone for proper records.
- Check logs and events.
- Check any filters.

After you have performed the preceding steps and verified that all server records are accurate, you need to capture the DNS traffic between the server and client(s) to further determine the problem.

2.9.4 Restoring Server Default Preferences

You might encounter situations in which DNS preferences have been changed and these changes adversely affect DNS server performance. If this is the case, you might need to restore the default server settings before troubleshooting further.

2.9.4.1 To restore default server preferences:

1. Open DNS.
2. In the console tree, right-click the applicable DNS server, and then click **Properties**.
3. Click the **Advanced** tab.
4. Click **Reset to Default**, and then click **OK**.

Clicking **Reset to Default** configures the DNS server with its initial configuration settings. The following table details these settings.

2.9.4.2 Property Setting

- Disable recursion Off
- BIND secondary On
- Fail on load if bad zone data Off
- Enable round robin On
- Enable netmask ordering On
- Secure cache against pollution On
- Name checking Multibyte (UTF8)
- Load zone data on startup From Active Directory and registry
- Enable automatic scavenging of stale records Off

2.9.4.3 How to Troubleshoot Host Records Registration

The primary reason why host records registration fails is that the primary DNS suffix does not match the zone name. For example, if the Active Directory domain and corresponding DNS domain are mydomain.com and the computer's primary DNS suffix is something different, such as sales.mydomain, the computer would try to register at sales.mydomain, which probably does not exist. You generally set this primary DNS suffix when the computer joins the Active Directory domain, but the user can change it.

To examine the primary DNS suffix:

1. In **Control Panel**, double-click **System** to open the **System Properties** dialog box.
2. In the **System Properties** dialog box, click the **Computer Name** tab.
3. Click **Change**.

If the computer is a domain controller, a dialog box appears stating that domain controllers cannot be moved from one domain to another. Click **OK**.

4. In the **Computer Name Changes** dialog box, click **More**.
5. Examine the DNS primary suffix.

2.9.4.4 How to Troubleshoot Dynamic Updates

Dynamic updates might not occur for the following reasons:

- The zone has not been configured to receive dynamic updates.
- The client is using a DNS product from a third party that does not support dynamic updates.
- Dynamic updates have been disabled on the client's side.

If dynamic updates are not occurring and you know that the zone is configured to receive dynamic updates, you need to check the settings on the client side.

To check dynamic update settings on the client's side:

1. In Control Panel, double-click Network Connections to open the Network Connections dialog box.
2. Open the Properties page of the network interface.
3. Open the Properties page for Internet Protocol (TCP/IP).
4. Click Advanced.
5. Click the DNS tab.
6. To dynamically register the interface IP address, the Register this connections address in DNS check box should be selected.

2.9.5 Diagnose & resolve issues related to client computer configuration

The three most common DNS problems are:

- Inability to resolve some names in the namespace.
- Inability to resolve names outside the DNS zone.
- Incorrect configuration of DNS client primary and secondary DNS servers.

2.9.5.1 Inability to Resolve Some Names in the Namespace

When the DNS server is unable to resolve some names in the namespace, it is frequently due to a missing or incorrectly entered delegation. There must be a valid NS record and a valid A (host) record for every server that is authoritative for the delegated zone.

Use the **New Delegation Wizard** to simplify delegation. As well, as we have discussed, you can use either DNSLint or Nslookup (or both) to help you in identifying and diagnosing incorrect delegations.

2.9.5.2 Inability to Resolve Names outside the DNS Zone

The primary reason why servers are unable to resolve names outside the DNS zone is that forwarders are missing. Most often, this is because individuals have a poor understanding of what forwarders are and how to use them.

In an Active Directory setting, you need to ensure network functionality outside of the Active Directory domain, such as browser requests for Internet addresses, and ensure that the DNS Server is configured to forward DNS requests to the appropriate outside or corporate DNS server or servers.

To troubleshoot forwarders on the DNS server:

1. Start the **DNS Management Console**.

2. Right-click the name of the server, and then click **Properties**.

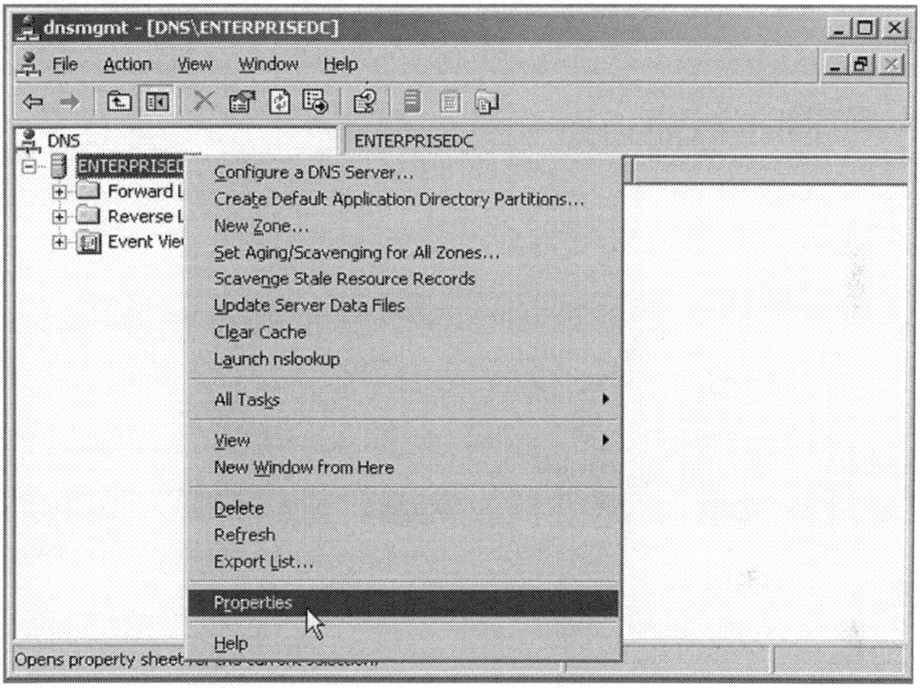

Figure 2—15: DNS Properties

3. Click the **Forwarders** tab.

4. Verify that the correct IP addresses are present for the DNS servers that you want to accept forwarded requests from this DNS server. The list reads in order from the top down, so if there is a preferred DNS server, make sure it is at the top of the list.

5. Click **OK** to accept the changes.

2.9.5.3 Incorrect Configuration of DNS Client Primary and Secondary DNS Servers

Incorrect configurations can occur on both domain controllers and workstations. Quite frequently, you will find that workstations will be configured for an ISP's DNS server rather than the corporate DNS server that hosts their Active Directory domain registrations. Make sure that you check the DNS server configuration on the computer in question.

2.9.6 Zone

2.9.6.1 Optimizing and Troubleshooting DNS

To troubleshoot forwarders on the DNS server:

1. Start the DNS Management console.
2. Right-click the name of the server, and then click Properties.
3. Click the Forwarders tab.
4. Select the Enable Forwarders check box.

If the Enable Forwarders check box is unavailable, the DNS server is attempting to host a root zone (usually identified by a zone named only with a period, or dot (".")). You must delete this zone to enable the DNS server to forward DNS requests. In a configuration in which the DNS server does not rely on an ISP DNS server or a corporate DNS server, you can use a root zone entry.

5. Ensure that the appropriate IP addresses are present for the DNS servers that will accept forwarded requests from this DNS server. The list reads in order from the top down; if there is a preferred DNS server, place it at the top of the list.
6. Click OK to accept the changes.

Incorrect configuration can occur on both domain controllers and workstations, which are often configured for their ISP's DNS server rather than their own DNS server that hosts their Active Directory domain registrations. You need to check the DNS server configuration on the computer in question.

Chapter 2: Review Questions

1. Which of the following isn't true about a proxy server?

   A. Proxy servers are the only firewall protection you need

   B. Proxy servers mask the IP address of internal hosts

   C. Proxy servers represent themselves to the web page

   D. Proxy servers function at the Application layer of the OSI model

---

2. Which of the following statements is false regarding ports?

   A. HTTP uses port 12

   B. A port is a logical connection place

   C. TCP and UDP use ports

   D. Ports 0-1023 are 'well-known' ports

3. Which of the following protocols does not use TCP?

   A. SNMP

   B. FTP

   C. HTTP

   D. NNTP

---

4. Which of the following will help secure your Windows 2003 DHCP services?

   A. Restrict access to the Enterprise Admins group

   B. Restrict access to root

   C. Use static addressing in your DMZ

   D. Use static addressing in your extranet

5. Which of the following URLs denotes SSL use?

    A. HTTPS://
    B. FTP://
    C. HTTP://
    D. HTTPX://

---

6. Which of the following describes NAT?

    A. NAT allows for use of one public IP address

    B. NAT maps host names to IP addresses

    C. NAT maps NetBIOS names to IP addresses

    D. NAT translates private IP addresses to a public IP address

    E. NAT acts as a firewall

7. You have a server to which clients can only connect using NAT. How can you make sure that the server won't accept file sharing network packets when they are changed during transmission?

A. Configure the local group policy on the server to enable the Digitally sign server communication (always) setting.

B. Configure the local group policy on the server to enable the Secure channel: Digitally encrypt or sign secure channel data (always) setting.

C. Configure the server and clients to use AH.

D. Configure the server and clients to use ESP.

---

8. Which of the following servers needs to be configured to accept L2TP connections from the Internet?

A. The NAT Server / External firewall

B. The RRAS Server in the DMZ

C. The Web Server in the DMZ

D. The RRAS Server in the intranet

9. Which of the following are advantages of supernetting?
    A. It helps to reduce the size of a routing table
    B. It reduces the need for Class B addresses in the corporate environment
    C. It helps to increase the size of a routing table
    D. It reduces the need for Class D addresses in the corporate environment
    E. It reduces the need for Class E addresses in the corporate environment

---

10. What is the associated address range of the 206.73.118.0/24 address?
    A. 206.73.118.111 to 206.73.118.254
    B. 206.73.118.1 to 206.73.118.254
    C. 206.73.118.1 to 206.73.118.2
    D. 206.73.118.112 to 206.73.118.254

11. What is the associated address range of the 131.107.0.0/16 address?

A. 131.107.0.1 to 131.107.255.254

B. 131.107.0.111 to 131.107.255.254

C. 131.107.0.112 to 131.107.255.254

D. 131.107.0.1 to 131.107.255.5

---

12. Which of the following statements regarding APIPA are true?

A. It uses an address that begins with 169.254

B. Clients using APIPA can't operate in a routed environment

C. It does not provide a default gateway

D. It uses an address that begins with 254.169

13. What actions can you take to disable APIPA?

    A. Add the following registry value:
    HKEY_LOCAL_MACHINE\SYSTEM\CurrentControlSet\Services\Tcpip\Parame
    ters\IPAutoconfigurationEnabled.

    B. You must assign a DWORD value of 3 to the registry entry.

    C. You must assign a DWORD value of 0 to the registry entry.

    D. You must assign a DWORD value of 2 to the registry entry.

14. Achieving maximum throughput depends on which of the following?

    A. The number of users on the network

    B. Hardware used with the operating system

    C. The frame size being used

    D. Amount of email read

15. What should be the average use and peak use percentage on your Ethernet network?
    A. 50 percent and 80 percent, respectively
    B. 90 percent and 100 percent, respectively
    C. 80 percent and 90 percent, respectively
    D. 100 percent and 80 percent, respectively

---

16. Which of the following is an acceptable collision rate on an Ethernet network?
    A. 20 percent
    B. 75 percent
    C. 50 percent
    D. 85 percent

Chapter 2: Review Answers

1. Which of the following isn't true about a proxy server?

*A. Proxy servers are the only firewall protection you need

B. Proxy servers mask the IP address of internal hosts

C. Proxy servers represent themselves to the web page

D. Proxy servers function at the Application layer of the OSI model

Explanation: A type of firewall that you may encounter is a proxy server, sometimes called an IP Proxy. The IP Proxy masks the IP address of internal hosts and represents itself instead. Proxy servers function at the Application layer of the OSI model.

---

2. Which of the following statements is false regarding ports?

*A. HTTP uses port 12

B. A port is a logical connection place

C. TCP and UDP use ports

D. Ports 0-1023 are 'well-known' ports

Explanation: A port is a logical connection place. The TCP/IP and UDP protocols use ports to allow a client program to specify a particular server program. Ports are a 16-bit number - numbered from 0 to 65,535 (totaling 65,536 ports). Ports 0-1023 (1024 total) are reserved as most HTTP services have an assigned standard port number. For example, a Web server (HTTP) uses port 80. This is called a well-known port. Well-known ports are used by HTTP to control the connection.

3. Which of the following protocols does not use TCP?

*A. SNMP

B. FTP

C. HTTP

D. NNTP

Explanation: FTP uses TCP and ports 20 and 21. TELNET uses TCP and port 23. SMTP uses TCP and port 25. WINS uses TCP and port 42. DNS uses TCP and port 53. BOOTP/DHCP use UDP and ports 67, 68. HTTP uses TCP and port 80. KERBEROS uses TCP and port 88. POP3 uses TCP and port 110. NNTP uses TCP and port 119. NETBIOS uses UDP and ports 137-139. LDAP uses UDP and port 389. SSL uses TCP and port 443. RADIUS uses TCP and ports 1645, 1646 for TCP connections. RADIUS also uses UDP and ports 1812 and 1813 for UDP connections.

---

4. Which of the following will help secure your Windows 2003 DHCP services?

*A. Restrict access to the Enterprise Admins group

B. Restrict access to root

C. Use static addressing in your DMZ

D. Use static addressing in your extranet

Explanation: There are even more DHCP server security features with Windows 2003 than with previous versions of Windows. Rogue DHCP servers cannot connect to your network and hand out addresses to gain sensitive information. DHCP servers have to be authorized within Active Directory.

5. Which of the following URLs denotes SSL use?

*A. HTTPS://

B. FTP://

C. HTTP://

D. HTTPX://

Explanation: By convention, clients requesting documents stored in SSL-enabled directories must use the https:// URL format instead of the standard http:// format. This means that when you visit a Web site, you will know it uses SSL technology if the URL begins with https://.

---

6. Which of the following describes NAT?

*A. NAT allows for use of one public IP address

B. NAT maps host names to IP addresses

C. NAT maps NetBIOS names to IP addresses

*D. NAT translates private IP addresses to a public IP address

*E. NAT acts as a firewall

Explanation: NAT (Network Address Translation) is the translation of an IP address used within an organization internally (private IP address) to an IP seen by the Internet (Public IP address). It allows for use of one public IP address for many private IP addresses. NAT also acts as a firewall, since it keeps the private IP addresses hidden from the outside world.

7. You have a server to which clients can only connect using NAT. How can you make sure that the server won't accept file sharing network packets when they are changed during transmission?

*A. Configure the local group policy on the server to enable the Digitally sign server communication (always) setting.

B. Configure the local group policy on the server to enable the Secure channel: Digitally encrypt or sign secure channel data (always) setting.

C. Configure the server and clients to use AH.

D. Configure the server and clients to use ESP.

Explanation: You have a server to which clients can only connect using NAT. To make sure that the server won't accept file sharing network packets when they are changed during transmission, configure the local group policy on the server to enable the Digitally sign server communication (always) setting.

---

8. Which of the following servers needs to be configured to accept L2TP connections from the Internet?

*A. The NAT Server / External firewall

B. The RRAS Server in the DMZ

C. The Web Server in the DMZ

D. The RRAS Server in the intranet

Explanation: The NAT Server (External firewall) needs to be configured to accept L2TP connections from the Internet.

9. Which of the following are advantages of supernetting?

*A. It helps to reduce the size of a routing table

*B. It reduces the need for Class B addresses in the corporate environment

C. It helps to increase the size of a routing table

D. It reduces the need for Class D addresses in the corporate environment

E. It reduces the need for Class E addresses in the corporate environment

Explanation: CIDR is based on subnetting, but eliminates most of subnetting's restrictions. By supernetting, or allowing the subnet boundary to move to the left into the network portion, you can use CIDR by combining groups of neighboring classful networks into single routing table entries, thus reducing the size of the tables through summation. It can also be used in assigning batches of 2, 4, 8, or 16 groups of Class C networks to meet the needs of organizations that would otherwise have requested the increasingly scarce Class B networks.

---

10. What is the associated address range of the 206.73.118.0/24 address?

A. 206.73.118.111 to 206.73.118.254

*B. 206.73.118.1 to 206.73.118.254

C. 206.73.118.1 to 206.73.118.2

D. 206.73.118.112 to 206.73.118.254

Explanation: 206.73.118.1 to 206.73.118.254 is the associated address range of the 206.73.118.0/24 address.

11. What is the associated address range of the 131.107.0.0/16 address?

*A. 131.107.0.1 to 131.107.255.254

B. 131.107.0.111 to 131.107.255.254

C. 131.107.0.112 to 131.107.255.254

D. 131.107.0.1 to 131.107.255.5

Explanation: 131.107.0.1 to 131.107.255.254 is the associated address range of the 131.107.0.0/16 address.

---

12. Which of the following statements regarding APIPA are true?

*A. It uses an address that begins with 169.254

*B. Clients using APIPA can't operate in a routed environment

*C. It does not provide a default gateway

D. It uses an address that begins with 254.169

Explanation: The APIPA address is selected from the IANA-reserved address block1 69.254.0.0/16. Because APIPA does not provide a default gateway IP address to the client, the client cannot operate in a routed network.

13. What actions can you take to disable APIPA?

*A. Add the following registry value: HKEY_LOCAL_MACHINE\SYSTEM\CurrentControlSet\Services\Tcpip\Parameters\IPAutoconfigurationEnabled.

B. You must assign a DWORD value of 3 to the registry entry.

*C. You must assign a DWORD value of 0 to the registry entry.

D. You must assign a DWORD value of 2 to the registry entry.

Explanation: To disable APIPA, you must add the following registry value:HKEY_LOCAL_MACHINE\SYSTEM\CurrentControlSet\Services\Tcpip\Parameters\IPAutoconfigurationEnabled. You must assign a DWORD value of 0 to the registry entry.

---

14. Achieving maximum throughput depends on which of the following?

*A. The number of users on the network

B. Hardware used with the operating system

*C. The frame size being used

D. Amount of email read

Explanation: The maximum throughput essentially depends on two variables: the number of users and frame size. The more users you have on a LAN, the more contention the channel has and the more collisions occur. The maximum throughput is reached with only two nodes on a LAN, also known as a switched connection. This assumes that both nodes are capable of generating the maximum frame rate. Ethernet throughput declines for smaller frames. Conversely, larger frames are more efficient, and they provide the added benefit of reducing opportunities for channel contention and collisions.

15. What should be the average use and peak use percentage on your Ethernet network?

*A. 50 percent and 80 percent, respectively

B. 90 percent and 100 percent, respectively

C. 80 percent and 90 percent, respectively

D. 100 percent and 80 percent, respectively

Explanation: Limit your shared Ethernets to no more than 50 percent average utilization and 80 percent peak utilization. Stay below 200 users for any shared LAN segment. A collision rate of up to 20 percent is acceptable.

---

16. Which of the following is an acceptable collision rate on an Ethernet network?

*A. 20 percent

B. 75 percent

C. 50 percent

D. 85 percent

Explanation: Limit your shared Ethernets to no more than 50 percent average utilization and 80 percent peak utilization. Stay below 200 users for any shared LAN segment. A collision rate of up to 20 percent is acceptable.

Planning, Implementing, and Maintaining Routing and Remote Access

The objective of this chapter is to provide the reader with an understanding of the following:

Plan a routing strategy.

- Identify routing protocols to use in a specified environment.
- Plan routing for IP multicast traffic.

Plan security for remote access users.

- Plan remote access policies.
- Analyze protocol security requirements.
- Plan authentication methods for remote access clients.

Implement secure access between private networks.

- Create and implement an IPSec policy.

Implement secure access between private networks.

- Create and implement an IPSec policy.

Troubleshoot TCP/IP routing. Tools might include

- Route
- Tracert
- Ping
- Pathping
- Netsh Commands
- Network Monitor

Chapter 3: Managing Routing and Remote Access

Introduction:

In this section, we are going to explore RRAS, the Routing and Remote Access Service. RRAS is most commonly used as a remote access service (the RAS part), whether that be dial-up or VPN. What is often overlooked, however, is the routing functionality that Microsoft has included with the service. Any computer with 2 NICs that is running Windows Server 2003 can be used as a full-featured router, either at the edge of the network or somewhere inside – perhaps serving as the router for a new subnet. In fact, when you think about the remote access side of the service, you can think of that as a router as well. In essence, dial-up users (modem, VPN, ISDN, etc.) are dialing in to a router, which has server functionality.

Getting Ready Questions

1. When would you choose RIPv1 instead of RIPv2?
2. Why would you use NAT instead of ICS?
3. RADIUS client refers to what part of a RADIUS solution?
4. Can IPSec be used in a heterogeneous environment?
5. What is the best way to configure IPSec policy in a homogenous environment?

Getting Ready Answers

1. RIPv2 is not available to older router operating systems, including Windows NT4

2. Any time you need the added configuration options, though the most common scenarios are multiple subnets and existing DHCP implementations.

3. The RADIUS client is the remote access server that is providing the actual connectivity.

4. Yes, as long as the operating systems in the environment support it. This includes the Windows 5.x family, as well as non-Windows operating systems.

5. If your environment is homogenous, that is all operating systems are Active Directory aware and enabled, then use a GPO (or three, if need be).

3.1 Identify routing protocols to use in a specified environment.

A routing protocol is used whenever you want to maintain the routing tables dynamically, which is definitely preferred in most situations. Routing protocols allow routers to share routing information. The two routing protocols supported by Windows Server 2003 are RIP and OSPF.

RIP, or Routing Information Protocol, is used in smaller networks. It does not scale well, but is very simple to implement. RIP is available in two versions, v.1 and v.2. Both use a routing table. RIPv.1 broadcasts its full table to its neighboring routers, while RIPv.2 can be configured to multicast instead of broadcast. Windows Server 2003 only supports RIPv.2, so you will need to ensure that all other routers also support version 2 if you plan to use RIP. Typically, RIP is used in networks with less than 50 servers, and less than 15 connected networks.

OSPF, or Open Shortest Path First, is known as a link state protocol. OSPF maintains a database of link states rather than a routing table, and rather than advertising its full database to all neighbors it only sends change messages. Because of this, it is a far more efficient routing protocol from the perspective of processor overhead and bandwidth utilization. Its main drawback is that it can be more complex to configure – though a default configuration on a network using entirely Windows Server 2003 can be quite effective. If, however, you have a mix of hardware routers and software routers running Windows 2000 Server or Windows Server 2003, you will need to be careful to configure all of the routers so that they properly communicate with each other.

3.1.1 Plan routing for IP multicast traffic.

Multicast is used for such things as streaming media, instead of either broadcast or unicast, because it is far more bandwidth efficient. In order to participate in multicast, a computer must be IGMP capable. Routers are required, as ever, when the multicast is outside the broadcast domain, though for multicast all routers must be multicast-capable.

According to Microsoft TechNet online, multicast-capable router must be able to:

- Listen for all multicast traffic on all attached networks. Upon receiving multicast traffic, forward the multicast packet to attached networks where nodes are listening or where downstream routers have nodes that are listening.
- In the Windows Server 2003 family, the ability to listen for all multicast traffic and forward multicast packets is provided by the TCP/IP protocol. The TCP/IP protocol uses a multicast-forwarding table to make decisions on where to forward incoming multicast traffic.
- Listen for IGMP Membership Report messages and update the TCP/IP multicast-forwarding table.
- In the Windows Server 2003 family, the ability to listen for IGMP Membership Report messages and update the TCP/IP multicast-forwarding table is provided by the IGMP routing protocol on an interface operating in IGMP router mode.
- Use a multicast routing protocol to propagate multicast group listening information to other multicast-capable routers.

Routing and Remote Access does not provide any multicast routing protocols. However, the Routing and Remote Access service is an extensible platform and can support multicast routing protocols.

It is very important to note that the IGMP protocol component included with RRAS is not the routing protocol side, but rather the multicast client component.

3.2 Plan security for remote access users

As you know, in any network environment, there are users who use computers directly connected to the LAN or Local Area Network. In some enterprises, there are users who are not directly connected to the LAN but rather access internal network resources from a remote location. Either these users will use an existing Internet connection to make a VPN or Virtual Private Networking connection to the LAN, or they will use a WAN technology to connect. In addition, some businesses have many locations connected to each other in the same way that remote users connect. In either case, a connection will need to be made between the remote computer or network and a remote access service connected to the LAN.

The Windows Server 2003 RRAS service can be used to provide this access, by choosing the VPN/Remote Access role or by configuring VPN/Remote Access in the Configure and Enable Routing and Remote Access wizard.

As is the case with configuring routing, it is a good idea to practice both methods. Using the wizard gives you more immediate granularity, but you can always go back and fine-tune your configuration after setting up the basics.

It is very important that you work from the minimum permissions needed principle when implementing remote access, as it opens a door to the world through which unscrupulous people may attempt to gain unauthorized access. Therefore, only enable what is needed – don't just open everything up because that is easier!

In a Windows Server 2003 remote access solution, there are many components that you need to configure. The obvious one is the remote access service itself, as well the clients that connect to it. In addition to this, however, you may need to support wireless clients, and you may need to configure Active Directory elements as well.

Before we get too far in, it is important to point out that every user who gains access to a network via the remote access server will need to have some kind of user account for authentication purposes. IF that user account is local to the remote access server, then it can be configured to either allow/deny remote access OR control access through remote access policy. If, however, the remote access server is a member of a domain and the account used is a domain account, then certain conditions need to be met in order to control access through remote access policy.

It can be said that there are four elements to any remote access solution – the Network Access Server, Network Access Clients, Authorization Service and Authentication Service.

We are first going to explore the Authorization Service aspect, which includes such things as the remote access policies and the protocol security requirements. Then we are going to look at the Authentication Service aspect, which can be as complex as RADIUS or as simple as accounts existing on the local Remote Access Server.

3.2.1 Plan remote access policies

In either Active Directory or the local SAM of a server, users can be configured to be allowed remote access, be denied remote access, or have their access controlled through remote access policy. Note that control access through remote access policy is not an option for domain accounts if the domain functional level is Windows 2000 Mixed. The domain functional level does not affect whether server local accounts can be configured to control access through remote access policy.

Once you have defined that a user account will have remote access controlled through remote access policies, you need to ensure that there is a policy in place that meets the requirements for that access.

With remote access policies, access is very cut and dried. Either you are allowed, or you are not. As with other permission types, unless you are explicitly allowed, you are denied. What is somewhat different between remote access policy processing and other permission processing is that once an "allow" determination is made, no further processing occurs. Thus, if you have 3 policies, two being the default and one being a custom that you have defined, and the custom is first in the processing order, then any access attempt which meets the conditions defined in the policy will be allowed.

Remember that the default policy setting is to deny everyone at all times of the day!

A remote access policy is made of three elements:

- Conditions
- Permissions
- Profile

Conditions are policy elements that include settings such as time of day, calling station ID, day of week, and even the groups in which a user is a member. When processing a policy, condition is evaluated first. If the conditions for a policy are not met, then processing moves to the next policy in the processing order. If it is the last policy in the processing order, then the result is an implicit deny because the calling station did not meet any of the conditions of access. When conditions for a policy ARE met, the policy processing moves to the next stage – permissions evaluation.

Permissions are policy elements that are evaluated as soon as a condition is met. For example, there is a second default remote access policy. This policy states that the Everyone group is denied access at all times of the day on all days of the week. Therefore, if users attempt a connection with the default remote access policy unmodified, they will meet the conditions of second default remote access policy. As a result, policy processing will determine the permission applied under those conditions -- in this case, "deny access" will be applied.

Remember that once an allow or a deny is reached, no additional policies are processed!

Figure 3-1 shows the second default remote access policy. This is where you would edit or add conditions, edit the profile, and define grant or deny remote access permission.

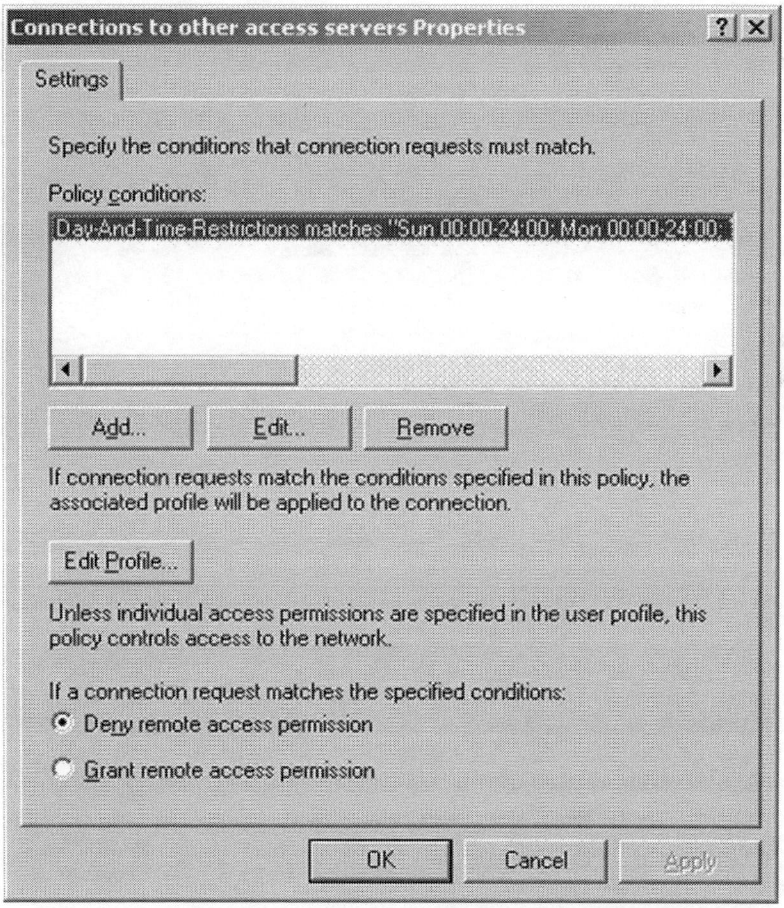

Figure 3—1: Default remote access policy

In the conditions section, you can add as many separate conditions as you would like. Remember that policy processing is an AND operation in a single policy, an OR operation between policies. Below are the conditions that can be set:

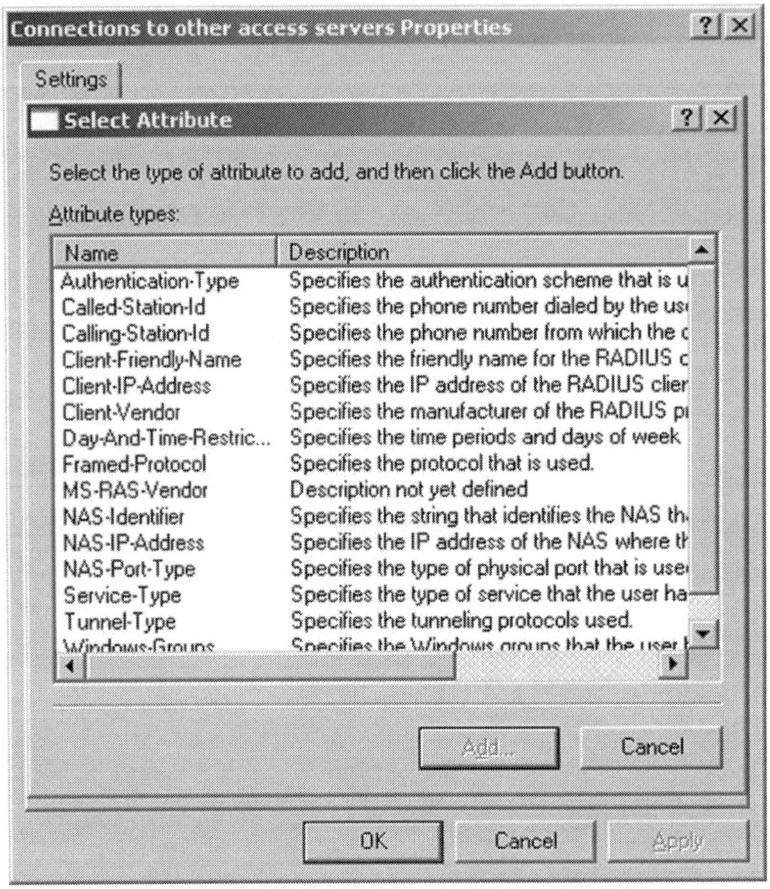

Figure 3—2: Remote Access Conditions

Some key conditions that you will likelybe using are:

- **Authentication-type**, which defines the authentication protocol.
- **Day-And-Time-Restrictions**, which defines when access is allowed OR denied.
- **Tunnel-Type**, which defines the tunneling protocol. If you are configuring a VPN link between two RRAS servers, for example, you must be sure that both are using the same tunneling protocol
- **Windows-Groups**, which defines which groups are allowed or explicitly denied access.

A remote access profile can be used to override the settings on the network access server, placing restrictions in a number of areas as shown below:

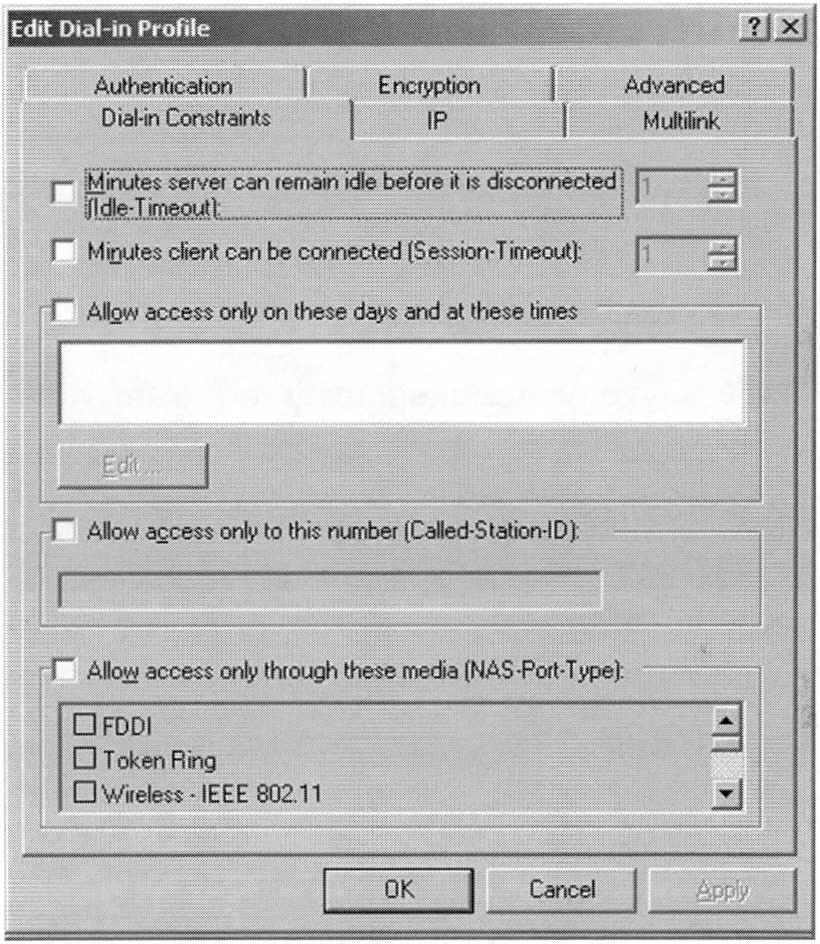

Figure 3—3: Remote Access Restrictions

As you can see, just on the Dial-in Constraints tab there are a number of configuration options. You will find that some condition elements are duplicated here. Since the conditions and permissions are processed before the profile, you may find that some contradictory settings still work. What you should do, however, is make the setting in one place or the other. If, for example, you want to control access based on time, then set that as a condition rather than a profile element. Remember that conditions and permissions are evaluated first, while the profile is applied only after an access attempt is authorized.

Configuring a policy is done using the RRAS Management console. Once you have configured and enabled RRAS on a server, whether it is to be used for LAN routing or Remote Access/VPN, there will be a section under that server called Remote Access Policies in the tree view portion of the console. Choose that object, and the policies defined on that server will be shown in the details pane. To edit a policy, you can double click on it, select it and right click, or select then choose properties from the action menu. From the context (right click) or action menu, you can also move a policy up or down in the processing order, as well as delete or rename a policy.

When the remote access policies object is selected, you can add a new policy, or modify the view of that portion of the management console.

3.2.2 Analyze protocol security requirements

When it comes to the authentication side of the process, you have many options available to you. Always choose the strongest method that does not pose an undue burden on the network and your users.

The recommended method for authentication is smart cards, which use a certificate-based system.

In order to use that method, however, there are a number of steps that need to be completed. You need to have a PKI (public key infrastructure) in place. You must install a computer certificate on the server providing remote access. You need to configure the Smart Card or other TLS (transport layer security) EAP (extensible authentication protocol) in the remote access policy. You must be able to USE remote access policies. As well, you must configure Smart Card authentication on all remote access clients that will use that method. Sounds like a lot? It is – but when you consider that it is, by far, the most secure access method, it is easily worth it.

In addition to EAP/TLS, the following authentication methods are supported:

- CHAP
- PAP
- SPAP
- MS-CHAP
- MS-CHAPv2
- PEAP
- MD-5 Challenge

CHAP stands for Challenge Handshake Authentication Protocol. It is probably the most widely supported, though not all that secure.

PAP stands for Password Authentication Protocol. A major drawback to this method is that the passwords are sent in plain text, which means that anyone with a sniffer between the client and the server can capture the password.

SPAP stands for Shiva Password Authentication Protocol, and is used primarily by Shiva LANRover systems. The password is encrypted, though lightly.

MS-CHAP stands for Microsoft Challenge Handshake Authentication Protocol. It is supported by Microsoft clients only, and then only from Windows 95 and up.

MS-CHAPv2 is the later version of the Microsoft Challenge Handshake Authentication Protocol, and is the default for Windows 2000 and later operating systems.

PEAP is Protected Extensible Authentication Protocol. It is used with 802.1x wireless systems. Of note is that access is granted based on user identity, rather than on a certificate. It also improves the encryption security for wireless networks.

MD-5 Challenge is Message Digest-5, and is used by EAP systems to provide authentication using standard name/password combinations.

You keep seeing this EAP character, too! EAP is Extensible Authentication Protocol, and extensible is just that. It provides a framework or infrastructure on which custom authentication solutions such as PEAP can be developed and implemented.

The big question, then, is when to use which approach?

Well, as with anything security related, you need to strike a balance between functionality and security. If, for example, your remote users were Windows 95, then you would be able to use CHAPv2. On the other hand, if your remote users were a mix of Mac and PC, then you may also need to use simple CHAP. Therefore, from the planning perspective, knowing which authentication protocol can be used under what conditions and what the strengths and weaknesses of those protocols are is the key.

3.2.3 Plan authentication methods for remote access clients

In addition to the protocols you can use, there is also the method by which users are authenticated. In large environments, you may want to use RADIUS or Remote Authentication Dial-In User Service. In medium and small environments, you may want to configure their user account to allow access or configure it to use Remote Access Policies, as seen below:

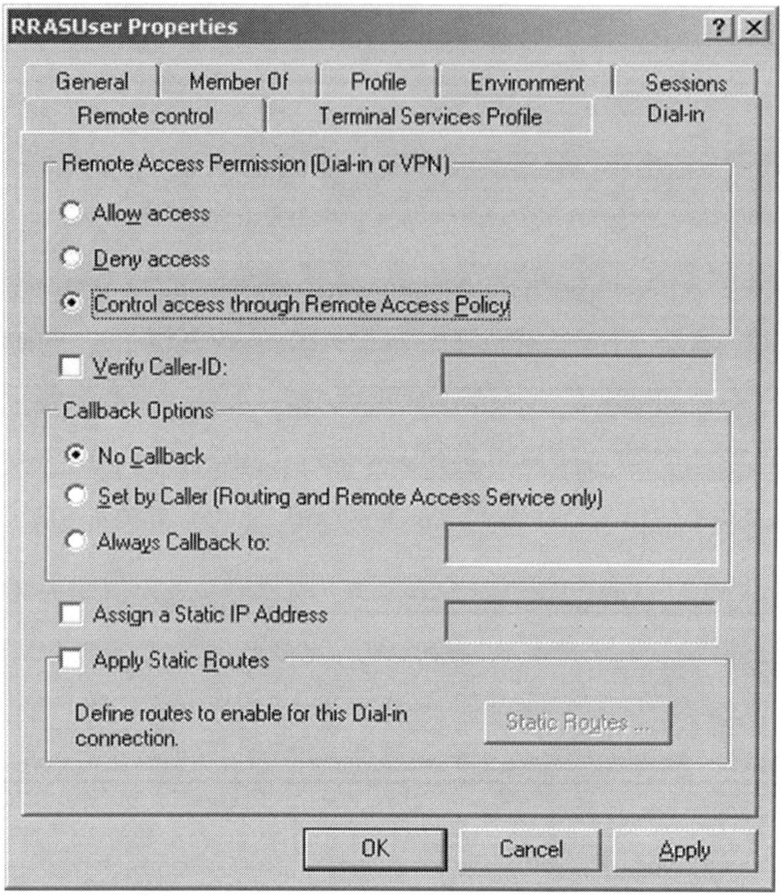

Figure 3—4: Domain user account Dial-in tab

Typically, in the small environments, configuring their account is fine IF you don't need to take advantage of the policy options mentioned earlier. On the other hand, if you have users with different remote access requirements, you will want to use policies because of their greater flexibility.

3.2.3.1 RADIUS

RADIUS is the tool of choice for larger environments. Windows Server 2003 IAS, or Internet Authentication Service, is an industry standard RADIUS implementation. So, before we get into configuring IAS for RRAS clients, let's look at what RADIUS.

RADIUS stands for Remote Authentication Dial-In User Service. As the name suggests, it is used for dial-up type access – which includes VPN. The purpose of RADIUS is to provide centralized authentication, accounting and access control for remote users.

It has been in use with ISPs for quite some time, but has been gaining popularity with use in corporate networks as a means of better managing remote access. Consider using RADIUS in medium to large networks with a significant remote user population.

There are three main components to a RADIUS solution:

- RADIUS Server
- RADIUS Client
- RADIUS Proxy

These names are not quite as self-explanatory as they seem! It is very important that you differentiate between the client and server components. Let's now look at each of the components.

A RADIUS Server is a server that handles authentication and accounting services. The server or servers use a centralized database that can be a Kerberos realm, a flat file, or a directory service. When using a file-based system, keep in mind that all RADIUS servers need to use the same file so that access is consistent. It is, after all, a means for centralized authentication!

A RADIUS client is an RRAS server – the server that actually provides the access. When an access attempt is made, the RADIUS client will send the authentication request to the configured RADIUS server or servers, rather than checking its local database. This can also be a WAP, or a RADIUS proxy. Anything that falls in the realm of remote access can be a RADIUS client providing it has the necessary hardware and software/firmware.

A RADIUS client is similarly an access server, but one that is configured as a go-between. Often this is used in solutions where there are multiple RADIUS servers that a RADIUS client can use. By pointing the RADIUS client to the RADIUS proxy, you can offload logic processing on the client to the proxy thereby freeing up resources for what the client does best – providing access.

Now let's look at IAS itself. Note that while RRAS is installed automatically, IAS is not. To install it, you must choose Internet Authentication Service from the Network Services portion of Add Windows Components in Add/Remove Programs. One of the biggest advantages to using IAS is centralized policies. When using remote access policies, they are stored on each RRAS server. If you have a couple of remote access servers, it is not too big of a deal to duplicate policies. If you have a large number of them, however, things can get somewhat rough! IAS can solve this for you because you can use the IAS server as the central policyholder. Bear in mind that if you do configure RRAS to use an IAS server, any policy on the RRAS server will no longer be used.

In addition, if your IAS server is a domain member, it will use domain credentials only, which provides a single sign on solution.

The authentication processing flow when using RADIUS/IAS is only slightly more complicated than that of a more traditional Windows solution. First, the user instantiates the access attempt with the network access server – which is also the RADIUS/IAS client. Then the client sends the authentication request to the RADIUS/IAS server or proxy, as the case may be. From there, either the proxy forwards the request to the server or the server uses its configured database to process the authentication request. If the server is a domain member, then it will send the authentication request to a domain controller. After authentication occurs or fails, the server responds to the client request with either an access-accept or an access-reject.

If there are policies in place on the server, then the same processing method that you learned earlier applies. The authentication occurs, and then the conditions are evaluated. Once there is a matching set of conditions, the permissions for that condition are evaluated. Once the permissions are determined to be "allow", the profile (if any) is added to the mix, after which the information is returned to the client.

While this seems like a lot of overhead, it doesn't really add that much time to an access request. In the end, it is time-efficient because it provides a centralized management infrastructure for RRAS administration.

In order to use Active Directory, an IAS server must be authorized in Active Directory – much the same way a DHCP or RIS server is. If you do, as part of the process the IAS Server computer account will be added to the RAS and IAS Servers security group. Don't remove them, because these groups have the necessary rights to access Active Directory user information.

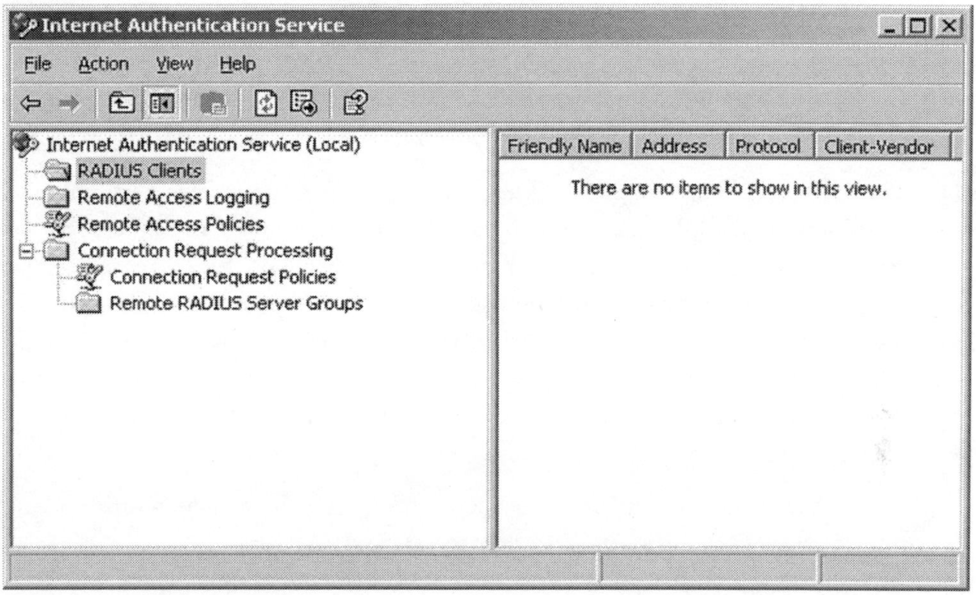

Figure 3—5: IAS console

Figure 3-5 shows the IAS console. As you may notice, this IAS server is not configured to process requests for any RADIUS clients, as there are no clients configured yet.

Adding a client is done much the same way you have done everything else so far. Right click on RADIUS clients or choose it, then click on the Action menu. From there, you choose to add a client.

When adding a RADIUS client, you need to specify (in order):

On the first screen of the wizard, you will configure:

Client Friendly Name – this is the name you will have this IAS server display in the IAS console.

Client Address – this can be either the IP address or DNS name of the client.

On the second screen of the wizard, you will configure:

Client Vendor – you have a drop down list where you choose the RADIUS client vendor. The default is standard, but you can specify a different vendor if necessary.

Shared Secret/Confirm Shared Secret – this is where you configure the RADIUS client's password so that it can be authenticated by the IAS server. The shared secret can be up to 255 characters long, and as with any password longer is more secure.

Request must contain the Message Authenticator attribute – here you can choose whether the RADIUS client includes a digital signature for PAP, CHAP and MS-CHAP authentication. IAS always requires the signature for EAP authentication, so if you are using EAS make sure to check this option.

On the RRAS server providing network access, or any other server type performing the same function, you will need to configure it to point to the IAS server you just configured. To do that with RRAS, click on the server name of the RRAS server, then either right click or action and then properties. Click on the security tab, and instead of Windows Authentication change it to RADIUS. Having chosen RADIUS for authentication (and optionally accounting as well), you will then need to configure the RADIUS server or servers to use. To do this, you will click on configure and then add. Fill in the IP address, configure the shared secret, and you are good to go!

Important! After configuring RRAS to use RADIUS for authentication, you will need to restart the service. Click on action, restart to restart the RRAS service.

Pop Quiz 3.1

Pop Quiz 3.1 Questions

1. Does Microsoft include the necessary components to make RRAS a multicast router?
2. Which routing protocol included with RRAS is a link-state protocol?
3. Can remote access policy be used with an account local to an RRAS server?
4. Once a condition has been met which results in an "allow" or "deny", will any remote access policies later in the processing order be checked?
5. When is it advantageous to control access through remote access policy in place of a simple allow?

Pop Quiz 3.1 Answers

1. Not entirely. RRAS can be used as a multicast router, but the specific IGMP routing protocol support must come from outside Microsoft at this time.

2. OSPF, or open shortest path first, is a link-state protocol.

3. Actually, it can! Local accounts, as well as those domain accounts in domains where the functional mode is Windows 2000 native or higher, can be configured to control remote access through remote access policy.

4. Nope! Once the conditions have been met which result in either an allow or a deny, RRAS stops looking at policies.

5. Any time you have an environment where you need to control access with greater configuration "granularity".

3.3 Implement secure access between private networks

3.3.1 Create and implement an IPSec policy

A particular IPSec configuration is called an IPSec policy. Each policy has rules and associated settings for those rules. The rules and settings allow for great flexibility, and many opportunities to take wrong turns if you are not careful during configuration.

You may use one or more of the following rules in your configuration. Each of these have a group of configurable settings you can apply as necessary for the particular needs of the situation. The rules are:

Rule	Description
IP filter list	Specifics what network traffic is secured, by using inbound and outbound filters
Filter action	Specifies how the matching traffic is handled, either dropped, passed, encrypted, etc.
Authentication methods	Specifies how two computers will authenticate to each other, such as Kerberos, preshared key or certificate
Tunnel endpoint	Defines a tunnel endpoint for IPSec tunnels
Connection type	Tells which type of connection to apply the rule to – LAN, WAN or both.

Table 3—1: IPSec Policy Rules

The rules for a policy are displayed in the Group Policy Object Editor. They include Computer Configuration, Windows Settings, Security Settings and IP Security Policies. The rules will appear in reverse alphabetical order based on the name of the filter list selected for each rule. You cannot control the order in which the rules are applied. They are automatically applied based on the most specific filter list to the least specific list. If you have a setting that has individual IP addresses, it would be applied before one that included all addresses on a subnet.

A sample setup rule follows. The Local Security Settings MMC is used, but the rule setup is the same. A tunnel endpoint will be selected and we will permit IP traffic to pass, but require security on the traffic. We'll use the wizard to set up the rule, so we don't miss anything.

From the properties of the default require security rule, the properties sheet was selected, and the add rule button was clicked. The Create IP Security Rule Wizard opens, as shown in Figure 3.3.1.

Figure 3—6: Security Rule Wizard

We click next to continue, and get to select a tunnel endpoint. As we want to connect two networks, we will select a specific endpoint, and give the IP address, as shown in Figure 3.3.2. We then click next to move to the network type selection.

In Figure 3.3.3, we select that this rule will apply to all network connections, and click next to move to the IP Filter List. In the IP filter list, we select what type of traffic we want to work with. In our case, all IP traffic was selected, as shown in Figure 3.3.4.

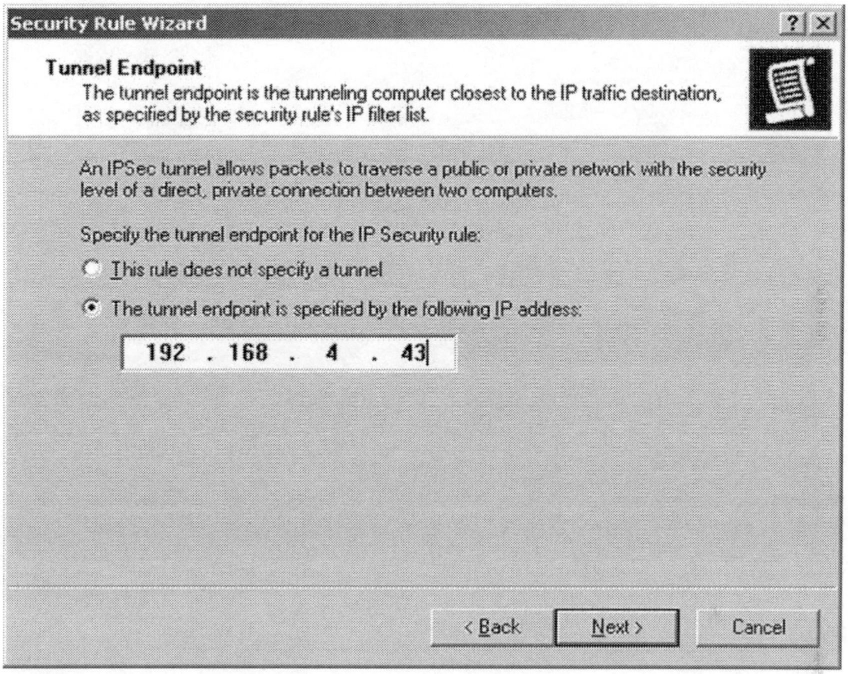

Figure 3—7: Tunnel Endpoint

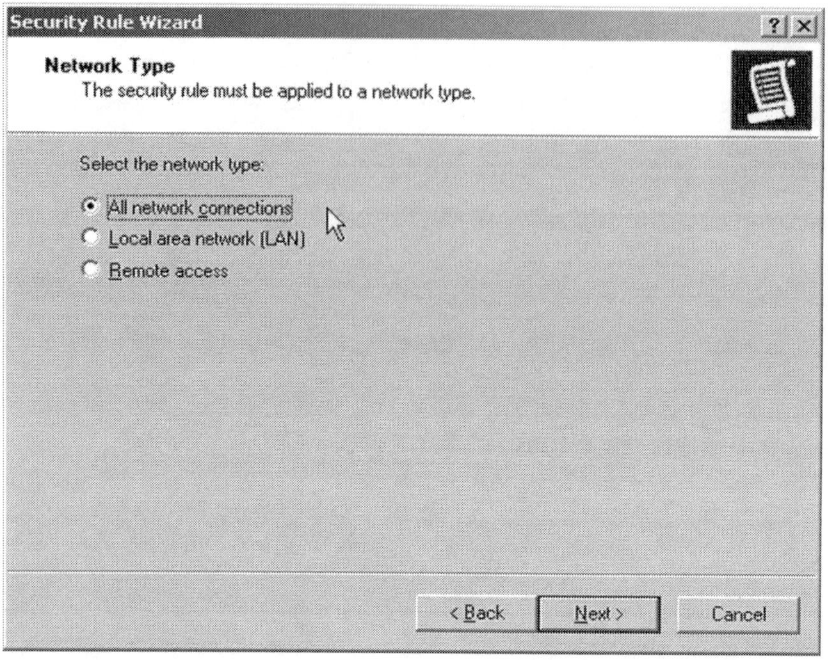

Figure 3—8: Network Type

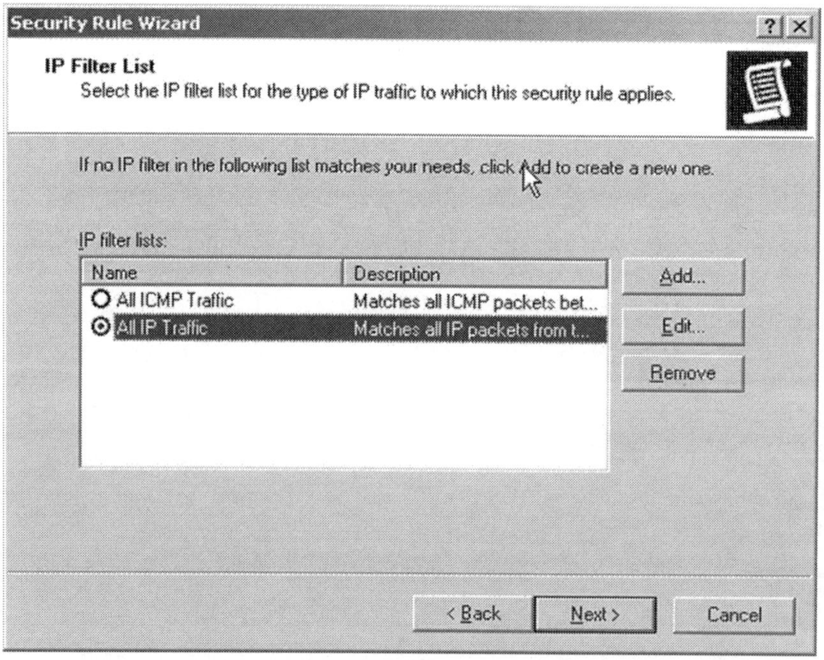

Figure 3—9: IP Filter List

After we select the filter list to use, we apply a filter action. Figure 3.3.5 shows the filter action screen, and require security is selected. When requires security is selected, the host will not communicate with another host, unless it is capable for providing security as well. We press next to continue to the authentication methods. Kerberos, the default Active Directory security authentication method is selected her, as shown in Figure 3.3.6. After clicking Next, we are taken to the final screen of the Add Rules Wizard. Click Finish to end the process.

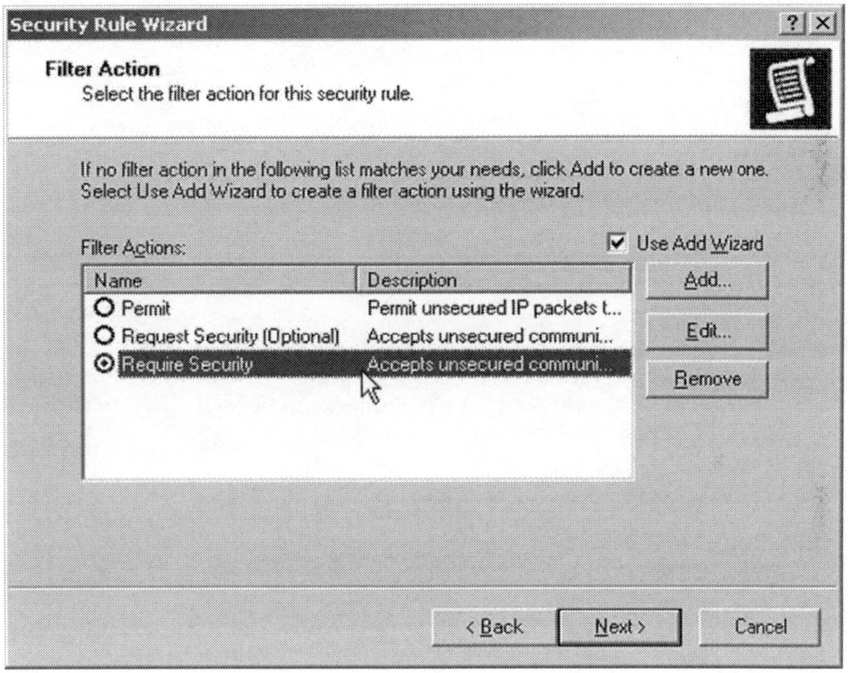

Figure 3—10: Filter Action

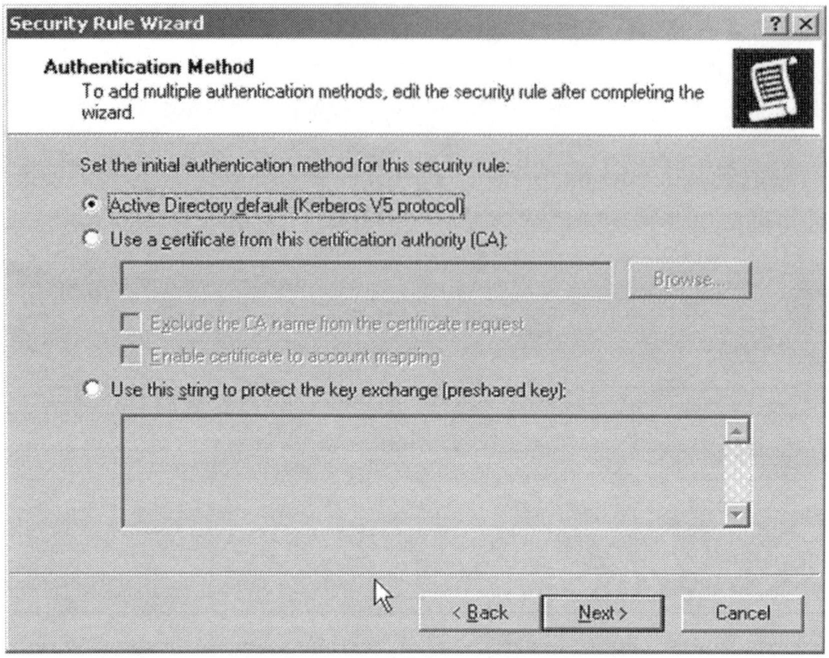

Figure 3—11: Authentication Method

Figure 3—12: Completing the Security Rule wizard

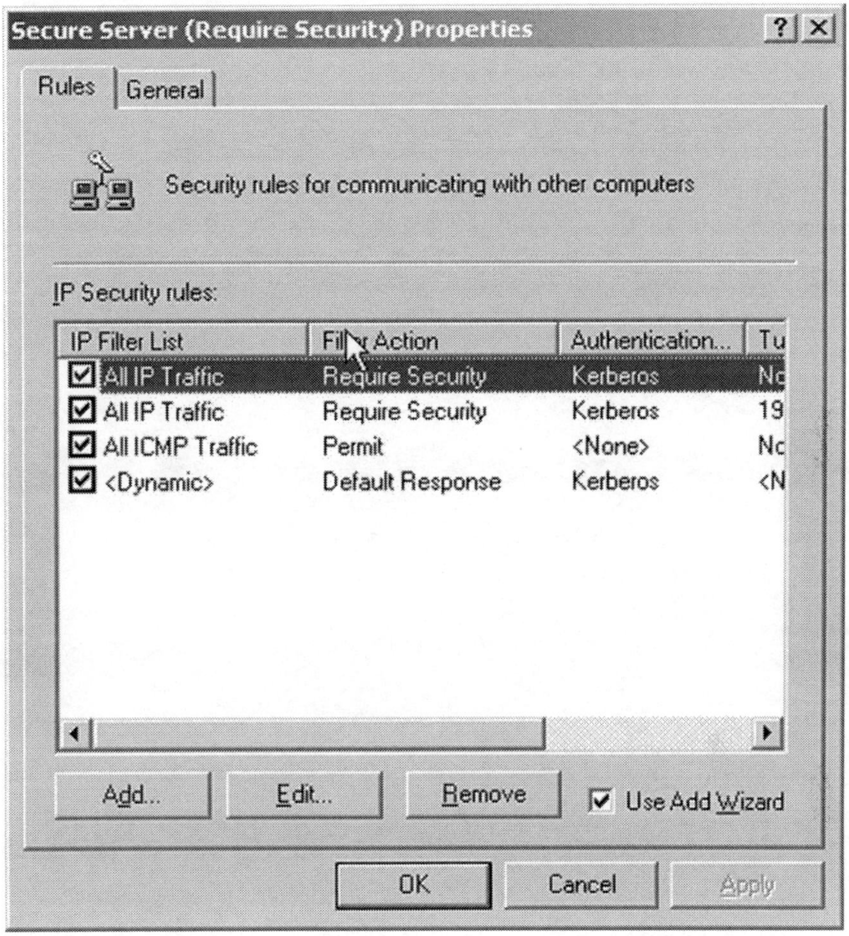

Figure 3—13: Rules

Figure 3.3.8 shows the properties sheet before we scroll to the right to see the tunnel endpoint, as shown in Figure 3.3.9.

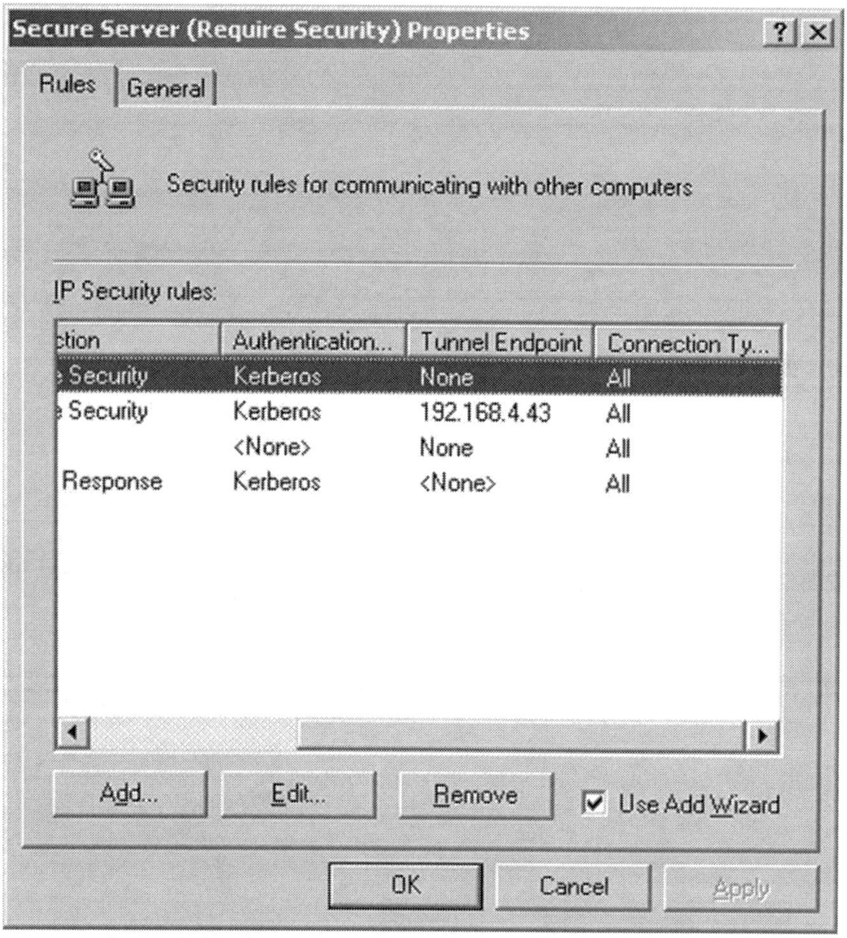

Figure 3—14: Security Kerberos

From this point, you make a connection to the remote network, and the tunnel sets itself up and secure communications occur.

3.3.2 Troubleshoot TCP/IP routing

Troubleshooting routing can be an interesting task, to say the least. So many different steps between "here" and "there" can be waiting to grab your poor unsuspecting packets and send them off to where ever lost packets go. Fortunately, Windows Server 2003 provides a wide range to tools to discover and correct the wide range of problems that could occur.

Things you need to discover to troubleshoot IP routing issues properly are the current TCP/IP configuration, the routing table for your host, connectivity issues between your host and the remote host, the route taken to get to the remote host, and where on that route a problem may be occurring.

3.3.2.1 The route

The route command allows you show the routing table for your host, and add or delete specific routes from the table. A typical routing table for Windows Server 2003 is shown in Figure 3.3.1

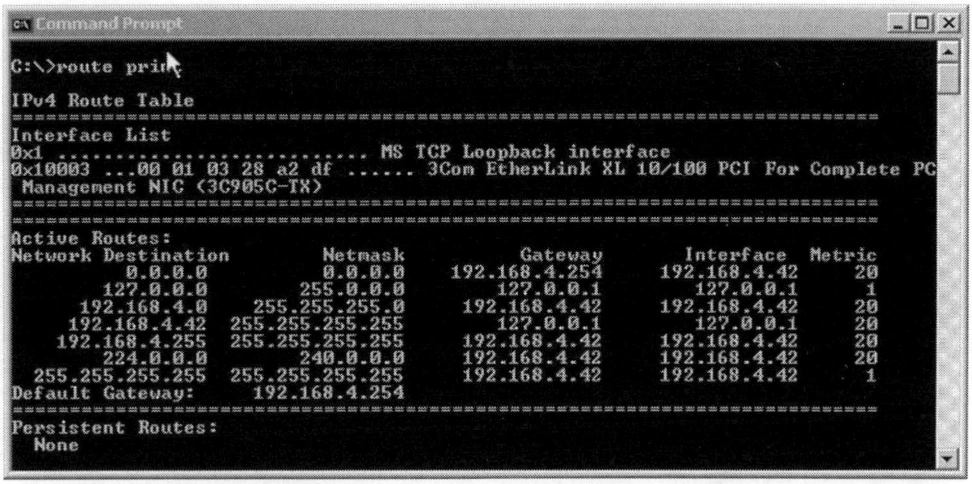

Figure 3—15: Route Table

The display shows the destination network and subnet mask (netmask) the gateway for that network, the local interface used to directly attach or route to that network.

By default, there should be an entry for each network interface card (NIC) and the network to which it is attached. There is one NIC in the machine shown, attached to the 192.168.4.0/24 network. There is an entry for the 127.0.0.0/8 for local diagnostics. There is an entry for the NIC itself, with a netmask of 255.255.255.255, for local broadcast. There is the local network broadcast of 192.168.4.255/32. There is the 224.0.0.0 for multicast, the all 255 for broadcast traffic, and the all 0 for the unknown destination. Note that the gateway for the 0.0.0.0 is the default gateway for that particular interface, or 192.168.4.254. Next, you need to check basic connectivity and communication to the default gateway.

3.3.2.2 Ping

Ping is used to test basic connectivity between hosts. It uses ICMP Echo Requests to verify the configuration of TCP/IP and the availability of a remote host. If your computer is properly configured and the proper DNS server or servers are available, you should be able to ping a remote host by its fully qualified domain name and get a response. Not only are you checking the availability of the remote host with this method, but you are testing host name resolution as well. Figure 3.3.2 shows a successful query of www.louisville.edu. Note that some hosts block ICMP Echo Requests as they can be used in denial of service (DOS) attacks on the host.

```
C:\>ping www.louisville.edu

Pinging www.louisville.edu [136.165.5.70] with 32 bytes of data:

Reply from 136.165.5.70: bytes=32 time=31ms TTL=245
Reply from 136.165.5.70: bytes=32 time=30ms TTL=245
Reply from 136.165.5.70: bytes=32 time=30ms TTL=245
Reply from 136.165.5.70: bytes=32 time=31ms TTL=245

Ping statistics for 136.165.5.70:
    Packets: Sent = 4, Received = 4, Lost = 0 (0% loss),
Approximate round trip times in milli-seconds:
    Minimum = 30ms, Maximum = 31ms, Average = 30ms

C:\>
```

Figure 3—16: Ping

Note that there is no way with ping to see the path taken to the remote host. Ping will measure packets lost and present statistics for the operation.

3.3.2.3 Tracert

Another useful addition to your TCP/IP troubleshooting toolbox is tracert, which will allow you to trace the path between your local and remote host, and will show you the timings involved at each router. If you have an issue at a particular router, you can attempt to correct the problem if you own the equipment. A sample tracert is shown in Figure 3.3.3

```
C:\>tracert www.louisville.edu

Tracing route to www.louisville.edu [136.165.5.70]
over a maximum of 30 hops:

  1    <1 ms    <1 ms    <1 ms  NATSERVER [192.168.1.254]
  2     1 ms     1 ms     1 ms  192.168.12.1
  3     4 ms     4 ms     4 ms  s2-0-7-0.cust-gw1.noc.win.net [24.235.1.73]
  4     5 ms     4 ms     4 ms  fa0-0.core-routera.noc.win.net [24.235.30.1]
  5    13 ms    14 ms    19 ms  64.242.63.153
  6    13 ms    15 ms    13 ms  at-0-2-901.usstls1-01.j20c.savvis.net [206.129.9
.89]
  7    18 ms    18 ms    18 ms  sl-gw31-chi-4-1.sprintlink.net [144.228.154.177]

  8    30 ms    32 ms    33 ms  sl-univlou-7-0.sprintlink.net [160.81.92.14]
  9    31 ms    32 ms    32 ms  uofl-belknap-g.kec.net [199.120.154.146]
 10    31 ms    31 ms    31 ms  center-gig-v306.bb.louisville.edu [136.165.254.1
02]
 11    31 ms    30 ms    31 ms  www.louisville.edu [136.165.5.70]

Trace complete.

C:\>
```

Figure 3—17: Tracert

3.3.2.4 Pathping

Pathping is a utility that combines the information provided by tracert and ping. Not only does it report the route to the remote host, it reports any packet losses along the way. Its report comes in two parts, first the path, then the timing stats. Figure 3.3.4 shows the way (again) to www.louisville.edu. The statistics sometimes take awhile to compute, so patience is in order if the path is somewhat long and involved. This utility can come into play to give a bit more detailed info than tracert, while giving you the timing info you can receive from ping without having to ping each separate router along the way.

```
C:\>pathping www.louisville.edu

Tracing route to www.louisville.edu [136.165.5.70]
over a maximum of 30 hops:
  0  tomw2k3.tomtest.msft [192.168.4.42]
  1  NATSERVER [192.168.1.254]
  2  192.168.12.1
  3  s2-0-7-0.cust-gw1.noc.win.net [24.235.1.73]
  4  fa0-0.core-routera.noc.win.net [24.235.30.1]
  5  64.242.63.153
  6  at-0-2-901.usstls1-01.j20c.savvis.net [206.129.9.89]
  7  sl-gw31-chi-4-1.sprintlink.net [144.228.154.177]
  8  sl-univlou-7-0.sprintlink.net [160.81.92.14]
  9  uofl-belknap-g.kec.net [199.120.154.146]
 10  center-gig-v306.bb.louisville.edu [136.165.254.102]
 11  www.louisville.edu [136.165.5.70]

Computing statistics for 275 seconds...
            Source to Here   This Node/Link
Hop  RTT    Lost/Sent = Pct  Lost/Sent = Pct  Address
  0                                           tomw2k3.tomtest.msft [192.168.4.42
]
                                0/ 100 =  0%   |
  1    0ms     0/ 100 =  0%     0/ 100 =  0%  NATSERVER [192.168.1.254]
                                0/ 100 =  0%   |
  2    1ms     0/ 100 =  0%     0/ 100 =  0%  192.168.12.1
                                0/ 100 =  0%   |
  3    5ms     0/ 100 =  0%     0/ 100 =  0%  s2-0-7-0.cust-gw1.noc.win.net [24.
235.1.73]
                                0/ 100 =  0%   |
  4   14ms     0/ 100 =  0%     0/ 100 =  0%  fa0-0.core-routera.noc.win.net [24
.235.30.1]
                                0/ 100 =  0%   |
  5   15ms     0/ 100 =  0%     0/ 100 =  0%  64.242.63.153
                                0/ 100 =  0%   |
  6   15ms     0/ 100 =  0%     0/ 100 =  0%  at-0-2-901.usstls1-01.j20c.savvis.
net [206.129.9.89]
                                0/ 100 =  0%   |
  7   25ms     0/ 100 =  0%     0/ 100 =  0%  sl-gw31-chi-4-1.sprintlink.net [14
4.228.154.177]
                                0/ 100 =  0%   |
  8   47ms     0/ 100 =  0%     0/ 100 =  0%  sl-univlou-7-0.sprintlink.net [160
.81.92.14]
                                0/ 100 =  0%   |
  9   33ms     0/ 100 =  0%     0/ 100 =  0%  uofl-belknap-g.kec.net [199.120.15
4.146]
                                0/ 100 =  0%   |
 10   33ms     0/ 100 =  0%     0/ 100 =  0%  center-gig-v306.bb.louisville.edu
[136.165.254.102]
                                0/ 100 =  0%   |
 11   34ms     0/ 100 =  0%     0/ 100 =  0%  www.louisville.edu [136.165.5.70]

Trace complete.

C:\>
```

Figure 3—18: pathping

3.3.2.5 Netsh commands

Netsh is a command-line scripting utility that allows you to display or modify the network configuration of either a local or a remote computer that is currently running. Netsh commands can also be scripted so that you can run a group of commands in batch mode against a specified computer. You can also save a configuration script in a text file for archival purposes. It may also be a helpful resource when you configure other servers.

Netsh uses features called a context, which is a specific group of commands associated with a networking component. If that particular component is installed, netsh uses a DLL to interact the specific component. For example, Dhcpmon.dll provides netsh the context and set of commands necessary to configure and manage DHCP servers. These extensive features allow you to configure and monitor networking components entirely from the command prompt. Thus, you can configure, display settings and monitor via command script.

To run a netsh command, you must start netsh from the Cmd.exe prompt and change to the context that contains the command you want to use. The contexts that are available to you depend on which networking components you have installed. For example, if you type dhcp at the Netsh command prompt, you change to the DHCP context. If you do not have DHCP installed, the following message appears:

The following command was not found: dhcp.

Another advantage to netsh is speed. While monitoring and configuring a remote server configured as a router, you don't have to worry about the overhead of a GUI utility while working over a slow WAN link.

3.3.2.6 Network Monitor

Network Monitor provides you with information about the traffic that flows to and from the network adapter or adapters of the computer on which it is installed. You can capture, examine, and analyze this traffic and either prevents or diagnoses and solves many types of problems.

The data can be filtered to examine packets from a particular host, or from a particular protocol type. You can configure Network Monitor to begin to capture data based on a particular set of circumstances arise. The data can be saved for later review as well.

The Network Monitor component that ships with Microsoft® Windows® Server 2003 captures frames that are sent to or from the computer where Network Monitor is installed. It will also capture any broadcast traffic, as broadcast traffic is addressed to all computers on the network segment. Any traffic that you would like to examine can be captured and saved by Network Monitor.

The information Network Monitor displays comes from the frames of information transmitted on the network. Data such as source and destination addresses, protocol types, and the contents of the data can be examined.

Chapter 3: Review Questions

1. Which of the following is not part of the CHAP process?

   A. IPSec is initiated between the authenticator and the client

   B. The authenticator sends a challenge to the client (after the link is established)

   C. The client responds to the challenge with a value calculated using a one-way hash function

   D. The authenticator verifies the value against what it expects the hash value to be (at this point the client is either authenticated or the connection is dropped)

---

2. Which of the following attacks would be performed on a smart card?

   A. Timing attack

   B. Man-in-the-middle attack

   C. TCP/IP hijacking

   D. Birthday attack

3. What types of attacks could be performed to break into a VPN?

   A. Breaking the encryption

   B. Spoofing

   C. Grab the passwords transmitted in cleartext

   D. Grab the information transmitted in cleartext

---

4. To what does the acronym RADIUS refer and what RFC document specifies its attributes?

   A. Remote Authentication Dial-In User Service (RFC 2138)

   B. Relaxed Authentication Dial-In User Service (RFC 1543)

   C. Remote Authentication Dynamic User Service (RFC 1238)

   D. Remote Authentication Dial-In User Stop (RFC 1492)

5. Which of the following remote protocols can be used with VPNs?

   A. PPTP

   B. PPP

   C. SLIP

   D. PAP

---

6. What are the security methods used with IPSec?

   A. ESP (Encapsulating Security Payload)

   B. AH (Authentication Header)

   C. ESP (Encrypting Security Payload)

   D. AH (Authoritative Header)

7. Which of the following remote protocols is a combination of L2F and PPTP?

   A. L2TP

   B. 2TP

   C. LTP

   D. LoTR

---

8. Which of the following VPN protocols is the most versatile working with most VPN hardware and software components?

   A. IPSec

   B. PPTP

   C. L2TP

   D. PPP

9. Which describe the PPTP protocol.

A. It enables highly private network links over the public Internet

B. It encrypts connections

C. Allows for secure transmission over TCP/IP networks

D. It does not encrypt connections

E. It does not allow for VPNs

---

10. Which of the following are true regarding L2TP?

A. The next version of PPTP

B. It does not require IP connectivity

C. It is used in conjunction with VPNs

D. L2F is not a part of L2TP

E. It functions at the Physical layer of the OSI model

11. Where is the ppp.log file stored by default?

    A. In the systemroot\Tracing folder

    B. In the systemroot\system32\Tracing folder

    C. In the systemroot\winnt\Tracing folder

    D. In the systemroot\windows\Tracing folder

---

12. Which of the following commands allows you to use the remote access diagnostic functions that are available in Windows Server 2003?

    A. netsh ras diag

    B. netsh ras diagnos

    C. netsh diag

    D. netsh ras

13. Which of the following would allow clients on one subnet or network segment to connect to clients on another subnet or network segment?

A. Setting up a server that connects the network segments to enable IP routing

B. Manually entering different default gateways on each of the clients

C. Setting up a server that uses the same IP addresses on both interfaces

D. Manually entering different subnet masks on each of the clients

---

14. When network connectivity is inconsistent between many routers in distant locations (i.e. Atlanta, GA, Los Angeles, CA, Houston, TX, and Philadelphia, PA), what command would you use to determine where packets are being dropped and what percentage of packets are being dropped?

A. pathping

B. ping

C. tracert

D. ipconfig

15. Multilink has to be set up both on the _________ and the _________. (select two)

A. RRAS server

B. Clients

C. ISP's server room

D. Modems

---

16. Which of the following protocol combinations would be the most secure for use with dial-in and Windows 2003 computers?

A. L2TP and IPSec

B. MS-CHAP v2 and MPPE

C. L2TP and MPPE

D. EAP-CHAP and MPPE

Chapter 3: Review Answers

1. Which of the following is not part of the CHAP process?

***A. IPSec is initiated between the authenticator and the client**

B. The authenticator sends a challenge to the client (after the link is established)

C. The client responds to the challenge with a value calculated using a one-way hash function

D. The authenticator verifies the value against what it expects the hash value to be (at this point the client is either authenticated or the connection is dropped)

Explanation: The CHAP (Challenge Handshake Authentication Protocol) protocol is used to dynamically encrypt a user's ID and password. The client' machine obtains a key from the CHAP server and proceeds to encrypt the user's ID and password before they are transmitted. The CHAP process involves the following steps: 1. The authenticator sends a challenge to the client (after the link is established), 2. The client responds to the challenge with a value calculated using a one-way hash function, 3. The authenticator verifies the value against what it expects the hash value to be (at this point the client is either authenticated or the connection is dropped), and 4. The process may be repeated more than once at various times after the initial process. The CHAP process is an important process, especially when you want to let the CHAP server know that you have the password without sending the actual password.

---

2. Which of the following attacks would be performed on a smart card?

***A. Timing attack**

B. Man-in-the-middle attack

C. TCP/IP hijacking

D. Birthday attack

Explanation: A timing attack requires the exact measurements of the processing time required to execute a cryptographic algorithm to acquire the key or the plaintext involved. Understanding the algorithm and its method of implementation is integral to this attack. This type of attack isn't generally performed in a networked situation, but rather when a smartcard that has fallen into the wrong hands. Extra processing steps can help prevent this type of attack. You can use EAP-TLS to tighten security with smart cards in a Windows 2003 environment.

3. What types of attacks could be performed to break into a VPN?

***A. Breaking the encryption**

***B. Spoofing**

C. Grab the passwords transmitted in cleartext

D. Grab the information transmitted in cleartext

Explanation: A VPN uses the Internet as the transport backbone to make secure links between such entities as business partners, main and regional offices, or vendors and suppliers in a supply chain. It is called virtual because it depends on the use of virtual, or temporary, connections that have no real physical presence but consist of packets routed over various machines on the Internet on an ad hoc basis. A VPN could be attacked if the encryption could be broken and, in some cases, spoofing might work too. This is relatively difficult to do, so VPNs are generally very secure.

---

4. To what does the acronym RADIUS refer and what RFC document specifies its attributes?

***A. Remote Authentication Dial-In User Service (RFC 2138)**

B. Relaxed Authentication Dial-In User Service (RFC 1543)

C. Remote Authentication Dynamic User Service (RFC 1238)

D. Remote Authentication Dial-In User Stop (RFC 1492)

Explanation: RADIUS (Remote Authentication Dial-In User Service), developed by Livingston Enterprises, is an access control protocol used in authentication that employs a challenge/response method. This protocol authenticates remote users to a network access server, which acts as a client to the RADIUS server. RADIUS is referred to in RFC 2138.

5. Which of the following remote protocols can be used with VPNs?

***A. PPTP**

B. PPP

C. SLIP

D. PAP

Explanation: PPTP (Point-to-Point Tunneling Protocol) provides enhancements over PPP. Even with all the improvements of PPP, it was not enough. PPTP provides secure transmission over TCP/IP networks. It enables highly private network links over the public Internet, encrypted connections, VPNs (Virtual Private Networks), RAS and Security.

---

6. What are the security methods used with IPSec?

***A. ESP (Encapsulating Security Payload)**

***B. AH (Authentication Header)**

C. ESP (Encrypting Security Payload)

D. AH (Authoritative Header)

Explanation: IPsec (Internet Protocol Security) is a framework of open standards for security at the network layer of the OSI model. It is designed to protect IP packets and defend against network attacks. It is used in conjunction with VPNs (Virtual Private Networks) and remote access for users who need access to resources on a private network. It is based on an end-to-end security model, meaning that only the computers, both sending and receiving, are aware of the IPsec transmission. It is transparent to the user. IPsec allows either ESP (Encapsulating Security Payload) or AH (Authentication Header). ESP, which is the highest security method, authenticates the sender and encrypts the data as well. AH only authenticates the user. Kerberos V5, certificates (like X.509) and preshared keys can be used for authentication with IPsec.

7. Which of the following remote protocols is a combination of L2F and PPTP?

***A. L2TP**

B. 2TP

C. LTP

D. LoTR

Explanation: L2TP (Layer Two Tunneling Protocol) is the next version of the Point-to-Point Tunneling Protocol (PPTP). Unlike PPTP, it does not require IP connectivity. It combines Cisco's Layer 2 Forwarding (L2F) with PPTP. It functions at the Data-link layer of the OSI model and is used with VPNs.

---

8. Which of the following VPN protocols is the most versatile working with most VPN hardware and software components?

***A. IPSec**

B. PPTP

C. L2TP

D. PPP

Explanation: Encryption protocols can be used with VPN, to offer security for the data being transmitted. PPTP, L2TP and IPSec fall into this category. IPSec is the most versatile of these protocols, in that it works with most VPN hardware and software components. It helps to create the 'tunnel' which defines the VPN.

9. Which describe the PPTP protocol.

***A. It enables highly private network links over the public Internet**

***B. It encrypts connections**

***C. Allows for secure transmission over TCP/IP networks**

D. It does not encrypt connections

E. It does not allow for VPNs

Explanation: PPTP (Point-to-Point Tunneling Protocol) provides enhancements over PPP. PPTP includes all the specifications of PPP plus secure transmission over TCP/IP networks. It enables highly private network links over the public Internet and encrypted connections. It is used to facilitate VPNs (Virtual Private Networks), RAS, and security.

---

10. Which of the following are true regarding L2TP?

***A. The next version of PPTP**

***B. It does not require IP connectivity**

***C. It is used in conjunction with VPNs**

D. L2F is not a part of L2TP

E. It functions at the Physical layer of the OSI model

Explanation: Layer Two Tunneling Protocol (L2TP) is the next version of the Point-to-Point Tunneling Protocol (PPTP). Unlike PPTP, it does not require IP connectivity. It combines Cisco's Layer 2 Forwarding (L2F) with PPTP. It functions at the Data-link layer of the OSI model and is used in conjunction with VPNs.

11. Where is the ppp.log file stored by default?

***A. In the systemroot\Tracing folder**

B. In the systemroot\system32\Tracing folder

C. In the systemroot\winnt\Tracing folder

D. In the systemroot\windows\Tracing folder

Explanation: The default location for the PPP log is in the systemroot\Tracing folder. It is stored as the ppp.log file.

---

12. Which of the following commands allows you to use the remote access diagnostic functions that are available in Windows Server 2003?

***A. netsh ras diag**

B. netsh ras diagnos

C. netsh diag

D. netsh ras

Explanation: When you run the netsh ras diag command, you can use the remote access diagnostic functions that are available in the Windows Server 2003 family.

13. Which of the following would allow clients on one subnet or network segment to connect to clients on another subnet or network segment?

***A. Setting up a server that connects the network segments to enable IP routing**

B. Manually entering different default gateways on each of the clients

C. Setting up a server that uses the same IP addresses on both interfaces

D. Manually entering different subnet masks on each of the clients

Explanation: **Enabling IP routing will allow IP packets to be routed to either subnet. Different default gateways and subnet masks on each client will only hinder or halt communication between the clients. The same is true if there aren't different IP addresses for each interface on the server being used as a router.**

---

14. When network connectivity is inconsistent between many routers in distant locations (i.e. Atlanta, GA, Los Angeles, CA, Houston, TX, and Philadelphia, PA), what command would you use to determine where packets are being dropped and what percentage of packets are being dropped?

***A. pathping**

B. ping

C. tracert

D. ipconfig

Explanation:

Pathping combines the functionality of the ping and tracert commands. Pathping also shows what percentage of packets is being dropped. Ping and Tracert don't show this information. An example of using pathping from Atlanta to test connectivity to Los Angeles, CA would be: pathping LOSANG01

15. Multilink has to be set up both on the _________ and the _________. (select two)

***A. RRAS server**

***B. Clients**

C. ISP's server room

D. Modems

Explanation: Multilink allows you to use multiple modems to use their combined connection speed. Multilink must be set up both on the server end and the client end. The ISP and the modems used have nothing to do with Multilink configuration.

---

16. Which of the following protocol combinations would be the most secure for use with dial-in and Windows 2003 computers?

***A. L2TP and IPSec**

B. MS-CHAP v2 and MPPE

C. L2TP and MPPE

D. EAP-CHAP and MPPE

Explanation:

L2TP is required for IPSec, which needs to be used by both the client and the server. MS-CHAP v2 and MPPE are good but aren't as secure as L2TP and IPSec. Windows 2003 supports EAP-TLS but not EAP-CHAP.

Planning, Implementing, and Maintaining Server Availability

The objective of this chapter is to provide the reader with an understanding of the following:

Plan services for high availability.

- Plan a high availability solution that uses clustering services.
- Plan a high availability solution that uses Network Load Balancing.

Identify system bottlenecks, including memory, processor, disk, and network related bottlenecks.

- Identify system bottlenecks by using System Monitor.

Implement a cluster server.

- Recover from cluster node failure.

Manage Network Load Balancing. Tools might include:

- Network Load Balancing Monitor Microsoft Management Console (MMC) snap-in
- WLBS cluster control utility.

Plan a backup and recovery strategy.

- Identify appropriate backup types. Methods include full, incremental, and differential.
- Plan a backup strategy that uses volume shadow copy.
- Plan system recovery that uses Automated System Recovery (ASR).

Chapter 4: Managing Server Availability

Introduction:

Server availability combines two important design concepts – that of services that are highly available, and the ability to recover when a disaster occurs. Windows Server 2003 provided tools in both of these areas to assist you in keeping network services available to the users. We'll look in detail at types of clustering and network load balancing as well as backup methods to protect your valuable data.

Other things to consider for server availability are things you can do to make the hardware less prone to failure. Having redundant power supplies, hardware raid and a UPS to protect and provide backup power will add to the resiliency of your server.

Getting Ready Questions

1. A _________ occurs when applications allocate memory for use but do not free that allocated memory when finished.

2. What new utilities allow Administrators to add, manage and delete user accounts from the command line.

3. List three backup methods.

4. Identify the latest graphical utility tool that allows administrators to check for strong passwords, scan IIS and SQL servers for security configuration problems.

Getting Ready Answers

1. Memory Leak

2. Utilities such as bsa, ldifde, csvde, dsadd, dsmod, and dsrm are available for Administrators to add, manage and delete user accounts from the command line.

3. Full Backup, Incremental Backup and Differential Backup

4. The MBSA 1.1 s is an excellent graphical utility tool that allows administrators to check for strong passwords, scan IIS and SQL servers for security configuration problems.

4.1 Plan services for high availability.

4.1.1 Plan a high availability solution that uses clustering services.

As mentioned earlier, Windows Server 2003 provides two clustering solutions to provide high availability and reliability. They are designed to help keep applications, not data available to the user. You must still have a good data protection and recovery plan. Clustering will not save you from viruses, software corruption, or human errors.

Microsoft cluster technologies guard against three specific types of failure:

- **Application and service failures** - Application software and essential network services are affected here.
- **System and hardware failures** - Here hardware components such as the CPU, memory, network adapters, drives and power supplies are affected.
- **Site failures in multisite organizations** - These problems can be created by natural disasters, power outages, or connectivity downtime.

The cluster technology you select in Windows Server 2003 depends on the services or applications you desire to run on the cluster. All applications and services must use TCP/IP for client-server communications. Server clusters are used for stateful applications. A stateful application has a long-running in-memory state, or large, frequently updated data states. Microsoft SQL Server is an excellent example of a stateful application.

A stateless application treats each client request as an independent event or operation. A stateless application may have read-only data, or infrequently changing data. Network Load Balancing (NLB) is intended for these types of applications. Some examples are Web front-end servers, VPNs (virtual private networks), and FTP (File Transfer Protocol) servers would typically use NLB.

Availability is enhanced by scaling out by adding more nodes to the cluster, or scaling up by adding ram and/or processors to existing nodes in the cluster. The following table shows some maximums in the different versions of Windows Server 2003.

Operating System	Nodes - NLB	Nodes – Cluster Service	Processors	Max RAM
Windows Server 2003 Standard	32	N/A	4	4 GB
Windows Server 2003 Enterprise	32	8	8	32 GB
Windows Server 2003 Data Center	32	8	32	64 GB

Table 4—1: Operating Systems

Note that NLB will run on all three editions of Windows Server 2003 listed in the table, while cluster services will only run on the Enterprise or Data Center Editions.

4.1.2 Plan a high availability solution that uses Network Load Balancing.

Here, high availability in a server cluster means that the application or applications being protected in the cluster will be available to the end users. The end user connects to a virtual server, which passes the request to a node in the cluster providing the application. That node retains the information about your server connection, and for the length of your connection to the application, your session will be served by that particular node.

The basic steps to creating a cluster are:

3. Choose the cluster model.
4. Select applications to run on the cluster.
5. Organize applications and resources into groups based on:
    a. Resource Dependencies
    b. Failover Policies
    c. Administrative Convenience
6. Determine the hardware capacity for each server in the cluster.
7. Plan network hardware.
8. Plan your system disks.
9. Plan your cluster disks.

Let's look at these in a bit of detail.

You need to select the cluster model from one of the following:

- ***Single node cluster*** – mainly used to test applications on a server cluster.
- ***Single quorum device cluster*** – more common in Windows Server 2003 setups, and the only type supported in Windows NT and 2000. This model has the quorum information on a single shared device connected to all nodes. This will cover a vast majority of clustering needs.
- ***Majority Node set cluster*** – each node keeps its copy of the configuration data, and the quorum is responsible for keeping that data consistent across the nodes. Good when the different nodes of the cluster are not physically located together.

Applications that can run on a cluster must meet three criteria:

- They must be IP Protocol based.
- The application has to be able to specify where its data is stored.
- Client applications that connect to the server side application must be able to try to recover from temporary network outages.

A resource group is the virtual server or servers in your cluster. Resources that depend upon each other need to be placed in the same resource group. These dependencies often had similar administrative requirements. Failover policies determine the manner and order resources are transferred from one node to another, and are based on the groups you develop.

After determining the cluster model, resource groups and the failover policies required by each resource, you next need to determine the hardware capacity required for each server in the cluster. Three major items should be considered, the cluster storage requirements, the CPU and RAM requirements.

Each cluster node needs enough persistent storage to store permanent copies of all applications and other resources to run all groups that node is required to cover. When calculating, assume all resources will be running on the node and plan the space accordingly.

Failover of resources can strain the CPU and RAM of the node. Without proper planning the surviving node's CPU and RAM can be pushed beyond their capacity. Of course, this will affect the responsiveness of the surviving node.

The nodes in the cluster need to be connected by at least two separate, independent networks.

In planning your system disks, it is best to use the same drive letter for each system disk in the cluster, and have the hardware as much the same as possible.

In planning your cluster disks, it is strongly recommended that you install the quorum resource on a separate disk, by itself, so that other applications cannot affect it. Be sure that the quorum disk has enough free space so that the Cluster service will be able to start and continue to write to the quorum log. To guard against the failure of your cluster disks, it is highly recommended that you implement a hardware RAID solution.

4.2 Identify system bottlenecks

What is a bottleneck? When speaking of network servers, a system bottleneck is something that is keeping one or more of the four major subsystems on the server from performing at its best.

4.2.1 System bottlenecks in memory

The most important subsystem to general server performance is server memory. If your server has insufficient random access memory (RAM) to hold needed data, it must temporarily store the data on the disk. This area of storage is called the paging file. The process of writing to the file is called paging. Some paging is acceptable, even expected. Disk access is much slower than RAM, so storing data on the disk can significantly degrade server performance by having to go to the page file frequently to read and write data, which also prevents the hard disk from accessing other needed data.

Lack of memory is the most common cause of serious performance problems in computer systems. Always check memory counters to rule out a memory shortage, even if you suspect other problems. Monitor server memory to assess the amount of available memory and the level of paging, and to observe the effects of a memory shortage. Proper monitoring of your server memory can help you determine whether any of the following conditions exist:

4.2.3.1 Memory bottleneck

Low memory conditions can slow the operation of applications and services on your server and can affect the performance of other resources on your server. For example, when your server is low on memory, paging can be prolonged, resulting in more work for your disks. Because it involves reading and writing to disk, this paging activity may compete with other disk transactions, thereby intensifying a disk bottleneck.

In turn, all this work by the disk can mean that the processor is used less or is doing unnecessary work, such as processing numerous interrupts due to repeated page faults. *Page faults* occur when the server cannot locate requested code or data in the physical memory that is available to the requesting process. As a result, applications and services become less responsive. Therefore, it is important to monitor memory regularly to detect memory bottlenecks.

4.2.3.2 Insufficient memory

Insufficient memory is the reason for the symptoms we encounter with low memory, and excessive paging. By monitoring server memory, you can use the baseline established to predict when you will need additional memory, and avoid some of these problems.

4.2.3.3 Excessive paging

The indication of memory shortage is frequent paging. *Paging* is the process of moving fixed-size blocks of code and data from RAM to disk by using units called *pages* to free memory for other uses. Although some paging is acceptable, because it enables you to use more memory than actually exists, constant paging slows server performance. Reducing paging significantly improves server responsiveness.

4.2.3.4 Memory leak

A memory leak occurs when applications allocate memory for use but do not free that allocated memory when finished. As a result, available memory is used up over time. This often causes the server to stop functioning properly.

Windows Server 2003 divides memory into two categories, paged and nonpaged. Paged RAM is virtual memory, where it appears that a full range of memory addresses is available to all applications. Windows Server 2003 does this by giving each application a private memory range called a virtual memory space and by mapping that virtual memory to physical memory. Nonpaged RAM cannot use this configuration. Data that is placed into nonpaged RAM must remain in memory and cannot be written to or retrieved from disk. For example, data structures that are used by interrupt routines or those that prevent multiprocessor conflicts within the operating system use nonpaged RAM.

The virtual memory system in Windows Server 2003 combines physical memory, the file system cache, and disk into an information storage and retrieval system. The system stores program code and data on disk until it is needed. It then moves it into physical memory. Code and data that are no longer in active use are written to disk. However, when a computer does not have enough memory, code and data must be written to and retrieved from the disk more frequently. This slow, resource-intensive process can become a system bottleneck.

The best indicator of a memory bottleneck is a sustained, high rate of hard page faults. Hard page faults occur when the data that a program requires is not found in its working set (the physical memory visible to the program) or elsewhere in physical memory, and must be retrieved from disk. Sustained hard page fault rates of over five per second indicate a memory bottleneck.

4.2.3.5 System monitor counters that help you identify memory problems include:

Pages/sec - This is the number of requested pages that were not immediately available in RAM, and thus were accessed from the disk or were written to the disk to make room in RAM for other pages. Generally, if the value of this counter is over five for extended periods, memory may be a bottleneck in the system.

Available Bytes - This is the amount of available physical memory. It is normally low, because Windows Disk Cache Manager uses extra memory for caching and then returns it when requests for memory occur. However, if this value is consistently below 5 percent of the total memory on a server, it is an indication that excessive paging is occurring.

Committed Bytes - This is the amount of virtual memory that is committed to either physical RAM for storage or to pagefile space. If the amount of committed bytes is larger than the amount of physical memory, more RAM may be required.

Pool Nonpaged Bytes - This is the amount of RAM in the nonpaged pool system memory area where space is acquired by operating system components as they accomplish their tasks. If the Pool Nonpaged Bytes value shows a steady increase without a corresponding increase in activity on the server, it may indicate that a process with a memory leak is running, and you should monitor it closely.

Page Faults/sec - Number of times a virtual page was not found in memory. If this number is consistently above five, too much memory has been allocated to an application and not enough to the server that you are running.

How these counters are used in system monitor is explained later in this chapter.

If memory is determined to be the problem, add more memory to the server, or correct the leaky application so that allocated memory is returned to the usable memory pool in the server.

4.2.2 System bottlenecks in processor

Processor activity is the most important data to monitor on your server, after memory consumption. To determine whether a busy processor is efficiently handling all the work on your computer or whether it is overwhelmed, you must examine the processor usage.

The most important aspect of processor performance is its level of usage. When an application or other software uses more than its share of the processor's cycles, all the other software that is running operates much more slowly.

High processor usage overall may not be a "bad thing" if the different applications on the server are all able to share the processor to complete their needed tasks.

The processor is involved in almost every activity on the server. The processor on an application server is generally busier than the processor on a file and print server. As a result, the level of processor activity, and what is considered normal, is different between the two types of servers. Two of the most common causes of processor bottlenecks are CPU-bound applications and drivers, and excessive interrupts that are generated by inadequate disk or network subsystem components.

4.2.2.1 System monitor counters that help you identify processor problems include:

% Processor Time - This counter measures the amount of time that the processor is busy. When processor usage consistently runs over 85 percent, the processor could be a system bottleneck. Analyze processor usage by monitoring individual processes to determine what is causing the processor activity.

System: Processor Queue Length - This is the number of requests in the queue for the processor. It indicates the number of threads that are ready to be executed and are waiting for processor time. Generally, a processor queue length that is consistently higher than two may indicate congestion. To determine the cause of the congestion, you must further analyze the individual processes that are making requests on the processor.

Server Work Queues: Queue Length - This is the number of requests in the queue for the selected processor. A consistent queue of over two indicates processor congestion.

Interrupts/sec - This is the number of interrupts that the processor is servicing from applications or from hardware devices. Windows Server 2003 can handle thousands of interrupts per second. A dramatic increase in this counter value without a corresponding increase in system activity indicates a hardware problem. The problem could be a device that is unable to keep up with the rest of the system, like a disk controller or network interface card (NIC). For example, if a conflict occurs between a hard disk controller and a network adapter card, monitor the disk controller and network adapter card.

Determine whether excessive requests are being generated by monitoring the queue lengths for the physical disk and the network interface. Generally, if the queue length is greater than two requests, check for slow disk drives or network adapters that could be causing the queue length backlog.

How these counters are used in system monitor is explained later in this chapter.

If the processor has been identified as the problem area, you may consider adding a second processor if the server is an application server, upgrading to a faster processor if the server is primarily a file and print server, or splitting the workload by moving an application to another server altogether. You should also look to various system components such as network interface, hard disk controllers, etc. to determine if they are 32-bit hardware, thus not overworking the processor with extra interrupt work.

4.2.3 System bottlenecks in disk

The access speed of the physical disk drive can greatly affect the speed at which applications operate and data is loaded. In addition, the disk storage space must be sufficient for you to install applications, store data, and have enough space for the paging file. You should monitor disks to insure your systems are working efficiently. You can also use the collected monitoring data to plan for future hardware and software upgrades.

A disk bottleneck exists when all of the following conditions occur:

10. There is a sustained rate of disk activity well above your baseline
11. There are persistent disk queues that are longer than two per disk
12. There is an absence of a significant amount of paging

If these three do not appear in at the same time, another subsystem (usually memory) is causing the disk to be overworked.

System monitor counters for disks include two objects the physical disk and logical disk. The logical disk counters monitor separate disk volumes, and can be used to monitor issues with each single volume, while the physical disk monitors over performance for that particular hard drive.

4.2.3.1 System monitor counters that help you identify disk problems include:

% Disk Time - This indicates the amount of time that the disk drive is busy servicing read and write requests. If this is consistently close to 100 percent, the disk is being used very heavily. Monitoring individual processes helps determine which process or processes are making the majority of the disk requests.

Current Disk Queue Length - This indicates the number of pending disk I/O requests for the disk drive. If this value is consistently over two, it indicates congestion.

Avg. Disk Bytes/Transfer - This is the average number of bytes transferred to or from the disk during write or read operations. The larger the transfer size, the more efficient the system is running.

Disk Bytes/sec - Bytes are transferred to or from the disk during write or read operations at this rate. The higher the average, the more efficient the system is running.

LogicalDisk\% Free Space - This is the amount of disk space available.

How these counters are used in system monitor is explained later in this chapter.

If you identify a disk bottleneck, you can do the following:

- Be sure there is a disk, not memory issue. Excessive paging will cause a disk to be overworked.
- Defragment the disk defragmenter in Computer Management.
- Add a faster controller, or upgrade to faster disks.
- In a RAID environment, add additional disks.
- Offload some of the server workload to another server.

4.2.4 Identify network related bottlenecks

The performance of your network is affected by the speed of both the hardware in your network infrastructure and the software that is running on your servers and clients. Network usage is the percentage of network bandwidth that is in use on the network segment that is being monitored. Network bottlenecks directly affect the experience of the user at the client workstation and the entire network. A network bottleneck limits the number of clients that can simultaneously access your server.

- Network bandwidth is measured in several different ways:
- The rate at which bytes are transferred to and from the server.
- The rate at which data packages are sent by the server.
- The rate at which files are sent and received by the server.

4.2.4.1 System monitor counters that help you identify network problems include:

Task Manager: % Network utilization. This is the percentage of the network bandwidth in use for the local network segment. You can use this counter to monitor the effect of various network operations on the network, such as user logon validation and domain account synchronization.

Network Interface: Bytes Sent/sec. This counter measures the number of bytes that are sent by using this network adapter card.

Network Interface: Bytes Total/sec. This counter measures the number of bytes that are sent and received by using this network adapter card. Use this counter to determine how the network adapter is performing. The Bytes Total/sec counter should report high values, to indicate a large number of successful transmissions.

Server: Bytes Received/sec. This compares the bytes received per second counter to the total bandwidth of your network adapter card to determine whether your network connection is creating a bottleneck. To allow room for spikes in traffic, you should usually use no more than 50 percent of capacity. If this number is very close to the capacity of the connection, and processor and memory use are moderate, the connection might be causing a problem.

How these counters are used in system monitor is explained later in this chapter.

If a network problem is identified, you should consider one of the following actions:

- You can add servers to the network, distributing the processing load.
- You can check and improve the physical layer components, such as routers, switches, and cabling.
- The network can be divided into multiple subnets or segments, attaching the server to each segment with a separate adapter. This method reduces congestion at the server by spreading server requests.
- The network traffic can be divided into appropriate segments. For example, configure your network so that systems that are shared by the same group of people are on the same subnet.
- Unbind network adapters that are used infrequently.
- For best performance, use adapters with the highest bandwidth that is available. Note, however, that increasing bandwidth increases the number of transmissions and in turn creates more work for your system. For example, the system must generate more interrupts. Remove unused network adapters to reduce overhead.
- Use offline folders to work on network applications without being connected to a network. Offline folders make use of client-side caching, thereby reducing network traffic.

4.2.5 Identify system bottlenecks by using System Monitor

In the sections above, we described System Monitor counters to use to determine if various system bottlenecks were occurring on your system. System Monitor is a part of the Performance applet in Windows Server 2003. It can be found by selecting Administrative Tools from the Start Menu, then selecting Performance. Counters can be selected and viewed in Graph, Histogram, or Report View.

Graph and Histogram are useful for real time information, while the Report view is helpful for looking at results over a period. Logs can also be created to trace results and review later, quite useful to collect baseline performance information.

A typical Graph View of the default counters is shown in Figure 4.2.1.

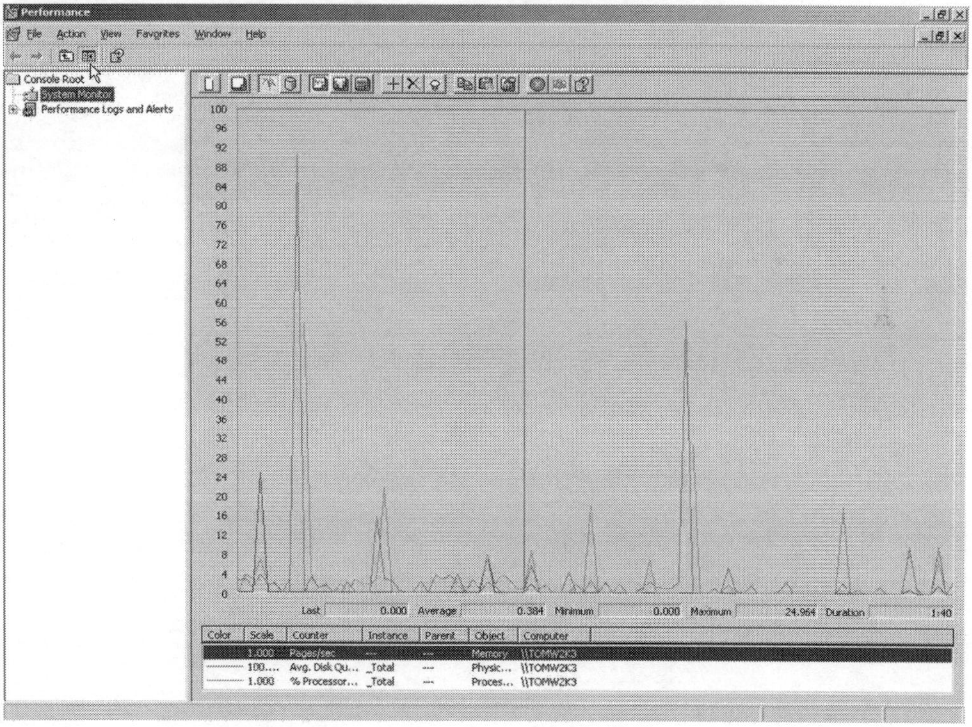

Figure 4—1: Graph View

The three default counters give a quick and dirty snapshot of very basic system health. You get a quick look at Processor: % Processor time, Physical Disk: Disk Queue Length and Memory: Pages Per Second. This allows us to see if any of the major subsystems on the server are having a problem. If one was, we could add a few other counters for that subsystem.

System monitor uses a system of objects and counters to provide you performance data for your system. The performance object maps to a subsystem or installed application on your server, such as network, memory, physical and logical disk, etc. The counter is a specific piece of information about the specific subsystem, such as disk free space, or % processor usage. If there is more than one instance of a subsystem on your server, such as more than one physical disk, or more than one processor, you can look at each instance in the subsystem, or the combined value for the entire subsystem.

For instance, if you have more than one processor, you would be concerned about the % processor on each processor and the total. Figure 4.2.2 shows adding counters to a graph.

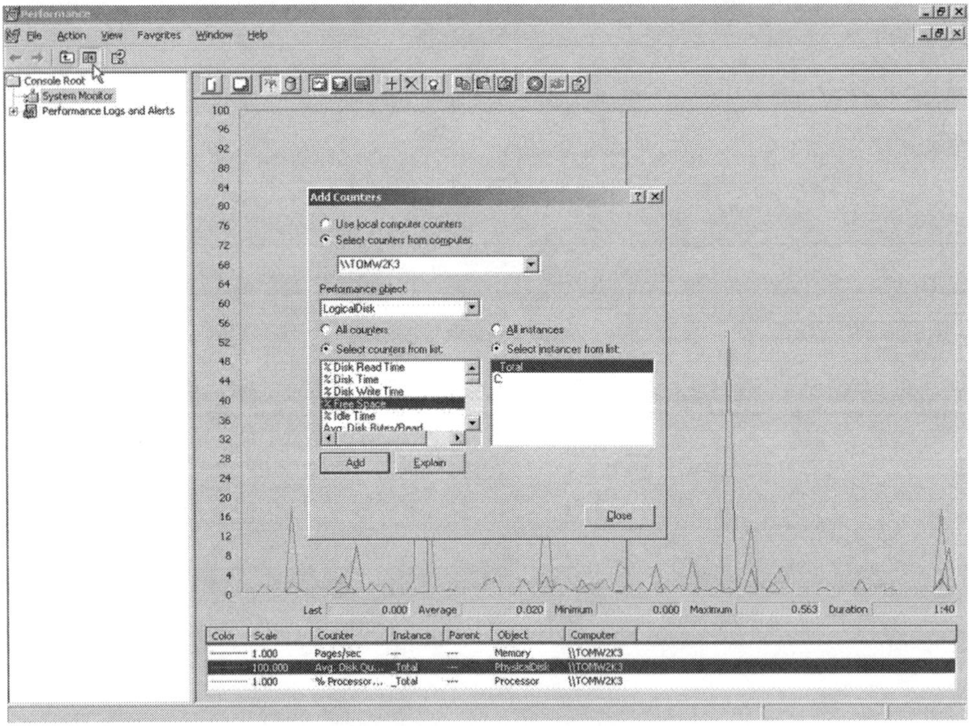

Figure 4—2: Adding Counters

Using the performance applet does degrade the performance of the system it is being run on. For this reason, you should monitor systems remotely to keep this from a minimum. Applications and other subsystems do not need to be installed on the system where performance is being run. You can select counters from any machine with which you can communicate across your network. This allows you to have a "central monitoring" machine monitoring several of your servers as necessary.

To look for a particular bottleneck, add the suggested counters in the previous sections, and observe. Go to report view and watch for values above or below the suggestions.

Pop Quiz 4.1

Pop Quiz 4.1 Questions

1. What are the three types of Clusters?
2. What indicates the number of pending disk I/O requests for the disk drive.
3. Is paging necessarily a bad thing?
4. What is a good indication that more RAM is needed?
5. What is a good indication that there is a memory leak?

Pop Quiz 4.1 Answers

1. ***Single node cluster*** **–** mainly used to test applications on a server cluster.

Single quorum device cluster **–** more common in Windows Server 2003 setups, and the only type supported in Windows NT and 2000. This model has the quorum information on a single shared device connected to all nodes. This will cover a vast majority of clustering needs.

Majority Node set cluster **–** each node keeps its copy of the configuration data, and the quorum is responsible for keeping that data consistent across the nodes. Good when the different nodes of the cluster are not physically located together.

2. **Current Disk Queue Length**

Note: If this value is consistently over two, it indicates congestion.

3. No - some paging will happen on every computer, regardless how much RAM there is.

4. Excessive page faults, where the operating system cannot find the data it requested from memory.

5. A steady increase in the Pool Nonpaged Bytes counter without a corresponding increase in server activity.

4.3 Implement a cluster server.

Recover from cluster node failure.

A major issue in cluster recovery is the loss of the quorum log or disk. To recover from this, use the following steps:

Stop the Cluster service on all nodes where it is running:

If the Cluster service is running, open the Services Applet from Computer Management or Administrative Tools and click on Cluster Service. Then on the Action menu, click Stop.

If you have a backup of the quorum log, restore it.

If you do not have a backup, then select a node. Then select the Cluster Service applet, right click and select the Action menu, and then click Properties. Now, under Service status, in Start parameters, specify /fixquorum, and then click Start.

Switch from the problematic quorum disk to another quorum resource. In Cluster Administrator, bring the new quorum resource disk online.

Now, run Chkdsk, using the switches **/f** and **/r**, on the quorum resource disk to determine whether the disk is corrupted. If no corruption is detected on the disk, it is likely that the log was corrupted. If corruption is detected, check the System Log in Event Viewer for possible hardware errors. Resolve any hardware errors before continuing.

Stop the Cluster service after Chkdsk is complete, following the previous instructions.

Make sure that **Cluster Service** is highlighted in the details pane. On the **Action** menu, click **Properties**. Under **Service status**, in **Start parameters**, specify **/resetquorumlog**, and then click **Start**. (Remove the /fixquorum switch) This restores the quorum log from the node's local database.

In the previous steps, it is important to start the Cluster service by clicking **Start** on the service control panel. You cannot click **OK** or **Apply** to commit these changes as this does not preserve the **/resetquorumlog** parameter.

Restart the Cluster service on all other nodes.

Remember these notes:

You must be a member of the Administrators group on the local computer, or you must have been delegated the appropriate authority to perform this procedure. As a security best practice, consider using Run as to perform it.

The quorum disk must be formatted with the NTFS file system.

4.4 Manage Network Load Balancing

4.4.1 Network Load Balancing Monitor

The Network Load Balancing Manager MMC allows you to perform administrative tasks from a central location. Tasks include creating a new cluster, adding hosts to an existing cluster, remove hosts from a cluster, configure all hosts and cluster properties, and diagnose problems with clusters. In one easy location, you can examine the cluster settings and change them as necessary.

4.4.3 WLBS cluster control utility.

NLB.exe replaces the older WLBS.exe command line control utility. It allows you to perform the same administrative chores from a command line. You can connect to the cluster and host and perform the necessary tasks, or incorporate them into a script.

4.4.2 Microsoft Management Console (MMC) snap-in

4.4.2.1 Overview

While scripting remains a powerful tool for automating the creation of objects on a large scale in Active Directory, the GUI consoles provided in the Administrative Tools is still a viable choice for small networks and for the occasional need to create groups in an Active Directory-enabled network. Active Directory Users and Computers is the primary tool for group creation and for modification of group settings or properties. In this section, we will look at the creation and the modification of groups.

4.4.2.2 Creating Groups Using Active Directory Users and Computers

To begin the creation of a group object, we first go to Administrative Tools and open Active Directory Users and Computers. Then we right-click on the appropriate container and choose the New|Group menu item, as shown below in Figure 8.

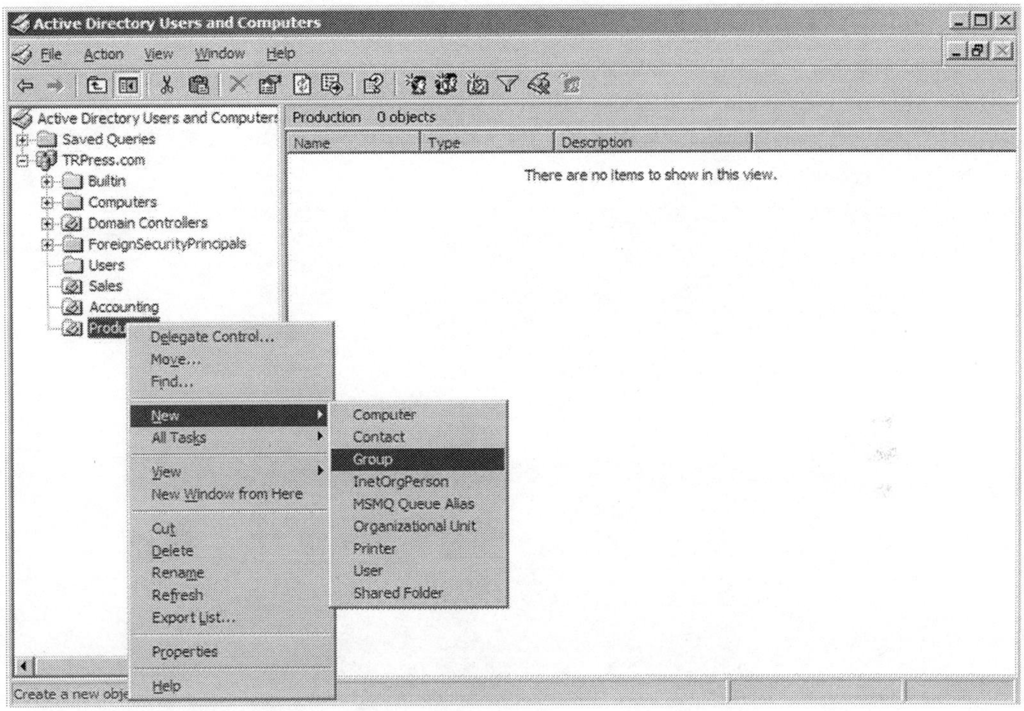

Figure 4—3: The New|Group Menu Selection

In the example below, we have chosen the Production OU as the container within which the new group object will be created. Selecting Group results in the opening of the Group creation dialog. Figure 9 shows the dialog, which allows us to choose the group scope, type and group name. In this example, the group being created is a Global security group named LargeAccountReps.

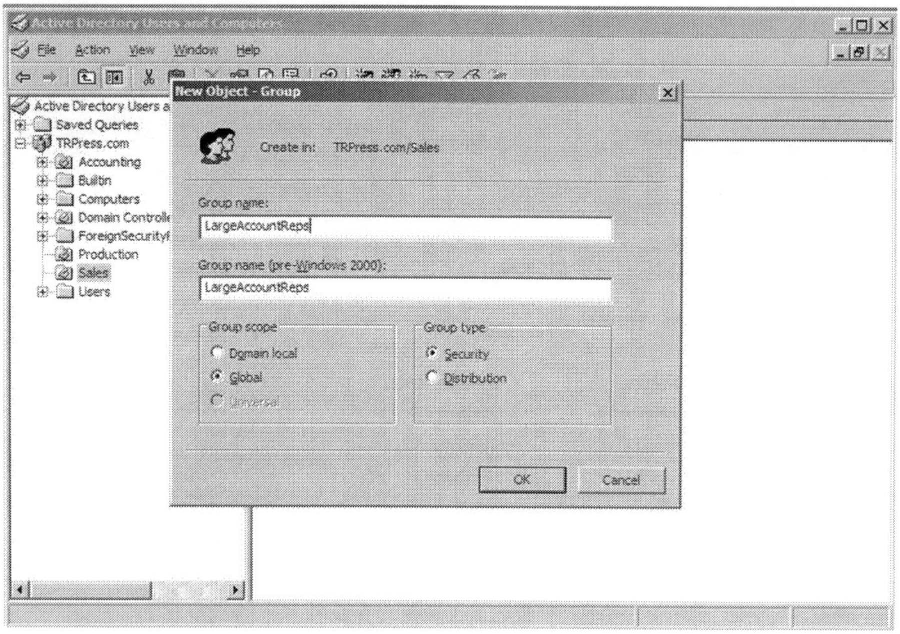

Figure 4—4: The New Group Creation Dialog

This is all there is to group creation. Unlike other object creation using wizards, with multiple dialog screens, there is only a single dialog to complete.

Figure 10 shows the contents of the Sales OU within which both a global and local group have been created.

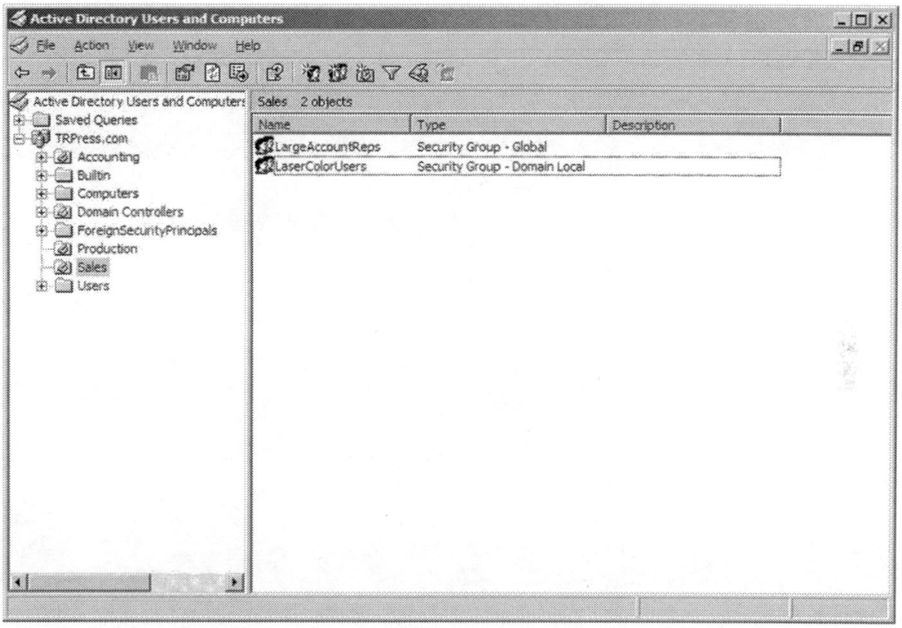

Figure 4—5: Results of group creation in the Sales OU

4.4.2.3 Modifying Group Membership Using the Active Directory Users and Computers MMC

The modification of groups involves either the addition of members or establishing a manager for the group. We will first look at the addition or removal of group members, which is the most common task. There are two different ways to modify group membership. In the first method, we start with the user and identify the group to which the user is to be added. The other method involves going into the group object's properties and modifying the Membership tab. We will look at the 'user' method first:

We start in Active Directory Users and Computers by right clicking on the user object whose membership we need to modify. Then we choose Add to a group from the pop-up menu as shown below in Figure 11.

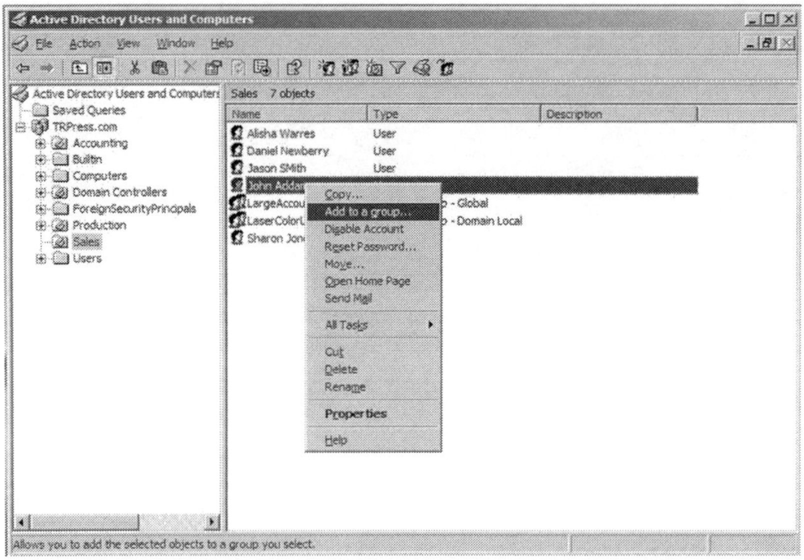

Figure 4—6: Add to a group using the Active Directory Users and Computers MMC

This action opens the Select Group dialog, within which we can choose any group in Active Directory, regardless of where container the group object resides.

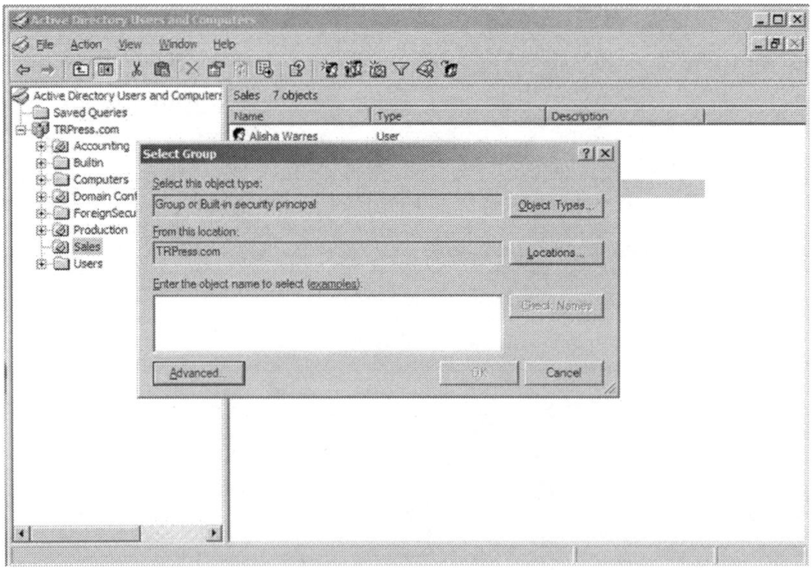

Figure 4—7: The Select Group Dialog

The Locations button allows you to select other domains if you are in a multiple-domain tree. Pressing the Advanced button in the lower bottom-left of the dialog expands the dialog window and provides a search dialog to help finding the appropriate group in Active Directory

In this example, we simply pressed the Find Now button without setting any search parameters. The resulting list shows all groups in the specified domain, in this example, TRPress.com. See the results in Figure 13 below.

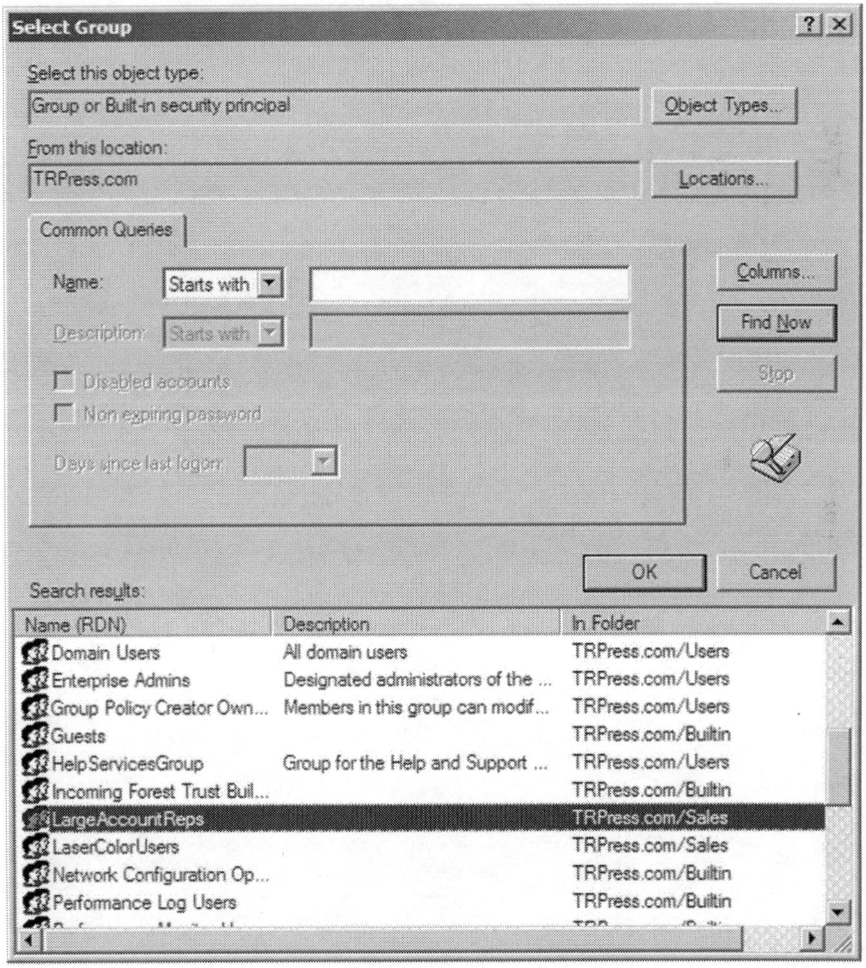

Figure 4—8: Advanced Search in the Select Group Dialog

In this example, we simply pressed the Find Now button without setting any search parameters. The resulting list shows all groups in the specified domain, in this example, TRPress.com.

Another method for modifying the membership of group objects is to go to the user object properties, choose the Member Of tab, and add the appropriate group. See figure 14 below.

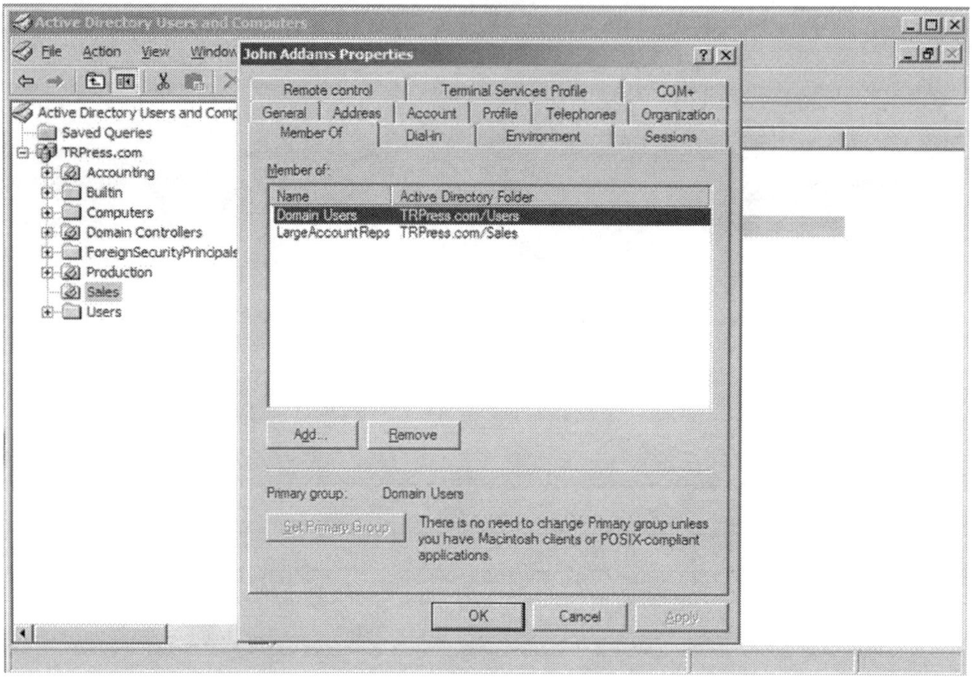

Figure 4—9: Member of tab in user properties

From here, the user can be added to groups or removed from groups. Simply press the Add button to access the search dialog to find the user or users to add to the group. To delete users, simply highlight the user and choose the Delete button.

The last method for modifying group membership is to go to the appropriate group object's Properties and choose the Members tab. Add and Remove can then be used to modify the group membership, as shown in Figure 15.

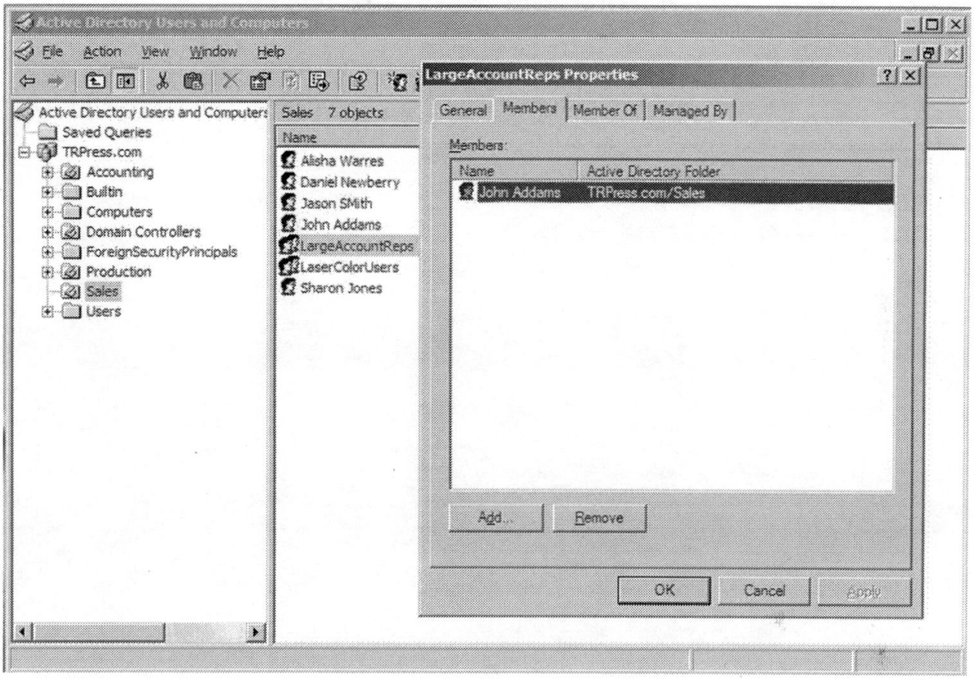

Figure 4—10: Add members from within the group object

4.4.2.4 Modifying the Management of Group Objects

The other property that can be modified is the Managed By property, allowing specified users to manage the group object. This is mostly meaningful if you wish to allow someone to add or remove members while not having other rights in Active Directory. To change the Manage by property, right-click on the group object and choose Properties. The last tab is the Managed by tab. From here, the Change button allows you to search for and select a user to manage the group.

The figure below, Figure 16, shows the selection of a user to manage the group.

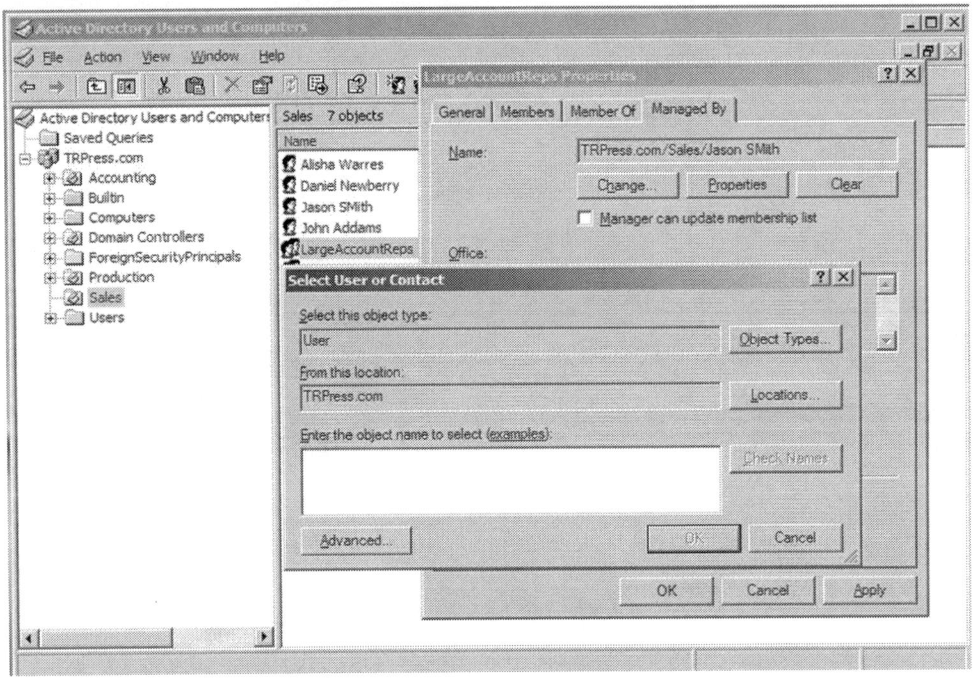

Figure 4—11: Modifying the Managed by property of a group

The Select User or Contact dialog works just as the search dialog did in the earlier example for adding users. Clicking on the Advanced tab offers an advanced search dialog for finding users within Active Directory. To allow the user to change the group membership, remember to check the Manager can update membership list check box.

4.4.2.5 Conclusion

The Active Directory Users and Computers MMC is the GUI administrative tool for creating and modifying groups in Active Directory. The GUI provides a simple interface, easy to use and easy to train others to use, for the management of group objects in Active Directory. Introduced in Windows 2000, the tool and the process have not changed in Server 2003. Group objects can be created or deleted, users added and group managers modified, all with a simple, intuitive GUI tool.

4.4.2.6 Create and modify user accounts by using the Active Directory Users and Computers MMC snap-in

Creating and managing users in Windows Server 2003 is much like that of its predecessor Windows 2000 Server. Accounts may be added using the Active Directory Users and Computer console or via the command prompt with a nifty utility called dsadd. Using this console is assuming you have Active Directory installed and properly running on the 2003 Server.

As I stated before much like Windows 2000 Server you can add users to the Windows Server 2003 machine using the Active Directory Users and Computer tool. This is assuming you have Active Directory installed and configured properly on your server. Click on the Start | Administrative Tools and then choose the Active Directory Users and Computers option. After the console is open, the domain should be viewable in the left pane of the console. The right pane of the console shows five objects:

13. Built-in - Container that includes all of the Built-in accounts such as Administrator,
14. Computers – Holds all computer names in the domain
15. Domain Controllers – Lists all domain controllers in domain
16. Foreign Security -
17. Users – Container for all users accounts.

4.4.2.7 Creating User Accounts

For this section, we will only be using the Users containers. You can add a user three ways in this console: Right Click Domain in the left pane choose New and choose user, Right click Users in the left pane | Choose New | Choose User as shown below in Figure 17 below.

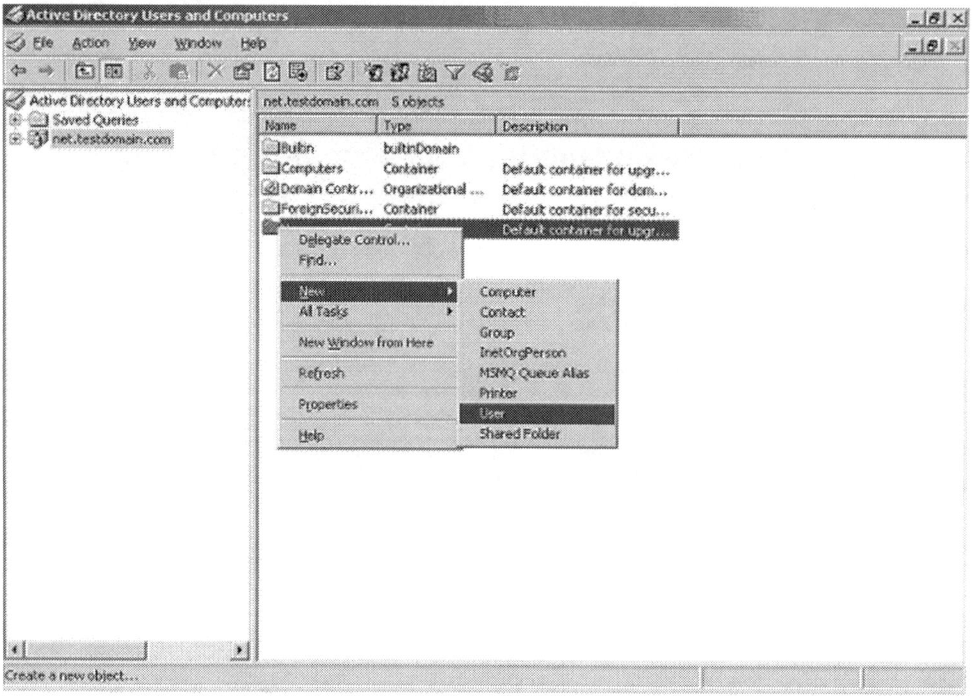

Figure 4—12: Creating a New user by right clicking on the User object in the Active Directory Users and Computers console.

Alternatively, you can choose the File menu | New | and User option. Know matter which option you choose they will all work in the same manner. Once the new user option has been selected, you will see a dialog box. The dialog box is shown below in figure 18.

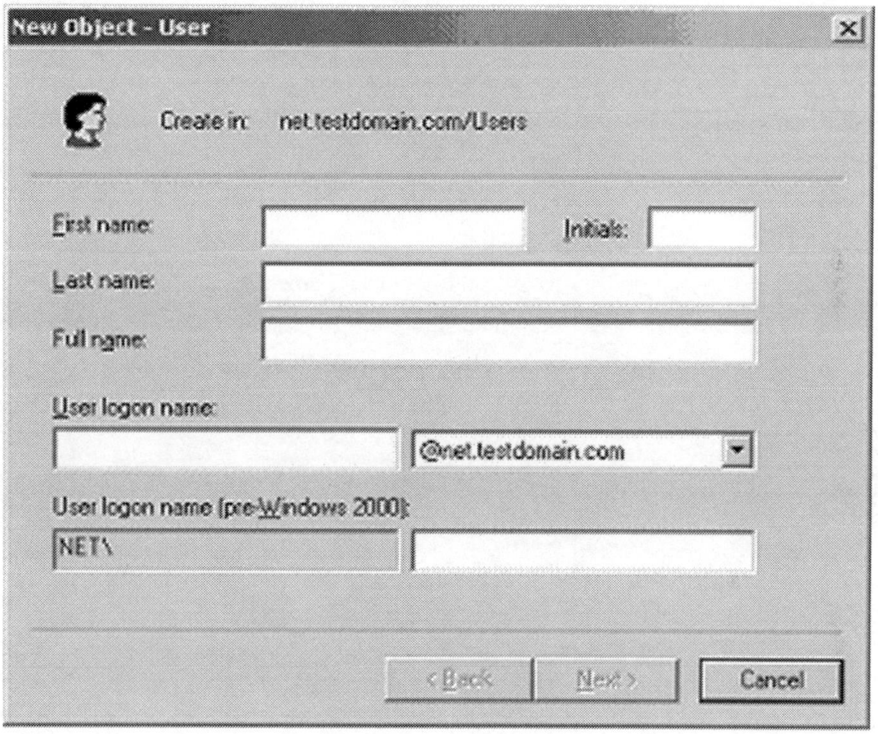

Figure 4—13: The New User Dialog Box in the Active Directory Users and Computers console.

It shows the create in domain and group, user first name, user initials, user last name, user Full Name, user login name, domain name, and also the pre-Windows 2000 login name. When creating user names remember the following rules:

Username	**Rule**
Character Type	Up to 20 characters, uppercase, lowercase or a combination of the two.
Special Characters	No " / \ [ ] : ; | = , + * ? < > characters may be used in the user name.
Other special characters	User name may include periods and spaces. However, it cannot entirely consist of spaces or periods. Try not to use spaces in user names because if you use command-line utilities or scripting these names have to be enclosed with quotations.
Local Account user names	User Name must be unique to the machine for local accounts
Domain Account user names	These can be the same name as a local user account name on a non-domain controller that is a member of the same domain. This is because they are entirely separate.

Table 4—2: User Name and Rules

Now that we have covered the basics for user name creation let's create a user account in our domain. The first name of the user is myuser. As you fill in the first name of the user, you will notice, as well, that the Full Name box and the user logon name box begin to fill with what you are typing.

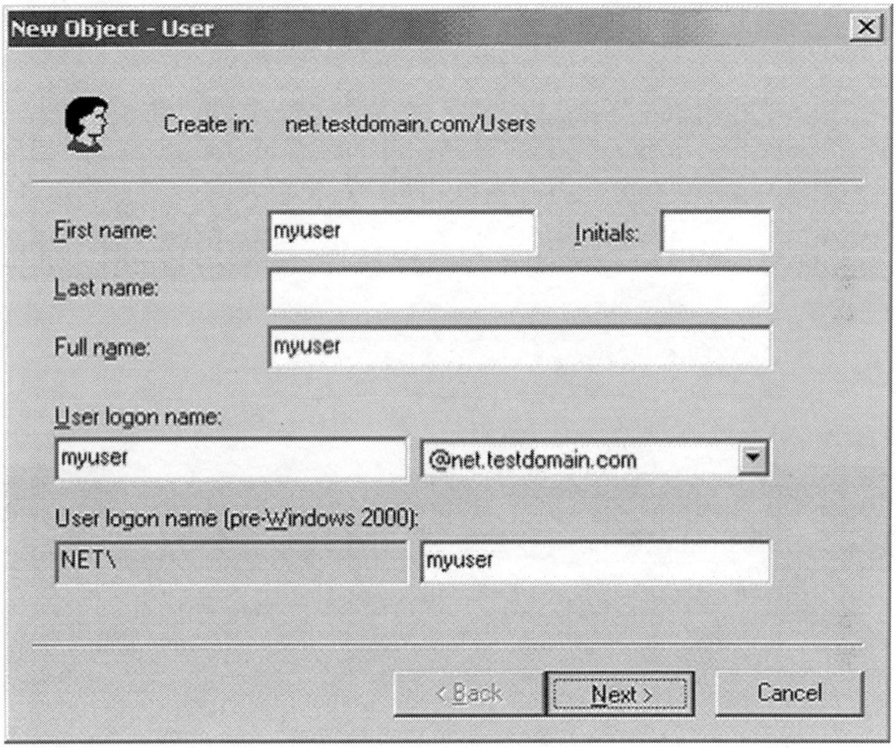

Figure 4—14: Entering the New User information.

Once all of the information has been entered, choose the Next button and the page shown in Figure 20 will be shown.

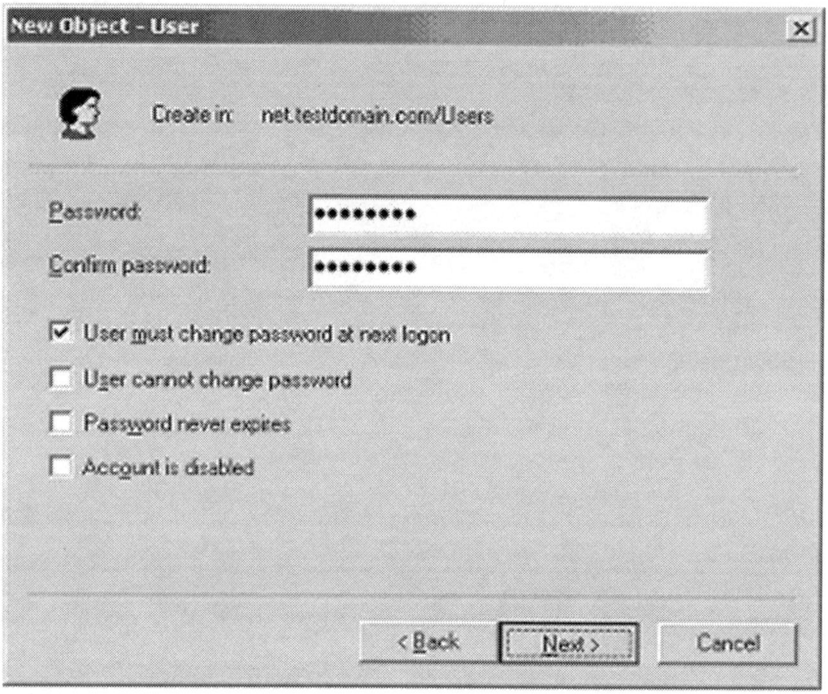

Figure 4—15: Entering a Password and choosing the password options for the new user.

Enter a password for the new user and then choose from the following options:

- User must change password at next logon – This will force the user to change their password at the next logon. Choosing this disables the "Password never expires" option.
- User cannot change password – This is helpful to use when you have user accounts that run server services like SQL Server or Exchange Server. When this option is chosen, the user cannot change the password.
- Password never expires – When this option is chosen the user account ignores any password policy that is in place. The password will never expire. Useful for IUSR_(servername) type accounts. Choosing this disables the "User must change password at next logon" option.
- Account is disabled – This is used in a couple of scenarios. Maybe your company has interns or temporary employees that come back between semesters or every few months. Instead of deleting and reading the user account each time they leave and return, you can just disable the account and enable the account as needed.

Once you have selected the Password option, choose the next button. The object will now be created as shown in Figure 21.

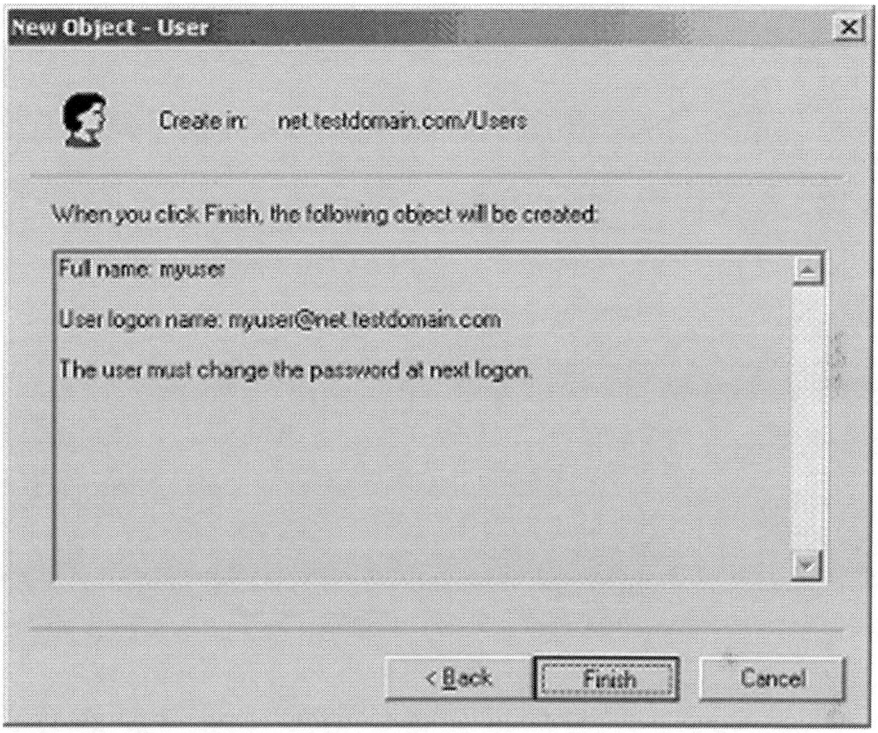

Figure 4—16: The new user account object.

The account will now be viewable in the user account container in the Active Directory Users and Computers console. You can view the user account by double clicking on the user container in the right side of the console as shown in Figure 22.

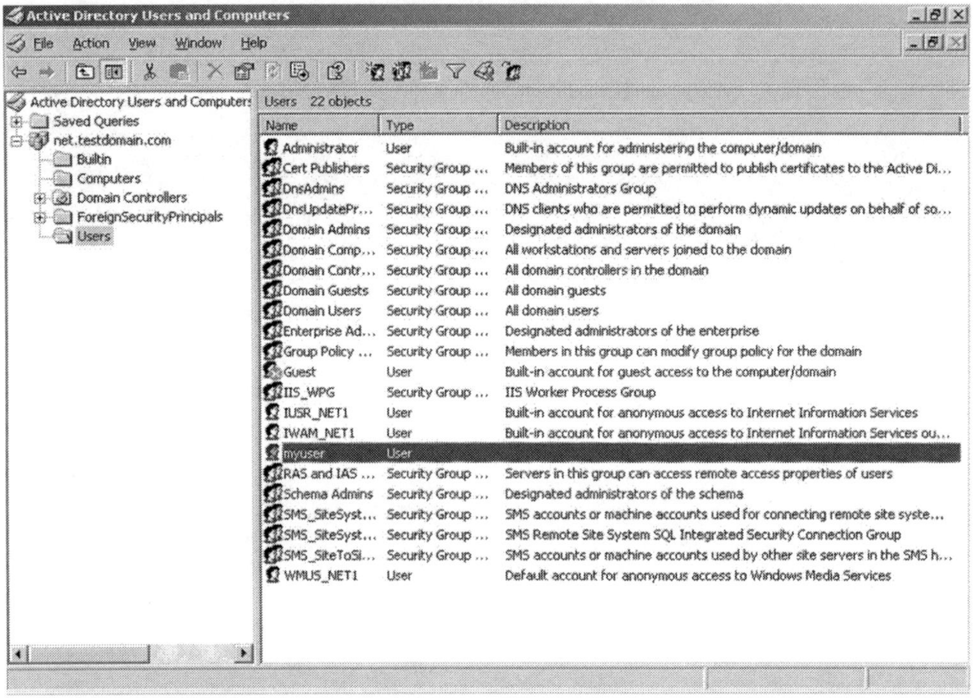

Figure 4—17: The newly added user in the User Container.

As you can see, the new user is listed along with additional user accounts, which are built-in to Windows 2003 Server. Depending on the additional installed software, such as Active Directory, IIS, SMS Server and Exchange Server you could see a variety of additional user accounts, which are not listed in this user container.

4.4.2.8 Manage User Accounts

Utilities such as bsa, ldifde, csvde, dsadd, dsmod, and dsrm are available in non-beta and beta mode at the time of this writing. These slick utilities allow Administrators to add, manage and delete user accounts from the command line. One great improvement in Windows Server 2003 is that you have additional command line utilities that were not available in previous network operating systems. Since some of these command line utilities are currently in beta mode I will not go into great depth with some of these utilities. In addition to command line utilities that are already included in the Windows Server 2003 the Support CD-Rom has many as well that can be installed.

4.4.2.9 Microsoft Baseline Security Analyzer

In December 2002, Microsoft released the Baseline Analyzer Version 1.1 (commonly referred to MBSA 1.1 or BSA). The MBSA 1.1 replaces the Microsoft Personal Security Advisor or MPSA and the HFNetChk tool that were used to scan security on local and remote computers and servers. It does not install on older Operating Systems such as Windows 95 and Windows 98. This utility only installs on Windows 2000 and XP machines. Another requirement is Internet Explorer version 5.01 at a minimum installed and the Workstation service running. If you do not have Internet Explorer 5.01 installed you will have to install an additional XML parser which is located at the following URL

http://msdn.microsoft.com/downloads/default.asp?url=/downloads/sample.asp?url=/msdn-files/027/001/772/msdncompositedoc.xml.

The MBSA 1.1 s is an excellent graphical utility tool that allows administrators to check for strong passwords, scan IIS and SQL servers for security configuration problems. It also has the ability to scan Microsoft Office applications for incorrectly configured security zone settings. This is a much more robust tool than the HFNetChk utility that only checks for service pack and security updates on local and remote computers and servers.

Use the table below to view what the MBSA v1.1 utility scans for in selected applications and operating systems.

Windows Operating System	**Flags for security**
Administrator Group Membership	Puts up flag if more than two local administrators are on machine.
Auditing	Is auditing turned on machine
AutoLogon	Is AutoLogon turned on machine
Domain Controller	Is this computer a domain controller?
File System	Checks to see what file system is in user NTFS or FAT.
Guest Account	Is the guest account enabled on the computer?
Local Account Password	Checks for common problems with local account passwords such as a blank password, password set to the word password, password with the word admin or administrator used, password same as the machine name.
OS Version	Check the operating system version
Shares	Checks to see if shares are located on the computer.
Unnecessary Services	Checks against the services.txt file which lists services such as MSFTP (FTP), TlntSvr(TELNET), W3SVC (WWW) and SMTPSVC(SMTP) for services that should not be running. These services are the default services listed and more can be added to the service.txt file for scanning.

Table 4—3: MBSA v1.1 security scans for Window machines.

This table just shows scans for Window machines and does not include the information for IIS, SQL server and Office Applications. The entire list may be viewed at the URL: http://www.microsoft.com/technet/treeview/default.asp?url=/technet/security/tools/Tools/mbsaqa.asp. The utility also can perform check security updates against a local SUS server. If this is chosen the utility will look for missing security updates on the SUS server rather than the mssecure.xml file located on Microsoft's website. The SUS Administrator may then mark updates approved and the MBSA tool will report the update information.

The MBSA v1.1 utility may be downloaded in English only at the URL: http://download.microsoft.com/download/e/5/7/e57f498f-2468-4905-aa5f-369252f8b15c/mbsasetup.msi. After the utility has been downloaded and installed open it by clicking on Start | All Programs | Microsoft Baseline Security Analyzer. It looks something the Figure 01:07 below.

4.4.2.10 dsadd, dsmod and dsrm

Utilities called dsadd, dsmod, and dsrm are available in beta mode at the time of this writing and they will allow Administrators to add, manage and delete user accounts from the command line. One great improvement in Windows Server 2003 is that you have additional command line utilities that were not available in previous network operating systems. Since this is currently in beta mode, I will not go into great depth with the utility.

Table 4.4, which shows some of the numerous commands and the syntax that may be used to manage user accounts, is listed below.

Command	Syntax	Explanation
Add a user	dsadd user *userdn* –samid *sam_name*	Userdn is the distinguished name of the user object you are adding. –samid is the security account name used for this object.
Entering the Password	dsadd user userdn–pwd *password*	The syntax password in italics represents the actual password to be used on the account.
Resetting a User Password	dsmod user user_dn-pwd *new_password*	The user_dn is the distinguished username and the new_password is the new password to be used.
Forcing a user to change password at next logon.	dsmod user *user_dn* –mustchpwd yes	This syntax will force a user to change their password at the next logon. If a password has not been assigned and they logon with a blank password then a dialog box will appear and tell them they are required to change their password.
Delete an account	dsmod user_dn	Simple syntax that allows you to delete an account from the prompt.

Table 4—4: Syntax to add, manage and delete user accounts from the command prompt.

To get additional information on these three commands just go to the command prompt on the Windows Server 2003 machine and type the command with the /? Command. It will list all switches relevant to the command. For example, to get more information on the dsrm command go to the command prompt and type dsrm /? The output will list all available switches with instructions. This tool also works if you have the Windows XP adminpak installed from the Windows Server 2003 CD-Rom, which was discussed earlier in this section. Microsoft also has an article number 322684 located at http://support.microsoft.com for further reference.

4.4.2.12 Import Accounts using the LDIFDE Command

Importing User accounts from the command line can be done with the ldifde utility.

The LDAP Data Interchange Format Directory Exchange or ldifde command line utility allows Administrators to create, modify, and delete directory objects on Window Server 2003 and Windows XP Professional machines. This utility also allows administrators to extend their Active Directory schema, populate, import and export user and/or group information from within Active Directory to additional applications and services.

Table 4.5 below shows some general import parameters that can be used with the ldifde command utility.

Switch Definition	**Switches**
Replace occurrence of FromDN to ToDN	-c From DN ToDN
Input or Output filename	-f
Turn on Import Mode (Export mode is the default mode)	-i
Log File location	-j
Server to bind to	-s
Port Number if you wish to change from default of 389	-t
Use Unicode Format	-u
Turn on Verbose Mode	-v
-?	Help

Table 4—5: Syntax to use with the LDIFDE utility.

To import user accounts from one Active Directory controller to another you must be logged in as the Administrator. If you log on using an account that does not have administrative privileges, you may not be able to perform export and import operations against the Active Directory. In the following steps, we will import a user account named John Doe using the ldifde command.

18. Click on Start | Run and type Notepad.
19. Name the blank notepad file myimport.ldf

On the first line of the Notepad file type the following exactly as it is shown in figure 23 below.

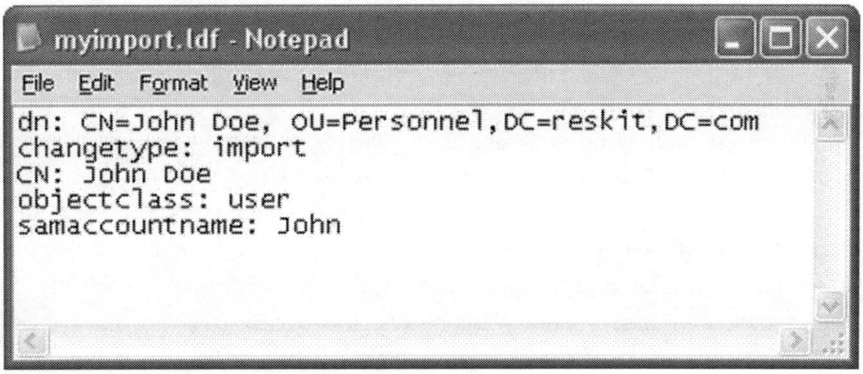

Figure 4—18: Myimport.ldf using Notepad

Creating the import file to use with ldifde

20. Click on the Start button, select Run and type cmd.
21. Once at the command prompt, use the following command:
    ldifde -v -i -s 2003svr -f myimport.ldf

To break it down bit by bit, look at the command closely. The –v displays the output in the verbose mode, -i is the import mode (you must use this to import because the command uses export by default), the –s command is the name of the server we are importing from and the –f is the name of the import file we created with notepad.

4.4.2.13 CSVDE

The CSVDE utility is much like the ldifde command but it uses a comma-separated format (CSV). This means that applications such as Microsoft Excel can read the output of the file. This is a great tool to use if you have a large number of accounts to import and you would like to view the output of the import file. However this utility does has its limitations it can only be used to import and export from Active Directory not to create and delete objects like the ldifde command is capable of doing. The command switches are just like the ones that were used in the ldifde command in the previous section so we are not going to list those here. An example of how to use this function is listed below. We will use this utility to create an LDAP search filter to import users with the surname smith. The import will be viewable in a filename we create called myimport.csv

22. Click on Start | Run | Type cmd
23. Type in the following command
24. Csvde –r –f –v –i –s 2003svr (and (objectClass=User)(sn=smith))

The –r command creates and LDAP search filter for the data export. The –f command identifies the name of the import file. The –v command displays the information verbose. The –i command must be used for importing (exporting is also used by default). The –s command specifies the server name. The object class specifies type of object, which in this case is the user, and the sn syntax represents the surname we are importing.

These are a few of the many tools available for use with the Windows Server 2003 network operating server. Enhancements to this network operating system allow administrators much more flexibility and control over their environment using command line utilities such as the ones listed in this section.

4.4.2.14 The IP Security Monitor Microsoft Management Console snap-in

The IPSec Monitor snap-in for mmc provides extensive monitoring and troubleshooting capabilities for the network administrator. You can view details about the IPSec process and examine IPSec policies in effect both locally and in the domain. See Figure 3.11.

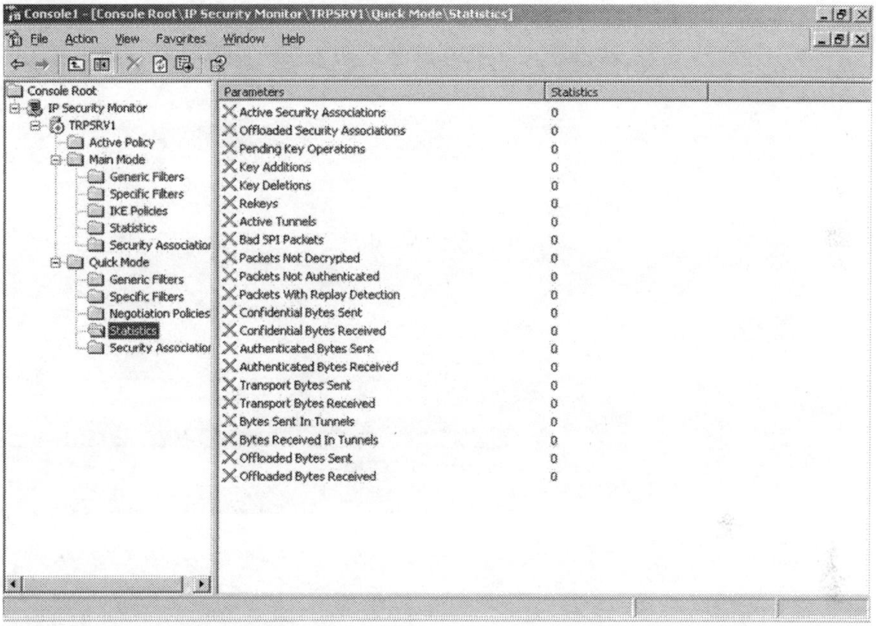

Figure 4—19: Preventing Fast Transfers

The first node, Active Policy, shows information relating to the active IPSec policy currently in effect. The other nodes allow for advanced troubleshooting of the IPSec process.

4.4.2.15 Modify groups by using the Active Directory Users and Computers Microsoft Management Console (MMC) snap-in

Modifying a Group using the Active Directory Users and Computer console is a simple task. Click on **Start | Administrative Tools | Active Directory Users and Computers.** Choose the Domain or OU, which contains the Group you wish to modify, and right-click the **Group.** Selecting Properties will display a dialog box similar to the one shown in Figure 2.10

Figure 4—20: Entering General information for Group settings.

This tab allows you to enter and select information for Groups such as Group Name, Description and E-mail information. It also will allow you to enter the Group Scope and Type and Notes pertaining to the group. Figure 2.11 below shows the Member information for the Group

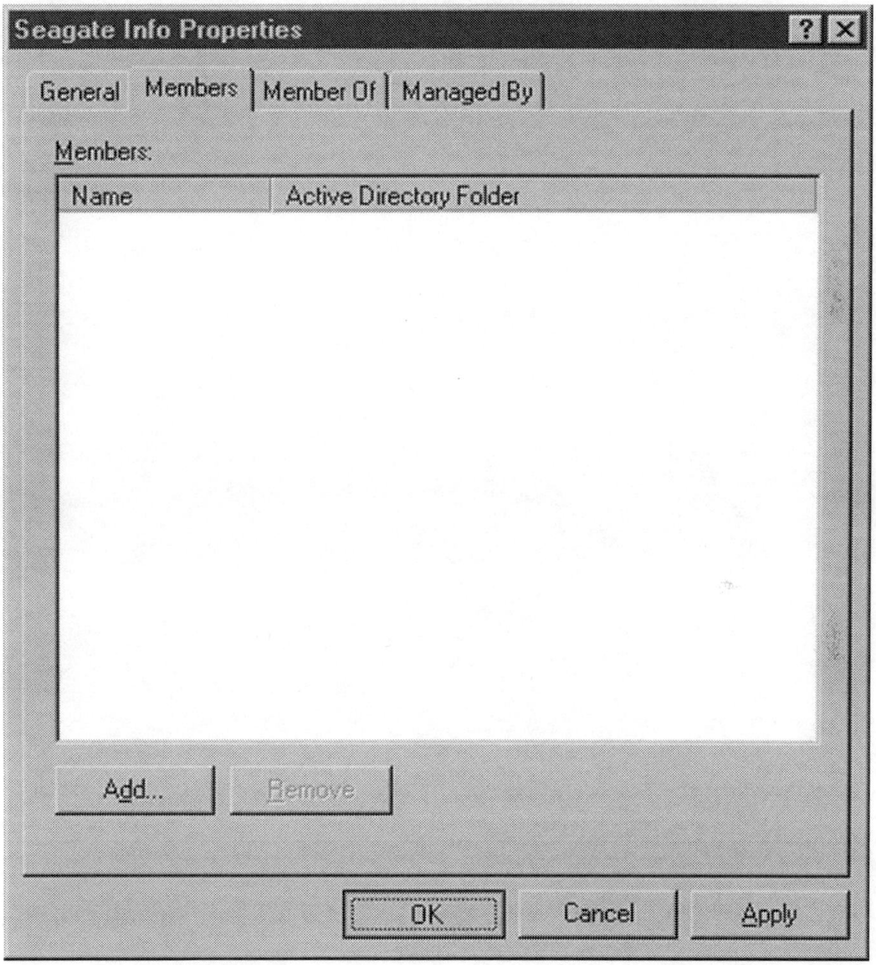

Figure 4—21: Member information for the Group.

Click the **Add** button to add additional members to this group then select **Apply.** Figure 2.12 shows the **Member of** which shows which users or computers belong to this group.

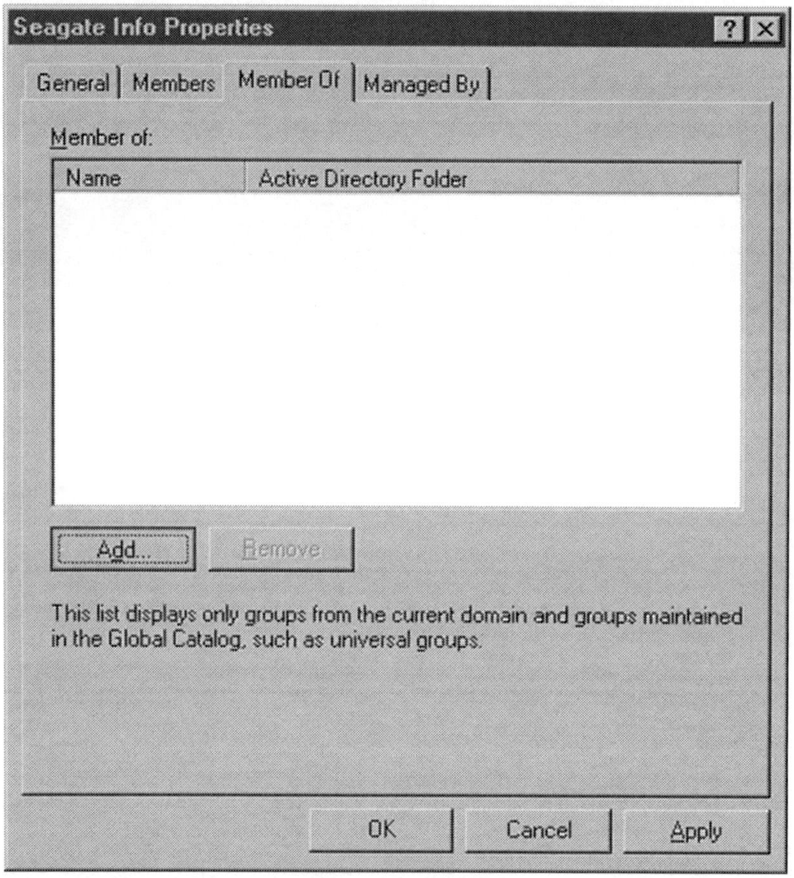

Figure 4—22: The Member of tab for Group settings.

The last tab is the Managed by tab shown in Figure 2.13.

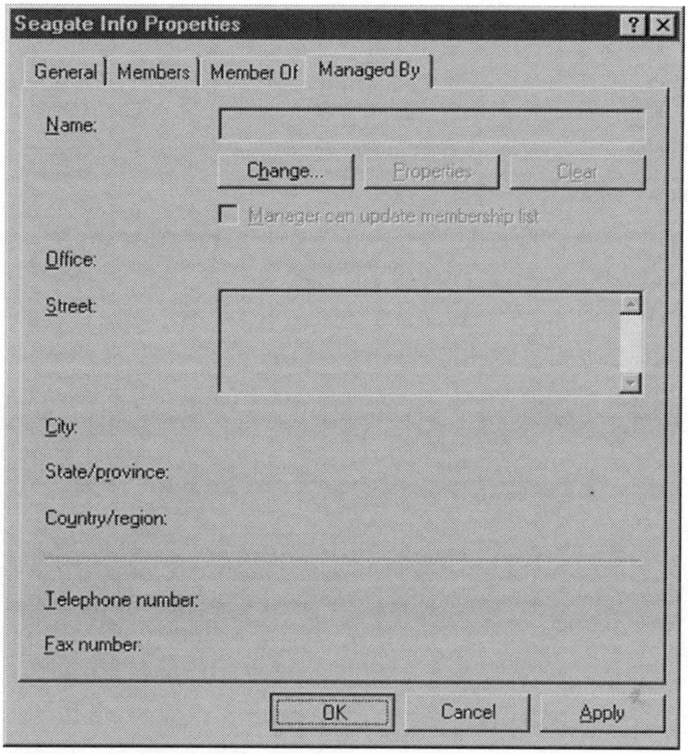

Figure 4—23: Managed By tab for Groups.

This screen allows you to enter the Name of the manager for this group, office information and can allow you to enable the Manager of the group to have the ability to update the membership list of the group.

Pop Quiz 4.2

Pop Quiz 4.2 Questions

1. What is the difference between group scope and group type?
2. What is the significance of the "Managed By" setting for an Active Directory object?
3. When would it be appropriate to set both "Password never expires" and "User cannot change password"?
4. What is a key difference between CSVDE and LDIFDE other than file format?

Pop Quiz 4.2 Answers

1. Active Directory groups have both a scope and a type, the. Scope is WHERE they can be used and where their membership can come from, while type relates to HOW a group can be used.

2. The managed by setting allows the delegation of authority over a single object without granting privileges over any other object in Active Directory.

3. You would use this primarily for service accounts, such as Exchange or SQL Server.

4. CSVDE can only be used to add objects, while LDIFDE can be used to add, modify existing, and delete.

4.5 Plan a backup and recovery strategy

Making sure you have the right backup strategy is very important to the quick restoration of your server to a useful state, i.e. as close as it was to the time of failure! Backing up all of your data on a regular basis is crucial! How you define "regular basis" will depend on the data and applications involved. Over the course of a day or a week, you could perform many different backups on a server or collection of servers. Developing the right mix will allow you to recover at once in a crisis.

Selecting what data to backup depends on the importance of the data, and the frequency of changes to it. The backup utility gives you the option of backing up the entire server, or selected portions. Then you can use different types of backups, depending on your specific need.

Windows Server 2003 provides several tools to allow us to build a successful recovery strategy for our operation. These include the backup utility, the system state backup from within the backup utility, volume shadow copy, and the Automated System Recovery (ASR) utility.

4.5.1 Identify appropriate backup types.

Why provide different type of backups? If everyone had 8 hours to complete a full backup of every file server in their organization, and could completely lock out any users from the system while they were doing it, this wouldn't be an issue. Most of us don't have that luxury of time or access control, so we have to examine different methods of backup.

4.5.2 Backup methods include

The different backup methods typically used in a recovery situation are a full backup, a differential backup, and an incremental backup. The different types allow you to make a complete backup of your selected data, or just changes in the data since the last time you made a backup. These different types target a specific category of data, such as all the files in a collection of folders, or all files on a selected volume that have changed since the last backup. This piece of magic involves the archive attribute. The archive attribute (or bit) is cleared or turned off every time a full backup or an incremental backup of a file is made. The archive bit is turned on (flipped on or switched on or flipped or toggled are also used to describe the action) every time a file or folder is changed after that backup. Other types of backups leave the archive bit alone. The differences are explained in the following sections. Then a couple of scenarios are presented to illustrate using the different methods together.

4.5.2.1 Full Backup

This method backs up all selected files, regardless of the archive bit setting. Upon completion, it clears the archive bit for future operations. If the file is modified later, the archive bit is then set. This indicates the file has been changed and needs to be backed up again. This method is used for a baseline for future backup jobs. The first time you create a backup set, it is strongly recommended that you use "full backup". It can be used alone, if you have enough time to backup all the selected data. A full backup is the easiest method from which to restore, as there is only one tape, or one set of tapes, to provide a complete recovery from failure.

4.5.2.2 Incremental Backup

This method of backup will back up all the selected files that have changed since the last incremental or full backup. It clears the archive bit on the files that were backed up. If you were to perform two incremental backups in a row, the files would not be backed up the second time, unless they were changed since the last incremental backup. This will take less media and less time per backup set, as you are not copying all the files changed since the last full backup (as in the differential), just the ones changed since incremental backup. Use this method on servers that require a faster backup time due to a small maintenance window. This method will take longer to restore that a full backup set and differentials, as to be sure you have the latest version of each file, you must restore the full backup set and the entire incremental backup sets.

4.5.2.3 Differential Backup

This method backs up all selected files and folders that were modified since the last full or incremental backup the files where the archive bit is turned on. The archive bit isn't modified, so you can perform other types of backups on these files again later. If you were to make another differential backup using the same selection set, you would backup the same file a second time. Using a differential backup with the full backup set lets you restore to a point in time of your last differential set by just restoring two sets, the full backup set, and then the last differential set. While your backup time increases, the restore time is shorter than restoring several incremental backup sets. This method allows for a faster restore, but increasingly longer backup times.

A comparison of ease of maintenance:

Method	Backup	Restore
Full	Easiest, but most time consuming as the entire group of selected data is always backed up.	Easiest and fastest, as only one media set is involved, the last full backup.
Incremental	Faster backup time than differential as each file that was changed after the full backup was made is only backed up again if it is changed again.	Slowest and more administratively complex, as to completely restore the files you must first restore the full backup set that is the basis for the incremental sets, then apply each and every incremental set in order.
Differential	Slower than incremental, as each file that was changed since the full backup set is backed up on each differential set. Eventually you can be taking as long as the full backup on which it is based.	Faster and less administratively complex than the incremental, as you have to restore the full backup set and only the last differential set to completely restore all files.

You can select the type of media on which to make your backup. The various storage devices and media that are supported include tape drives, removable disks, recordable CD-ROM drives and logical drives on your local system.

You can combine different types of backups to allow for shorter backup times or shorter recovery times. The best scenario would be to make a complete backup of the system each day. Then to restore your system you just need to restore that day's backup. You can also combine a normal or full backup with a differential or incremental backup. You should base your decision for a proper mix of types on the amount of time you can spend creating the backup, and the amount of time your can use to restore. Some sample scenarios follow.

Scenario One: Normal backup weekly combined with incremental backups every day.

On Sunday evening, you perform a normal (full) backup. The archive bit on ALL files is reset. Each evening on Monday through Saturday, you perform an incremental backup. Each backup saves the files changed that day, and resets the archive bit on those files that were backed up. The evening backup on Monday through Saturday is done rather quickly (compared to the full backup on Sunday) as just the files changed that day are backed up.

If something were to happen to your server hardware on Saturday, to recover your files to the state of the last known good backup (made on Friday), first you must restore the full backup from the previous Sunday, and then each incremental backup made on Monday through Friday evening. This would insure your would get all the files that were changed during the week, as the files that were changed were only backed up on the day that they were changed.

Scenario Two: Normal backup weekly combined with differential backups every day

On Sunday evening, you perform a normal (full) backup. The archive bit on ALL files is reset. Each evening on Monday through Saturday, you perform a differential backup. Each backup saves the files changed since the full backup made on Sunday. The archive bits on these files are not changed. This way, on Monday you backup the files changed on Monday. On Tuesday, you backup the files changed on Monday and Tuesday, and so on through the week. The evening backup takes somewhat longer each evening, as you are backing up all files changed through the entire week.

Again, something happens to the server on Saturday, and you need to restore to the state the files were in on Friday evening when the backup was made. Here you need to restore the full backup made on Sunday, and the last differential backup made on Friday. Why just the two? Unlike the incremental backups made in scenario one, the last differential backup on Friday has all the files that were changed that week on one media set. Recovery time is reduced as compared to scenario one.

4.5.3 Plan a backup strategy that uses volume shadow copy

The Volume Shadow Copy service provides the backup application a method to copy open files, insuring a complete backup of all selected files. Previously, with Windows 2000 and Windows NT, if the file was open due to an application using the file, such as a word processing document, that file was skipped. Now open files in Windows Server 2003 are backed up by using the Volume Shadow Copy service. This behavior is turned on by default.

When a backup application that is aware of Volume Shadow Copy service starts a backup, the Volume Shadow Copy service makes a read only shadow copy of the volume to be backed up. The backup application uses this copy to make the backup, and when it is completed, deletes that shadow copy. Of course, your backup media has the backed up data stored on it. Applications continue to access the data on the volume while the backup is proceeding.

Windows Server 2003 will consume free disk space on a volume to make the shadow copy. The size of the space consumed depends on the amount of data changing during the backup. If there is not enough free space on the volume, the shadow copy will fail and the backup will continue in the "old way" i.e. files are read only from the regular volume, and open files are skipped.

A backup application must work with (be aware of) the Volume Shadow Copy service. The Windows Server 2003 backup program is able to work with Volume Shadow Copy service. Be care of third party backup applications, and be sure that they are Volume Shadow Copy service aware.

4.5.4 Plan system recovery that uses Automated System Recovery (ASR)

Automated System Recovery (ASR) is a tool that will help you collect information needed to repair and reconstruct your operating system and other system state files in case of a failure. The ASR is a set of a single floppy and a backup on removable media (or network file). ASR does not try to place all the necessary recovery information on a diskette, instead it makes a system backup and creates three information files on the floppy that describe the disk configurations, locations of various plug and play devices and system files on your server.

The ASR set is easy to make, and should be done BEFORE you implement a major change to your server as a fallback method, or final recovery. A major change may be defined as anything done in control panel, such as Add/Remove Programs or Windows Components, or any change to the hard disk configuration. Another possibility is to create a set after you install the basic operating system and before the applications are installed. Saving this set would allow you to "start over" with a fresh server without the fun of completing reinstalling Windows.

The ASR diskette is not bootable, and it must be used with your original operating system CD or setup diskettes during the setup program. The ASR set only gets system files, not any applications or data. You must be very careful to insure you have another method of backing up that data.

To restore a server using ASR, you would have two major tasks, repair / restore the operating system, and restore applications and data. To restore the operating system using the ASR follow these steps:

Locate the following items:

- ASR floppy disk and backup media.
- Windows Server 2003 Operating System installation CD.
- Any separate driver diskettes you may have for a mass storage controller that does not appear on the operating system CD.

1. Place the installation CD in your CD drive and restart your computer. You may be prompted to press a key to start from CD.
2. If you have a separate driver file as mentioned above, press F6 when prompted in setup and insert the diskette as requested.
3. When the text-only portion of setup begins, press F2. You will then be prompted to insert the ASR floppy that matches the media you wish to restore.
4. At this point, follow the instructions on screen. The system will re-boot.
5. If you used a separate driver file as in step 2 above, press F6 again to use the diskette. Place the driver diskette in the floppy drive and follow the instructions on screen as you did in step 2.
6. Restore any necessary program or data backups.

Chapter 4: Review Questions

1. Which are valid backups methods in a Windows 2003 Server environment?

    A. Normal (Full) and Incremental

    B. Differential and Incremental

    C. Normal (Full) and Differential

    D. Differential only

---

2. When using a normal and differential backup method, how many tapes will be required to restore the server?

    A. 2

    B. 1

    C. 3

    D. 4

3. You probably need to replace your hard drive if System Monitor indicates which of the following?

    A. Avg. Disk sec/Transfer is 3.132

    B. Average % Processor Time is 87%

    C. Average Pages/Sec 27.322

    D. Network Interface: Bytes Total/sec is 241.322

---

4. You probably need to upgrade your processor if System Monitor indicates which of the following?

    A. Average % Processor Time is 87%

    B. Avg. Disk sec/Transfer is 3.132

    C. Average Pages/Sec 27.322

    D. Network Interface:Bytes Total/sec is 241.322

5. You probably need to upgrade your RAM if System Monitor indicates which of the following?
   A. Average Pages/Sec 27.322
   B. Avg. Disk sec/Transfer is 3.132
   C. Average % Processor Time is 87%
   D. Network Interface: Bytes Total/sec is 241.322

---

6. Hard page faults are corrected by a/an _________ upgrade.
   A. RAM
   B. Processor
   C. Hard Drive
   D. Operating System

7. Which of the following commands will show you the hops to a destination?
    - A. Tracert
    - B. Pathping
    - C. Ping
    - D. Arp

---

8. When network connectivity is inconsistent between many routers in distant locations (i.e. - Atlanta, GA, Los Angeles, CA, Houston, TX and Philadelphia, PA), what commands would you use to determine the number of hops?
    - A. pathping
    - B. ipconfig
    - C. tracert
    - D. ping

9. In what instances would using shadow copies be helpful?
    A. Recovery of files that were accidentally deleted
    B. Your Server 2003 OS kernel is corrupted
    C. You accidentally overwrite a file
    D. You need to convert back to FAT32

---

10. Which of the following executables starts the Volume Shadow Copy service?
    A. Vssadmin.exe
    B. Sssadmin.exe
    C. Vscadmin.exe
    D. Vsscopy.exe

11. How can you access shadow copies in 2003 Server?

A. With the Shadow Copies tab of the Local Disk Properties dialog box.

B. In Computer Management, right-click Shares, point to All Tasks, and then click Configure Shadow Copies.

C. With the Copies tab of the Local Disk Properties dialog box.

D. In Device Manager, right-click Shares, point to All Tasks, and then click Configure Shadow Copies.

---

12. How do you create an ASR floppy disk from an ASR backup set in Windows 2003 Server?

A. Start the backup wizard

B. Copy the Asr.sif file to the A: drive

C. Copy the Asrpnp.sif file to the A: drive

D. Start the ASR wizard

13. Which of the following counters can monitor your hard disk?
    A. Physical Disk\ Disk Reads/sec
    B. Physical Disk\ Disk Writes/sec
    C. LogicalDisk\ % Free Space
    D. Memory\ Page Reads/sec
    E. Server\ Pool Paged Bytes

---

14. Which of the following counters can monitor your memory?
    A. Memory\ Available Bytes
    B. Memory\ Pages/sec
    C. Memory\ Transition Faults/sec
    D. Network Interface\ Packets/sec
    E. System\Context switches/sec

15. Which of the following counters can monitor your network performance?
    A. Network Interface\ Bytes total/sec
    B. Server\ Bytes Total/sec
    C. Server\ Bytes Received/sec
    D. System\Context switches/sec

16. Which of the following counters can monitor your processor performance?
    A. Processor\ % Processor Time
    B. System\Context switches/sec
    C. System\ Processor Queue Length
    D. Server\ Bytes Received/sec

Chapter 4: Review Answers

1. Which are valid backups methods in a Windows 2003 Server environment?

***A. Normal (Full) and Incremental**

B. Differential and Incremental

***C. Normal (Full) and Differential**

D. Differential only

Explanation: The Normal (Full) backup will back up all data on the server. This method will require the largest size storage media, but will be the easiest to restore. This type of backup is usually performed weekly. The Differential backup is used for backing up only the files that have changed since the last Normal (Full) backup. An archive bit is used to identify the files that have changed. When recovering from a failure, both the differential backup tape and the last Normal (Full) backup tape copies will need to be used. Differential only backs up files since last Normal (Full) backup. Each backup takes a little longer, but restore requires only two tapes (most recent Normal (Full) backup and most recent differential backup). The Incremental backup is used for daily backups. This will reduce the amount of time needed to perform backups to the server, because only the data that has changed since the last incremental backup will be copied. This method also uses an archive bit to identify that files have changed. To restore, the last Normal (Full) backup and the most recent incremental backup tapes will be needed. Incremental only backs up files added or changed since the last backup. Incremental backups are quick to execute, but restore requires multiple tapes (last Normal (Full) backup tape plus all incremental tapes since the last Normal (Full) backup).

---

2. When using a normal and differential backup method, how many tapes will be required to restore the server?

***A. 2**

B. 1

C. 3

D. 4

Explanation: When using a normal and differential backup method, two tapes will be required to restore the server. The normal backup tape catches everything, and the differential tape records the difference since the last normal backup tape.

3. You probably need to replace your hard drive if System Monitor indicates which of the following?

***A. Avg. Disk sec/Transfer is 3.132**

B. Average % Processor Time is 87%

C. Average Pages/Sec 27.322

D. Network Interface: Bytes Total/sec is 241.322

Explanation: An Avg. Disk sec/Transfer of 3.132 would indicate that the hard drive needs to be replaced, since it should be much lower (less than 1.0.) If Average % Processor Time were 87%, this would indicate a need for a processor upgrade. If Average Pages/Sec were 27.322, then more RAM is needed, since the average should be more like 15 or less. Network Interface: Bytes Total/sec is 241.322 and this is within the normal parameters for a NIC card.

---

4. You probably need to upgrade your processor if System Monitor indicates which of the following?

***A. Average % Processor Time is 87%**

B. Avg. Disk sec/Transfer is 3.132

C. Average Pages/Sec 27.322

D. Network Interface:Bytes Total/sec is 241.322

Explanation: An Avg. Disk sec/Transfer of 3.132 would indicate that the hard drive needs to be replaced, since it should be much lower (less than 1.0.) If Average % Processor Time were 87%, this would indicate a need for a processor upgrade. If Average Pages/Sec were 27.322, then more RAM is needed, since the average should be more like 15 or less. Network Interface: Bytes Total/sec is 241.322 and this is within the normal parameters for a NIC card.

5. You probably need to upgrade your RAM if System Monitor indicates which of the following?

***A. Average Pages/Sec 27.322**

B. Avg. Disk sec/Transfer is 3.132

C. Average % Processor Time is 87%

D. Network Interface: Bytes Total/sec is 241.322

Explanation: An Avg. Disk sec/Transfer of 3.132 would indicate that the hard drive needs to be replaced, since it should be much lower (less than 1.0.) If Average % Processor Time were 87%, this would indicate a need for a processor upgrade. If Average Pages/Sec were 27.322, then more RAM is needed, since the average should be more like 15 or less. Network Interface: Bytes Total/sec is 241.322 and this is within the normal parameters for a NIC card.

---

6. Hard page faults are corrected by a/an _________ upgrade.

***A. RAM**

B. Processor

C. Hard Drive

D. Operating System

Explanation: Hard page faults, which are satisfied by the hard drive, are corrected by a RAM upgrade. Processor load is reduced with more RAM and hard page faults decrease.

7. Which of the following commands will show you the hops to a destination?

***A. Tracert**

***B. Pathping**

C. Ping

D. Arp

Explanation: Tracert and Pathping will both show the hops to a destination. Pathping will also show the packet loss at each hop.

---

8. When network connectivity is inconsistent between many routers in distant locations (i.e. - Atlanta, GA, Los Angeles, CA, Houston, TX and Philadelphia, PA), what commands would you use to determine the number of hops?

***A. pathping**

B. ipconfig

***C. tracert**

D. ping

Explanation: Pathping and tracert both show the number of hops to the destination. Ping only indicates if a computer is reachable. Ipconfig only shows IP information on the computer where the command is run.

9. In what instances would using shadow copies be helpful?

***A. Recovery of files that were accidentally deleted**

B. Your Server 2003 OS kernel is corrupted

***C. You accidentally overwrite a file**

D. You need to convert back to FAT32

Explanation: The Shadow Copies feature provides point-in-time copies of files on network shares. With shadow copies of shared folders, you can view the contents of network folders as they existed at points of time in the past. This is very helpful if you want to recover files that were accidentally deleted. This is the network equivalent of the Recycle Bin functionality. If you accidentally delete a file, you can open an old version of the file, and then copy it to a safe location. Shadow copies of shared folders can recover files that are deleted by any mechanism, as long as the required history folder exists. Do you want to recover a file after you accidentally overwrite it? Shadow copies of shared folders can be very useful in environments where you commonly create new files by opening an existing file, making modifications, and then saving the file with a new name. You can use a shadow copy of the shared folder to recover the previous version of the file. Do you want to check different versions of the same file while you are working on the file? You could use shadow copies of shared folders during the normal work cycle when you want to determine what has changed between two versions of the same file. For example, you might want to see what your original text looked like before you spent time editing the file.

---

10. Which of the following executables starts the Volume Shadow Copy service?

***A. Vssadmin.exe**

B. Sssadmin.exe

C. Vscadmin.exe

D. Vsscopy.exe

Explanation: You can access shadow copies of shared folders on the Shadow Copies tab of the Local Disk Properties dialog box. You can also view the same dialog box in the Computer Management snap-in. To do so, right-click Shares, point to All Tasks, and then click Configure Shadow Copies. The Vssadmin.exe tool is the command-line equivalent tool for the Volume Shadow Copy service.

11. How can you access shadow copies in 2003 Server?

***A. With the Shadow Copies tab of the Local Disk Properties dialog box.**

***B. In Computer Management, right-click Shares, point to All Tasks, and then click Configure Shadow Copies.**

C. With the Copies tab of the Local Disk Properties dialog box.

D. In Device Manager, right-click Shares, point to All Tasks, and then click Configure Shadow Copies.

Explanation: You can access shadow copies of shared folders on the Shadow Copies tab of the Local Disk Properties dialog box. You can also view the same dialog box in the Computer Management snap-in. To do so, right-click Shares, point to All Tasks, and then click Configure Shadow Copies. The Vssadmin.exe tool is the command-line equivalent tool of the Volume Shadow Copy service.

---

12. How do you create an ASR floppy disk from an ASR backup set in Windows 2003 Server?

***A. Start the backup wizard**

***B. Copy the Asr.sif file to the A: drive**

***C. Copy the Asrpnp.sif file to the A: drive**

D. Start the ASR wizard

Explanation: Insert a blank, pre-formatted floppy disk into your computer's floppy drive. Click Start, point to All Programs, point to Accessories, point to System Tools, and then click Backup. The Backup Wizard starts. Click Advanced Mode. On the Welcome tab, click Restore Wizard (Advanced). The Restore Wizard starts. Click Next. On the What to Restore page, click to select the check box next to the media that contains the ASR backup. Expand the ASR backup set that corresponds to the ASR floppy disk that you want to create. Expand the second instance of the drive letter that contains the system files, expand Windows_Folder, and then expand the Repair folder. In the right pane, click to select the check boxes next to Asr.sif and Asrpnp.sif, and then click Next. On the Completing the Restore Wizard page, click Advanced. On the Where to Restore page, click Single Folder in the Restore files to box, type A:\ in the Folder name box, and then click Next. Follow the instructions on the remaining pages of the wizard.

13. Which of the following counters can monitor your hard disk?

***A. Physical Disk\ Disk Reads/sec**

***B. Physical Disk\ Disk Writes/sec**

***C. LogicalDisk\ % Free Space**

D. Memory\ Page Reads/sec

E. Server\ Pool Paged Bytes

Explanation: The following counters can be monitored when you need to observer hard disk performance: Physical Disk\ Disk Reads/sec, Physical Disk\ Disk Writes/sec, and LogicalDisk\ % Free Space.

---

14. Which of the following counters can monitor your memory?

***A. Memory\ Available Bytes**

***B. Memory\ Pages/sec**

***C. Memory\ Transition Faults/sec**

D. Network Interface\ Packets/sec

E. System\Context switches/sec

Explanation: The following counters can be monitored when you need to observe memory performance: Memory\ Available Bytes, Memory\ Cache Bytes, Memory\ Pages/sec, Memory\ Page Reads/sec, Memory\ Transition Faults/sec, Memory\ Pool Paged Bytes, and Memory\ Pool Nonpaged Bytes.

15. Which of the following counters can monitor your network performance?

***A. Network Interface\ Bytes total/sec**

***B. Server\ Bytes Total/sec**

***C. Server\ Bytes Received/sec**

D. System\Context switches/sec

Explanation: The following counters can be monitored when you need to observe network performance: Network Interface\ Bytes total/sec, Network Interface\ Packets/sec, Server\ Bytes Total/sec, Server\ Bytes Transmitted/sec, and Server\ Bytes Received/sec.

---

16. Which of the following counters can monitor your processor performance?

***A. Processor\ % Processor Time**

***B. System\Context switches/sec**

***C. System\ Processor Queue Length**

D. Server\ Bytes Received/sec

Explanation: The following counters can be monitored when you need to observe processor performance: Processor\ % Processor Time, System\ Processor Queue Length, Processor\ Interrupts/sec, and System\Context switches/sec.

Planning and Maintaining Network Security

The objective of this chapter is to provide the reader with an understanding of the following:

Configure network protocol security.

- Configure protocol security in a heterogeneous client computer environment.
- Configure protocol security by using IPSec policies.

Configure security for data transmission.

- Configure IPSec policy settings.

Plan for network protocol security.

- Specify the required ports and protocols for specified services.
- Plan an IPSec policy for secure network communications.

Plan secure network administration methods.

- Create a plan to offer Remote Assistance to client computers.
- Plan for remote administration by using Terminal Services.

Plan security for wireless networks.

Plan security for data transmission.

- Secure data transmission between client computers to meet security requirements.
- Secure data transmission by using IPSec.

Troubleshoot security for data transmission. Tools might include:

- IP Security Monitor MMC snap-in
- Resultant Set of Policy (RSoP) MMC snap-in.

Chapter 5: Managing Network Security

Getting Ready Questions

1. To ensure security in TCP/IP networks, Microsoft includes which protocol with their Windows 2003 server family?

2. While IPSec can be managed locally on each computer, what is the recommended method for delivering IPSec settings to network computers?

3. In terms of securing communications, what are the two major needs?

4. How does IPSec provide for full encryption of IP datagram contents?

5. What snap-in tool for MMC has been introduced with Windows 2003 to troubleshoot IPSec policies?

Getting Ready Answers

1. Microsoft includes IPSec with their Windows 2003 server family to help secure TCP/IP communications.

2. The recommended method for delivering IPSec settings to network computers is through the use of Group Policy Objects (GPO).

3. The two major needs in securing network communications are authentication and encryption. Authentication is used to ensure integrity in the communications process; that is, to ensure that communications have not been "spoofed" or been subjected to a man-in-the-middle attack.

4. IPSec provides for full encryption of IP datagram contents by using ESP, Encapsulating Security Protocol?

5. Microsoft introduced the IPSec Monitor snap-in to MMC with Windows 2003 and Windows XP to aid in the troubleshooting of IPSec conflicts and problems.

5.1 Configure network protocol security

In this new era of networking, network protocol security has begun to focus on IPSec, an industry-standard encryption and security protocol. IPSec provides for end-to-end secure transport of IP datagrams through a network infrastructure. Whether in the intranet or over the Internet, computers can use IPSec to improve their transmission's security. IPSec settings can be set locally, that is, on the computer, or domain-wide, as in a Windows 2003 network using Group Policy Objects. As with other GPO settings, the local settings will be overwritten by the GPO settings during startup, if there are GPO settings in effect.

5.1.1 Configure protocol security in a heterogeneous client computer environment

Responding to the promise of IPSec, Microsoft collaborated with Cisco Systems in development and deployment of the IPSec solution in Windows 2000 Professional and Windows XP Professional, in the Windows 2000 server family and in the Windows 2003 server family. Whether the IPSec settings (called rules) are applied through local configuration or through a GPO, the computers that are attempting to connect to each other will need to use the settings (rules) to negotiate the establishment of the IPSec session.

5.1.2 Configure protocol security by using IPSec policies

Microsoft Group Policy includes three IPSec policies, Client, Server and Secure Server. By creating the settings in a GPO and then linking the GPO with the appropriate OU, a standard approach to securing IP transmissions can be achieved in networks. See Figure 5.1 below:

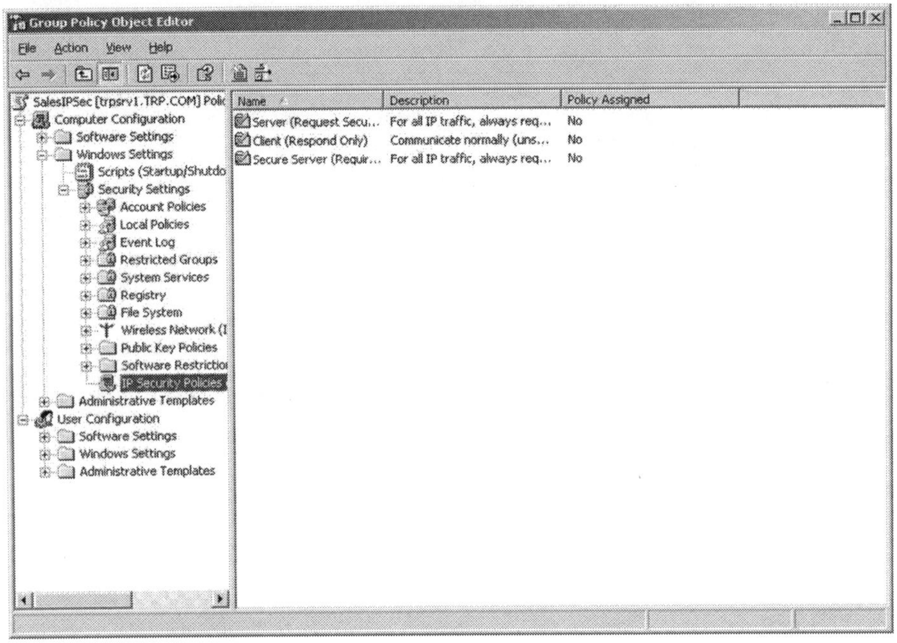

Figure 5—1: IPSec Policies

While Microsoft provides three policies as a starting point in configuring IPSec, there are numerous settings within IPSec policies that can be used to fine tune the security configuration. These policies are designed for intranet use, and those who need IPSec settings for Internet clients' connections will need to create custom IPSec policies and configure those policies accordingly.

IPSec policies are collections of settings, called rules, that govern the computer's behavior when connecting or accepting a connection. The rules are filter list, filter action, authentication methods, tunnel endpoint and connection type. The default policies are pre-configured in rules settings, with none requiring a tunnel endpoint, which essentially means no encryption of datagrams. This is why these policies are inadequate for securing transmissions outside your intranet.

Let's take a moment to clarify the five rules areas. Filter lists and filter actions rule go hand-in-hand. Together they create a firewall-like ability on the computer. Filter lists allow the administrator to specify the type of traffic that will be affected by the IPSec rule. Figure 5-2 below shows some of these settings:

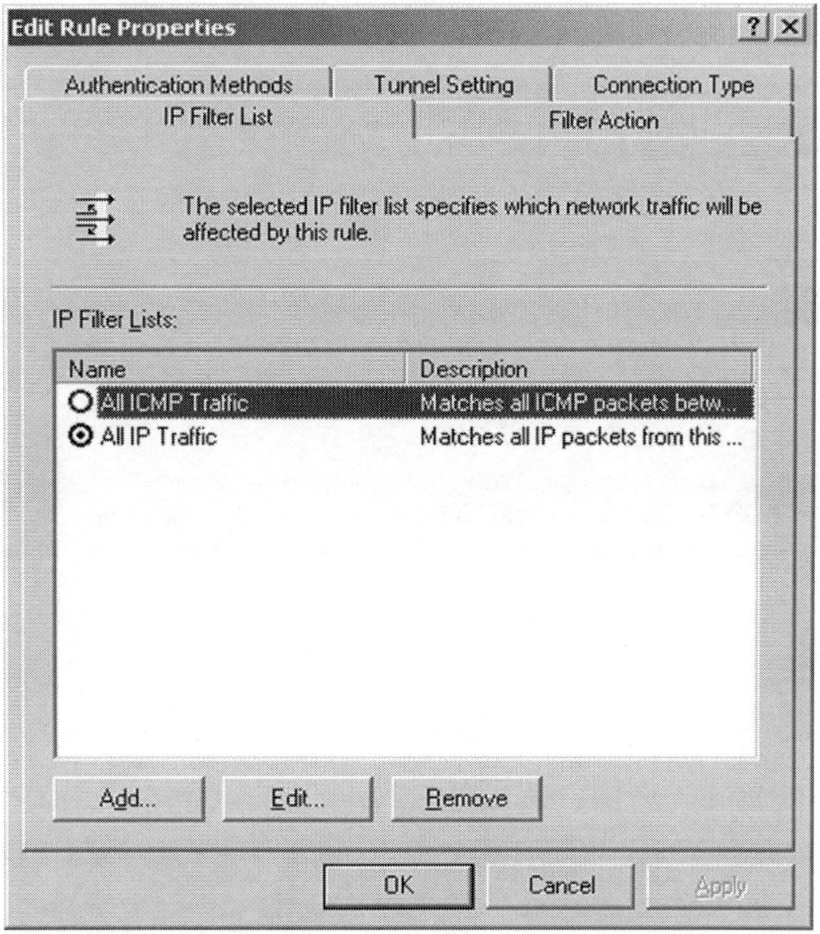

Figure 5—2: IPSec Policy Rules

The filter actions then tell the computer what to do when a packet matches a filter list entry. Filter actions include permit, block or negotiate security. While permit and block are clear, negotiate security takes some clarification. This setting allows the IP traffic to be secured using Authentication Header (AH) or Encapsulating Security Payload (ESP) protocols. In either case, additional decisions are required in terms of how the security will be achieved.

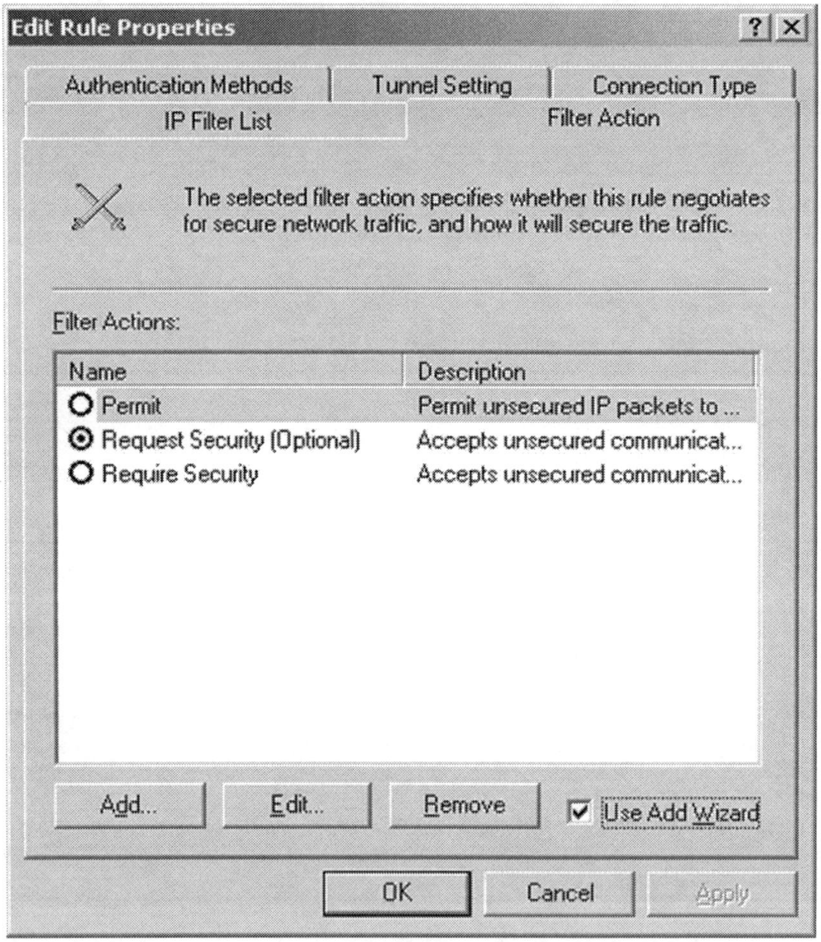

Figure 5—3: IPSec Filter Action Rule

The choices include cryptographic and hashing algorithms and the session key regeneration settings to be used. These settings govern key exchange during Internet Key Exchange (IKE).

The authentication methods rule defaults to Kerberos, but also includes settings for the use of certificates from a certificate authority or a pre-shared key for encryption of the authentication credentials. Figure 5-4 shows the Authentication tab from within an IPSec policy.

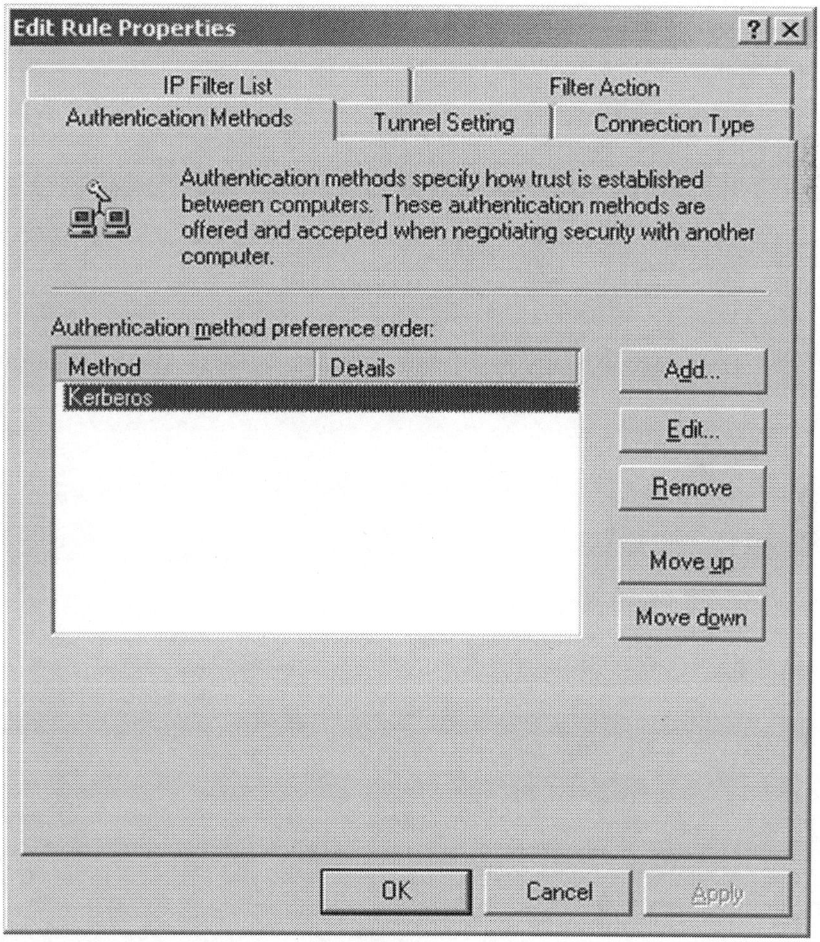

Figure 5—4: IPSec Authentication Methods

The tunnel endpoint rule specifies whether tunneling is being used, and sets the IP address of the endpoint of the tunnel. The last rule, connection type, is used to state whether the rule applies to LAN traffic, remote traffic or both.

5.2 Configure security for data transmission

In securing data transmissions, the need is typically for tunneling and encryption. Usually used in network environments that are not secure (like the Internet), IPSec can be configured for ESP or AH, and used in combination with L2TP to increase the level of security, particularly in VPN implementations.

5.2.1 Configure IPSec policy settings

The policy settings that need configuration particularly in securing these transmissions are found deep within the IPSec policy, actually buries within the filter action rule, as shown in Figure 5-5.

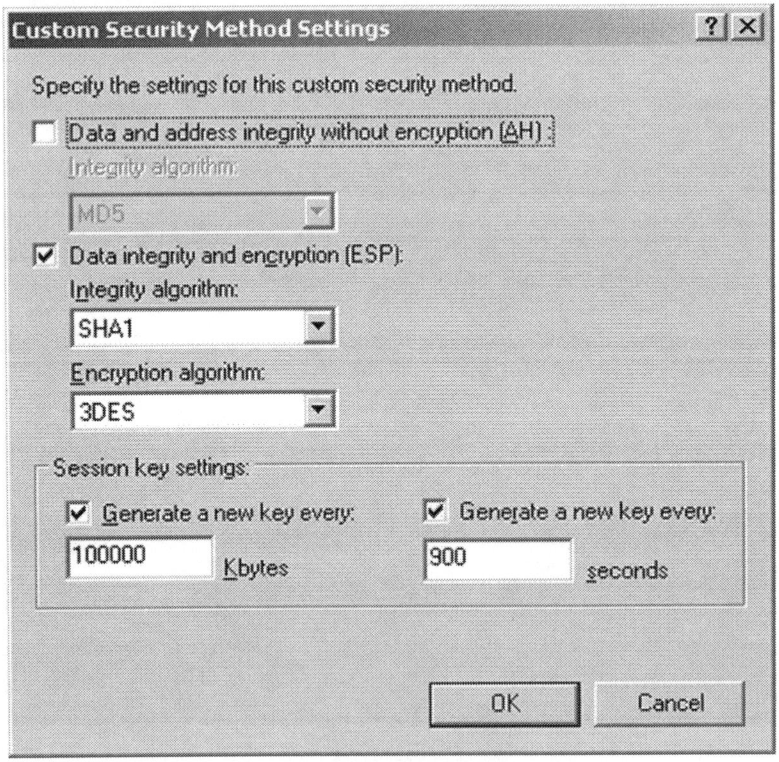

Figure 5—5: Securing Data Transmissions with IPSec

The algorithms for AH integrity include MD5 and SHA1. AH integrity ensures that a transmission has not been modified, and that the transmission indeed comes from the entity that it is supposed to come from. That is the basis of an authentication process. For encryption of the entire packet using ESP, you have a choice of DES or 3DES, with 3DES providing strong encryption of the packet contents.

5.3 Plan for network protocol security.

The filter lists and filter action rules allow the IPSec policy to create a firewall capability. Both settings areas include wizards for simplification of the configuration process. The result allows the computer to control the flow of traffic through the network connection based on the settings.

5.3.1 Specify the required ports and protocols for specified services.

Within the filter list, you can specify quite exactly the traffic you wish to have either permitted, blocked, or for which you want security negotiated. The next figure, Figure 5-6, shows the detailed tabs for configuring filter lists.

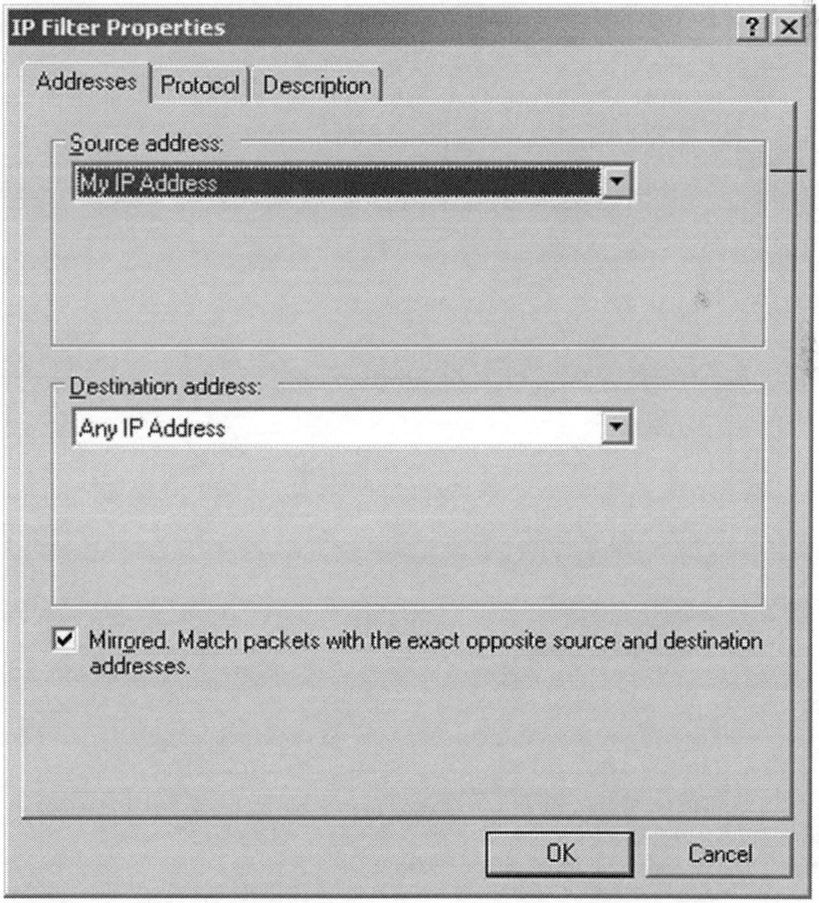

Figure 5—6: IPSec Filter Lists

The address tab allows for specification of source or destination address. The protocol tab allows for the choice of protocol and then the specific port within each protocol. This is packet filtering at its simplest level. In preparing for the Microsoft certification exam, be sure to know the well-known ports used in IP networking. When a firewall or filtering router exists between IPSec peers, it must be configured to forward IPSec traffic on UDP source and destination port 500, IP protocol 50 (ESP), or IP protocol 51 (AH). In addition to the more common ports through which services are provided, know that Kerberos uses port 88 and domain controllers use port 389 for LDAP queries.

5.3.2 Plan an IPSec policy for secure network communications

Within an intranet environment, Microsoft provides three IPSec policies as a starting point for securing network communications. Keep in mind that all three are intended to be copied and then modified to fit your particular needs. None of the three actually encrypts the contents of the IP packets. Client, Server and Secure Server are increasingly restrictive IPSec policies that increase the authentication requirements and the IPSec negotiation process. If encryption is necessary, then these policies will need changes as noted above to create an encrypted tunnel

Pop Quiz 5.1

Pop Quiz 5.1 Questions

1. If you had to configure an IPSec filter during a migration from Windows NT 4.0 to Windows Server 2003, what filter setting would you use to ensure communication during the migration?
2. If your environment required both the data integrity to be secure and the data to be encrypted, what protocol would be used?
3. 3DES (also known as Triple DES) is used under what condition?
4. What would you configure to provide basic firewall capability?
5. The Secure Server IPSec policy provides what security functionality?

Total Recall

Pop Quiz 5.1 Answers

1. Request Security (Optional), as this allows for secure and insecure communication.
2. ESP, or Encapsulating Security Protocol.
3. 3DES is used as an encryption algorithm for encrypting data when ESP is being used.
4. IP or IPSec filter rules and filter action rules.
5. Secure Server only allows communication with computers that use IPSec.

5.4 Plan secure network administration methods

Network administration is often remote in nature. That is, an administrator does not sit down at a computer console physically, but rather the administrator uses various tools to take a remote session on the target computer an then perform the tasks necessary. This ability saves enormous amounts of time for administrators, but then creates potential security risks in the network.

5.4.1 Create a plan to offer Remote Assistance to client computers

When a Windows XP Professional client needs help from administration, the user can "ask" for help through a new feature of Windows XP – Remote Assistance. To get assistance, the user must send an e-mail request to the administrator that contains a hyperlink allowing the administrator to attempt a remote connection to the user's computer. The user then grants the administrator permission to take a remote administration session. This is the fundamental approach to securing Remote Assistance. Additionally, in Active Directory networks, Remote Assistance is controlled through Group Policy settings, offering additional control and security. From the client, there are two areas to set, Remote Assistance which allows requests to be sent, ad Remote Desktop, where the client specifies who can initiate a remote session. See Figure 5-7.

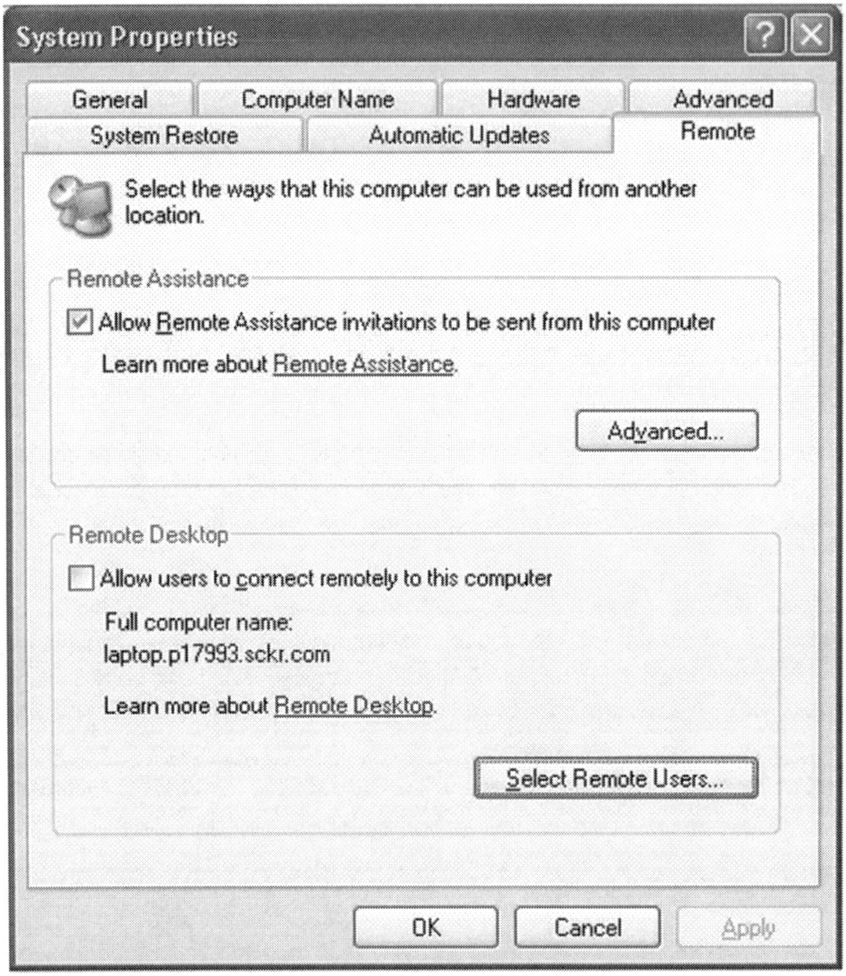

Figure 5—7: Remote Assistance and Remote Desktop

5.4.2 Plan for remote administration by using Terminal Services

Terminal Services can be set for remote administration of a Windows server, but for Windows 2003 servers, this is no longer in favor. The same capability that has come with Windows XP is available in Windows 2003 server, that is, Remote Assistance and Remote Desktop. Terminal Services can still be used, but are no longer recommended by Microsoft. If Terminal Services is used, it requires an authentication, which can be encrypted during the connection process. The session can be controlled through various methods, including session timeout settings, terminal services policies,

5.5 Plan security for wireless networks

Windows 2003 provides secure access to networking using 802.11 and 802.1x protocols in combination with RADIUS. 802.11 uses shared keys for authentication, which many suggest is not secure enough to scale to a corporate LAN. For business environments that require secure connections, the additional use of 802.1x and RADIUS is recommended.

Wireless networking using 802.11 will secure the connection using WEP (Wired Equivalent Privacy), which uses a shared key to secure the authentication process and then secure transmissions through encryption of packet contents. Content encryption can be strengthened through the addition of the use of a shared key, however, makes this scheme inherently weak for larger network environments.

In larger networks, 802.1x provides for RADIUS (Microsoft provides IAS) for centralized authentication services. Married with EAP or other key management strategies, the client connection can be authenticated and a unique (rather than shared) key generated for security. Note that it is possible to use EAP and other key management strategies for packet-level security in WEP, but the use of shared keys for the authentication process is its major limitation.

5.6 Plan security for data transmission

5.6.1 Secure data transmission between client computers to meet security requirements

In this new era of networking, network protocol security has begun to focus on IPSec, an industry-standard encryption and security protocol.

5.6.2 Secure data transmission by using IPSec

IPSec provides for end-to-end secure transport of IP datagrams through a network infrastructure. Whether in the intranet or over the Internet, computers can use IPSec to ensure their transmission's security. IPSec settings can be set locally, that is, on the computer, or domain-wide, as in a Windows 2003 network using Group Policy Objects. As with other GPO settings, the local settings will be overwritten by the GPO settings during startup, if there are GPO settings in effect.

Pop Quiz 5.2

Pop Quiz 5.2 Questions

1. What feature allows an end-user using a Windows XP computer to ask for help from an administrator without the administrator being present?
2. What is considered a liability of WEP (Wired Equivalent Privacy)?

Pop Quiz 5.2 Answers

1. Remote Assistance. Remote Desktop allows a Windows XP computer to host one remote session, though this also locks out the local desktop at the same time.
2. The use of a shared key for all aspects of communication including authentication.

5.7 Troubleshoot security for data transmission

5.7.1 Tools might include

5.7.1.1 IP Security Monitor MMC snap-in

The IPSec Monitor snap-in for MMC provides extensive monitoring and troubleshooting capabilities for the network administrator. You can view details about the IPSec process and examine IPSec policies in effect both locally and in the domain. See Figure 5-8.

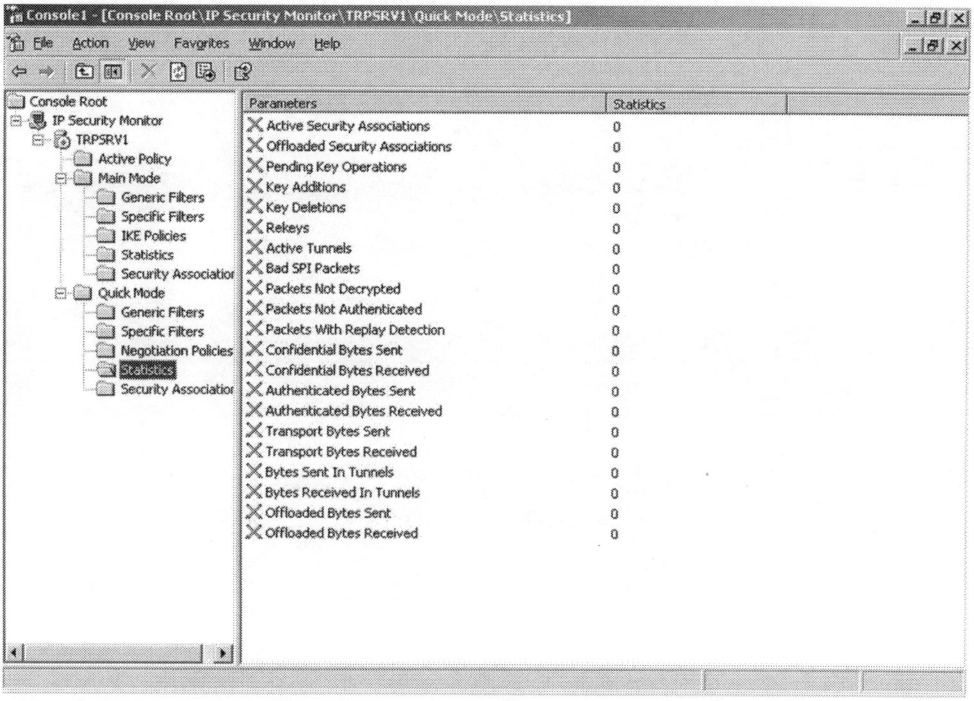

Figure 5—8: IPSec Monitor Snap-in for MMC

The first node, Active Policy, shows information relating to the active IPSec policy currently in effect. The other nodes allow for advanced troubleshooting of the IPSec process.

5.7.1.2 Resultant Set of Policy (RSoP) MMC snap-in

Improper configuration of IPSec policies can result in major problems in a network infrastructure. Microsoft released with Windows 2003 the Resultant Set of Policy snap-in for MMC. This tool, RSOP, is used to query Active Directory and report the results of the query back to the administrator. It can be used to see the effects of existing GPOs in terms of IPSec settings, or planned IPSec policies in terms of their impact. RSoP provides two types of queries: logging mode queries (for viewing IPSec policy assignments for a computer) and planning mode queries (for viewing IPSec policy assignments for members of a Group Policy container). The console is activated through a right-click, which starts a wizard to begin the query process. See Figure 5-9.

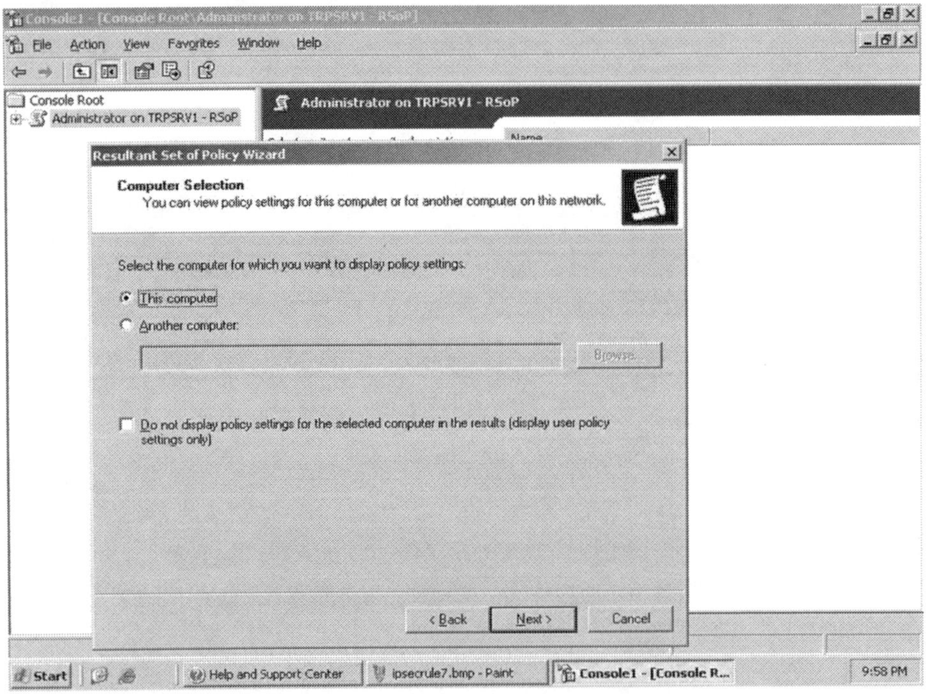

Figure 5—9: RSOP with Wizard Started

The RSoP console simplifies the task of determining which IPSec policy is being applied. It displays the following information for each Group Policy object that contains an IPSec policy assignment:

- the name of the IPSec policy,
- the name of the Group Policy object to which the IPSec policy is assigned,
- the IPSec policy precedence (the lower the number, the higher the precedence), and
- the name of the site, domain, and organizational unit to which the Group Policy object containing the IPSec policy applies (that is, the scope of management for the Group Policy object).

Chapter 5: Review Questions

1. Which of the following ports and protocols does Telnet use?

   A. UDP, 110

   B. TCP, 23

   C. TCP, 80

   D. UDP, 23

---

2. Which of the following ports and protocols does SMTP use?

   A. TCP, 80

   B. UDP, 110

   C. TCP, 25

   D. UDP, 23

3. Which of the following ports and protocols does WINS use?
    A. TCP, 80
    B. UDP, 110
    C. TCP, 42
    D. UDP, 23

---

4. Which of the following ports and protocols does DNS use?
    A. TCP, 80
    B. UDP, 110
    C. TCP, 53
    D. UDP, 23

5. Which of the following ports does BOOTP/DHCP use?

A. 68

B. 23

C. 67

D. 80

E. 65

---

6. Which of the following ports and protocols does HTTP use?

A. TCP, 80

B. TCP, 69

C. UDP, 21

D. TCP, 443

7. What steps should you take to secure POP3 traffic?

    A. Install an IPSec certificate on all computers that need POP3 access as well as your Exchange server.

    B. Install an IPSec certificate on just your Exchange server.

    C. On each of the clients, create an IPSec policy that uses ESP (Encapsulating Security Payload) encryption to all traffic sent to the POP3 port on the Exchange server.

    D. On each of the clients, create an IPSec policy that uses TTL (Time To Live) encryption to all traffic sent to the POP3 port on the Exchange server.

---

8. You have an 802.11b WAN and you want to use WEP (Wired Equivalent Privacy) on it. You also want your clients to be able to connect automatically to the wireless LAN while keeping unauthorized computers from using or viewing the wireless LAN. What actions should you take?

    A. Set the authentication type to Shared Key.

    B. On the clients, add the SSID for them to access the wireless LAN.

    C. Disable SSID Broadcast and enable MAC filtering on all wireless access points.

    D. Set the authentication type to Open System.

9. If a server, with which clients often communicate, is configured with the IPSec Secure Server (Require Security) policy, which of the following policies would make the clients that communicate with it the most secure, securing both communications with the server and other clients?

   A. Have the clients use the IPSec Secure Server (Require Security) policy

   B. Have the clients use the IPSec Server (Require Security) policy

   C. Have the clients use the IPSec Secure Server (Request Security) policy

   D. Have the clients use the IPSec Server (Request Security) policy

---

10. Which of the following is true regarding IPSec tunnel secured traffic over the Internet?

    A. IPSec tunnels always require multiple filters

    B. IPSec tunnels don't provide higher security

    C. An IPSec tunnel needs to be setup between the internal local interfaces of two gateways.

    D. IPSec tunnels aren't based on IP traffic

11. You have a network with two forests in which an external trust is established between them (domain1.com trusts domain2.com). What should you do to use IPSec to encrypt traffic to the domain controller in domain2.com?

    A. Configure a custom IPSec policy on both domain controllers in each forest root that uses ESP (Encapsulating Security Payload) and Kerberos.

    B. Make it so that the IPSec policies use certificate-based authentication and use a root CA to get IPSec certificates for them.

    C. Configure a custom IPSec policy on both domain controllers in each forest root that uses ESP (Encapsulating Security Payload) only.

    D. Configure a custom IPSec policy on both domain controllers in each forest root that uses Kerberos only.

    E. Make it so that the IPSec policies use AH.

---

12. Which of the following would help to properly secure your payroll department's wireless LAN?

    A. Have it use a unique SSID

    B. Disable SSID Broadcast for the wireless access point of the payroll department

    C. Enable MAC filtering for the wireless access point of the payroll department

    D. Enable SSID Broadcast for the wireless access point of the payroll department

    E. Disable MAC filtering for the wireless access point of the payroll department

13. You have a RRAS server that sales people access with laptops. You have configured the laptops with both a user and computer certificate to authenticate to the RRAS server. You receive the following error, 'Error 792: The L2TP connection attempt because security negotiation times out.' What do you need to do to fix this?
    A. Verify that the IPSec Policy Agent is started on the RRAS server
    B. On the RRAS server, install a computer certificate that is issued by the same CA that issued the user certificates installed on the laptops.
    C. On the RRAS server, install a computer certificate that is issued by a different CA than the one that issued the user certificates installed on the laptops.
    D. Verify that the IPSec Policy Agent is stopped on the RRAS server

---

14. You have a DMZ (Demilitarized Zone) that is comprised of an external firewall performing NAT, an internal firewall and a RRAS server between the two. What do you do to allow L2TP/IPSec connections through the external firewall to the RRAS server.
    A. Use packet filters that allow ESP and IKE traffic to the RRAS server.
    B. Adjust the network addressing scheme in the DMZ to use a public Internet address.
    C. Do not use packet filters that allow ESP and IKE traffic to the RRAS server.
    D. Leave the network addressing scheme in the DMZ alone.

15. You have an 802.11a wireless LAN that uses WEP and MAC filtering. You also use EAP-TLS and have an IAS server. How can you ensure that only domain users can connect to the wireless LAN and you that computers don't connect to the wireless LAN when a user is not logged on to the computer?

A. Enable 802.1x network access control on the clients

B. Clear the Authenticate as computer when computer information is available option and configure the EAP type as Smart Card or other Certificate.

C. Set up the clients as RADIUS clients that use the IAS server as a RADIUS server

D. Set up the IAS server as a RADIUS client

---

16. Which of the following will protect a server from inspection but will allow the clients to authenticate to it?

A. Have the server use the IPSec Secure Server (Require Security) policy and have the clients use the Client (Respond Only) policy

B. Have the server use the IPSec Client (Respond Only) policy and have the clients use the Client (Respond Only) policy

C. Have the server use the IPSec Secure Server (Require Security) policy and have the clients use the IPSec Secure Server (Require Security) policy

D. Have the server use the IPSec Secure Server (Request Security) policy and have the clients use the Client (Respond Only) policy

17. Which would enable four encryption methods on all computers in the domain with the least administrative overhead (each type of computer is held in its respective OU, clients in Clients, server in Servers, etc.)?
    A. Create a single GPO, link it to the domain, and configure its IPSec policy to use the encryption methods

    B. Create a GPO for each OU, link them, and configure its IPSec policy to use the encryption methods for each OU

    C. Create a single GPO, link it to all the OUs, and configure its IPSec policy to use the encryption methods

    D. Create three GPOs per OU, link them all to the domain, and configure its IPSec policy to use the encryption methods

---

18. How can Telnet session traffic be encrypted and users who are not a part of a selected group (the Marketing group) be prevented from intercepting the Telnet traffic?
    A. Set up ESP in a custom IPSec policy for connections to the Telnet server on TCP port 23 from any IP address or port.

    B. Place all applicable user accounts in the OU affected by the GPO that defines this IPSec encryption.

    C. Set up ESP in a custom IPSec policy for connections to the Telnet server on TCP port 25 from any IP address or port.

    D. Set up ESP in a custom IPSec policy for connections to the Telnet server on TCP port 27 from any IP address or port.

Chapter 5: Review Answers

1. Which of the following ports and protocols does Telnet use?
    A. UDP, 110

***B. TCP, 23**

    C. TCP, 80

    D. UDP, 23

Explanation: FTP uses TCP and ports 20 and 21. TELNET uses TCP and port 23. SMTP uses TCP and port 25. WINS uses TCP and port 42. DNS uses TCP and port 53. BOOTP/DHCP use UDP and ports 67, 68. HTTP uses TCP and port 80. KERBEROS uses TCP and port 88. POP3 uses TCP and port 110. NNTP uses TCP and port 119. NETBIOS uses UDP and ports 137-139. LDAP uses UDP and port 389. SSL uses TCP and port 443. RADIUS uses TCP and ports 1645, 1646 for TCP connections. RADIUS also uses UDP and ports 1812 and 1813 for UDP connections.

---

2. Which of the following ports and protocols does SMTP use?
    A. TCP, 80

    B. UDP, 110

***C. TCP, 25**

    D. UDP, 23

Explanation: FTP uses TCP and ports 20 and 21. TELNET uses TCP and port 23. SMTP uses TCP and port 25. WINS uses TCP and port 42. DNS uses TCP and port 53. BOOTP/DHCP use UDP and ports 67, 68. HTTP uses TCP and port 80. KERBEROS uses TCP and port 88. POP3 uses TCP and port 110. NNTP uses TCP and port 119. NETBIOS uses UDP and ports 137-139. LDAP uses UDP and port 389. SSL uses TCP and port 443. RADIUS uses TCP and ports 1645, 1646 for TCP connections. RADIUS also uses UDP and ports 1812 and 1813 for UDP connections.

3. Which of the following ports and protocols does WINS use?

A. TCP, 80

B. UDP, 110

***C. TCP, 42**

D. UDP, 23

Explanation: FTP uses TCP and ports 20 and 21. TELNET uses TCP and port 23. SMTP uses TCP and port 25. WINS uses TCP and port 42. DNS uses TCP and port 53. BOOTP/DHCP use UDP and ports 67, 68. HTTP uses TCP and port 80. KERBEROS uses TCP and port 88. POP3 uses TCP and port 110. NNTP uses TCP and port 119. NETBIOS uses UDP and ports 137-139. LDAP uses UDP and port 389. SSL uses TCP and port 443. RADIUS uses TCP and ports 1645, 1646 for TCP connections. RADIUS also uses UDP and ports 1812 and 1813 for UDP connections.

---

4. Which of the following ports and protocols does DNS use?

A. TCP, 80

B. UDP, 110

***C. TCP, 53**

D. UDP, 23

Explanation: FTP uses TCP and ports 20 and 21. TELNET uses TCP and port 23. SMTP uses TCP and port 25. WINS uses TCP and port 42. DNS uses TCP and port 53. BOOTP/DHCP use UDP and ports 67, 68. HTTP uses TCP and port 80. KERBEROS uses TCP and port 88. POP3 uses TCP and port 110. NNTP uses TCP and port 119. NETBIOS uses UDP and ports 137-139. LDAP uses UDP and port 389. SSL uses TCP and port 443. RADIUS uses TCP and ports 1645, 1646 for TCP connections. RADIUS also uses UDP and ports 1812 and 1813 for UDP connections.

5. Which of the following ports does BOOTP/DHCP use?

***A. 68**

B. 23

***C. 67**

D. 80

E. 65

Explanation: FTP uses TCP and ports 20 and 21. TELNET uses TCP and port 23. SMTP uses TCP and port 25. WINS uses TCP and port 42. DNS uses TCP and port 53. BOOTP/DHCP use UDP and ports 67, 68. HTTP uses TCP and port 80. KERBEROS uses TCP and port 88. POP3 uses TCP and port 110. NNTP uses TCP and port 119. NETBIOS uses UDP and ports 137-139. LDAP uses UDP and port 389. SSL uses TCP and port 443. RADIUS uses TCP and ports 1645, 1646 for TCP connections. RADIUS also uses UDP and ports 1812 and 1813 for UDP connections.

---

6. Which of the following ports and protocols does HTTP use?

***A. TCP, 80**

B. TCP, 69

C. UDP, 21

D. TCP, 443

Explanation: FTP uses TCP and ports 20 and 21. TELNET uses TCP and port 23. SMTP uses TCP and port 25. WINS uses TCP and port 42. DNS uses TCP and port 53. BOOTP/DHCP use UDP and ports 67, 68. HTTP uses TCP and port 80. KERBEROS uses TCP and port 88. POP3 uses TCP and port 110. NNTP uses TCP and port 119. NETBIOS uses UDP and ports 137-139. LDAP uses UDP and port 389. SSL uses TCP and port 443. RADIUS uses TCP and ports 1645, 1646 for TCP connections. RADIUS also uses UDP and ports 1812 and 1813 for UDP connections.

7. What steps should you take to secure POP3 traffic?

***A. Install an IPSec certificate on all computers that need POP3 access as well as your Exchange server.**

B. Install an IPSec certificate on just your Exchange server.

***C. On each of the clients, create an IPSec policy that uses ESP (Encapsulating Security Payload) encryption to all traffic sent to the POP3 port on the Exchange server.**

D. On each of the clients, create an IPSec policy that uses TTL (Time To Live) encryption to all traffic sent to the POP3 port on the Exchange server.

Explanation: To secure POP3 traffic, install an IPSec certificate on all computers that need POP3 access as well as your Exchange server. On each of the clients, create an IPSec policy that uses ESP (Encapsulating Security Payload) encryption to all traffic sent to the POP3 port on the Exchange server.

---

8. You have an 802.11b WAN and you want to use WEP (Wired Equivalent Privacy) on it. You also want your clients to be able to connect automatically to the wireless LAN while keeping unauthorized computers from using or viewing the wireless LAN. What actions should you take?

***A. Set the authentication type to Shared Key.**

***B. On the clients, add the SSID for them to access the wireless LAN.**

***C. Disable SSID Broadcast and enable MAC filtering on all wireless access points.**

D. Set the authentication type to Open System.

Explanation: You have an 802.11b WAN and you want to use WEP (Wired Equivalent Privacy) on it. You also want your clients to be able to connect automatically to the wireless LAN while keeping unauthorized computers from using or viewing the wireless LAN. Set the authentication type to Shared Key. Disable SSID Broadcast and enable MAC filtering on all wireless access points. On the clients, add the SSID for them to access the wireless LAN.

9. If a server, with which clients often communicate, is configured with the IPSec Secure Server (Require Security) policy, which of the following policies would make the clients that communicate with it the most secure, securing both communications with the server and other clients?

***A. Have the clients use the IPSec Secure Server (Require Security) policy**

B. Have the clients use the IPSec Server (Require Security) policy

C. Have the clients use the IPSec Secure Server (Request Security) policy

D. Have the clients use the IPSec Server (Request Security) policy

Explanation: If a server, with which clients often communicate is configured with the IPSec Secure Server (Require Security) policy, have the clients use the IPSec Secure Server (Require Security) policy to make the clients that communicate with it the most secure, securing both communications with the server and other clients.

---

10. Which of the following is true regarding IPSec tunnel secured traffic over the Internet?

A. IPSec tunnels always require multiple filters

B. IPSec tunnels don't provide higher security

***C. An IPSec tunnel needs to be setup between the internal local interfaces of two gateways.**

D. IPSec tunnels aren't based on IP traffic

Explanation: To secure Internet traffic, an IPSec tunnel needs to be setup between the internal local interfaces of two gateways.

11. You have a network with two forests in which an external trust is established between them (domain1.com trusts domain2.com). What should you do to use IPSec to encrypt traffic to the domain controller in domain2.com?

***A. Configure a custom IPSec policy on both domain controllers in each forest root that uses ESP (Encapsulating Security Payload) and Kerberos.**

***B. Make it so that the IPSec policies use certificate-based authentication and use a root CA to get IPSec certificates for them.**

C. Configure a custom IPSec policy on both domain controllers in each forest root that uses ESP (Encapsulating Security Payload) only.

D. Configure a custom IPSec policy on both domain controllers in each forest root that uses Kerberos only.

E. Make it so that the IPSec policies use AH.

Explanation: You have a network with two forests in which an external trust is established between the two (domain1.com trusts domain2.com). You want to use IPSec to encrypt traffic to the domain controller in domain2.com. Configure a custom IPSec policy on both domain controllers in each forest root that uses ESP (Encapsulating Security Payload) and Kerberos. Also, make the IPSec policies use certificate-based authentication. Use a root CA to get IPSec certificates for them.

---

12. Which of the following would help to properly secure your payroll department's wireless LAN?

***A. Have it use a unique SSID**

***B. Disable SSID Broadcast for the wireless access point of the payroll department**

***C. Enable MAC filtering for the wireless access point of the payroll department**

D. Enable SSID Broadcast for the wireless access point of the payroll department

E. Disable MAC filtering for the wireless access point of the payroll department

Explanation: To properly secure your payroll department's wireless LAN, have it use a unique SSID, disable SSID Broadcast for the wireless access point of the payroll department, and enable MAC filtering for the wireless access point of the payroll department.

13. You have a RRAS server that sales people access with laptops. You have configured the laptops with both a user and computer certificate to authenticate to the RRAS server. You receive the following error, 'Error 792: The L2TP connection attempt because security negotiation times out.' What do you need to do to fix this?

***A. Verify that the IPSec Policy Agent is started on the RRAS server**

***B. On the RRAS server, install a computer certificate that is issued by the same CA that issued the user certificates installed on the laptops.**

C. On the RRAS server, install a computer certificate that is issued by a different CA than the one that issued the user certificates installed on the laptops.

D. Verify that the IPSec Policy Agent is stopped on the RRAS server

Explanation: You have a RRAS server that sales people access with laptops. You have configured the laptops with both a user and computer certificate to authenticate to the RRAS server. You receive the following error, 'Error 792: The L2TP connection attempt because security negotiation times out.' Verify that the IPSec Policy Agent is started on the RRAS server. On the RRAS server, install a computer certificate that is issued by the same CA that issued the user certificates installed on the laptops.

---

14. You have a DMZ (Demilitarized Zone) that is comprised of an external firewall performing NAT, an internal firewall and a RRAS server between the two. What do you do to allow L2TP/IPSec connections through the external firewall to the RRAS server.

***A. Use packet filters that allow ESP and IKE traffic to the RRAS server.**

***B. Adjust the network addressing scheme in the DMZ to use a public Internet address.**

C. Do not use packet filters that allow ESP and IKE traffic to the RRAS server.

D. Leave the network addressing scheme in the DMZ alone.

Explanation: You have a DMZ (Demilitarized Zone) that is comprised of an external firewall performing NAT, an internal firewall and a RRAS server between the two. To allow L2TP/IPSec connections through the external firewall to the RRAS server, use packet filters that allow ESP and IKE traffic to the RRAS server and adjust the network addressing scheme in the DMZ to use a public Internet address (since NAT blows away the IP header on L2TP/IPSec).

15. You have an 802.11a wireless LAN that uses WEP and MAC filtering. You also use EAP-TLS and have an IAS server. How can you ensure that only domain users can connect to the wireless LAN and you that computers don't connect to the wireless LAN when a user is not logged on to the computer?

***A. Enable 802.1x network access control on the clients**

***B. Clear the Authenticate as computer when computer information is available option and configure the EAP type as Smart Card or other Certificate.**

***C. Set up the clients as RADIUS clients that use the IAS server as a RADIUS server**

D. Set up the IAS server as a RADIUS client

Explanation: You have an 802.11a wireless LAN that uses WEP and MAC filtering. You also use EAP-TLS and have an IAS server. To ensure that only domain users can connect to the wireless LAN and that computers don't connect to the wireless LAN when a user is not logged on to the computer, enable 802.1x network access control on the clients. Clear the Authenticate as computer when computer information is available option and configure the EAP type as Smart Card or other Certificate. Set up the clients as RADIUS clients that use the IAS server as a RADIUS server.

---

16. Which of the following will protect a server from inspection but will allow the clients to authenticate to it?

***A. Have the server use the IPSec Secure Server (Require Security) policy and have the clients use the Client (Respond Only) policy**

B. Have the server use the IPSec Client (Respond Only) policy and have the clients use the Client (Respond Only) policy

C. Have the server use the IPSec Secure Server (Require Security) policy and have the clients use the IPSec Secure Server (Require Security) policy

D. Have the server use the IPSec Secure Server (Request Security) policy and have the clients use the Client (Respond Only) policy

Explanation: Using the IPSec Secure Server (Require Security) policy for the server and using the Client (Respond Only) policy for the clients will protect a server from inspection but will allow clients to authenticate to it.

17. Which would enable four encryption methods on all computers in the domain with the least administrative overhead (each type of computer is held in its respective OU, clients in Clients, server in Servers, etc.)?

***A. Create a single GPO, link it to the domain, and configure its IPSec policy to use the encryption methods**

B. Create a GPO for each OU, link them, and configure its IPSec policy to use the encryption methods for each OU

C. Create a single GPO, link it to all the OUs, and configure its IPSec policy to use the encryption methods

D. Create three GPOs per OU, link them all to the domain, and configure its IPSec policy to use the encryption methods

Explanation: You want to enable four encryption methods (DES, 3DES, etc.) on all computers in the domain (each type of computer is held in its respective OU, clients in Clients, server in Servers, etc). Create a single GPO, link it to the domain, and configure its IPSec policy to use the encryption methods.

---

18. How can Telnet session traffic be encrypted and users who are not a part of a selected group (the Marketing group) be prevented from intercepting the Telnet traffic?

***A. Set up ESP in a custom IPSec policy for connections to the Telnet server on TCP port 23 from any IP address or port.**

***B. Place all applicable user accounts in the OU affected by the GPO that defines this IPSec encryption.**

C. Set up ESP in a custom IPSec policy for connections to the Telnet server on TCP port 25 from any IP address or port.

D. Set up ESP in a custom IPSec policy for connections to the Telnet server on TCP port 27 from any IP address or port.

Explanation: To encrypt Telnet session traffic and prevent users not a part of a selected group (the Marketing group) from intercepting the traffic, set up ESP in a custom IPSec policy for connections to the Telnet server on TCP port 23 from any IP address or port. Place all applicable user accounts in the OU affected by the GPO that defines this IPSec encryption.

Planning, Implementing, and Maintaining Security Infrastructure

The objective of this chapter is to provide the reader with an understanding of the following:

Configure the Active Directory directory services for certificate publication.

Plan a public key infrastructure (PKI) that uses Certificate Services.

- **Identify the appropriate type of certificate authority to support certificate issuance requirements.**
- **Plan the enrollment and distribution of certificates.**
- **Plan for the use of smart cards for authentication.**

Plan a framework for planning and implementing security.

- **Plan for security monitoring.**
- **Plan a change and configuration management framework for security.**

Plan a security update infrastructure. Tools might include:

- **Microsoft Baseline Security Analyzer**
- **Microsoft Software Update Services.**

Chapter 6: Security Infrastructure

Introduction:

Certificate services provide for authentication of users and services, and for encryption of data transmission. Digital certificates provide the mechanism for authentication, while public/private key pairs provide the mechanism for encryption/decryption of data. The keys can be minted and digital certificates issued by an external Certificate Authority or by the Certificate Authority that ships with Windows 2003. While some aspects of these PKI services are automated, others will require the creation of a Certificate Authority, a CA hierarchy, or the use of an external CA like VeriSign or GTE CyberTrust. The starting point is to determine which applications or services will need to be secured by the use of certificates. S/MIME for secure e-mail, SSL or TLS for authentication to web sites, smart cards and EFS are all examples of solutions that use certificate services for security.

Certificates, often called digital certificates, are used in PKI settings to distribute the public key from a public-private key pair in a secure fashion. The public key is included in the certificate, which is digitally signed by a Certificate Authority (CA). The signing of the certificate ensures that the public key has not been altered, and so is safe to use. Once a recipient has validated the authenticity of the certificate, they can then use the public key to encrypt and secure communications with the owner of the corresponding private key. Most certificate services (PKI) environments use X.509 certificates, sometimes issued by an internally managed CA, but often procured from an external CA.

Getting Ready Questions

1. What are the two primary concerns when securing communications?
2. What is the means used to deliver public keys to trusted entities in PKI?
3. What are the main concerns in the area of certificate management?
4. What Microsoft tool can be used to scan computers for common security vulnerabilities?
5. What has Microsoft done to help in the deployment of critical security patches and fixes?

Getting Ready Answers

1. The two primary concerns when securing communications are authentication (ensuring that the sender is who they say they are) and encryption, to ensure that the contents of the communications cannot be intercepted and read.

2. Public keys are embedded and then distributed with digital certificates in a PKI infrastructure.

3. Certificate management revolves around enrollment, distribution, and expiration or revocation.

4. The Microsoft Baseline Security Analyzer (MBSA) is a security assessment tool that allows users to scan one or more Windows®-based computers for common security misconfigurations.

5. To help centralize the deployment of patches and fixes, Microsoft has released Software Update Services (SUS).

6.1 Plan a public key infrastructure (PKI) that uses Certificate Services

6.1.1 Identify the appropriate type of certificate authority to support certificate issuance requirements

In Windows 2003, you may choose to use either your own managed, private CA or an external or commercial CA. Typically a commercial CA is used when the company is dealing mainly with outside users or organizations that need secure access, and the company wishes to outsource the expertise of a third-party company. For those settings where internal expertise is available, the company can create a stand-alone CA. A stand-alone CA is a private CA with a stand-alone policy, which enables the issuance and maintenance of certificates independent of Active Directory. For internal needs, companies would create a private CA with an enterprise CA policy (often referred to as creating an enterprise CA). For enterprise CAs, if a CA hierarchy is being created, then the determination needs to be made of which CA will function as the Root CA and which will be subordinate. In Certificate Authority hierarchies, the Root CA should be maintained offline, to further secure the server, while subordinate CAs provide for issuance and maintenance of certificates.

CA hierarchies are for use in large organizations, or in settings where the use of certificates needs to be managed separately, Windows 2003 allows for the creation of Certificate Authority hierarchies. Organized by usage, organizational structure or function, hierarchies consist of a Root CA and subordinate CAs organized with parent/child relationships. The need for certificates to secure SSL or TLS connections as well as to deliver secure e-mail through S/MIME may drive the creation of a usage-based hierarchy. Organizations that need to use Certificate Services across different bases of user, contractors, staff and temporary employees, might create a hierarchy based upon organizational structure. Companies that operate in countries with different regulations regarding the use of PKI will need to create hierarchies based on location.

6.1.2 Plan the enrollment and distribution of certificates

Certificate management revolves around enrollment, distribution, and expiration or revocation. In a CA hierarchy, the Root CA certifies the subordinate CAs, while the subordinate CAs are used to issue certificates to users. Users will trust certificates from the subordinate CAs as long as they trust the Root CA. In the enrollment process, users issue a CSR (certificate signing request) to the CA. Then the CA verifies the information from the CSR (like the identity of the requestor, etc.) and issues a digital certificate along with the public key back to the requestor.

Certificates can be made available using certificate templates. See Figure 6-1 below:

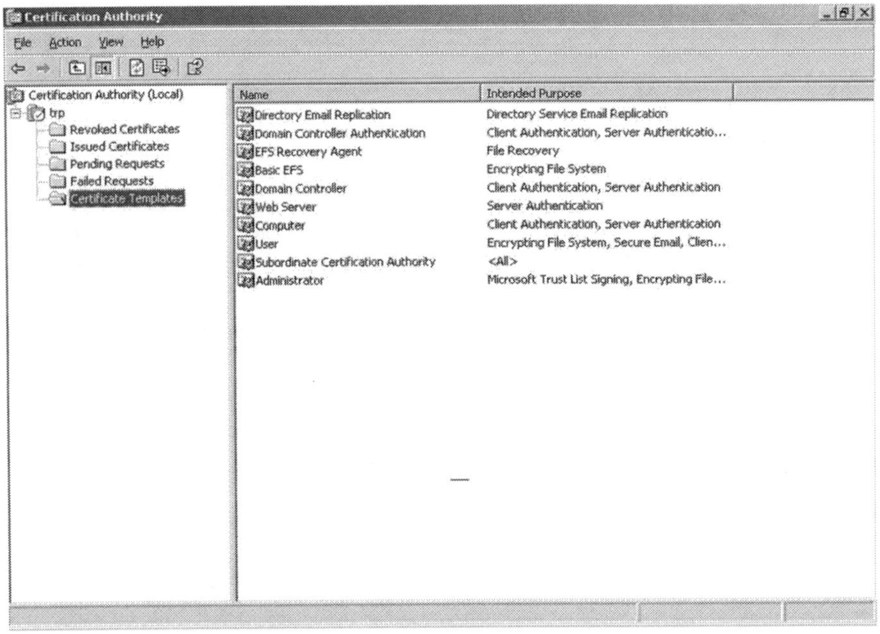

Figure 6—1: Certificate Templates in the Certificate Authority MMC

For a user, a computer or a service to obtain a certificate for use, autoenrollment can be set in Group Policy. In the User or Computer node of Group Policy, then under Windows Settings|Security Setings|PKI Settings, in the details pane, double-click Autoenrollment Settings and choose Enroll certificates automatically.

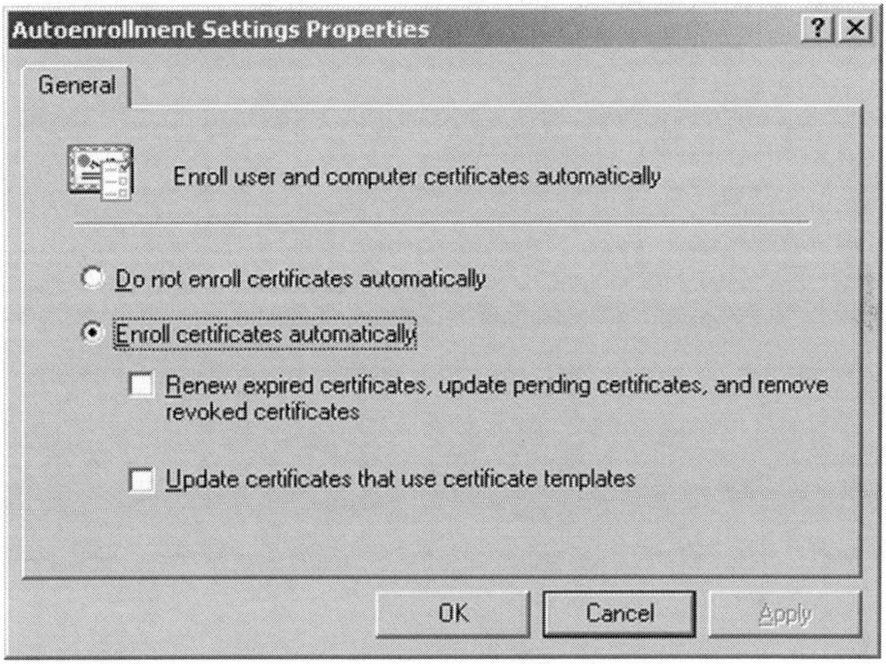

Figure 6—2: Autoenrollment Setting in Group Policy

Also, select the "Renew expired certificates, update pending certificates, and remove revoked certificates" check box, and select the "Update certificates that use certificate templates" check box and click OK.

Once certificate enrollment is enabled, the certificates are then published in Active Directory automatically for users in their user object.

Certificates can be mapped to Active Directory user accounts. Certificate mapping can be one-to-one or many-to-one. The one-to-one mapping scheme would require much more administration than the many-to-one scheme, since each user would need a unique certificate. Consider many-to-one mappings to streamline the mapping process. For internal users, you could map their user accounts to a single account that uses the necessary certificate for authentication (and probably encryption), while outside consultants or contractors could use a certificate that is mapped to a user account specially created for that purpose.

6.1.3 Plan for the use of smart cards for authentication

Smart card logon is integrated with the Kerberos version 5 authentication protocol implemented in Windows Server 2003. When smart card logon is enabled, the system recognizes a smart-card insertion event as an alternative to the standard Ctrl + Alt + Del sequence to initiate a logon. The user is then prompted for the smart card PIN. In this system, the smart card also contains a copy of the certificate of the user (issued by an enterprise CA).

Smart cards enhance security by allowing you to store extremely strong credentials in an easy-to-use form. Requiring a physical smart card for authentication virtually eliminates the potential for spoofing the identities of your users across a network, as well as the possibility of password theft, dictionary attacks, etc.

Pop Quiz 6.1

Pop Quiz 6.1 Questions

1. When using an Enterprise CA, it is recommended that end-user certificates be issued from what level of the hierarchy?

2. If using certificates for authentication in Active Directory, which mapping scheme is recommended and why?

3. Why is the use of a smart card recommended for mobile users?

Pop Quiz 6.1 Answers

1. It is recommended that end-user certificates be issued from subordinate CAs, while the root issues certificates to the subordinates only.

2. It is recommended that you use the many-to-one mapping scheme, because the one-to-one mapping scheme would cause far more administrative overhead.

3. Because it is much harder to impersonate a physical card than to guess a users password.

6.2 Plan a framework for planning and implementing security.

The implementation of Active Directory adds tremendous capability in the securing of computers in a Windows 2003 network. Security settings for computers can be created using security templates provided by Microsoft, adding incremental security templates, or by creating custom templates. The settings can then be applied to multiple computers by placing computers in Active Directory containers and using Group Policy objects to push the security template settings. It is important to identify the different roles that the various Windows computers play in the network. Clearly, domain controllers have different security requirements than do file servers, as laptops have different risks associated with their use than do kiosks. Then each resource must be evaluated in terms of security needs. Shares, files, printers are all examples of common resources in a network environment. Each resource has to be identified and the security risks identified. Then the appropriate security measures have to be recommended. For many of these resources, Active Directory containers or group nesting will provide the focal point of access, and the resource will have a DACL or ACL that provides an interface for setting permissions.

Certificates expire based upon certain predetermined dates, or they can be revoked if the manager feels that security of the keys has been compromised. The status of a certificate is updated when it is revoked or when it expires by placing the certificate on a Certificate Revocation List (CRL), which can be published in Active Directory. The list will then be checked whenever a certificate is presented to assure that the certificate is still valid.

6.2.1 Plan for security monitoring

There can be many elements to a plan for security monitoring. Auditing can be enabled in many areas of the network to ensure that unauthorized access is not being attempted, or that intrusion is not occurring. The Microsoft Baseline Security Analyzer, described below, can be used to ensure that systems are up-to-date in terms of patches and fixes, and not prone to vulnerabilities.

6.2.2 Plan a change and configuration management framework for security.

Change and configuration management encompasses the documentation of what is currently in place, and procedures and processes for planning and implementing changes in the existing infrastructure. This aspect of planning calls for detailed network diagrams, inventory, Active Directory diagrams, tables of DACL assignments, lists of servers and their specific settings, and on and on. Sample documentation can be found from many sources to begin this process. Once the details of what security currently looks like in the network is complete, then detailed procedures on how to asses the impact of proposed changes and how to roll out proposed changes need to be developed. This part of security planning is not exciting, but is critical to ensure that a secure network does not "drift" into a non-secure state.

6.3 Plan a security update infrastructure

Tools might include

6.3.1 Microsoft Baseline Security Analyzer

The Microsoft Baseline Security Analyzer (MBSA) is a security assessment tool that allows users to scan one or more Windows®-based computers for common security misconfigurations. MBSA will scan a Windows-based computer and check the operating system and other installed components -- such as Internet Information Services (IIS) and SQL Server™ -- for security misconfigurations. It will also verify whether they are up-to-date with respect to recommended security updates. See Figure 6-3 below:

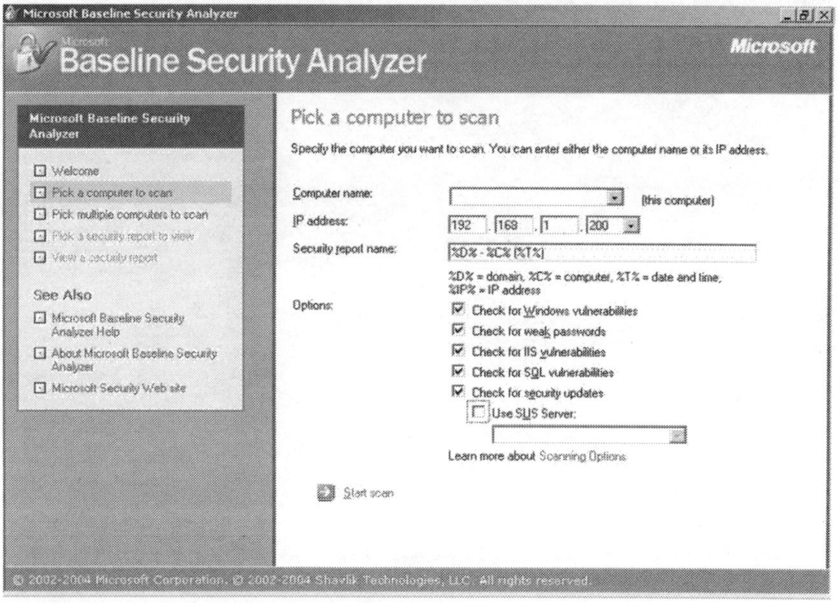

Figure 6—3: Microsoft Security Baseline Analyzer

The tool will check for specific vulnerabilities for the Windows operating system, for Internet Information Server, for SQL server, for desktop applications and their known areas of vulnerability. This is done by downloading an xml file named mssecure.xml from Microsoft's web site, comparing registry settings, file versions, and checksums form the computer to the contents of Microsoft's mssecure.xml. Differences are reported in a scan report after the tool runs. This tool is quite comprehensive, and can scan for a wide range of potential security problems, both on a local computer, or on network computers.

6.3.2 Microsoft Software Update Services

To help centralize the deployment of patches and fixes, Microsoft has released Software Update Services (SUS). With SUS, an organization can have a single internal server serve as a central point for downloading and then updating all other servers and workstations. Multiple servers can be used to provide fault tolerance and load balancing for this service in larger implementations. Not only can this provide efficiencies in the update process, since most of the updates can be delivered across high-speed infrastructure, but it can also provide for better control over who and what updates can and are applied throughout the network. Software Update Services behavior is best managed through Group Policy settings, as shown in Figure 6-4 next:

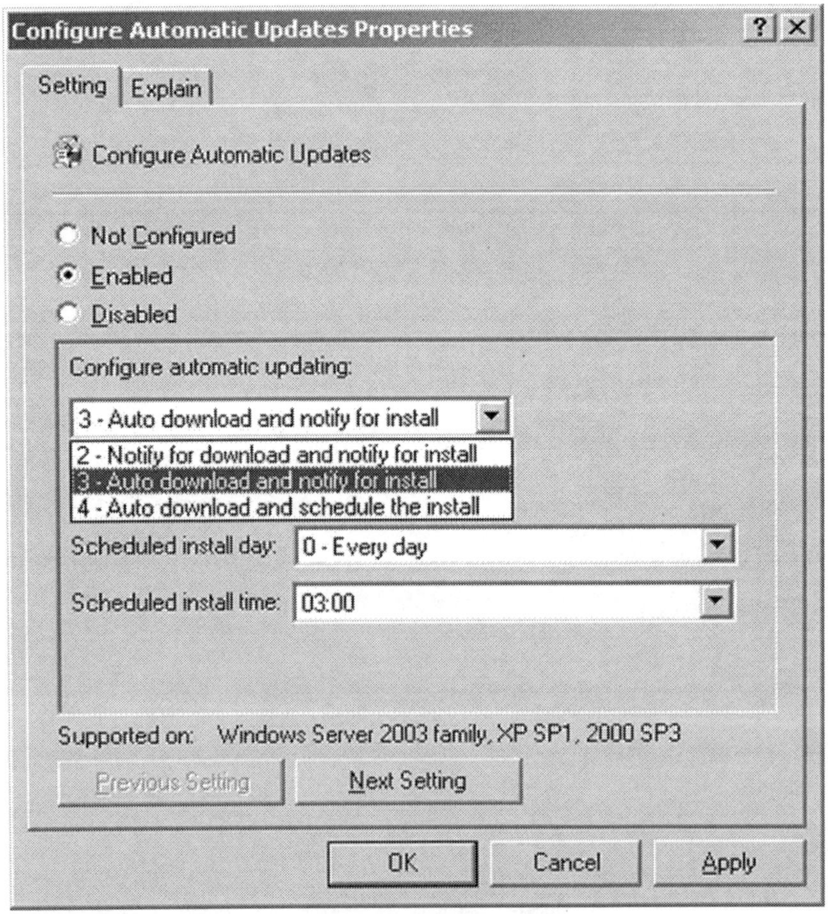

Figure 6—4: Group Policy Software Update Settings

Not only can client update be scheduled, but the server to which the client connects can also be specified in Group Policy, as shown in the next figure:

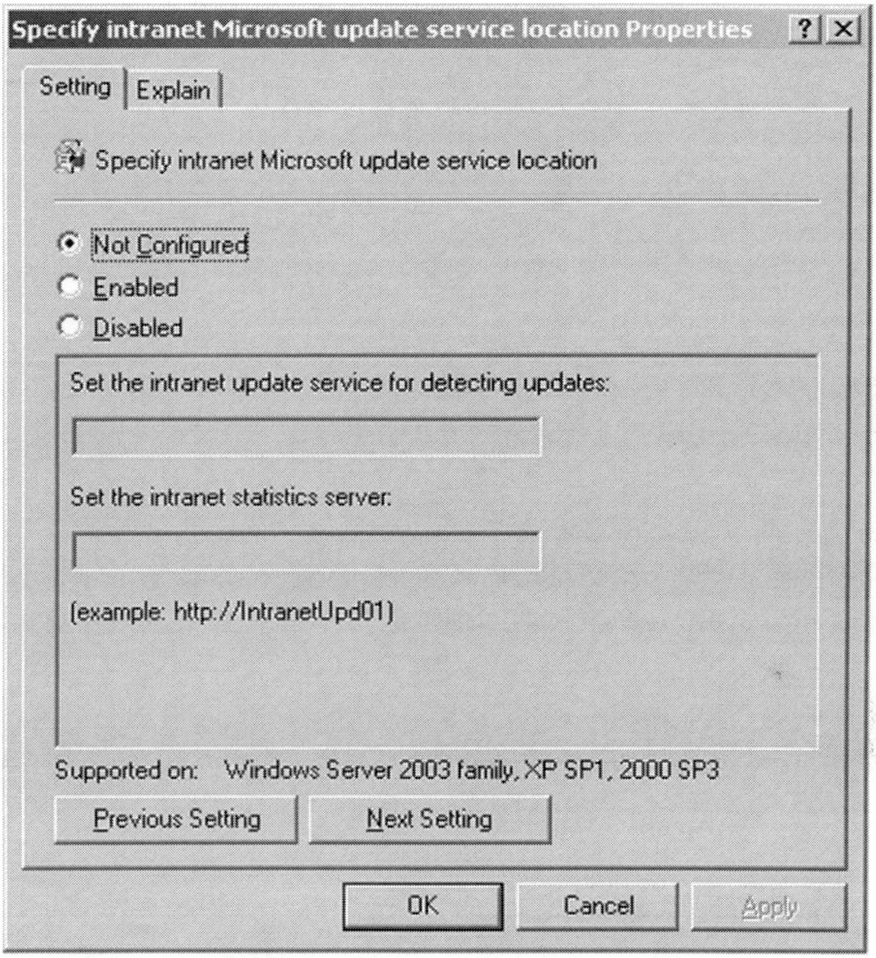

Figure 6—5: Group Policy Settings for the Update Server

Together, the MBSA and SUS can be used to assure that critical security patches and fixes are applied and in a consistent and controlled manner.

Chapter 6 Review Questions

1. Which of the following tools can help you assess whether you have the latest and greatest hot fixes and service packs applied?
   A. HFNetChk
   B. MBSA
   C. netdom
   D. Netdiag
   E. ipconfig

---

2. How can you allow external users to connect to an IIS server in your DMZ with HTTPS while administrators connect using certificate based authentication?
   A. Configure a filter to allow HTTPS connections
   B. Configure a filter to negotiate security for all traffic
   C. Install an IPSec certificate on the IIS server
   D. Configure a filter to allow FTP connections

3. Which of the following actions are necessary when you need to enable SSL encryption on your Web site and allow content inspection on all traffic passing through your Web server?
   A. Import your .pfx file to the Web server
   B. Redirect SSL traffic as HTTP requests on the Web server
   C. Export your .pfx file to the Web server
   D. Redirect SSL traffic as SSL requests on the Web server

---

4. From where do you need to obtain your Web Server certificates if clients outside of the Windows 2003 domain will access the Web server?
   A. A commercial CA (Certification Authority)
   B. A private CA (Certification Authority) in the Windows 2003 domain
   C. A stand-alone CA (Certification Authority) in the Windows 2003 domain
   D. An enterprise CA (Certification Authority) in the Windows 2003 domain

5. If you have an IIS Server in your DMZ, and it transmits data to a SQL server in your LAN, which of the following would secure the data being transmitted from the IIS server to the SQL server?

   A. On the IIS server, install a Web server certificate

   B. Configure IIS to require SSL encryption for all connections to the application

   C. Configure IIS to require SSL encryption for all connections for the Default Web site

   D. On the IIS server, remove any Web server certificates

---

6. When working with VPNs in a Windows 2003 environment, which of the following rules do you need to remember?

   A. You cannot combine NAT and PPTP

   B. You cannot combine NAT and ESP

   C. You cannot combine NAT and L2TP/IPSec

   D. You cannot combine NAT and PPP

7. Which of the following utilities will allow you to publish a certificate in Active Directory?
   A. Certutil.exe
   B. Certpub.exe
   C. Certreq.exe
   D. Certlaunch.exe

---

8. Your PKI infrastructure consists of an offline root CA (RootCA) and an offline intermediate CA (PolicyCA). You plan to install an enterprise CA subordinate to PolicyCA (IssuingCA). You submit a certificate request to the PolicyCA from the Issuing CA, but you can't start Certificate Services on the Issuing CA. How can you initiate certificate services on the Issuing CA?
   A. On PolicyCA, issue the pending certificate request
   B. On RootCA, issue the pending certificate request
   C. Install the issued certificate in the Certificate Authority console and start Certificate Services
   D. On IssuingCA, issue the pending certificate request

9. If you have a user leaving your company who has access to a Web site with an extranet, what steps should be taken to prevent the user from being able to access the Web site?

    A. Disable the user's account

    B. Revoke all certificates issued to the user

    C. Make sure to publish the CRL

    D. Give the user's account to someone else without making changes

---

10. You have a stand-alone CA that you recently upgraded to Windows 2003. You want to convert this CA to an enterprise CA that can manage existing certificates?

    A. Backup the stand-alone CA by using the Certificate Authority console and remove Certification Services

    B. Reinstall Certificate Services as an Enterprise CA by using the existing key pair and certificate saved by the backup from the Certificate Authority console

    C. Restore the CA database in the Certificate Authority console

    D. Create a new key pair and certificate

11. Which will run a command-line version of MBSA?
    A. mbsacli.exe
    B. hfnetchk.exe
    C. runas
    D. net use

---

12. The full version of Network Monitor installs a service called Monitor Control Service (mcsvc). How can you find out if the mcsvc service is installed on a computer in the domain?
    A. Edit a text file named msservices to include the mcsvc service
    B. Run MBSA
    C. Run dcpromo
    D. Run sigverif.exe
    E. Run hfnetchk.exe

13. How can you ensure that certificates will be used when a domain user authenticates to your intranet web site?

    A. Set up certificate authentication on the IIS server and use a Web server certificate on it

    B. Request user certificates for each user account

    C. Set the IIS server up to use the Windows directory service mapper and clear all authentication methods for the web site

    D. Request computer certificates for each user account

---

14. What do you need to do to recover lost e-mail messages or digitally sign messages?

    A. Export the certificate and private key into a PKCS#12 format file

    B. Export the certificate and private key into a CS#8 format file

    C. Delete the mail encryption private keys from the KMS (Key Management Services)

    D. Recover the mail encryption private keys from the KMS (Key Management Services)

15. How are Software Update Services installed?

    A. Download Software Update Services from http://www.microsoft.com/windows2000/windowsupdate/sus/default.asp.

    B. Download Software Update Services from http://www.technet.com/windows2000/windowsupdate/sus/default.asp.

    C. Double-click the SUS101SP1.exe file to begin the installation process and follow the prompts in the wizard.

    D. Double-click the SU.exe file to begin the installation process and follow the prompts in the wizard.

---

16. Which of the following actions should you take if, while you are working with Software Updates Services, you receive the 'http 500-12: Application Restarting' error when attempting to browse to the administration Web site?

    A. Press F5 to refresh your browser

    B. Reinstall Software Updates Services

    C. Reinstall your 2003 Server

    D. Press F9 to refresh your browser

Chapter 6 Review Answers

1. Which of the following tools can help you assess whether you have the latest and greatest hot fixes and service packs applied?

***A. HFNetChk**

***B. MBSA**

C. netdom

D. Netdiag

E. ipconfig

Explanation: The HFNetChk tool and the MBSA tool can help you assess whether you have the latest and greatest hot fixes and service packs applied.

---

2. How can you allow external users to connect to an IIS server in your DMZ with HTTPS while administrators connect using certificate based authentication?

***A. Configure a filter to allow HTTPS connections**

***B. Configure a filter to negotiate security for all traffic**

***C. Install an IPSec certificate on the IIS server**

D. Configure a filter to allow FTP connections

Explanation: You can allow external users to connect to an IIS server in your DMZ with HTTPS while administrators connect using certificate based authentication by configuring a filter to allow HTTPS connections and configuring a filter to negotiate security for all traffic. Install an IPSec certificate on the IIS server.

3. Which of the following actions are necessary when you need to enable SSL encryption on your Web site and allow content inspection on all traffic passing through your Web server?

***A. Import your .pfx file to the Web server**

***B. Redirect SSL traffic as HTTP requests on the Web server**

C. Export your .pfx file to the Web server

D. Redirect SSL traffic as SSL requests on the Web server

Explanation: Importing your .pfx file to the Web server and redirecting SSL traffic as HTTP requests on the Web server are necessary when you need to enable SSL encryption on your Web site and allow content inspection on all traffic passing through your Web server.

---

4. From where do you need to obtain your Web Server certificates if clients outside of the Windows 2003 domain will access the Web server?

***A. A commercial CA (Certification Authority)**

B. A private CA (Certification Authority) in the Windows 2003 domain

C. A stand-alone CA (Certification Authority) in the Windows 2003 domain

D. An enterprise CA (Certification Authority) in the Windows 2003 domain

Explanation: You need to obtain your Web Server certificates from a commercial CA (Certification Authority) if clients outside of the Windows 2003 domain will access the Web server.

5. If you have an IIS Server in your DMZ, and it transmits data to a SQL server in your LAN, which of the following would secure the data being transmitted from the IIS server to the SQL server?

***A. On the IIS server, install a Web server certificate**

***B. Configure IIS to require SSL encryption for all connections to the application**

C. Configure IIS to require SSL encryption for all connections for the Default Web site

D. On the IIS server, remove any Web server certificates

Explanation: You have an IIS Server in your DMZ, and it transmits data to a SQL server in your LAN. On the IIS server, install a Web server certificate and configure IIS to require SSL encryption for all connections to the application. These actions would secure the data being transmitted from the IIS server to the SQL server.

---

6. When working with VPNs in a Windows 2003 environment, which of the following rules do you need to remember?

A. You cannot combine NAT and PPTP

B. You cannot combine NAT and ESP

***C. You cannot combine NAT and L2TP/IPSec**

D. You cannot combine NAT and PPP

Explanation: You cannot combine NAT and L2TP/IPSec when working with VPNs in a Windows 2003 environment.

7. Which of the following utilities will allow you to publish a certificate in Active Directory?

***A. Certutil.exe**

B. Certpub.exe

C. Certreq.exe

D. Certlaunch.exe

Explanation: Certutil.exe will allow you to publish a certificate in Active Directory.

---

8. Your PKI infrastructure consists of an offline root CA (RootCA) and an offline intermediate CA (PolicyCA). You plan to install an enterprise CA subordinate to PolicyCA (IssuingCA). You submit a certificate request to the PolicyCA from the Issuing CA, but you can't start Certificate Services on the Issuing CA. How can you initiate certificate services on the Issuing CA?

***A. On PolicyCA, issue the pending certificate request**

B. On RootCA, issue the pending certificate request

***C. Install the issued certificate in the Certificate Authority console and start Certificate Services**

D. On IssuingCA, issue the pending certificate request

Explanation: Your PKI infrastructure consists of an offline root CA (RootCA) and an offline intermediate CA (PolicyCA). You plan to install an enterprise CA subordinate to PolicyCA (IssuingCA). You submit a certificate request to the PolicyCA from the Issuing CA, but you can't start Certificate Services on the Issuing CA. To initiate certificate services on the Issuing CA, issue the pending certificate request on PolicyCA. In addition, you should install the issued certificate in the Certificate Authority console and start Certificate Services.

9. If you have a user leaving your company who has access to a Web site with an extranet, what steps should be taken to prevent the user from being able to access the Web site?

***A. Disable the user's account**

***B. Revoke all certificates issued to the user**

***C. Make sure to publish the CRL**

D. Give the user's account to someone else without making changes

Explanation: If you have a user leaving your company that has access to a Web site with an extranet, prevent the user from being able to access the Web site by disabling the user's account, revoking all certificates issued to the user, and publishing the CRL so the revocation sticks.

---

10. You have a stand-alone CA that you recently upgraded to Windows 2003. You want to convert this CA to an enterprise CA that can manage existing certificates?

***A. Backup the stand-alone CA by using the Certificate Authority console and remove Certification Services**

***B. Reinstall Certificate Services as an Enterprise CA by using the existing key pair and certificate saved by the backup from the Certificate Authority console**

***C. Restore the CA database in the Certificate Authority console**

D. Create a new key pair and certificate

Explanation: You have a stand-alone CA that you recently upgraded to Windows 2003. To convert this CA to an enterprise CA that can manage existing certificates, backup the stand-alone CA by using the Certificate Authority console and remove Certification Services. Reinstall Certificate Services as an Enterprise CA by using the existing key pair and certificate saved by the backup from the Certificate Authority console. Restore the CA database in the Certificate Authority console.

11. Which will run a command-line version of MBSA?

***A. mbsacli.exe**

B. hfnetchk.exe

C. runas

D. net use

Explanation: The mbsacli executable is the command-line version of the MBSA (Microsoft Baseline Security Analyzer).

---

12. The full version of Network Monitor installs a service called Monitor Control Service (mcsvc). How can you find out if the mcsvc service is installed on a computer in the domain?

***A. Edit a text file named msservices to include the mcsvc service**

***B. Run MBSA**

C. Run dcpromo

D. Run sigverif.exe

E. Run hfnetchk.exe

Explanation: The full version of Network Monitor installs a service called Monitor Control Service (mcsvc). To find out if the mcsvc service is installed on a computer in the domain, edit a text file named msservices to include the mcsvc service and run MBSA.

13. How can you ensure that certificates will be used when a domain user authenticates to your intranet web site?

***A. Set up certificate authentication on the IIS server and use a Web server certificate on it**

***B. Request user certificates for each user account**

***C. Set the IIS server up to use the Windows directory service mapper and clear all authentication methods for the web site**

D. Request computer certificates for each user account

Explanation: To ensure certificates will be used when a domain user authenticates to your intranet web site, set up certificate authentication on the IIS server and use a Web server certificate on it. Request user certificates for each user account. Set the IIS server up to use the Windows directory service mapper and clear all authentication methods for the web site.

---

14. What do you need to do to recover lost e-mail messages or digitally sign messages?

***A. Export the certificate and private key into a PKCS#12 format file**

B. Export the certificate and private key into a CS#8 format file

C. Delete the mail encryption private keys from the KMS (Key Management Services)

***D. Recover the mail encryption private keys from the KMS (Key Management Services)**

Explanation: If you want to recover lost e-mail messages or digitally sign messages, recover the mail encryption private keys from the KMS (Key Management Services) and export the certificate and private key into a PKCS#12 format file.

15. How are Software Update Services installed?

***A. Download Software Update Services from http://www.microsoft.com/windows2000/windowsupdate/sus/default.asp.**

B. Download Software Update Services from http://www.technet.com/windows2000/windowsupdate/sus/default.asp.

***C. Double-click the SUS101SP1.exe file to begin the installation process and follow the prompts in the wizard.**

D. Double-click the SU.exe file to begin the installation process and follow the prompts in the wizard.

Explanation: If you want to set up Software Update Services on your Windows 2003 Server, download Software Update Services from http://www.microsoft.com/windows2000/windowsupdate/sus/default.asp. Double-click the SUS101SP1.exe file to begin the installation process. In the Setup Wizard, on the Welcome page, click Next. Read and accept the End User License Agreement. Select the Typical check box. Click Install, and then click Finish in the Setup Wizard to open the Software Update Services administration Web site in Internet Explorer.

---

16. Which of the following actions should you take if, while you are working with Software Updates Services, you receive the 'http 500-12: Application Restarting' error when attempting to browse to the administration Web site?

***A. Press F5 to refresh your browser**

B. Reinstall Software Updates Services

C. Reinstall your 2003 Server

D. Press F9 to refresh your browser

Explanation: When using SUS (Software Updates Services), if you try to browse to the administration Web site and you receive the 'http 500-12: Application Restarting' error, press F5 to refresh your browser.

List of Tables and Figures

I Listing of all Tables

II Listing of all Figures

Glossary

A

AC-3

The coding system used by Dolby Digital. A standard for high quality digital audio that is used for the sound portion of video stored in digital format.

Accelerated Graphics Port (AGP)

A type of expansion slot that is solely for video cards. Designed by Intel and supported by Windows 2000, AGP is a dedicated bus that provides fast, high-quality video and graphics performance.

Access control entry (ACE)

An entry in an access control list (ACL) containing the security ID (SID) for a user or group and an access mask that specifies which operations by the user or group are allowed, denied, or audited.

See also *access control list*; *access mask*; *security descriptor*.

Access control list (ACL)

A list of security protections that apply to an entire object, a set of the object's properties, or an individual property of an object. There are two types of access control lists: discretionary and system.

See also *access control entry*; *discretionary access control list*; *security descriptor*; *system access control list*.

Access mask

A 32-bit value that specifies the rights that are allowed or denied in an access control entry (ACE) of an access control list (ACL). An access mask is also used to request access rights when an object is opened.

See also *access control entry*.

Access token

A data structure containing security information that identifies a user to the security subsystem on a computer running Windows 2000 or Windows NT. An access token contains a user's security ID, the security IDs for groups that the user belongs to, and a list of the user's privileges on the local computer.

See also *privilege*; *security ID*.

Accessibility

The quality of a system incorporating hardware or software to engage a flexible, customizable user interface, alternative input and output methods, and greater exposure of screen elements to make the computer usable by people with cognitive, hearing, physical, or visual disabilities.

Accessibility status indicators

Icons on the system status area of the taskbar of the Windows desktop that let the user know which accessibility features are activated.

Accessibility Wizard

An interactive tool that makes it easier to set up commonly used accessibility features by specifying options by type of disability, rather than by numeric value changes.

ACPI

See *Advanced Configuration and Power Interface.*

Active Accessibility

A core component in the Windows operating system that is built on COM and defines how applications can exchange information about user interface elements.

Active Directory

The directory service included with Windows 2000 Server. It stores information about objects on a network and makes this information available to users and network administrators. Active Directory gives network users access to permitted resources anywhere on the network using a single logon process. It provides network administrators with an intuitive hierarchical view of the network and a single point of administration for all network objects.

See also *directory*; *directory service.*

ActiveX

A set of technologies that enable software components to interact with one another in a networked environment, regardless of the language in which the components were created.

Administrator

See *system administrator.*

Advanced Configuration and Power Interface (ACPI)

An open industry specification that defines power management on a wide range of mobile, desktop, and server computers and peripherals. ACPI is the foundation for the OnNow industry initiative that allows system manufacturers to deliver computers that will start at the touch of a keyboard. ACPI design is essential to take full advantage of power management and Plug and Play in Windows 2000. Check the manufacturer's documentation to verify that a computer is ACPI-compliant.

See also *Plug and Play*.

Advanced Power Management (APM)

A software interface (designed by Microsoft and Intel) between hardware-specific power management software (such as that located in a system BIOS) and an operating system power management driver.

Advertisement

In Windows 2000, the Software Installation snap-in generates an application advertisement script and stores this script in the appropriate locations in Active Directory and the Group Policy object.

Allocation unit

In file systems an allocation unit is the smallest amount of disk space that can be allocated to hold a file. All file systems used by Windows 2000 organize hard disks based on allocation units. The smaller the allocation unit size, the more efficiently a disk stores information. If no allocation unit size is specified during formatting, Windows 2000 chooses default sizes based on the size of the volume and the file system used. These defaults are selected to reduce the amount of space lost and the amount of fragmentation on the volume. Also called cluster.

American Standard Code for Information Interchange (ASCII)

A standard single byte character-encoding scheme used for text-based data. ASCII uses designated 7-bit or 8-bit number combinations to represent either 128 or 256 possible characters. Standard ASCII uses 7 bits to represent all uppercase and lowercase letters, the numbers 0 through 9, punctuation marks, and special control characters used in U.S. English. Most current x86 systems support the use of extended (or "high") ASCII. Extended ASCII allows the eighth bit of each character to identify an additional 128 special symbol characters, foreign-language letters, and graphic symbols.

See also *Unicode*.

Answer file

A text file that you can use to provide automated input for unattended installation of Windows 2000. This input includes parameters to answer the questions required by Setup for specific installations. In some cases, you can use this text file to provide input to wizards, such as the Active Directory Installation wizard, which is used to add Active Directory to Windows 2000 Server through Setup. The default answer file for Setup is known as Unattend.txt.

API

See *application programming interface.*

APM

See *Advanced Power Management.*

Application media pool

A data repository that determines which media can be accessed by which applications and that sets the policies for that media. There can be any number of application media pools in a Removable Storage system. Applications create application media pools.

Application programming interface (API)

A set of routines that an application uses to request and carry out lower-level services performed by a computer's operating system. These routines usually carry out maintenance tasks such as managing files and displaying information.

Assistive technology

System extensions, programs, devices, and utilities added to a computer to make it more accessible to users with disabilities.

Asynchronous communication

A form of data transmission in which information is sent and received at irregular intervals, one character at a time. Because data is received at irregular intervals, the receiving modem must be signaled to inform it when the data bits of a character begin and end. This is done by means of start and stop bits.

Asynchronous Transfer Mode (ATM)

A high-speed connection-oriented protocol used to transport many different types of network traffic.

ATM

See *Asynchronous Transfer Mode*.

Attribute (object)

In Active Directory, an attribute describes characteristics of an object and the type of information an object can hold. For each object class, the schema defines what attributes an instance of the class must have and what additional attributes it might have.

Auditing

To track the activities of users by recording selected types of events in the security log of a server or a workstation.

Authentication

A basic security function of cryptography. Authentication verifies the identity of the entities that communicate over the network. For example, the process that verifies the identity of a user who logs on to a computer either locally, at a computer's keyboard, or remotely, through a network connection.

See also *cryptography*; *confidentiality*; *integrity*; *Kerberos authentication protocol*; *nonrepudiation*; *NTLM authentication protocol*.

Authentication Header (AH)

A header that provides integrity, authentication, and anti-replay for the entire packet (both the IP header and the data payload carried in the packet).

Authoritative

In the Domain Name System (DNS), the use of zones by DNS servers to register and resolve a DNS domain name. When a DNS server is configured to host a zone, it is authoritative for names within that zone. DNS servers are granted authority based on information stored in the zone.

See also *zone*.

Automated installation

An unattended setup using one or more of several methods such as Remote Installation Services, bootable CD, and SysPrep.

Automatic caching

A method of automatically storing network files on a user's hard disk drive whenever a file is open so the files can be accessed when the user is not connected to the network.

Automatic Private IP Addressing (APIPA)

A feature of Windows 2000 TCP/IP that automatically configures a unique IP address from the range 169.254.0.1 to 169.254.255.254 and a subnet mask of 255.255.0.0 when the TCP/IP protocol is configured for dynamic addressing and a Dynamic Host Configuration Protocol (DHCP) Server is not available.

Available state

A state in which media can be allocated for use by applications.

Averaging counter

A type of counter that measures a value over time and displays the average of the last two measurements over some other factor (for example, PhysicalDisk\Avg. Disk Bytes/Transfer).

B

Backup

A duplicate copy of a program, a disk, or data, made either for archiving purposes or for safeguarding valuable files from loss should the active copy be damaged or destroyed. Some application programs automatically make backup copies of data files, maintaining both the current version and the preceding version.

Backup operator

A type of local or global group that contains the user rights needed to back up and restore files and folders. Members of the Backup Operators group can back up and restore files and folders regardless of ownership, access permissions, encryption, or auditing settings.

See also *auditing*; *global group*; *local group*; *user rights.*

Backup types

A type that determines which data is backed up and how it is backed up. There are five backup types: copy, daily, differential, incremental, and normal.

See also *copy backup*; *daily backup*; *differential backup*; *incremental backup*; *normal backup*.

Bad block

A disk sector that can no longer be used for data storage, usually due to media damage or imperfections.

Bandwidth

In analog communications, the difference between the highest and lowest frequencies in a given range. For example, a telephone line accommodates a bandwidth of 3,000 Hz, the difference between the lowest (300 Hz) and highest (3,300 Hz) frequencies it can carry. In digital communications, the rate at which information is sent expressed in bits per second (bps).

Barcode

A machine-readable label that identifies an object, such as physical media.

Base file record

The first file record in the master file table (MFT) for a file that has multiple file records. The base file record is the record to which the file's file reference corresponds.

Baseline

A range of measurements derived from performance monitoring that represents acceptable performance under typical operating conditions.

Basic disk

A physical disk that contains primary partitions or extended partitions with logical drives used by Windows 2000 and all versions of Windows NT. Basic disks can also contain volume, striped, mirror, or RAID-5 sets that were created using Windows NT 4.0 or earlier. As long as a compatible file format is used, MS-DOS, Windows 95, Windows 98, and all versions of Windows NT can access basic disks.

Basic input/output system (BIOS)

The set of essential software routines that tests hardware at startup, assists with starting the operating system, and supports the transfer of data among hardware devices. The BIOS is stored in read-only memory (ROM) so that it can be executed when the computer is turned on. Although critical to performance, the BIOS is usually invisible to computer users.

Basic volume

A volume on a basic disk. Basic volumes include primary partitions, logical drives within extended partitions, as well as volume, striped, mirror, or RAID-5 sets that were created using Windows NT 4.0 or earlier. Only basic disks can contain basic volumes. Basic and dynamic volumes cannot exist on the same disk.

Batch program

An ASCII (unformatted text) file containing one or more Windows NT or Windows 2000 commands. A batch program's filename has a .BAT extension. When you type the filename at the command prompt, the commands are processed sequentially. "Script" is often used interchangeably with "batch program" in the Windows NT and Windows 2000 environment.

Bi-directional communication

Communication that occurs in two directions simultaneously. Bi-directional communication is useful in printing where jobs can be sent and printer status can be returned at the same time.

Binding

A process by which software components and layers are linked together. When a network component is installed, the binding relationships and dependencies for the components are established. Binding allows components to communicate with each other.

Binding order

The sequence in which software components, network protocols and network adapters are linked together. When a network component is installed, the binding relationships and dependencies for the components are established.

BIOS

See *basic input/output system.*

BIOS parameter block (BPB)

A series of fields containing data on disk size, geometry variables, and the physical parameters of the volume. The BPB is located within the boot sector.

Boot sector

A critical disk structure for starting your computer, located at sector 1 of each volume or floppy disk. It contains executable code and data that is required by the code, including information used by the file system to access the volume. The boot sector is created when you format the volume.

Bootable CD

An automated installation method that runs Setup from a CD-ROM. This method is useful for computers at remote sites with slow links and no local IT department.

See also *automated installation.*

Bottleneck

A condition, usually involving a hardware resource, which causes the entire system to perform poorly.

BounceKeys

A keyboard filter that assists users whose fingers bounce on the keys when pressing or releasing them.

Bound trap

In programming, a problem in which a set of conditions exceeds a permitted range of values that causes the microprocessor to stop what it is doing and handle the situation in a separate routine.

Browsing

The process of creating and maintaining an up-to-date list of computers and resources on a network or part of a network by one or more designated computers running the Computer Browser service.

See also *Computer Browser service.*

Bulk encryption

A process in which large amounts of data, such as files, e-mail messages, or online communications sessions, are encrypted for confidentiality. It is usually done with a symmetric key algorithm.

See also *encryption*; *symmetric key encryption.*

C

Cable modem

A modem that provides broadband Internet access in the range of 10 to 30 Mbps.

Cache

For DNS and WINS, a local information store of resource records for recently resolved names of remote hosts. Typically, the cache is built dynamically as the computer queries and resolves names; it helps optimize the time required to resolve queried names.

See also *cache file*; *naming service*; *resource record.*

Cache file

A file used by the Domain Name System (DNS) server to preload its names cache when service is started. Also known as the "root hints" file because resource records stored in this file are used by the DNS service to help locate root servers that provide referral to authoritative servers for remote names. For Windows DNS servers, the cache file is named Cache.dns and is located in the %SystemRoot%\System32\Dns folder.

See also *authoritative*; *cache*; *systemroot.*

Caching

The process of storing recently-used data values in a special pool in memory where they are temporarily held for quicker subsequent accesses. For DNS, the ability of DNS servers to store information about the domain namespace learned during the processing and resolution of name queries. In Windows 2000, caching is also available through the DNS client service (resolve) as a way for DNS clients to keep a cache of name information learned during recent queries.

Caching resolve

For Windows 2000, a client-side Domain Name System (DNS) name resolution service that performs caching of recently learned DNS domain name information. The caching resolve service provides system-wide access to DNS-aware programs for resource records obtained from DNS servers during the processing of name queries. Data placed in the cache is used for a limited period of time and aged according to the active Time To Live (TTL) value. You can set the TTL either individually for each resource record (RR) or default to the minimum TTL set in the start of authority RR for the zone.

See also *cache*; *caching*; *expire interval*; *minimum TTL*; *resolve*; *resource record*; *Time To Live (TTL).*

Callback number

The number that a RAS server uses to call back a user. This number can be preset by the administrator or specified by the user at the time of each call, depending on how the administrator configures the user's callback status. The callback number should be the number of the phone line to which the user's modem is connected.

Card Bus

A 32-bit PC Card.

Cartridge

A unit of media of a certain type, such as 8mm tape, magnetic disk, optical disk, or CD-ROM, used by Removable Storage.

Central Processing Unit (CPU)

The part of a computer that has the ability to retrieve, interpret, and execute instructions and to transfer information to and from other resources over the computer's main data-transfer path, the bus. By definition, the CPU is the chip that functions as the "brain" of a computer.

Certificate

A digital document that is commonly used for authentication and secure exchange of information on open networks, such as the Internet, extranets, and intranets. A certificate securely binds a public key to the entity that holds the corresponding private key. Certificates are digitally signed by the issuing certification authority and can be issued for a user, a computer, or a service. The most widely accepted format for certificates is defined by the ITU-T X.509 version 3 international standard.

See also *certification authority*; *private key*; *public key*.

Certificate Services

The Windows 2000 service that issues certificates for a particular CA. It provides customizable services for issuing and managing certificates for the enterprise.

See also *certificate*; *certification authority*.

Certification authority (CA)

An entity responsible for establishing and vouching for the authenticity of public keys belonging to users (end entities) or other certification authorities. Activities of a certification authority can include binding public keys to distinguished names through signed certificates, managing certificate serial numbers, and certificate revocation.

See also *certificate*; *public key*.

Certified-for-Windows Logo

A specification that addresses the requirements of computer users with disabilities to ensure quality and consistency in assertive devices.

Challenge Handshake Authentication Protocol (CHAP)

A challenge-response authentication protocol for PPP connections documented in RFC 1994 that uses the industry-standard Message Digest 5 (MD5) one-way encryption scheme to hash the response to a challenge issued by the remote access server.

Change journal

A feature new to Windows 2000 that tracks changes to NTFS volumes, including additions, deletions, and modifications. The change journal exists on the volume as a sparse file.

Changer

The robotic element of an online library unit.

CHAP

See *Challenge Handshake Authentication Protocol.*

Child object

An object that is the immediate subordinate of another object in a hierarchy. A child object can have only one immediate superior, or parent, object. In Active Directory, the schema determines what classes of objects can be child objects of what other classes of objects. Depending on its class, a child object can also be the parent of other objects.

See also *object*; *parent object.*

CIM (COM Information Model) Object Manager (CIMOM)

A system service that handles interaction between network management applications and providers of local or remote data or system events.

Cipher text

Text that has been encrypted using an encryption key. Cipher text is meaningless to anyone who does not have the decryption key.

See also *decryption*; *encryption*; *encryption key*; *plaintext.*

Client

Any computer or program connecting to, or requesting services of, another computer or program.

See also *server.*

Cluster

A group of independent computer systems known as nodes or hosts, that work together as a single system to ensure that mission-critical applications and resources remain available to clients. A server cluster is the type of cluster that the Cluster service implements. Network Load Balancing provides a software solution for clustering multiple computers running Windows 2000 Server that provides networked services over the Internet and private intranets.

In file systems a cluster is the smallest amount of disk space that can be allocated to hold a file. All file systems used by Windows 2000 organize hard disks based on clusters. The smaller the cluster size, the more efficiently a disk stores information. If no cluster size is specified during formatting, Windows 2000 chooses default sizes based on the size of the volume and the file system used. These defaults are selected to reduce the amount of space lost and the amount of fragmentation on the volume. Also called allocation units.

Cluster recapping

A recovery technique used when Windows 2000 returns a bad sector error to NTFS. NTFS dynamically replaces the cluster containing the bad sector and allocates a new cluster for the data. If the error occurs during a read, NTFS returns a read error to the calling program, and the data is lost. If the error occurs during a write, NTFS writes the data to the new cluster, and no data is lost.

Code page

A page that maps character codes to individual characters. Different code pages include different special characters, typically customized for a language or a group of languages. The system uses code pages to translate keyboard input into character values for non-Unicode based applications, and to translate character values into characters for non-Unicode based output displays.

COM

See *Component Object Model.*

COM port

Short for communications port, the logical address assigned by MS-DOS (versions 3.3 and higher) and Microsoft Windows (including Windows 95, Windows 98, Windows NT and Windows 2000) to each of the four serial ports on an IBM Personal Computer or a PC compatible. COM ports are also known as the actual serial ports on a PC where peripherals, such as printers, scanners, and external modems, are plugged in.

Commit a transaction

To record in the log file the fact that a transaction is complete and has been recorded in the cache.

Common Internet File System (CIFS)

A protocol and a corresponding API used by application programs to request higher level application services. CIFS was formerly known as SMB (Server Message Block).

Compact Disc File System (CDFS)

A 32-bit protected-mode file system that controls access to the contents of CD-ROM drives in Windows 2000.

Compact disc-record able (CD-R)

A type of CD-ROM that can be written once on a CD recorder and read on a CD-ROM drive.

Compact disc-rewritable (CD-RW)

A type of CD-ROM that can be written many times on a CD recorder and read on a CD-ROM drive.

Complementary metal-oxide semiconductor (CMOS)

The battery-packed memory that stores information, such as disk types and amount of memory, used to start the computer.

Component Object Model (COM)

An object-based programming model designed to promote software interoperability; it allows two or more applications or components to easily cooperate with one another, even if they were written by different vendors, at different times, in different programming languages, or if they are running on different computers running different operating systems. COM is the foundation technology upon which broader technologies can be built. Object linking and embedding (OLE) technology and ActiveX are both built on top of COM.

Computer Browser service

A service that maintains an up-to-date list of computers and provides the list to applications when requested. The Computer Browser service provides the computer lists displayed in the My Network Places, Select Computer, and Select Domain dialog boxes and (for Windows 2000 Server only) in the Server Manager window.

Confidentiality

A basic security function of cryptography. Confidentiality provides assurance that only authorized users can read or use confidential or secret information. Without confidentiality, anyone with network access can use readily available tools to eavesdrop on network traffic and intercept valuable proprietary information. For example, an Internet Protocol security service that ensures a message is disclosed only to intended recipients by encrypting the data.

See also *cryptography*; *authentication*; *integrity*; *nonrepudiation*.

Console tree

The tree view pane in a Microsoft Management Console (MMC) that displays the hierarchical namespace. By default it is the left pane of the console window, but it can be hidden. The items in the console tree (for example, Web pages, folders, and controls) and their hierarchical organization determine the management capabilities of a console.

See also *Microsoft Management Console (MMC)*; *namespace*.

Container object

An object that can logically contain other objects. For example, a folder is a container object.

See also *no container object*; *object*.

Copy backup

A backup that copies all selected files but does not mark each file as having been backed up (that is, the archive bit is not set). A copy backup is useful between normal and incremental backups because copying does not affect these other backup operations.

See also *daily backup*; *differential backup*; *incremental backup*; *normal backup*.

CPU

See *Central Processing Unit*.

Cryptography

The art and science of information security. It provides four basic information security functions: confidentiality, integrity, authentication, and no repudiation.

See also *confidentiality*; *integrity*; *authentication*; *no repudiation*.

D

Daily backup

A backup that copies all selected files that have been modified the day the daily backup is performed. The backed-up files are not marked as having been backed up (that is, the archive bit is not set).

See also *copy backup*; *differential backup*; *incremental backup*; *normal backup*.

Data confidentiality

A service provided by cryptographic technology to assure that data can be read only by authorized users or programs. In a network, data confidentiality ensures that intruders cannot read data. Windows 2000 uses access control mechanisms and encryption, such as DES, 3DES and RSA encryption algorithms, to ensure data confidentiality.

Data Encryption Standard (DES)

An encryption algorithm that uses a 56-bit key, and maps a 64-bit input block to a 64-bit output block. The key appears to be a 64-bit key, but one bit in each of the 8 bytes is used for odd parity, resulting in 56 bits of usable key.

Data integrity

A service provided by cryptographic technology that ensures data has not been modified. In a network environment, data integrity allows the receiver of a message to verify that data has not been modified in transit. Windows 2000 uses access control mechanisms and cryptography, such as RSA public-key signing and shared symmetric key one way hash algorithms, to ensure data integrity.

Data Link Control (DLC)

A protocol used primarily for IBM mainframe computers and printer connectivity.

Data packet

A unit of information transmitted as a whole from one device to another on a network.

Deallocate

To return media to the available state after they have been used by an application.

Decommissioned state

A state that indicates that media have reached their allocation maximum.

Decryption

The process of making encrypted data readable again by converting ciphertext to plaintext.

See also *ciphertext*; *encryption*; *plaintext*.

Default gateway

A configuration item for the TCP/IP protocol that is the IP address of a directly reachable IP router. Configuring a default gateway creates a default route in the IP routing table.

Defragmentation

The process of rewriting parts of a file to contiguous sectors on a hard disk to increase the speed of access and retrieval. When files are updated, the computer tends to save these updates on the largest continuous space on the hard disk, which is often on a different sector than the other parts of the file. When files are thus fragmented, the computer must search the hard disk each time the file is opened to find all of the parts of the file, which slows down response time. In Active Directory, defragmentation rearranges how the data is written in the directory database file to compact it.

See also *fragmentation*.

Desktop

The on-screen work area in which windows, icons, menus, and dialog boxes appear.

Destination directory

The directory (or folder) to which files are copied or moved.

See also *source directory*.

Device driver

A program that allows a specific device, such as a modem, network adapter, or printer, to communicate with Windows 2000. Although a device can be installed on a system, Windows 2000 cannot use the device until the appropriate driver has been installed and configured. If a device is listed in the Hardware Compatibility List (HCL), a driver is usually included with Windows 2000. Device drivers load (for all enabled devices) when a computer is started, and thereafter run invisibly.

See also *Hardware Compatibility List (HCL)*.

Device Manager

An administrative tool that can be used to manage the devices on your computer. Use Device Manager to view and change device properties, update device drivers, configure device settings, and remove devices.

Device Tree

A hierarchical tree that contains the devices configured on the computer.

Differential backup

A backup that copies files created or changed since the last normal or incremental backup. It does not mark files as having been backed up (that is, the archive bit is not set). If you are performing a combination of normal and differential backups, restoring files and folders requires that you have the last normal as well as the last differential backup.

See also *copy backup*; *daily backup*; *incremental backup*; *normal backup*.

Digital audio tape (DAT)

A magnetic medium for recording and storing digital audio data.

Digital certificate

See *certificate*.

Digital linear tape (DLT)

A magnetic medium for backing up data. DLT can transfer data faster than many other types of tape media.

Digital signature

A means for originators of a message, file, or other digitally encoded information to bind their identity to the information. The process of digitally signing information entails transforming the information, as well as some secret information held by the sender, into a tag called a signature. Digital signatures are used in public key environments and they provide no repudiation and integrity services.

See also *public key cryptography*.

Digital subscriber line (DSL)

A special communication line that uses modulation technology to maximize the amount of data that can be sent over copper wires. DSL is used for connections from telephone switching stations to a subscriber rather than between switching stations.

Direct hosting

A feature that allows Windows 2000 computers using Microsoft file and print sharing to communicate over a communications protocol, such as TCP or IPX, bypassing the NetBIOS layer.

Direct memory access (DMA)

Memory access that does not involve the microprocessor. DMA is frequently used for data transfer directly between memory and a peripheral device, such as a disk drive.

Directory

An information source that contains information about computer files or other objects. In a file system, a directory stores information about files. In a distributed computing environment (such as a Windows 2000 domain), the directory stores information about objects such as printers, applications, databases, and users.

Directory service

Both the directory information source and the service that make the information available and usable. A directory service enables the user to find an object given any one of its attributes.

See also *Active Directory*; *directory*.

Disable

To make a device nonfunctional. For example, if a device in a hardware profile is disabled, the device cannot be used while using that hardware profile. Disabling a device frees the resources that were allocated to the device.

Discretionary access control list (DACL)

The part of an object's security descriptor that grants or denies specific users and groups permission to access the object. Only the owner of an object can change permissions granted or denied in a DACL; thus access to the object is at the owner's discretion.

See also *access control entry*; *object*; *security descriptor*; *system access control list*.

Disk bottleneck

A condition that occurs when disk performance is reduced to the extent that overall system performance is affected.

Disk quota

The maximum amount of disk space available to a user.

Dismount

To remove a removable tape or disc from a drive.

See also *library*.

Distinguished name

A name that uniquely identifies an object by using the relative distinguished name for the object, plus the names of container objects and domains that contain the object. The distinguished name identifies the object as well as its location in a tree. Every object in Active Directory has a distinguished name. An example of a distinguished name is CN=MyName,CN=Users,DC=Reskit,DC=Com. This distinguished name identifies the "MyName" user object in the reskit.com domain.

Distributed file system (DFS)

A Windows 2000 service consisting of software residing on network servers and clients that transparently links shared folders located on different file servers into a single namespace for improved load sharing and data availability.

Distribution folder

The folder created on the Windows 2000 distribution server to contain the Setup files.

DMA

See *direct memory access*.

DNS

See *Domain Name System*.

DNS server

A computer that runs DNS server programs containing name-to-IP address mappings, IP address-to-name mappings, information about the domain tree structure, and other information. DNS servers also attempt to resolve client queries.

DNS zone

In a DNS database, a zone is a contiguous portion of the DNS tree that is administered as a single separate entity, by a DNS server. The zone contains resource records for all the names within the zone.

Domain

In Windows 2000 and Active Directory, a collection of computers defined by the administrator of a Windows 2000 Server network that share a common directory database. A domain has a unique name and provides access to the centralized user accounts and group accounts maintained by the domain administrator. Each domain has its own security policies and security relationships with other domains and represents a single security boundary of a Windows 2000 computer network. Active Directory is made up of one or more domains, each of which can span more than one physical location. For DNS, a domain is any tree or sub tree within the DNS namespace. Although the names for DNS domains often correspond to Active Directory domains, DNS domains should not be confused with Windows 2000 and Active Directory networking domain.

Domain controller

For a Windows NT Server or Windows 2000 Server domain, the server that authenticates domain logons and maintains the security policy and the security accounts master database for a domain. Domain controllers manage user access to a network, which includes logging on, authentication, and access to the directory and shared resources.

Domain local group

A Windows 2000 group only available in native mode domains that can contain members from anywhere in the forest, in trusted forests, or in a trusted pre-Windows 2000 domain. Domain local groups can only grant permissions to resources within the domain in which they exist. Typically, domain local groups are used to gather security principals from across the forest to control access to resources within the domain.

Domain name

In Windows 2000 and Active Directory, the name given by an administrator to a collection of networked computers that share a common directory. For DNS, domain names are specific node names in the DNS namespace tree. DNS domain names use singular node names, known as "labels," joined together by periods (.) that indicate each node level in the namespace.

See also *Domain Name System (DNS)*; *namespace*.

Domain Name System (DNS)

A hierarchical naming system used for locating domain names on the Internet and on private TCP/IP networks. DNS provides a service for mapping DNS domain names to IP addresses, and vice versa. This allows users, computers, and applications to query the DNS to specify remote systems by fully qualified domain names rather than by IP addresses.

See also *domain*; *Ping*.

Domain tree

In DNS, the inverted hierarchical tree structure that is used to index domain names. Domain trees are similar in purpose and concept to the directory trees used by computer filing systems for disk storage.

See also *domain name*; *namespace*.

DOT4

See *IEEE 1284.4*

Dual boot

A computer configuration that can start two different operating systems.

See also *multiple boot*.

DVD decoder

A hardware or software component that allows a digital video disc (DVD) drive to display movies on your computer screen.

See also *DVD disc*; *DVD drive*.

DVD disc

A type of optical disc storage technology. A digital video disc (DVD) looks like a CD-ROM disc, but it can store greater amounts of data. DVD discs are often used to store full-length movies and other multimedia content that requires large amounts of storage space.

See also *DVD decoder*; *DVD drive*.

DVD drive

A disk storage device that uses digital video disc (DVD) technology. A DVD drive reads both CD-ROM and DVD discs; however, a DVD decoder is necessary to display DVD movies on your computer screen.

See also *DVD decoder*; *DVD disc*.

Dvorak keyboard

An alternative keyboard with a layout that makes the most frequently typed characters more accessible to people who have difficulty typing on the standard QWERTY layout.

Dynamic disk

A physical disk that is managed by Disk Management. Dynamic disks can contain only dynamic volumes (that is, volumes created by using Disk Management). Dynamic disks cannot contain partitions or logical drives, nor can MS-DOS access them.

See also *dynamic volume*; *partition*.

Dynamic Host Configuration Protocol (DHCP)

A networking protocol that provides safe, reliable, and simple TCP/IP network configuration and offers dynamic configuration of Internet Protocol (IP) addresses for computers. DHCP ensures that address conflicts do not occur and helps conserve the use of IP addresses through centralized management of address allocation.

Dynamic priority

The priority value to which a thread's base priority is adjusted to optimize scheduling.

Dynamic volume

A logical volume that is created using Disk Management. Dynamic volumes include simple, spanned, striped, mirrored, and RAID-5 volumes. Dynamic volumes must be created on dynamic disks.

See also *dynamic disk*; *volume*.

Dynamic-link library (DLL)

A feature of the Microsoft Windows family of operating systems and the OS/2 operating system. DLLs allow executable routines, generally serving a specific function or set of functions, to be stored separately as files with .dll extensions, and to be loaded only when needed by the program that calls them.

E

EAP

See *Extensible Authentication Protocol*

EIDE

See *Enhanced Integrated Drive Electronics*

Embedded object

Information created in another application that has been pasted inside a document. When information is embedded, you can edit it in the new document by using toolbars and menus from the original program. When you double-click the embedded icon, the toolbars and menus from the program used to create the information appear. Embedded information is not linked to the original file. If you change information in one place, it is not updated in the other.

See also *linked object.*

Emergency repair disk (ERD)

A disk, created by the Backup utility, that contains copies of three of the files stored in the %SystemRoot%/Repair folder, including Setup. log that contains a list of system files installed on the computer. This disk can be used during the Emergency Repair Process to repair your computer if it will not start or if your system files are damaged or erased.

Encapsulating security payload (ESP)

An IPSec protocol that provides confidentiality, in addition to authentication, integrity, and anti-replay. ESP can be used alone, in combination with AH, or nested with the Layer Two Tunneling Protocol (L2TP). ESP does not normally sign the entire packet unless it is being tunneled. Ordinarily, just the data payload is protected, not the IP header.

Encrypting File System (EFS)

A new feature in Windows 2000 that protects sensitive data in files that is stored on disk using the NTFS file system. It uses symmetric key encryption in conjunction with public key technology to provide confidentiality for files. It runs as an integrated system service, which makes EFS easy to manage, difficult to attack, and transparent to the file owner and to applications.

Encryption

The process of disguising a message or data in such a way as to hide its substance.

Encryption key

A bit string that is used in conjunction with an encryption algorithm to encrypt and decrypt data.

See also *public key*; *private key*; *symmetric key.*

Enhanced Integrated Drive Electronics (EIDE)

An extension of the IDE standard, EIDE is a hardware interface standard for disk drive designs that houses control circuits in the drives themselves. It allows for standardized interfaces to the system bus, while providing for advanced features, such as burst data transfers and direct data access.

Enterprise Resource Planning (ERP)

A software system designed to support and automate the processes of an organization, including manufacturing and distribution, accounting, project management and personnel functions.

Environment variable

A string consisting of environment information, such as a drive, path, or filename, associated with a symbolic name that can be used by Windows NT and Windows 2000. Use the System option in Control Panel or the set command from the command prompt to define environment variables.

ERD

See *emergency repair disk.*

Ethernet

An IEEE 802.3 standard for contention networks. Ethernet uses a bus or star topology and relies on the form of access known as Carrier Sense Multiple Access with Collision Detection (CSMA/DC) to regulate communication line traffic. Network nodes are linked by coaxial cable, fiber-optic cable, or by twisted-pair wiring. Data is transmitted in variable-length frames containing delivery and control information and up to 1,500 bytes of data. The Ethernet standard provides for base band transmission at 10 megabits (10 million bits) per second.

Exabytes

Approximately one quintillion bytes, or one billion billion bytes.

Expire interval

For DNS, the number of seconds that DNS servers operating as secondary masters for a zone use to determine if zone data should be expired when the zone is not refreshed and renewed.

See also *zone*.

Explicit trust relationship

A trust relationship from Windows NT in which an explicit link is made in one direction only. Explicit trusts can also exist between Windows NT domains and Windows 2000 domains, and between forests.

Export

In NFS, to make a file system available by a server to a client for mounting.

Extended Industry Standard Architecture (EISA)

A 32-bit bus standard introduced in 1988 by a consortium of nine computer-industry companies. EISA maintains compatibility with the earlier Industry Standard Architecture (ISA) but provides for additional features.

Extended partition

A portion of a basic disk that can contain logical drives. To have more than four volumes on your basic disk, you need to use an extended partition. Only one of the four partitions allowed per physical disk can be an extended partition, and no primary partition needs to be present to create an extended partition. You can create extended partitions only on basic disks.

See also *basic disk*; *logical drive*; *partition*; *primary partition*; *unallocated space*.

Extensible Authentication Protocol (EAP)

An extension to PPP that allows for arbitrary authentication mechanisms to be employed for the validation of a PPP connection.

Extensible Markup Language (XML)

A meta-markup language that provides a format for describing structured data. This facilitates more precise declarations of content and more meaningful search results across multiple platforms. In addition, XML will enable a new generation of Web-based data viewing and manipulation applications.

F

FAT32

A derivative of the file allocation table file system. FAT32 supports smaller cluster sizes than FAT in the same given disk space, which results in more efficient space allocation on FAT32 drives.

See also *file allocation table*; *NTFS file system.*

Fault tolerance

The assurance of data integrity when hardware failures occur. On the Windows NT and Windows 2000 platforms, fault tolerance is provided by the Ftdisk.sys driver.

Fiber Distributed Data Interface (FDDI)

A type of network media designed to be used with fiber-optic cabling.

See also LocalTalk; Token Ring.

File allocation table (FAT)

A file system based on a file allocation table (FAT) maintained by some operating systems, including Windows NT and Windows 2000, to keep track of the status of various segments of disk space used for file storage.

File record

The row in the master file table (MFT) that corresponds to a particular disk file. The file record is identified by its file reference.

File system

In an operating system, the overall structure in which files are named, stored, and organized. NTFS, FAT, and FAT32 are types of file systems.

File system cache

An area of physical memory that holds frequently used pages. It allows applications and services to locate pages rapidly and reduces disk activity.

File Transfer Protocol (FTP)

A protocol that defines how to transfer files from one computer to another over the Internet. FTP is also a client/server application that moves files using this protocol.

Filter

In IPSec, a rule that provides the ability to trigger security negotiations for a communication based on the source, destination, and type of IP traffic.

See also search filter.

FilterKeys

A Windows 2000 accessibility feature that allows people with physical disabilities to adjust keyboard response time.

See also *BounceKeys*; *RepeatKeys*; *SlowKeys*.

Firewall

A combination of hardware and software that provides a security system, usually to prevent unauthorized access from outside to an internal network or intranet. A firewall prevents direct communication between network and external computers by routing communication through a proxy server outside of the network. The proxy server determines whether it is safe to let a file pass through to the network. A firewall is also called a security-edge gateway.

Folder redirection

A Group Policy option that allows you to redirect designated folders to the network.

Foreground boost

A mechanism that increases the priority of a foreground application.

Forest

A collection of one or more Windows 2000 Active Directory trees, organized as peers and connected by two-way transitive trust relationships between the root domains of each tree. All trees in a forest share a common schema, configuration, and Global Catalog. When a forest contains multiple trees, the trees do not form a contiguous namespace.

Fragmentation

The scattering of parts of the same disk file over different areas of the disk. Fragmentation occurs as files on a disk are deleted and new files are added. It slows disk access and degrades the overall performance of disk operations, although usually not severely.

See also *defragmentation*.

Free media pool

A logical collection of unused data-storage media that can be used by applications or other media pools. When media are no longer needed by an application, they are returned to a free media pool so that they can be used again.

See also *media pool*; *Removable Storage*.

G

Gatekeeper

A server that uses a directory to perform name-to-IP address translation, admission control and call management services in H.323 conferencing.

Gateway

A device connected to multiple physical TCP/IP networks, capable of routing or delivering IP packets between them. A gateway translates between different transport protocols or data formats (for example, IPX and IP) and is generally added to a network primarily for its translation ability.

See also *IP address*; *IP router*.

Global Catalog

A domain controller that contains a partial replica of every domain directory partition in the forest as well as a full replica of its own domain directory partition and the schema and configuration directory partitions. The Global Catalog holds a replica of every object in Active Directory, but each object includes a limited number of its attributes. The attributes in the Global Catalog are those most frequently used in search operations (such as a user's first and last names) and those attributes that are required to locate a full replica of the object. The Global Catalog enables users and applications to find objects in Active Directory given one or more attributes of the target object, without knowing what domain holds the object. The Active Directory replication system builds the Global Catalog automatically. The attributes replicated into the Global Catalog include a base set defined by Microsoft. Administrators can specify additional properties to meet the needs of their installation.

Global group

For Windows 2000 Server, a group that can be used in its own domain, in member servers and in workstations of the domain, and in trusting domains. In all those places a global group can be granted rights and permissions and can become a member of local groups. However, a global group can contain user accounts only from its own domain.

See also *group*; *local group*.

Globally unique identifier (GUID)

A 16-byte value generated from the unique identifier on a device, the current date and time, and a sequence number. A GUID is used to identify a particular device or component.

Graphical Identification and Authentication (GINA)

A DLL loaded during the Windows 2000 Winlogon process, which displays the standard logon dialog box, collects, and processes user logon data for verification.

Graphical user interface (GUI)

A display format, like that of Windows, which represents a program's functions with graphic images such as buttons and icons. GUIs allow a user to perform operations and make choices by pointing and clicking with a mouse.

Group

A collection of users, computers, contacts, and other groups. Groups can be used as security or as e-mail distribution collections. Distribution groups are used only for e-mail. Security groups are used both to grant access to resources and as e-mail distribution lists. In a server cluster, a group is a collection of resources, and the basic unit of failover.

See also *domain local group*; *global group*; *native mode*; *universal group*.

Group Identification (GID)

A group identifier that uniquely identifies a group of users. UNIX uses the GID to identify the group ownership of a file, and to determine access permissions.

Group memberships

The groups to which a user account belongs. Permissions and rights granted to a group are also provided to its members. In most cases, the actions a user can perform in Windows 2000 are determined by the group memberships of the user account to which the user is logged on.

See also *group*.

Group Policy

An administrator's tool for defining and controlling how programs, network resources, and the operating system operate for users and computers in an organization. In an Active Directory environment, Group Policy is applied to users or computers on the basis of their membership in sites, domains, or organizational units.

Group Policy object

A collection of Group Policy settings. Group Policy objects are the documents created by the Group Policy snap-in. Group Policy objects are stored at the domain level, and they affect users and computers contained in sites, domains, and organizational units. Each Windows 2000-based computer has exactly one group of settings stored locally, called the local Group Policy object.

H

H.323

The ITU-T standard for multimedia communications over networks that do not provide a guaranteed quality of service. This standard provides specifications for workstations, devices, and services to carry real-time video, audio, and data or any combination of these elements.

See also *QoS*.

Hardware abstraction layer (HAL)

A thin layer of software provided by the hardware manufacturer that hides, or abstracts, hardware differences from higher layers of the operating system. Through the filter provided by the HAL, different types of hardware all look alike to the rest of the operating system. This allows Windows NT and Windows 2000 to be portable from one hardware platform to another. The HAL also provides routines that allow a single device driver to support the same device on all platforms. The HAL works closely with the kernel.

Hardware Compatibility List (HCL)

A list of the devices supported by Windows 2000, available from the Microsoft Web site.

Hardware malfunction message

A character-based, full-screen error message displayed on a blue background. It indicates the microprocessor detected a hardware error condition from which the system cannot recover.

Hardware profile

A set of changes to the standard configuration of devices and services (including drivers and Win32 services) loaded by Windows 2000 when the system starts. For example, a hardware profile can include an instruction to disable (that is, not load) a driver, or an instruction not to connect an undocked laptop computer to the network. Because of the instructions in this subkey, users can modify the service configuration for a particular use while preserving the standard configuration unchanged for more general uses.

Hardware type

A classification for similar devices. For example, Imaging Device is a hardware type for digital cameras and scanners.

Heartbeat thread

A thread initiated by the Windows NT Virtual DOS Machine (NTVDM) process that interrupts every 55 milliseconds to simulate a timer interrupt.

Hop

In data communications, one segment of the path between routers on a geographically dispersed network. A hop is comparable to one "leg" of a journey that includes intervening stops between the starting point and the destination. The distance between each of those stops (routers) is a communications hop.

Hosts

A local text file in the same format as the 4.3 Berkeley Software Distribution (BSD) UNIX/etc/hosts file. This file maps host names to IP addresses. In Windows 2000, this file is stored in the \%SystemRoot%\System32\Drivers\Etc folder.

Hot keys

A Windows feature that allows quick activation of specified accessibility features through a combination of keys pressed in unison.

HTML+Time

A new feature in Microsoft Internet Explorer 5 that adds timing and media synchronization support to HTML pages. Using a few Extensible Markup Language (XML)-based elements and attributes, you can add images, video, and sounds to an HTML page, and synchronize them with HTML text elements over a specified amount of time. In short, you can use HTML+TIME technology to quickly and easily create multimedia-rich, interactive presentations, with little or no scripting.

Human Interface Device (HID)

A firmware specification that is a new standard for input and output devices such as drawing tablets, keyboards, USB speakers, and other specialized devices designed to improve accessibility.

Hypertext Markup Language (HTML)

A simple markup language used to create hypertext documents that are portable from one platform to another. HTML files are simple ASCII text files with embedded codes (indicated by markup tags) to indicate formatting and hypertext links. HTML is used for formatting documents on the World Wide Web.

Hypertext Transfer Protocol (HTTP)

The protocol used to transfer information on the World Wide Web. An HTTP address (one kind of Uniform Resource Locator [URL]) takes the form: http://www.microsoft.com.

I

I/O request packet (IRP)

Data structures that drivers use to communicate with each other.

ICM

See *Image Color Management.*

IDE

See *integrated device electronics.*

IEEE 1284.4

An IEEE specification, also called DOT4, for supporting multi-function peripherals (MFPs). Windows 2000 has a driver called DOT4 that creates different port settings for each function of an MFP, enabling Windows 2000 print servers to simultaneously send data to multiple parts of an MFP.

IEEE 1394 (Firewire)

A standard for high-speed serial devices such as digital video and digital audio editing equipment.

IIS

See *Internet Information Services.*

ILS

See *Internet locator service.*

Image Color Management (ICM)

The process of image output correction. ICM attempts to make the output more closely match the colors that are input or scanned.

Impersonation

A circumstance that occurs when Windows NT or Windows 2000 allows one process to take on the security attributes of another.

Import media pool

A repository where Removable Storage puts media when it recognizes the on-media identifier (OMID), but does not have the media cataloged in the current Removable Storage database.

Incremental backup

A backup that copies only those files created or changed since the last normal or incremental backup. It marks files as having been backed up (that is, the archive bit is set). If a combination of normal and incremental backups is used to restore your data, you need to have the last normal backup and all subsequent incremental backup sets.

See also *copy backup*; *daily backup*; *differential backup*; *normal backup*.

Independent software vendors (ISVs)

A third-party software developer; an individual or an organization that independently creates computer software.

Industry Standard Architecture (ISA)

A bus design specification that allows components to be added as cards plugged into standard expansion slots in IBM Personal Computers and IBM compatible computers. Originally introduced in the IBM PC/XT with an 8-bit data path, ISA was expanded in 1984, when IBM introduced the PC/AT, to permit a 16-bit data path. A 16-bit ISA slot consists of two separate 8-bit slots mounted end-to-end so that a single 16-bit card plugs into both slots. An 8-bit expansion card can be inserted and used in a 16-bit slot (it occupies only one of the two slots), but a 16-bit expansion card cannot be used in an 8-bit slot.

See also *Extended Industry Standard Architecture*.

Infrared (IR)

Light that is beyond red in the color spectrum. While the light is not visible to the human eye, infrared transmitters and receivers can send and receive infrared signals.

See also *Infrared Data Association*; *infrared device*; *infrared port*.

Infrared Data Association (IrDA)

A networking protocol used to transmit data created by infrared devices. Infrared Data Association is also the name of the industry organization of computer, component, and telecommunications vendors who establish the standards for infrared communication between computers and peripheral devices, such as printers.

See also *infrared*; *infrared device*; *infrared port*.

Infrared device

A computer, or a computer peripheral such as a printer, that can communicate using infrared light.

See also *infrared*.

Infrared port

An optical port on a computer that enables communication with other computers or devices by using infrared light, without cables. Infrared ports can be found on some portable computers, printers, and cameras.

See also *infrared device*.

Input/Output (I/O) port

A channel through which data is transferred between a device and the microprocessor. The port appears to the microprocessor as one or more memory addresses that it can use to send or receive data.

Insert/Eject (IE) port

IE ports, also called "mailslots," offer limited access to the cartridges in a library managed by Removable Storage. When an administrator adds cartridges to a library through an IE port, the cartridges are placed in the IE port and then the library uses the transport to move the cartridges from the IE port to a slot. Some libraries have no IE ports; others have several. Some IE ports handle only one cartridge at a time; others can handle several at one time.

Instantaneous counter

A type of counter that displays the most recent measurement taken by the Performance console.

Institute of Electrical and Electronics Engineers (IEEE)

An organization of engineering and electronics professionals that are notable for developing standards for hardware and software.

Integrated device electronics (IDE)

A type of disk-drive interface in which the controller electronics reside on the drive itself, eliminating the need for a separate adapter card. IDE offers advantages such as look-ahead caching to increase overall performance.

Integrated Services Digital Network (ISDN)

A type of phone line used to enhance WAN speeds. ISDN lines can transmit at speeds of 64 or 128 kilobits per second, as opposed to standard phone lines, which typically transmit at 28.8 kilobits per second. The phone company must install an ISDN line at both the server site and the remote site.

See also *wide area network.*

Integrity

A basic security function of cryptography. Integrity provides verification that the original contents of information have not been altered or corrupted. Without integrity, someone might alter information or the information might become corrupted, but the alteration can go undetected. For example, an Internet Protocol security property that protects data from unauthorized modification in transit, ensuring that the data received is exactly the same as the data sent. Hash functions sign each packet with a cryptographic checksum, which the receiving computer checks before opening the packet. If the packet-and therefore signature-has changed, the packet is discarded.

See also *cryptography*; *authentication*; *confidentiality*; *no repudiation.*

IntelliMirror

A set of Windows 2000 features used for desktop change and configuration management. When IntelliMirror is used in both the server and client, the users' data, applications, and settings follow them when they move to another computer.

Interactive logon

A network logon from a computer keyboard, when the user types information in the Logon Information dialog box displayed by the computer's operating system.

Internet

A worldwide public TCP/IP internetwork consisting of thousands of networks, connecting research facilities, universities, libraries, and private companies.

Internet Control Message Protocol (ICMP)

A required maintenance protocol in the TCP/IP suite that reports errors and allows simple connectivity. The Ping tool uses ICMP to perform TCP/IP troubleshooting.

Internet Information Services (IIS)

Software services that support Web site creation, configuration, and management, along with other Internet functions. Internet Information Services include Network News Transfer Protocol (NNTP), File Transfer Protocol (FTP), and Simple Mail Transfer Protocol (SMTP).

See also *File Transfer Protocol*; *Network News Transfer Protocol*; *Simple Mail Transfer Protocol.*

Internet Key Exchange (IKE)

A protocol that establishes the security association and shared keys necessary for two parties to communicate with Internet Protocol security.

Internet locator service (ILS)

An optional component of Microsoft Site Server that creates a dynamic directory of videoconferencing users.

Internet Printing Protocol (IPP)

The protocol that uses the Hypertext Transfer Protocol (HTTP) to send print jobs to printers throughout the world. Windows 2000 supports Internet Printing Protocol (IPP) version 1.0.

Internet Protocol (IP)

A routable protocol in the TCP/IP protocol suite that is responsible for IP addressing, routing, and the fragmentation and reassembly of IP packets.

Internet Protocol security (IPSec)

A set of industry-standard, cryptography-based protection services and protocols. IPSec protects all protocols in the TCP/IP protocol suite and Internet communications using L2TP.

See also *Layer Two Tunneling Protocol.*

Internet service provider (ISP)

A company that provides individuals or companies access to the Internet and the World Wide Web. An ISP provides a telephone number, a user name, a password, and other connection information so users can connect their computers to the ISP's computers. An ISP typically charges a monthly and/or hourly connection fee.

Internetwork Packet Exchange (IPX)

A network protocol native to NetWare that controls addressing and routing of packets within and between LANs. IPX does not guarantee that a message will be complete (no lost packets).

See also *Internetwork Packet Exchange / Sequenced Packet Exchange.*

Internetwork Packet Exchange / Sequenced Packet Exchange (IPX/SPX)

Transport protocols used in Novell NetWare and other networks.

Interrupt

A request for attention from the processor. When the processor receives an interrupt, it suspends its current operations, saves the status of its work, and transfers control to a special routine known as an interrupt handler, which contains the instructions for dealing with the particular situation that caused the interrupt.

Interrupt request (IRQ)

A signal sent by a device to get the attention of the processor when the device is ready to accept or send information. Each device sends its interrupt requests over a specific hardware line, numbered from 0 to 15. Each device must be assigned a unique IRQ number.

Intranet

A network within an organization that uses Internet technologies and protocols but is available only to certain people, such as employees of a company. An intranet is also called a private network.

IP address

A 32-bit address used to identify a node on an IP internetwork. Each node on the IP internetwork must be assigned a unique IP address, which is made up of the network ID, plus a unique host ID. This address is typically represented with the decimal value of each octet separated by a period (for example, 192.168.7.27). In Windows 2000, the IP address can be configured manually or dynamically through DHCP.

See also *Dynamic Host Configuration Protocol*; *node.*

IP router

A system connected to multiple physical TCP/IP networks that can route or deliver IP packets between the networks.

See also *packet*; *router*; *routing*; *Transmission Control Protocol/Internet Protocol.*

IPP

See *Internet Printing Protocol.*

IPSec

See *Internet Protocol security.*

IPSec driver

A driver that uses the IP Filter List from the active IPSec policy to watch for outbound IP packets that must be secured and inbound IP packets that need to be verified and decrypted.

IPSec filter

A part of IPSec security rules that make up an IPSec security policy. IPSec filters determine whether a data packet needs an IPSec action and what the IPSec action is, such as permit, block, or secure. Filters can classify traffic by criteria including source IP address, source subnet mask, destination IP address, IP protocol type, source port, and destination port. Filters are not specific to a network interface.

See also *IPSec security rules.*

IPSec security rules

Rules contained in the IPSec policy that govern how and when an IPSec is invoked. A rule triggers and controls secure communication when a particular source, destination, or traffic type is found. Each IPSec policy may contain one or many rules; any of which may apply to a particular packet. Default rules are provided which encompass a variety of clients and server-based communications or rules can be modified to meet custom requirements.

Irtran-p

A protocol that transfers images from cameras to Windows 2000 computers using infrared transmissions, making a physical cable connection unnecessary.

IrDA

See *Infrared Data Association.*

IRP

See *I/O request packet.*

Isochronous

Time dependent. Refers to processes where data must be delivered within certain time constraints. Multimedia streams require an isochronous transport mechanism to ensure that data is delivered as fast as it is displayed, and to ensure that the audio is synchronized with the video.

J

Job object

A feature in the Win32 API set that makes it possible for groups of processes to be managed with respect to their processor usage and other factors.

K

Kerberos authentication protocol

An authentication mechanism used to verify user or host identity. The Kerberos v5 authentication protocol is the default authentication service for Windows 2000. Internet Protocol security and the QoS Admission Control Service use the Kerberos protocol for authentication.

See also *Internet Protocol security*; *NTLM authentication protocol*; *QoS Admission Control Service*.

Kernel

The core of layered architecture that manages the most basic operations of the operating system and the computer's processor for Windows NT and Windows 2000. The kernel schedules different blocks of executing code, called threads, for the processor to keep it as busy as possible and coordinates multiple processors to optimize performance. The kernel also synchronizes activities among Executive-level subcomponents, such as I/O Manager and Process Manager, and handles hardware exceptions and other hardware-dependent functions. The kernel works closely with the hardware abstraction layer.

Key

A secret code or number required to read, modify, or verify secured data. Keys are used in conjunction with algorithms to secure data. Windows 2000 automatically handles key generation. For the registry, a key is an entry in the registry that can contain both subkeys and entries. In the registry structure, keys are analogous to folders, and entries are analogous to files. In the Registry Editor window, a key appears as a file folder in the left pane. In an answer file, keys are character strings that specify parameters from which Setup obtains the needed data for unattended installation of the operating system.

Keyboard filters

Special timing and other devices that compensate for erratic motion tremors, slow response time, and other mobility impairments.

L

L2TP

See *Layer Two Tunneling Protocol.*

LAN

See *local area network.*

Last Known Good Configuration

A hardware configuration available by pressing F8 during startup. If the current hardware settings prevent the computer from starting, the Last Known Good Configuration can allow the computer to be started and the configuration to be examined. When the Last Known Good Configuration is used, later configuration changes are lost.

Layer 2 forwarding (L2F)

Permits the tunneling of the link layer of higher-level protocols. Using these tunnels, it is possible to separate the location of the initial dial-up server from the physical location at which the dial-up protocol connection is terminated and access to the network is provided.

See also *Layer Two Tunneling Protocol*; *tunnel.*

Layer two Tunneling Protocol (L2TP)

A tunneling protocol that encapsulates PPP frames to be sent over IP, X.25, Frame Relay, or ATM networks. L2TP is a combination of the Point-to-Point Tunneling Protocol (PPTP) and Layer 2 Forwarding (L2F), a technology proposed by Cisco Systems, Inc.

Legend

The area of the System Monitor graph or histogram display that shows computer name, object name, counter name, instances, and other information as a reference to the lines in the graph or the bars in the histogram.

Library

A data-storage system, usually managed by Removable Storage. A library consists of removable media (such as tapes or discs) and a hardware device that can read from or write to the media. There are two major types of libraries: robotic libraries (automated multiple-media, mutative devices) and stand-alone drive libraries (manually operated, single-drive devices). A robotic library is also called a jukebox or changer.

See also *Removable Storage.*

Library request

A request for an online library or stand-alone drive to perform a task. This request can be issued by an application or by Removable Storage.

Lightweight Directory Access Protocol (LDAP)

A directory service protocol that runs directly over TCP/IP and the primary access protocol for Active Directory. LDAP version 3 is defined by a set of Proposed Standard documents in Internet Engineering Task Force (IETF) RFC 2251.

See also *Lightweight Directory Access Protocol application programming interface*.

Lightweight Directory Access Protocol application programming interface (LDAP API)

An API for experienced programmers who want to enable new or existing applications to connect to, search, and update LDAP servers. You can use the LDAP API to write directory-enabled applications that allow LDAP client applications to search for and retrieve information from an LDAP server. LDAP API enables the modification of directory objects, where such modifications are permitted. There are also functions that provide access control for servers, by allowing clients to authenticate themselves.

Line Printer

A connectivity tool that runs on client systems and is used to print files to a computer running an LPD server.

See also *Line Printer Daemon*.

Line Printer Daemon (LPD)

A service on the print server that receives documents (print jobs) from line printer remote (LPR) tools running on client systems.

See also *Line Printer*.

Line Printer Port Monitor

A port monitor that is used to send jobs over TCP/IP from the client running Lprmon.dll to a print server running an LPD (Line Printer Daemon) service. Line Printer Port Monitor can be used to enable Internet printing, UNIX print servers, or Windows 2000 print servers over a TCP/IP network.

Line Printer Remote (LPR)

See *Line Printer*.

Linked object

An object that is inserted into a document but still exists in the source file. When information is linked, the new document is updated automatically if the information in the original document changes.

See also *embedded object*.

Local area network (LAN)

A communications network connecting a group of computers, printers, and other devices located within a relatively limited area (for example, a building). A LAN allows any connected device to interact with any other on the network.

See also *wide area network*.

Local computer

A computer that can be accessed directly without using a communications line or a communications device, such as a network adapter or a modem. Similarly, running a local program means running the program on your computer, as opposed to running it from a server.

Local group

For computers running Windows 2000 Professional and member servers, a group that is granted permissions and rights from its own computer to only those resources on its own computer on which the group resides.

See also *global group*.

Local Security Authority (LSA)

A protected subsystem that authenticates and logs users onto the local system. In addition, the LSA maintains information about all aspects of local security on a system (collectively known as the local security policy), and provides various services for translation between names and identifiers.

Local user profile

A computer-based record maintained about an authorized user that is created automatically on the computer the first time a user logs on to a computer running Windows 2000.

Localmon.dll

The standard print monitor for use with printers connected directly to your computer. If you add a printer to your computer using a serial or parallel port (such as COM1 or LPT1), this is the monitor that is used.

LocalTalk

The Apple networking hardware built into every Macintosh computer. LocalTalk includes the cables and connector boxes to connect components and network devices that are part of the AppleTalk network system. LocalTalk was formerly known as the AppleTalk Personal Network.

Locator service

In a distributed system, a feature that allows a client to find a shared resource or server without providing an address or full name. Generally associated with Active Directory, which provides a locator service.

Logical drive

A volume created within an extended partition on a basic disk. You can format and assign a drive letter to a logical drive. Only basic disks can contain logical drives. A logical drive cannot span multiple disks.

See also *basic disk*; *basic volume*; *extended partition.*

Logical volume

A volume created within an extended partition on a basic disk. You can format and assign a drive letter to a logical drive. Only basic disks can contain logical drives. A logical drive cannot span multiple disks.

See also *basic disk*; *basic volume*; *extended partition.*

Logon script

Files that can be assigned to user accounts. Typically a batch file, a logon script runs automatically every time the user logs on. It can be used to configure a user's working environment at every logon, and it allows an administrator to influence a user's environment without managing all aspects of it. A logon script can be assigned to one or more user accounts.

See also *batch program.*

Long file name (LFN)

A folder name or file name on the FAT file system that is longer than the 8.3 file name standard (up to eight characters followed by a period and an extension of up to three characters). Windows 2000 supports long file names up to the file-name limit of 255 characters. Macintosh users can assign long names to files and folders on the server and, using Services for Macintosh, long names to Macintosh-accessible volumes can be assigned when created. Windows 2000 automatically translates long names of files and folders to 8.3 names for MS-DOS and Windows 3.*x* users.

See also *name mapping*.

Loopback address

The address of the local computer used for routing outgoing packets back to the source computer. This address is used primarily for testing.

M

MAC

See *media access control.*

Magazine

A collection of storage locations, also called "slots," for cartridges in a library managed by Removable Storage. Magazines are usually removable.

Magneto-optic (MO) disk

A high-capacity, erasable storage medium which uses laser beams to heat the disk and magnetically arrange the data.

Magnifier

A screen enlarger that magnifies a portion of the screen in a separate window for users with low vision and for those who require occasional screen magnification for such tasks as editing art.

Manual caching

A method of manually designating network files and folders so they are stored on a user's hard disk and accessible when the user is not connected to the network.

Master Boot Record (MBR)

The first sector on a hard disk, this data structure starts the process of booting the computer. It is the most important area on a hard disk. The MBR contains the partition table for the disk and a small amount of executable code called the master boot code.

Master file table (MFT)

The database that tracks the contents of an NTFS volume. The MFT is a table whose rows correspond to files on the volume and whose columns correspond to the attributes of each file.

Maximum password age

The period of time a password can be used before the system requires the user to change it.

Media

The physical material on which information is recorded and stored.

Media access control

A sublayer of the IEEE 802 specifications that defines network access methods and framing.

Media label library

A dynamic-link library (DLL) that can interpret the format of a media label written by a Removable Storage application.

Media pool

Logical collections of removable media that have the same management policies. Media pools are used by applications to control access to specific tapes or discs within libraries managed by Removable Storage. There are four media pools: Unrecognized, Import, Free, and application-specific. Each media pool can only hold either media or other media pools.

See also *Removable Storage.*

Media states

Descriptions of conditions in which Removable Storage has placed a cartridge that it is managing. The states include Idle, In Use, Mounted, Loaded, and Unloaded.

Memory leak

A condition that occurs when applications allocate memory for use but do not free allocated memory when finished.

Metric

A number used to indicate the cost of a route in the IP routing table to enable the selection of the best route among possible multiple routes to the same destination.

MFP

See *multi-function peripherals.*

Microsoft Challenge Handshake Authentication Protocol version 1 (MS-CHAP v1)

An encrypted authentication mechanism for PPP connections similar to CHAP. The remote access server sends a challenge to the remote access client that consists of a session ID and an arbitrary challenge string. The remote access client must return the user name and a Message Digest 4 (MD4) hash of the challenge string, the session ID, and the MD4-hashed password.

Microsoft Challenge Handshake Authentication Protocol version 2 (MS-CHAP v2)

An encrypted authentication mechanism for PPP connections that provides stronger security than CHAP and MS-CHAP v1. MS-CHAP v2 provides mutual authentication and asymmetric encryption keys.

Microsoft Indexing Service

Software that provides search functions for documents stored on disk, allowing users to search for specific document text or properties.

Microsoft Internet Directory

A Web site provided and maintained by Microsoft used by applications such as NetMeeting to locate people to call on the Internet. The Microsoft Internet Directory is operated through an ILS server.

Microsoft Management Console (MMC)

A framework for hosting administrative consoles. A console is defined by the items on its console tree, which might include folders or other containers, World Wide Web pages, and other administrative items. A console has one or more windows that can provide views of the console tree and the administrative properties, services, and events that are acted on by the items in the console tree. The main MMC window provides commands and tools for authoring consoles. The authoring features of MMC and the console tree might be hidden when a console is in User Mode.

See also *console tree*.

Microsoft Point-to-Point Encryption (MPPE)

A 128/40-bit encryption algorithm using RSA RC4. MPPE provides for packet security between the client and the tunnel server and is useful where IPSec is not available. The 40-bit version addresses localization issues based on current export restrictions. MPPE is compatible with Network Address Translation.

See also *IPSec*.

Microsoft Tape Format (MTF)

The data format used for tapes supported by the Backup application in Windows 2000. There are three major components to MTF: a Tape Data Block (Tape DBLK), otherwise known as the tape header; one or more Data Sets; and On Tape Catalog Information (On Tape Catalog Inf).

Minidrivers

Relatively small, simple drivers or files that contain additional instructions needed by a specific hardware device, to interface with the universal driver for a class of devices.

Minimum TTL

A default Time To Live (TTL) value set in seconds for use with all resource records in a zone. This value is set in the start of authority (SOA) resource record for each zone. By default, the DNS server includes this value in query answers to inform recipients how long it can store and use resource records provided in the query answer before they must expire the stored records data. When TTL values are set for individual resource records, those values will override the minimum TTL.

See also *Time To Live*.

Mirrored volume

A fault-tolerant volume that duplicates data on two physical disks. The mirror is always located on a different disk. If one of the physical disks fails, the data on the failed disk becomes unavailable, but the system continues to operate by using the unaffected disk. A mirrored volume is slower than a RAID-5 volume in read operations but faster in write operations. Mirrored volumes can only be created on dynamic disks. In Windows NT 4.0, a mirrored volume was known as a mirror set.

See also *dynamic disk*; *dynamic volume*; *fault tolerance*; *redundant array of independent disks*; *volume*.

Mixed mode

The default mode setting for domains on Windows 2000 domain controllers. Mixed mode allows Windows 2000 domain controllers and Windows NT backup domain controllers to co-exist in a domain. Mixed mode does not support the universal and nested group enhancements of Windows 2000. You can change the domain mode setting to Windows 2000 native mode after all Windows NT domain controllers are either removed from the domain or upgraded to Windows 2000.

See also *native mode*.

Mode Pruning

A Windows 2000 feature that can be used to remove display modes that the monitor cannot support.

Mount

To place a removable tape or disc into a drive.

See also *library*.

MouseKeys

A feature in Microsoft Windows that allows use of the numeric keyboard to move the mouse pointer.

MP3

Audio compressed in the MPEG1 Layer 3 format

MPEG-2

A standard of video compression and file format developed by the Moving Pictures Experts Group. MPEG-2 offers video resolutions of 720 x 480 and 128 x 720 at 60 frames per second, with full CD-quality audio.

MS-CHAPv2

See *Microsoft Challenge Handshake Authentication Protocol version 2.*

Multicast IP

IP packets sent from a single destination IP address but received and processed by multiple IP hosts, regardless of their location on an IP internetwork.

Multicasting

The process of sending a message simultaneously to more than one destination on a network.

Multihomed computer

A computer that has multiple network adapters or that has been configured with multiple IP addresses for a single network adapter.

Multiple boot

A computer configuration that runs two or more operating systems. For example, Windows 98, MS-DOS, and Windows 2000 operating systems can be installed on the same computer. When the computer is started, any one of the operating systems can be selected.

See also *dual boot*.

N

Name devolution

A process by which a DNS resolver appends one or more domain names to an unqualified domain name, making it a fully qualified domain name, and then submits the fully qualified domain name to a DNS server.

Namespace

A set of unique names for resources or items used in a shared computing environment. The names in a namespace can be resolved to the objects they represent. For Microsoft Management Console (MMC), the namespace is represented by the console tree, which displays all of the snap-ins and resources that are accessible to a console. For Domain Name System (DNS), namespace is the vertical or hierarchical structure of the domain name tree. For example, each domain label, such as "host1" or "example," used in a fully qualified domain name, such as "host1.example.microsoft.com," indicates a branch in the domain namespace tree. For Active Directory, namespace corresponds to the DNS namespace in structure, but resolves Active Directory object names.

Naming service

A service, such as that provided by WINS or DNS, that allows friendly names to be resolved to an address or other specially defined resource data that is used to locate network resources of various types and purposes.

Narrator

A synthesized text-to-speech utility for users who have low vision. Narrator reads aloud most of what the screen displays.

Native mode

The condition in which all domain controllers within a domain are Windows 2000 domain controllers and an administrator has enabled native mode operation (through Active Directory Users and Computers).

See also *mixed mode*.

NDIS miniport drivers

A type of minidriver that interfaces network class devices to NDIS.

Nested groups

A Windows 2000 capability available only in native mode that allows the creation of groups within groups. See also domain local group; forest; global group; trusted forest; universal group.

NetBEUI

See *NetBIOS Extended User Interface*.

NetBIOS Extended User Interface (NetBEUI)

A network protocol native to Microsoft Networking that is usually used in local area networks of one to 200 clients. NetBEUI uses Token Ring source routing as its only method of routing. It is the Microsoft implementation of the NetBIOS standard.

NetBIOS over TCP/IP (NetBT)

A feature that provides the NetBIOS programming interface over the TCP/IP protocol. It is used for monitoring routed servers that use NetBIOS name resolution.

NetWare

Novell's network operating system.

Network adapter

Software or a hardware plug-in board that connects a node or host to a local area network.

Network basic input/output system (NetBIOS)

An application programming interface (API) that can be used by applications on a local area network or computers running MS-DOS, OS/2, or some version of UNIX. NetBIOS provides a uniform set of commands for requesting lower level network services.

Network Control Protocol (NCP)

A protocol within the PPP protocol suite that negotiates the parameters of an individual LAN protocol such as TCP/IP or IPX.

Network Driver Interface Specification (NDIS)

A software component that provides Windows 2000 network protocols a common interface for communications with network adapters. NDIS allows more than one transport protocol to be bound and operate simultaneously over a single network adapter card.

Network file system (NFS)

A service for distributed computing systems that provides a distributed file system, eliminating the need for keeping multiple copies of files on separate computers.

Network Information Service (NIS)

Formerly known as Yellow Pages, NIS is a distributed database service that allows for a shared set of system configuration files on UNIX-based systems, including password, hosts, and group files.

Network News Transfer Protocol (NNTP)

A member of the TCP/IP suite of protocols, used to distribute network news messages to NNTP servers and clients, or newsreaders, on the Internet. NNTP is designed so that news articles are stored on a server in a central database, and the user selects specific items to read.

See also *Transmission Control Protocol/Internet Protocol.*

Network security administrators

Users who manage network and information security. Network security administrators should implement a security plan that addresses network security threats.

Node

In tree structures, a location on the tree that can have links to one or more items below it. In local area networks (LANs), a device that is connected to the network and is capable of communicating with other network devices. In a server cluster, a server that has Cluster service software installed and is a member of the cluster.

See also *local area network.*

Noncontainer object

An object that cannot logically contain other objects. A file is a noncontainer object.

See also *container object*; *object.*

Nonrepudiation

A basic security function of cryptography. Nonrepudiation provides assurance that a party in a communication cannot falsely deny that a part of the communication occurred. Without nonrepudiation, someone can communicate and then later deny the communication or claim that the communication occurred at a different time.

See also *cryptography*; *authentication*; *confidentiality*; *integrity.*

Nonresident attribute

A file attribute whose value is contained in one or more runs, or extents, outside the master file table (MFT) record and separate from the MFT.

Nontransitive trust relationship

A type of trust relationship that is bounded by the two domains in the relationship. For example, if domain A trusts domain B and domain B trusts domain C, there is no trust relationship between domain A and domain C. A nontransitive trust relationship can be a one-way or two-way relationship. It is the only type of trust relationship that can exist between a Windows 2000 domain and a Windows NT domain or between Windows 2000 domains in different forests.

See also *trust relationship*; *transitive trust relationship*.

Normal backup

A backup that copies all selected files and marks each file as backed up (that is, the archive bit is set). With normal backups, only the most recent copy of the backup file or tape is needed to restore all of the files. A normal backup is usually performed the first time a backup set is created.

See also *copy backup*; *daily backup*; *differential backup*; *incremental backup*.

Novell Directory Services (NDS)

On networks running Novell NetWare 4.*x* and NetWare 5.*x*, a distributed database that maintains information about every resource on the network and provides access to these resources.

NT-1 (Network Terminator 1)

A device that terminates an ISDN line at the connection location, commonly through a connection port.

NTFS file system

A recoverable file system designed for use specifically with Windows NT and Windows 2000. NTFS uses database, transaction-processing, and object paradigms to provide data security, file system reliability, and other advanced features. It supports file system recovery, large storage media, and various features for the POSIX subsystem. It also supports object-oriented applications by treating all files as objects with user-defined and system-defined attributes.

NTLM

A security package that provides authentication between clients and servers.

See also *NTLM authentication protocol.*

NTLM authentication protocol

A challenge/response authentication protocol. The NTLM authentication protocol was the default for network authentication in Windows NT version 4.0 and earlier. The protocol continues to be supported in Windows 2000 but no longer is the default.

See also *authentication.*

NWLink

An implementation of the Internetwork Packet Exchange (IPX), Sequenced Packet Exchange (SPX), and NetBIOS protocols used in Novell networks. NWLink is a standard network protocol that supports routing and can support NetWare client/server applications, where NetWare-aware Sockets-based applications communicate with IPX/SPX Sockets-based applications.

See also *Internetwork Packet Exchange*; *network basic input/output system.*

O

Object

An entity, such as a file, folder, shared folder, printer, or Active Directory object, described by a distinct, named set of attributes. For example, the attributes of a File object include its name, location, and size; the attributes of an Active Directory User object might include the user's first name, last name, and e-mail address. For OLE and ActiveX objects, an object can also be any piece of information that can be linked to, or embedded into, another object.

See also *attribute*; *child object*; *container object*; *noncontainer object*; *parent object*.

Object linking and embedding (OLE)

A method for sharing information among applications. Linking an object, such as a graphic, from one document to another inserts a reference to the object into the second document. Any changes you make in the object in the first document will also be made in the second document. Embedding an object inserts a copy of an object from one document into another document. Changes you make in the object in the first document will not be updated in the second unless the embedded object is explicitly updated.

See also *ActiveX*.

Offline media

Media that are not connected to the computer and require external assistance to be accessed.

On-media identifier (OMID)

A label that is electronically recorded on each medium in a Removable Storage system. Removable Storage uses on-media identifiers to track media in the Removable Storage database. An application on-media identifier is a subset of the media label.

On-screen keyboard

A utility that displays a virtual keyboard on a computer screen and allows users with mobility impairments to type using a pointing device or joystick.

OnNow

See *Advanced Configuration and Power Interface*.

Open database connectivity (ODBC)

An application programming interface (API) that enables database applications to access data from a variety of existing data sources.

Open Host Controller Interface (OHCI)

Part of the IEEE 1394 standard. In Windows 2000 Professional, only OHCI-compliant host adapters are supported.

OpenType fonts

Outline fonts that are rendered from line and curve commands, and can be scaled and rotated. OpenType fonts are clear and readable in all sizes and on all output devices supported by Windows 2000. OpenType is an extension of TrueType font technology.

See also *font*; *TrueType fonts*.

Operator request

A request for the operator to perform a task. This request can be issued by an application or by Removable Storage.

Original equipment manufacturer (OEM)

The maker of a piece of equipment. In making computers and computer-related equipment, manufacturers of original equipment typically purchase components from other manufacturers of original equipment and then integrate them into their own products.

Overclocking

Setting a microprocessor to run at speeds above the rated specification.

P

Package

An icon that represents embedded or linked information. That information can consist of a complete file, such as a Paint bitmap, or part of a file, such as a spreadsheet cell. When a package is chosen, the application used to create the object either plays the object (if it is a sound file, for example) or opens and displays the object. If the original information is changed, linked information is then updated. However, embedded information needs to be manually updated. In Systems Management Server, an object that contains the files and instructions for distributing software to a distribution point.

See also *embedded object*; *linked object*; *object linking and embedding*.

Packet

A transmission unit of fixed maximum size that consists of binary information. This information represents both data and a header containing an ID number, source and destination addresses, and error-control data.

Packet assembler/disassembler (PAD)

A connection used in X.25 networks. X.25 PAD boards can be used in place of modems when provided with a compatible COM driver.

PAD

See *packet assembler/disassembler*.

Page fault

An error that occurs when the requested code or data cannot be located in the physical memory that is available to the requesting process.

Page-description language (PDL)

A computer language that describes the arrangement of text and graphics on a printed page.

See also *printer control language*; *PostScript*.

Paging

The process of moving virtual memory back and forth between physical memory and the disk. Paging occurs when physical memory limitations are reached and only occurs for data that is not already "backed" by disk space. For example, file data is not paged out because it already has allocated disk space within a file system.

See also *virtual memory*.

paging file

A hidden file on the hard disk that Windows 2000 uses to hold parts of programs and data files that do not fit in memory. The paging file and physical memory, or RAM, comprise virtual memory. Windows 2000 moves data from the paging file to memory as needed and moves data from memory to the paging file to make room for new data. Also called a swap file.

See also *random access memory*; *virtual memory*.

PAP

See *Password Authentication Protocol*.

Parallel connection

A connection that simultaneously transmits both data and control bits over wires connected in parallel. In general, a parallel connection can move data between devices faster than a serial connection.

Parallel device

A device that uses a parallel connection.

Parallel ports

The input/output connector for a parallel interface device. Printers are generally plugged into a parallel port.

Parent object

The object that is the immediate superior of another object in a hierarchy. A parent object can have multiple subordinate, or child, objects. In Active Directory, the schema determines what objects can be parent objects of what other objects. Depending on its class, a parent object can be the child of another object.

See also *child object*; *object*.

Partition

A logical division of a hard disk. Partitions make it easier to organize information. Each partition can be formatted for a different file system. A partition must be completely contained on one physical disk, and the partition table in the Master Boot Record for a physical disk can contain up to four entries for partitions.

Password authentication protocol (PAP)

A simple, plaintext authentication scheme for authenticating PPP connections. The user name and password are requested by the remote access server and returned by the remote access client in plaintext.

Path

A sequence of directory (or folder) names that specifies the location of a directory, file, or folder within the Windows directory tree. Each directory name and file name within the path must be preceded by a backslash (\). For example, to specify the path of a file named Readme.doc located in the Windows directory on drive C, type C:\Windows\Readme.doc.

PC Card

A removable device, approximately the size of a credit card, that can be plugged into a PCMCIA (Personal Computer Memory Card International Association) slot in a portable computer. PCMCIA devices can include modems, network adapters, and hard disk drives.

PCI

See *Peripheral Component Interconnect.*

PCNFS Daemon (PCNFSD)

A program that receives requests from PC-NFS clients for authentication on remote machines.

Peer-to-peer network

See *workgroup.*

Performance counter

In System Monitor, a data item associated with a performance object. For each counter selected, System Monitor presents a value corresponding to a particular aspect of the performance that is defined for the performance object.

See also *performance object.*

Performance object

In System Monitor, a logical collection of counters that is associated with a resource or service that can be monitored. See also performance counter.

Peripheral

A device, such as a disk drive, printer, modem, or joystick, that is connected to a computer and is controlled by the computer's microprocessor.

Peripheral component interconnect (PCI)

A specification introduced by Intel Corporation that defines a local bus system that allows up to 10 PCI-compliant expansion cards to be installed in the computer.

Permission

A rule associated with an object to regulate which users can gain access to the object and in what manner. Permissions are granted or denied by the object's owner.

See also *access control list*; *object*; *privilege*; *user rights*.

Physical location

The location designation assigned to media managed by Removable Storage. The two classes of physical locations include libraries and offline media physical locations. The offline media physical location is where Removable Storage lists the cartridges that are not in a library. The physical location of cartridges in an online library is the library in which it resides.

Physical media

A storage object that data can be written to, such as a disk or magnetic tape. A physical medium is referenced by its physical media ID (PMID).

Physical object

An object, such as an ATM card or smart card used in conjunction with a piece of information, such as a PIN number, to authenticate users. In two-factor authentication, physical objects are used in conjunction with another secret piece of identification, such as a password, to authenticate users. In two-factor authentication, the physical object might be an ATM card that is used in combination with a PIN to authenticate the user.

Ping

A tool that verifies connections to one or more remote hosts. The ping command uses the ICMP Echo Request and Echo Reply packets to determine whether a particular IP system on a network is functional. Ping is useful for diagnosing IP network or router failures.

See also *Internet Control Message Protocol.*

Pinning

To make a network file or folder available for offline use.

Plaintext

Data that is not encrypted. Sometimes also called clear text.

See also *ciphertext*; *encryption*; *decryption.*

Plug and Play

A set of specifications developed by Intel that allows a computer to automatically detect and configure a device and install the appropriate device drivers.

Point and Print

A way of installing network printers on a user's local computer. Point and Print allows users to initiate a connection to a network printer and loads any required drivers onto the client's computer. When users know which network printer they want to use, Point and Print greatly simplifies the installation process.

Point of presence (POP)

The local access point for a network provider. Each POP provides a telephone number that allows users to make a local call for access to online services.

Point-to-Point Protocol (PPP)

An industry standard suite of protocols for the use of point-to-point links to transport multiprotocol datagrams. PPP is documented in RFC 1661.

Point-to-Point Tunneling Protocol (PPTP)

A tunneling protocol that encapsulates Point-to-Point Protocol (PPP) frames into IP datagrams for transmission over an IP-based internetwork, such as the Internet or a private intranet.

Portable Operating System Interface for UNIX (POSIX)

An IEEE (Institute of Electrical and Electronics Engineers) standard that defines a set of operating-system services. Programs that adhere to the POSIX standard can be easily ported from one system to another. POSIX was based on UNIX system services, but it was created in a way that allows it to be implemented by other operating systems.

POST

See *power-on self test.*

PostScript

A page-description language (PDL) developed by Adobe Systems for printing with laser printers. PostScript offers flexible font capability and high-quality graphics. It is the standard for desktop publishing because it is supported by image setters, the high-resolution printers used by printing services for commercial typesetting.

See also *printer control language*; *page-description language.*

Power-on self test (POST)

A set of routines stored in read-only memory (ROM) that tests various system components such as RAM, the disk drives, and the keyboard, to see if they are properly connected and operating. If problems are found, these routines alert the user with a series of beeps or a message, often accompanied by a diagnostic numeric value. If the POST is successful, it passes control to the bootstrap loader.

PPTP

See *Point-to-Point Tunneling Protocol.*

Primary partition

A volume created using unallocated space on a basic disk. Windows 2000 and other operating systems can start from a primary partition. As many as four primary partitions can be created on a basic disk, or three primary partitions and an extended partition. Primary partitions can be created only on basic disks and cannot be subpartitioned.

See also *basic disk*; *dynamic volume*; *extended partition*; *partition.*

Printer control language (PCL)

The page-description language (PDL) developed by Hewlett Packard for their laser and inkjet printers. Because of the widespread use of laser printers, this command language has become a standard in many printers.

See also *page-description language*; *PostScript.*

Priority

A precedence ranking that determines the order in which the threads of a process are scheduled for the processor.

Priority inversion

The mechanism that allows low-priority threads to run and complete execution rather than being preempted and locking up a resource such as an I/O device.

Private branch exchange (PBX)

An automatic telephone switching system that enables users within an organization to place calls to each other without going through the public telephone network. Users can also place calls to outside numbers.

Private key

The secret half of a cryptographic key pair that is used with a public key algorithm. Private keys are typically used to digitally sign data and to decrypt data that has been encrypted with the corresponding public key.

See also *public key*.

Privilege

A user's right to perform a specific task, usually one that affects an entire computer system rather than a particular object. Administrators assign privileges to individual users or groups of users as part of the security settings for the computer.

See also *access token*; *permission*; *user rights*.

Privileged mode

Also known as kernel mode, the processing mode that allows code to have direct access to all hardware and memory in the system.

Process throttling

A method of restricting the amount of processor time a process consumes, for example, using job object functions.

Processor queue

An instantaneous count of the threads that are ready to run on the system but are waiting because the processor is running other threads.

Protocol

A set of rules and conventions by which two computers pass messages across a network. Networking software usually implements multiple levels of protocols layered one on top of another. Windows NT and Windows 2000 include NetBEUI, TCP/IP, and IPX/SPX-compatible protocols.

Proxy server

A firewall component that manages Internet traffic to and from a local area network and can provide other features, such as document caching and access control. A proxy server can improve performance by supplying frequently requested data, such as a popular Web page, and can filter and discard requests that the owner does not consider appropriate, such as requests for unauthorized access to proprietary files.

See also *firewall*.

Public key

The non-secret half of a cryptographic key pair that is used with a public key algorithm. Public keys are typically used to verify digital signatures or decrypt data that has been encrypted with the corresponding private key.

See also *private key*.

Public key cryptography

A method of cryptography in which two different but complimentary keys are used: a public key and a private key for providing security functions. Public key cryptography is also called asymmetric key cryptography.

See also *cryptography*; *public key*; *private key*.

Public switched telephone network (PSTN)

Standard analog telephone lines, available worldwide.

Q

QoS

See *Quality of Service*.

QoS Admission Control Service

A software service that controls bandwidth and network resources on the subnet to which it is assigned. Important applications can be given more bandwidth, less important applications less bandwidth. The QoS Admission Control Service can be installed on any network-enabled computer running Windows 2000.

Quality of Service (QoS)

A set of quality assurance standards and mechanisms for data transmission, implemented in Windows 2000.

Quantum

Also known as a time slice, the maximum amount of time a thread can run before the system checks for another ready thread of the same priority to run.

Quarter-inch cartridge (QIC)

An older storage technology used with tape backup drives and cartridges. A means of backing up data on computer systems, QIC represents a set of standards devised to enable tapes to be used with drives from different manufacturers. The QIC standards specify the length of tape, the number of recording tracks, and the magnetic strength of the tape coating, all of which determine the amount of information that can be written to the tape. Older QIC-80 drives can hold up to 340 MB of compressed data. Newer versions can hold more than 1 GB of information.

R

RAID-5 volume

A fault-tolerant volume with data and parity striped intermittently across three or more physical disks. Parity is a calculated value that is used to reconstruct data after a failure. If a portion of a physical disk fails, you can recreate the data that was on the failed portion from the remaining data and parity. Also known as a striped volume with parity.

Raster fonts

Fonts that are stored as bitmaps; also called bit-mapped fonts. Raster fonts are designed with a specific size and resolution for a specific printer and cannot be scaled or rotated. If a printer does not support raster fonts, it will not print them.

Rate counter

Similar to an averaging counter, a counter type that samples an increasing count of events over time; the change in the count is divided by the change in time to display a rate of activity.

Read-only memory (ROM)

A semiconductor circuit that contains information that cannot be modified.

Recoverable file system

A file system that ensures that if a power outage or other catastrophic system failure occurs, the file system will not be corrupted and disk modifications will not be left incomplete. The structure of the disk volume is restored to a consistent state when the system restarts.

Recovery Console

A startable, text-mode command interpreter environment separate from the Windows 2000 command prompt that allows the system administrator access to the hard disk of a computer running Windows 2000, regardless of the file format used, for basic troubleshooting and system maintenance tasks.

Redundant array of independent disks (RAID)

A method used to standardize and categorize fault-tolerant disk systems. Six levels gauge various mixes of performance, reliability, and cost. Windows 2000 provides three of the RAID levels: Level 0 (striping) which is not fault-tolerant, Level 1 (mirroring), and Level 5 (striped volume with parity).

See also *fault tolerance*; *mirrored volume*; *RAID-5 volume*; *striped volume*.

Registry

In Windows 2000, Windows NT, Windows 98, and Windows 95, a database of information about a computer's configuration. The registry is organized in a hierarchical structure and consists of subtrees and their keys, hives, and entries.

Relative ID (RID)

The part of a security ID (SID) that uniquely identifies an account or group within a domain.

See also *security ID*.

Remote access server

A Windows 2000 Server-based computer running the Routing and Remote Access service and configured to provide remote access.

Remote procedure call (RPC)

A message-passing facility that allows a distributed application to call services that are available on various computers in a network. Used during remote administration of computers.

Removable Storage

A service used for managing removable media (such as tapes and discs) and storage devices (libraries). Removable Storage allows applications to access and share the same media resources.

See also *library*.

Reparse points

New NTFS file system objects that have a definable attribute containing user-controlled data and are used to extend functionality in the input/output (I/O) subsystem.

Repeat Keys

A feature that allows users with mobility impairments to adjust the repeat rate or to disable the key-repeat function on the keyboard.

See also *FilterKeys*.

Request for Comments (RFC)

A document that defines a standard. RFCs are published by the Internet Engineering Task Force (IETF) and other working groups.

Resident attribute

A file attribute whose value is wholly contained in the file's file record in the master file table (MFT).

Resolver

DNS client programs used to look up DNS name information. Resolvers can be either a small "stub" (a limited set of programming routines that provide basic query functionality) or larger programs that provide additional lookup DNS client functions, such as caching.

See also *caching*; *caching resolver*.

Resource publishing

The process of making an object visible and accessible to users in a Windows 2000 domain. For example, a shared printer resource is published by creating a reference to the printer object in Active Directory.

Resource record (RR)

Information in the DNS database that can be used to process client queries. Each DNS server contains the resource records it needs to answer queries for the portion of the DNS namespace for which it is authoritative.

Response time

The amount of time required to do work from start to finish. In a client/server environment, this is typically measured on the client side.

RGB

The initials of red, green, blue. Used to describe a color monitor or color value.

Roaming user profile

A server-based user profile that is downloaded to the local computer when a user logs on and is updated both locally and on the server when the user logs off. A roaming user profile is available from the server when logging on to any computer that is running Windows 2000 Professional or Windows 2000 Server.

ROM

See *read-only memory.*

Route table

See *routing table.*

Router

A network device that helps LANs and WANs achieve interoperability and connectivity and that can link LANs that have different network topologies, such as Ethernet and Token Ring.

Routing

The process of forwarding a packet through an internetwork from a source host to a destination host.

Routing Information Protocol (RIP)

An industry standard distance vector routing protocol used in small to medium sized IP and IPX internetworks.

Routing table

A database of routes containing information on network IDs, forwarding addresses, and metrics for reachable network segments on an internetwork.

RPC

See *Remote Procedure Call.*

Rules

An IPSec policy mechanism that governs how and when an IPSec policy protects communication. A rule provides the ability to trigger and control secure communication based on the source, destination, and type of IP traffic. Each rule contains a list of IP filters and a collection of security actions that take place upon a match with that filter list.

S

Safe Mode

A method of starting Windows 2000 using basic files and drivers only, without networking. Safe Mode is available by pressing the F8 key when prompted during startup. This allows the computer to start when a problem prevents it from starting normally.

Screen-enlargement utility

A utility that allows the user to magnify a portion of the screen for greater visibility. (Also called a screen magnifier or large-print program.)

Script

A type of program consisting of a set of instructions to an application or utility program. A script usually expresses instructions by using the application's or utility's rules and syntax, combined with simple control structures such as loops and if/then expressions. "Batch program" is often used interchangeably with "script" in the Windows environment.

SCSI

See *Small Computer System Interface.*

SCSI connection

A standard high-speed parallel interface defined by the X3T9.2 committee of the American National Standards Institute (ANSI). A SCSI interface is used to connect microcomputers to SCSI peripheral devices, such as many hard disks and printers, and to other computers and local area networks.

Search filter

An argument in an LDAP search that allows certain entries in the subtree and excludes others. Filters allow you to define search criteria and give you better control to achieve more effective and efficient searches.

Secure Sockets Layer (SSL)

A proposed open standard developed by Netscape Communications for establishing a secure communications channel to prevent the interception of critical information, such as credit card numbers. Primarily, it enables secure electronic financial transactions on the World Wide Web, although it is designed to work on other Internet services as well.

Security Accounts Manager (SAM)

A protected subsystem that manages user and group account information. In Windows NT 4.0, both local and domain security principals are stored by SAM in the registry. In Windows 2000, workstation security accounts are stored by SAM in the local computer registry, and domain controller security accounts are stored in Active Directory.

Security association (SA)

A set of parameters that define the services and mechanisms necessary to protect Internet Protocol security communications.

See also *Internet Protocol security.*

Security descriptor

A data structure that contains security information associated with a protected object. Security descriptors include information about who owns the object, who may access it and in what way, and what types of access will be audited.

See also *access control list*; *object.*

Security event types

Different categories of events about which Windows 2000 can create auditing events. Account logon or object access are examples of security event types.

Security ID (SID)

A data structure of variable length that uniquely identifies user, group, service, and computer accounts within an enterprise. Every account is issued a SID when the account is first created. Access control mechanisms in Windows 2000 identify security principals by SID rather than by name.

See also *relative ID*; *security principal.*

Security method

A process that determines the Internet Protocol security services, key settings, and algorithms that will be used to protect the data during the communication.

Security Parameters Index (SPI)

A unique, identifying value in the SA used to distinguish among multiple security associations existing at the receiving computer.

Security principal

An account-holder, such as a user, computer, or service. Each security principal within a Windows 2000 domain is identified by a unique security ID (SID). When a security principal logs on to a computer running Windows 2000, the Local Security Authority (LSA) authenticates the security principal's account name and password. If the logon is successful, the system creates an access token. Every process executed on behalf of this security principal will have a copy of its access token.

See also *access token*; *security ID*; *security principal name*.

Security principal name

A name that uniquely identifies a user, group, or computer within a single domain. This name is not guaranteed to be unique across domains.

See also *security principal*.

Seek time

The amount of time required for a disk head to position itself at the right disk cylinder to access requested data.

Serial Bus Protocol (SBP-2)

A standard for storage devices, printers, and scanners that is a supplement to the IEEE 1394 specification.

Serial connection

A connection that exchanges information between computers or between computers and peripheral devices one bit at a time over a single channel. Serial communications can be synchronous or asynchronous. Both sender and receiver must use the same baud rate, parity, and control information.

Serial device

A device that uses a serial connection.

SerialKeys

A Windows feature that uses a communications aid interface device to allow keystrokes and mouse controls to be accepted through a computer's serial port.

Server

A computer that provides shared resources to network users.

Server Message Block (SMB)

A file-sharing protocol designed to allow networked computers to transparently access files that reside on remote systems over a variety of networks. The SMB protocol defines a series of commands that pass information between computers. SMB uses four message types: session control, file, printer, and message.

Service access point

A logical address that allows a system to route data between a remote device and the appropriate communications support.

Service Pack

A software upgrade to an existing software distribution that contains updated files consisting of patches and fixes.

Service Profile Identifier (SPID)

A 14-digit number that identifies a specific ISDN line. When establishing ISDN service, your telephone company assigns a SPID to your line.

See also *ISDN*.

Service provider

In TAPI, a dynamic link library (DLL) that provides an interface between an application requesting services and the controlling hardware device. TAPI supports two classes of service providers, media service providers and telephony service providers.

Session key

A key used primarily for encryption and decryption. Session keys are typically used with symmetric encryption algorithms where the same key is used for both encryption and decryption. For this reason, session and symmetric keys usually refer to the same type of key.

See also *symmetric key encryption*.

Sfmmon

A port monitor that is used to send jobs over the AppleTalk protocol to printers such as LaserWriters or those configured with AppleTalk or any AppleTalk spoolers.

Shared folder permissions

Permissions that restrict a shared resource's availability over the network to certain users.

See also *permission*.

Shiva Password Authentication Protocol (SPAP)

A two-way, reversible encryption mechanism for authenticating PPP connections employed by Shiva remote access servers.

Shortcut key navigation indicators

Underlined letters on a menu or control. (Also called access keys or quick-access letters.)

ShowSounds

A global flag that instructs programs to display captions for speech and system sounds to alert users with hearing impairments or people who work in a noisy location such as a factory floor.

Simple Mail Transfer Protocol (SMTP)

A protocol used on the Internet to transfer mail. SMTP is independent of the particular transmission subsystem and requires only a reliable, ordered, data stream channel.

Simple Network Management Protocol (SNMP)

A network management protocol installed with TCP/IP and widely used on TCP/IP and Internet Package Exchange (IPX) networks. SNMP transports management information and commands between a management program run by an administrator and the network management agent running on a host. The SNMP agent sends status information to one or more hosts when the host requests it or when a significant event occurs.

Single-switch device

An alternative input device, such as a voice activation program, that allows a user to scan or select using a single switch.

Slot

Storage locations for cartridges in a library managed by Removable Storage.

SlowKeys

A Windows feature that instructs the computer to disregard keystrokes that are not held down for a minimum period of time, which allows the user to brush against keys without any effect.

See also *FilterKeys*.

Small Computer System Interface (SCSI)

A standard high-speed parallel interface defined by the X3T9.2 committee of the American National Standards Institute (ANSI). A SCSI interface is used for connecting microcomputers to peripheral devices, such as hard disks and printers, and to other computers and local area networks.

Small Office/Home Office (SOHO)

An office with a few computers that can be considered a small business or part of a larger network.

Smart card

A credit card-sized device that is used with a PIN number to enable certificate-based authentication and single sign-on to the enterprise. Smart cards securely store certificates, public and private keys, passwords, and other types of personal information. A smart card reader attached to the computer reads the smart card.

See also *authentication*; *certificate*; *nonrepudiation*.

SNMP

See *Simple Network Management Protocol*.

Software trap

In programming, an event that occurs when a microprocessor detects a problem with executing an instruction, which causes it to stop.

SoundSentry

A Windows feature that produces a visual cue, such as a screen flash or a blinking title bar instead of system sounds.

Source directory

The folder that contains the file or files to be copied or moved.

See also *destination directory*.

SPAP

See *Shiva Password Authentication Protocol.*

Sparse file

A file that is handled in a way that requires less disk space than would otherwise be needed by allocating only meaningful non-zero data. Sparse support allows an application to create very large files without committing disk space for every byte.

Speech synthesizer

An assistive device that produces spoken words, either by splicing together prerecorded words or by programming the computer to produce the sounds that make up spoken words.

Stand-alone drive

An online drive that is not part of a library unit. Removable Storage treats stand-alone drives as online libraries with one drive and a port.

Status area

The area on the taskbar to the right of the taskbar buttons. The status area displays the time and can also contain icons that provide quick access to programs, such as Volume Control and Power Options. Other icons can appear temporarily, providing information about the status of activities. For example, the printer icon appears after a document has been sent to the printer and disappears when printing is complete.

StickyKeys

An accessibility feature built into Windows that causes modifier keys such as SHIFT, CTRL, WINDOWS LOGO, or ALT to stay on after they are pressed, eliminating the need to press multiple keys simultaneously. This feature facilitates the use of modifier keys for users who are unable to hold down one key while pressing another.

Stop error

A serious error that affects the operating system and that could place data at risk. The operating system generates an obvious message, a screen with the Stop message, rather than continuing on, and possibly corrupting data. Also known as a fatal system error.

See also *Stop message.*

Stop message

A character-based, full-screen error message displayed on a blue background. A Stop message indicates that the Windows 2000 kernel detected a condition from which it cannot recover. Each message is uniquely identified by a Stop error code (a hexadecimal number) and a string indicating the error's symbolic name. Stop messages are usually followed by up to four additional hexadecimal numbers, enclosed in parentheses, which identify developer-defined error parameters. A driver or device may be identified as the cause of the error. A series of troubleshooting tips are also displayed, along with an indication that, if the system was configured to do so, a memory dump file was saved for later use by a kernel debugger.

See also *Stop error*.

Streaming media servers

Software (such as Microsoft Media Technologies) that provides multimedia support, allowing you to deliver content by using Advanced Streaming Format over an intranet or the Internet.

Streams

A sequence of bits, bytes, or other small structurally uniform units.

Striped volume

A volume that stores data in stripes on two or more physical disks. Data in a striped volume is allocated alternately and evenly (in stripes) to these disks. Striped volumes offer the best performance of all volumes available in Windows 2000, but they do not provide fault tolerance. If a disk in a striped volume fails, the data in the entire volume is lost. You can create striped volumes only on dynamic disks. Striped volumes cannot be mirrored or extended. In Windows NT 4.0, a striped volume was known as a stripe set.

See also *dynamic disk*; *dynamic volume*; *fault tolerance*; *volume*.

Subkey

In the registry, a key within a key. Subkeys are analogous to subdirectories in the registry hierarchy. Keys and subkeys are similar to the section header in .ini files; however, subkeys can carry out functions.

See also *key*.

Subnet

A subdivision of an IP network. Each subnet has its own unique subnetted network ID.

Subnet mask

A 32-bit value expressed as four decimal numbers from 0 to 255, separated by periods (for example, 255.255.0.0). This number allows TCP/IP to determine the network ID portion of an IP address.

Subnet prioritization

The ordering of multiple IP address mappings from a DNS server so that the resolver orders local resource records first. This reduces network traffic across subnets by forcing computers to connect to network resources that are closer to them.

Subpicture

A data stream contained within a DVD. The Subpicture stream delivers the subtitles and any other add-on data, such as system help or director's comments, which can be displayed while playing multimedia.

Symmetric key

A single key that is used with symmetric encryption algorithms for both encryption and decryption.

See also *bulk encryption*; *encryption*; *decryption*; *session key*.

Symmetric key encryption

An encryption algorithm that requires the same secret key to be used for both encryption and decryption. This is often called secret key encryption. Because of its speed, symmetric encryption is typically used rather than public key encryption when a message sender needs to encrypt large amounts of data.

Synchronization Manager

In Windows 2000, the tool used to ensure that a file or directory on a client computer contains the same data as a matching file or directory on a server.

Syntax

The order in which a command must be typed and the elements that follow the command.

System access control list (SACL)

The part of an object's security descriptor that specifies which events are to be audited per user or group. Examples of auditing events are file access, logon attempts, and system shutdowns.

See also *access control entry*; *discretionary access control list*; *object*; *security descriptor*.

System administrator

A person that administers a computer system or network, including administering user accounts, security, storage space, and backing up data.

System files

Files that are used by Windows to load, configure, and run the operating system. Generally, system files must never be deleted or moved.

System media pool

A pool used to hold cartridges that are not in use. The free pool holds unused cartridges that are available to applications, and the unrecognized and import pools are temporary holding places for cartridges that have been newly placed in a library.

System policy

In network administration, the part of Group Policy that is concerned with the current user and local computer settings in the registry. In Windows 2000, system policy is sometimes called software policy and is one of several services provided by Group Policy, a Microsoft Management Console (MMC) snap-in. The Windows NT 4.0 System Policy Editor, Poledit.exe, is included with Windows 2000 for backward compatibility. That is, administrators need it to set system policy on Windows NT 4.0 and Windows 95 computers.

See also *Microsoft Management Console*; *registry*.

System Policy Editor

The utility Poledit.exe, used by administrators to set system policy on Windows NT 4.0 and Windows 95 computers.

System state data

A collection of system-specific data that can be backed up and restored. For all Windows 2000 operating systems, the System State data includes the registry, the class registration database, and the system boot files.

System volume

The volume that contains the hardware-specific files needed to load Windows 2000. The system volume can be (but does not have to be) the same volume as the boot volume.

See also *volume*.

Systemroot

The path and folder name where the Windows 2000 system files are located. Typically, this is C:\Winnt, although a different drive or folder can be designated when Windows 2000 is installed. The value %systemroot% can be used to replace the actual location of the folder that contains the Windows 2000 system files. To identify your systemroot folder, click Start, click Run, and then type %systemroot%.

T

Taskbar

The bar that contains the Start button and appears by default at the bottom of the desktop. You can use the taskbar buttons to switch between the programs you are running. The taskbar can be hidden, moved to the sides or top of the desktop, or customized in other ways.

See also *desktop*; *taskbar button*; *status area.*

Taskbar button

A button that appears on the taskbar when an application is running.

Tcpmon.ini

The file that specifies whether a device supports multiple ports. If the Tcpmon.ini file indicates that a device can support multiple ports, users a prompted to pick which port should be used during device installation.

Telephony API (TAPI)

An application programming interface (API) used by communications programs to communicate with telephony and network services.

See also *Internet Protocol.*

Terabyte

Approximately one trillion bytes, or one million million bytes.

Terminal Services

Software services that allow client applications to be run on a server so that client computers can function as terminals rather than independent systems. The server provides a multisession environment and runs the Windows-based programs being used on the clients.

See also *client.*

Thread

A type of object within a process that runs program instructions. Using multiple threads allows concurrent operations within a process and enables one process to run different parts of its program on different processors simultaneously. A thread has its own set of registers, its own kernel stack, a thread environment block, and a user stack in the address space of its process.

Thread state

A numeric value indicating the execution state of the thread. Numbered 0 through 5, the states seen most often are 1 for ready, 2 for running, and 5 for waiting.

Throughput

For disks, the transfer capacity of the disk system.

Time To Live (TTL)

A timer value included in packets sent over TCP/IP-based networks that tells the recipients how long to hold or use the packet or any of its included data before expiring and discarding the packet or data.

For DNS, TTL values are used in resource records within a zone to determine how long requesting clients should cache and use this information when it appears in a query response answered by a DNS server for the zone.

Timer bar

The colored bar that moves across the screen according to the frequency of the data-collection update interval.

ToggleKeys

A Windows feature that beeps when one of the locking keys (CAPS LOCK, NUM LOCK, or SCROLL LOCK) is turned on or off.

Token Ring

A type of network media that connects clients in a closed ring and uses token passing to allow clients to use the network.

See also *Fiber Distributed Data Interface*.

Total instance

A unique instance that contains the performance counters that represent the sum of all active instances of an object.

Transitive trust relationship

The trust relationship that inherently exists between Windows 2000 domains in a domain tree or forest, or between trees in a forest, or between forests. When a domain joins an existing forest or domain tree, a transitive trust is automatically established. In Windows 2000 transitive trusts are always two-way relationships.

See also *domain tree*; *forest*; *nontransitive trust relationship*.

Transmission Control Protocol / Internet Protocol (TCP/IP)

A set of software networking protocols widely used on the Internet that provide communications across interconnected networks of computers with diverse hardware architectures and operating systems. TCP/IP includes standards for how computers communicate and conventions for connecting networks and routing traffic.

Transmitting Station ID string (TSID)

A string that specifies the Transmitter Subscriber ID sent by the fax machine when sending a fax to a receiving machine. This string is usually a combination of the fax or telephone number and the name of the business. It is often the same as the Called Subscriber ID.

Transport Layer Security (TLS)

A standard protocol that is used to provide secure Web communications on the Internet or intranets. It enables clients to authenticate servers or, optionally, servers to authenticate clients. It also provides a secure channel by encrypting communications.

Transport protocol

A protocol that defines how data should be presented to the next receiving layer in the Windows NT and Windows 2000 networking model and packages the data accordingly. The transport protocol passes data to the network adapter driver through the network driver interface specification (NDIS) interface and to the redirector through the Transport Driver Interface (TDI).

TrueType fonts

Fonts that are scalable and sometimes generated as bitmaps or soft fonts, depending on the capabilities of your printer. TrueType fonts are device-independent fonts that are stored as outlines. They can be sized to any height, and they can be printed exactly as they appear on the screen.

See also *font*.

Trust relationship

A logical relationship established between domains that allows pass-through authentication in which a trusting domain honors the logon authentications of a trusted domain. User accounts and global groups defined in a trusted domain can be granted rights and permissions in a trusting domain, even though the user accounts or groups do not exist in the trusting domain's directory.

See also *authentication*; *domain*; *two-way trust relationship*.

Trusted forest

A forest that is connected to another forest by explicit or transitive trust.

See also *explicit trust relationship*; *forest*; *transitive trust relationship*.

TSID

See *Transmitting Station ID string*.

Tunnel

The logical path by which the encapsulated packets travel through the transit internetwork.

TWAIN

An acronym for Technology Without An Interesting Name. An industry-standard software protocol and API that provides easy integration of image data between input devices, such as scanners and still image digital cameras, and software applications.

Two-way trust relationship

A link between domains in which each domain trusts user accounts in the other domain to use its resources. Users can log on from computers in either domain to the domain that contains their account.

See also *trust relationship*.

Type 1 fonts

Scalable fonts designed to work with PostScript devices.

See also *font*; *PostScript*.

U

UART

See *Universal Asynchronous Receiver/Transmitter.*

Unallocated space

Available disk space that is not allocated to any partition, logical drive, or volume. The type of object created on unallocated space depends on the disk type (basic or dynamic). For basic disks, unallocated space outside partitions can be used to create primary or extended partitions. Free space inside an extended partition can be used to create a logical drive. For dynamic disks, unallocated space can be used to create dynamic volumes. Unlike basic disks, the exact disk region used is not selected to create the volume.

See also *basic disk*; *dynamic disk*; *extended partition*; *logical drive*; *partition*; *primary partition*; *volume.*

Unicode

A fixed-width, 16-bit character-encoding standard capable of representing the letters and characters of the majority of the world's languages. A consortium of U.S. computer companies developed Unicode.

UniDriver

The UniDriver (or Universal Print Driver) carries out requests (such as printing text, rendering bitmaps, or advancing a page) on most types of printers. The UniDriver accepts information from a printer specific minidriver and uses this information to complete tasks.

Uniform Resource Locator (URL)

An address that uniquely identifies a location on the Internet. A URL for a World Wide Web site is preceded with http://, as in the fictitious URL http://www.example.microsoft.com/. A URL can contain more detail, such as the name of a page of hypertext, usually identified by the file name extension .html or .htm.

See also *HTML*; *HTTP*; *IP address.*

Universal Asynchronous Receiver/Transmitter (UART)

An integrated circuit (silicon chip) that is commonly used in microcomputers to provide asynchronous communications. The UART does parallel-to-serial conversion of data to be transmitted and serial-to-parallel conversion of data received.

See also *asynchronous communication.*

Universal Disk Format (UDF)

A file system defined by the Optical Storage Technology Association (OSTA) that is the successor to the CD-ROM file system (CDFS). UDF is targeted for removable disk media like DVD, CD, and Magneto-Optical (MO) discs.

Universal group

A Windows 2000 group only available in native mode that is valid anywhere in the forest. A universal group appears in the Global Catalog but contains primarily global groups from domains in the forest. This is the simplest form of group and can contain other universal groups, global groups, and users from anywhere in the forest.

See also *domain local group*; *forest*; *Global Catalog*.

Universal Naming Convention (UNC)

A convention for naming files and other resources beginning with two backslashes (\), indicating that the resource exists on a network computer. UNC names conform to the \\SERVERNAME\SHARENAME syntax, where SERVERNAME is the server's name and SHARENAME is the name of the shared resource. The UNC name of a directory or file can also include the directory path after the share name, with the following syntax:
\\SERVERNAME\SHARENAME\DIRECTORY\FILENAME.

Universal Serial Bus (USB)

A serial bus with a bandwidth of 1.5 megabits per second (Mbps) for connecting peripherals to a microcomputer. USB can connect up to 127 peripherals, such as external CD-ROM drives, printers, modems, mice, and keyboards, to the system through a single, general-purpose port. This is accomplished by daisy chaining peripherals together. USB supports hot plugging and multiple data streams.

UNIX

A powerful, multi-user, multitasking operating system initially developed at AT&T Bell Laboratories in 1969 for use on minicomputers. UNIX is considered more portable—that is, less computer-specific—than other operating systems because it is written in C language. Newer versions of UNIX have been developed at the University of California at Berkeley and by AT&T.

Unrecognized pool

A repository for blank media and media that are not recognized by Removable Storage.

Upgrade

When referring to software, to update existing program files, folders, and registry entries to a more recent version. Upgrading, unlike performing a new installation, leaves existing settings and files in place.

URL

See *Uniform Resource Locator.*

USB

See *Universal Serial Bus.*

User account

A record that consists of all the information that defines a user to Windows 2000. This includes the user name and password required for the user to log on, the groups in which the user account has membership, and the rights and permissions the user has for using the computer and network and accessing their resources. For Windows 2000 Professional and member servers, user accounts are managed by using Local Users and Groups. For Windows 2000 Server domain controllers, user accounts are managed by using Microsoft Active Directory Users and Computers.

See also *domain controller*; *group*; *user name.*

User Identification (UID)

A user identifier that uniquely identifies a user. UNIX-bases systems use the UID to identify the owner of files and processes, and to determine access permissions.

User mode

The processing mode in which applications run.

User name

A unique name identifying a user account to Windows 2000. An account's user name must be unique among the other group names and user names within its own domain or workgroup.

User principal name (UPN)

A friendly name assigned to security principals (users and groups) that is shorter than the distinguished name and easier to remember. The default user principal name is composed of the security principal name for the user and the DNS name of the root domain where the user object resides. The user principal name is the preferred logon name for Windows 2000 users and is independent of the distinguished name, so a User object can be moved or renamed without affecting the user's logon name.

See also *distinguished name.*

User profile

A file that contains configuration information for a specific user, such as desktop settings, persistent network connections, and application settings. Each user's preferences are saved to a user profile that Windows NT and Windows 2000 use to configure the desktop each time a user logs on.

User rights

Tasks a user is permitted to perform on a computer system or domain. There are two types of user rights: privileges and logon rights. An example of a privilege is the right to shut down the system. An example of a logon right is the right to log on to a computer locally (at the keyboard). Administrators assign both types to individual users or groups as part of the security settings for the computer.

See also *permission*; *privilege.*

User rights policy

Security settings that manage the assignment of rights to groups and user accounts.

Utility Manager

A function of Windows 2000 that allows administrators to review the status of applications and tools and to customize features and add tools more easily.

V

Value bar

The area of the System Monitor graph or histogram display that shows last, average, minimum and maximum statistics for the selected counter.

Vector fonts

Fonts rendered from a mathematical model, in which each character is defined as a set of lines drawn between points. Vector fonts can be cleanly scaled to any size or aspect ratio.

Video for Windows (VfW)

A format developed by Microsoft for storing video and audio information. Files in this format have an .avi extension. AVI files are limited to 320 x 240 resolution at 30 frames per second, neither of which is adequate for full-screen, full-motion video.

Video Port Extensions (VPE)

A DirectDraw extension to support direct hardware connections from a video decoder and autoflipping in the graphics frame buffer. VPE allows the client to negotiate the connection between the MPEG or NTSC decoder and the video port. VPE also allows the client to control effects in the video stream, such as cropping, scaling, and so on.

Virtual Device Driver (VxD)

Software for Windows that manages a hardware or software system resource. The middle letter in the abbreviation indicates the type of device; x is used where the type of device is not under discussion.

Virtual memory

The space on the hard disk that Windows 2000 uses as memory. Because of virtual memory, the amount of memory taken from the perspective of a process can be much greater than the actual physical memory in the computer. The operating system does this in a way that is transparent to the application, by paging data that does not fit in physical memory to and from the disk at any given instant.

Virtual private network (VPN)

The extension of a private network that encompasses links across shared or public networks, such as the Internet.

Virus scanner

Software used to scan for and eradicate computer viruses, worms, and Trojan horses.

Volume

A portion of a physical disk that functions as though it were a physically separate disk. In My Computer and Windows Explorer, volumes appear as local disks, such as drive C or drive D.

Volume mount points

New system objects in the version of NTFS included with Windows 2000 that represent storage volumes in a persistent, robust manner. Volume mount points allow the operating system to graft the root of a volume onto a directory.

W

WDM Streaming class

The means by which Windows 2000 Professional supports digital video and audio. Enables support for such components as DVD decoders, MPEG decoders, video decoders, tuners, and audio codecs.

Wide area network (WAN)

A communications network connecting geographically separated computers, printers, and other devices. A WAN allows any connected device to interact with any other on the network.

See also *local area network.*

Windows 2000 Multilanguage Version

A version of Windows 2000 that extends the native language support in Windows 2000 by allowing user interface languages to be changed on a per user basis. This version also minimizes the number of language versions you need to deploy across the network.

Windows File Protection (WFP)

A Windows 2000 feature that runs in the background and protects your system files from being overwritten. When a file in a protected folder is modified, WFP determines if the new file is the correct Microsoft version or if the file is digitally signed. If not, the modified file is replaced with a valid version.

Windows Internet Name Service (WINS)

A software service that dynamically maps IP addresses to computer names (NetBIOS names). This allows users to access resources by name instead of requiring them to use IP addresses that are difficult to recognize and remember. WINS servers support clients running Windows NT 4.0 and earlier versions of Windows operating systems.

See also *Domain Name System.*

Windows Update

A Microsoft-owned Web site from which Windows 98 and Windows 2000 users can install or update device drivers. By using an ActiveX control, Windows Update compares the available drivers with those on the user's system and offers to install new or updated versions.

WINS

See *Windows Internet Name Service*.

Winsock

An application programming interface standard for software that provides TCP/IP interface under Windows. Short for Windows Sockets.

See also *TCP/IP*.

Work queue item

A job request of an existing library, made by an application that supports Removable Storage, which is placed in a queue and processed when the library resource becomes available.

Workgroup

A simple grouping of computers intended only to help users find such things as printers and shared folders within that group. Workgroups in Windows 2000 do not offer the centralized user accounts and authentication offered by domains.

Working set

For a process, the amount of physical memory assigned to a process by the operating system.

X

X.25

X.25 is a standard that defines the communications protocol for access to packet-switched networks.

X.400

What is an ISO and ITU standard for addressing and transporting e-mail messages. It conforms to layer 7 of the OSI model and supports several types of transport mechanisms, including Ethernet, X.25, TCP/IP, and dial-up lines.

X.500

The X.500 is the standard for defining a distributed directory service standard and was developed by the International Standards Organization (ISO). This ISO and ITU standard defines how global directories should be structured. X.500 directories are hierarchical, which means that they have different levels for each category of information, such as country, state, and city. X.500 supports X.400 systems.

X Window System

X Windows is a standard set of display-handling routines developed at MIT for UNIX workstations. These routines are used to create hardware-independent graphical user interfaces for UNIX systems.

Y

Ymodem

Ymodem is a variation of the Xmodem file transfer protocol that includes the following enhancements:

1. The ability to transfer information in 1-kilobyte (1,024-byte) blocks

2. The ability to send multiple files (batch file transmission)

3. Cyclical redundancy checking (CRC)

4. The ability to abort transfer by transmitting two CAN (cancel) characters in a row.

Z

ZIPI

A MIDI-like serial data format for musical instruments. ZIPI provides a hierarchical method for addressing instruments and uses an extensible command set.

Zero Wait State

The condition of random access memory (RAM) that is fast enough to respond to the processor without requiring a wait states.

Z axis (X axis)

Used in defining specific graphical display locations. The optical axis that is perpendicular to X and Y axes

Index

TotalRecall Gives You *Four* Levels of Computer Certification Practice Exams, Books, and eBooks

Study formats and prices vary so you can choose one that best fits your level of knowledge and skills.

Each format offers you either free or discounted access to our popular BeachFront Quizzer test engine. See description below.

ALL come with our exclusive Money-Back Guarantee—pass the exam your first time or get money back!

- **1. InsideScoop Certification Success Series**

Paperback books in the InsideScoop series offer a package of comprehensive study manual and CD-ROM of the BeachFront Quizzer test engine with answers/ explanations linked to relevant chapters in an integrated eBook. The study manual includes detailed information about each core exam topic with pre/post assessment quizzes; an abundance of figures, diagrams and photos; chapter summaries; helpful tips and time management techniques for test taking; lists of useful websites, articles and other learning resources; and an extensive glossary of 600 computer, IT, and telecommunications terms.

Books are $89.99

- **2. InsidersChoice Certification Success Series**

Paperback books in the InsidersChoice series offer a package of comprehensive study manual and FREE download of the BeachFront Quizzer test engine with answers/ explanations linked to relevant chapters in an integrated eBook. The study manual includes detailed information about each core exam topic with pre/post assessment quizzes; an abundance of figures, diagrams and photos; chapter summaries; helpful tips and time management techniques for test taking; lists of useful websites, articles and other learning resources; and an extensive glossary of 600 computer, IT, and telecommunications terms.

Paperbacks are $59.99 and eBooks are $44.99

3. ExamInsight IT Certification System Series

Paperback books and eBooks in the ExamInsight series offer a package of compact study guide and 50% discount to purchase a download of the BeachFront Quizzer test engine with answers/ explanations linked to relevant chapters in an integrated eBook. The study guide includes compact information about each core exam topic with pre/post assessment quizzes; an abundance of figures, diagrams and photos; chapter summaries; helpful tips and time management techniques for test taking; and lists of useful websites, articles and other learning resources

Paperbacks are $39.99 and eBooks are $29.99

- **4. ExamWise IT Question Book Series**

Paperback books and eBooks in the ExamWise series offer a package of Q&A workbook and 30-Day FREE access to a BeachFront Quizzer online practice exam. Each ExamWise Q&A workbook offers you approximately 300 practice questions organized by core exam topic. Questions are arranged in a unique format of two questions per right and page, with answers and brief explanations on the reverse page.

Paperbacks are $39.99 and eBooks are $29.99

The BeachFront Quizzer Test Engine Makes Passing Certification Exams as Easy as a Day at the Beach...

The BeachFront Quizzer test engine was pioneered in 1995 by Bruce Moran, an ex-NASA IT professional turned vocational computer instructor and certification trainer before launching his own book publishing operation in 2002. This popular test engine introduced interactive and adaptive features that other publishers have since tried to imitate, but never duplicate. It offers you four helpful study formats:

1) Adaptive technology generates 15-25 questions in 30-minute sessions to help you identify your strengths and weaknesses for each exam topic.

2) Study sessions help strengthen your weakest exam topics by generating up to 250 questions per topic until you can answer each correctly. Explanations for each question are linked to relevant chapters in an eBook study manual and often to web sites to help you develop a complete understanding of why an answer is correct. By focusing on your rough spots, we'll get you certified fast—guaranteed or get money back!

3) Simulated exams generate randomized questions about core exam topics in 60-90 minute sessions and then provide a score summary by topic. Taking multiple practice exams will build your confidence and ability to concentrate during the real deal!

4) Flash card drills present questions to answer mentally and then allow you to click F4 to display the correct answer.

Visit our web sites for more information:

www.TotalRecallPress.com / www.bfq.com

Total Recall

TotalRecall Certification Publications Microsoft

InsideScoop: TotalRecall's Complete Certification System Series:

InsideScoop to MCP / MCSE Certification: **Exam 70-210**
Managing Microsoft Windows 2000 Professional

InsideScoop to MCP / MCSE Certification: **Exam 70-216**
Implementing and Administering a Microsoft Windows 2000 Network Infrastructure

InsideScoop to MCP / MCSE Certification: **Exam 70-217**
Managing a Microsoft Directory Services Infrastructure

InsideScoop to MCP / MCSE Certification: **Exam 70-219**
Designing a Windows 2000 Directory Services Infrastructure

InsideScoop to MCP / MCSE Certification: **Exam 70-220**
Designing Security for a Microsoft Windows 2000 Network

InsideScoop to MCP / MCSE Certification: **Exam 70-221**
Designing a Microsoft Windows 2000 Network Infrastructure

InsideScoop to MCP / MCSE Certification: **Exam 70-227**
Installing, Configuring, and Administering Microsoft Internet Security and Acceleration (ISA) Server 2000, Enterprise Edition

InsideScoop to MCP / MCSE Certification: **Exam 70-270**
Installing, Configuring, and Administering Microsoft Windows XP Professional

InsideScoop to MCP / MCSE Certification: **Exam 70-290**
Managing and Maintaining a Microsoft Windows Server 2003 Environment

InsideScoop to MCP / MCSE Certification: **Exam 70-291**
Managing, and Maintaining a Microsoft Windows Server 2003 Network Infrastructure

InsideScoop to MCP / MCSE Certification: **Exam 70-292**
Managing and Maintaining a Microsoft Windows Server 2003 Environment for an MCSA Certified on Windows 2000

InsideScoop to MCP / MCSE Certification: **Exam 70-293**
Planning and Maintaining a Microsoft Windows Server 2003 Network Infrastructure

InsideScoop to MCP / MCSE Certification: **Exam 70-294**
Plan and Maintain a Microsoft Windows Server 2003 Active Directory Infrastructure

InsideScoop to MCP / MCSE Certification: **Exam 70-296**
Planning, Implementing, and Maintaining a Microsoft Windows Server 2003 Environment for an MCSE Certified on Windows

InsideScoop to MCP / MCSE Certification: **Exam 70-297**
Designing Microsoft Windows Server 2003 Active Directory and Network Infrastructure

InsideScoop to MCP / MCSE Certification: **Exam 70-298**
Designing Security for a Microsoft Server 2003 Network

InsideScoop to MCP / MCSE Certification: **Exam 70-299**
Implementing and Administering Security in a Microsoft Windows Server 2003 Network

ExamInsight: TotalRecall IT Insight Certification Book Series:

ExamInsight For MCP / MCSE Certification: **Exam 70-210**
Managing Microsoft Windows 2000 Professional

ExamInsight For MCP / MCSE Certification: **Exam 70-216**
Implementing and Administering a Microsoft Windows 2000 Network Infrastructure

ExamInsight For MCP / MCSE Certification: **Exam 70-217**
Managing a Microsoft Directory Services Infrastructure

ExamInsight For MCP / MCSE Certification: **Exam 70-219**
Designing a Windows 2000 Directory Services Infrastructure

ExamInsight For MCP / MCSE Certification: **Exam 70-220**
Designing Security for a Microsoft Windows 2000 Network

ExamInsight For MCP / MCSE Certification: **Exam 70-221**
Designing a Microsoft Windows 2000 Network Infrastructure

ExamInsight For MCP / MCSE Certification: **Exam 70-227**
Installing, Configuring, and Administering Microsoft Internet Security and Acceleration (ISA) Server 2000, Enterprise Edition

ExamInsight For MCP / MCSE Certification: **Exam 70-270**
Installing, Configuring, and Administering Microsoft Windows XP Professional

ExamInsight For MCP / MCSE Certification: **Exam 70-290**
Managing and Maintaining a Microsoft Windows Server 2003 Environment

ExamInsight For MCP / MCSE Certification: **Exam 70-291**
Managing, and Maintaining a Microsoft Windows Server 2003 Network Infrastructure

ExamInsight For MCP / MCSE Certification: **Exam 70-292**
Managing and Maintaining a Microsoft Windows Server 2003 Environment for an MCSA Certified on Windows 2000

ExamInsight For MCP / MCSE Certification: **Exam 70-293**
Planning and Maintaining a Microsoft Windows Server 2003 Network Infrastructure

ExamInsight For MCP / MCSE Certification: **Exam 70-294**
Plan and Maintain a Microsoft Windows Server 2003 Active Directory Infrastructure

ExamInsight For MCP / MCSE Certification: **Exam 70-296**
Planning, Implementing, and Maintaining a Microsoft Windows Server 2003 Environment for an MCSE Certified on Windows

ExamInsight For MCP / MCSE Certification: **Exam 70-297**
Designing Microsoft Windows Server 2003 Active Directory and Network Infrastructure

ExamInsight For MCP / MCSE Certification: **Exam 70-298**
Designing Security for a Microsoft Server 2003 Network:

ExamInsight For MCP / MCSE Certification: **Exam 70-299**
Implementing and Administering Security in a Microsoft Windows Server 2003 Network

InsidersChoice: TotalRecall's Insiders Certification System Series:

InsidersChoice to MCP / MCSE Certification: Exam 70-270
Installing, Configuring, and Administering Microsoft Windows XP Professional

InsidersChoice to MCP / MCSE Certification: Exam 70-290
Managing and Maintaining a Microsoft Windows Server 2003 Environment

InsidersChoice to MCP / MCSE Certification: Exam 70-291
Managing, and Maintaining a Microsoft Windows Server 2003 Network Infrastructure

InsidersChoice to MCP / MCSE Certification: Exam 70-292
Managing and Maintaining a Microsoft Windows Server 2003
Environment for an MCSA Certified on Windows 2000

InsidersChoice to MCP / MCSE Certification: Exam 70-293
Planning and Maintaining a Microsoft Windows Server 2003 Network Infrastructure

InsidersChoice to MCP / MCSE Certification: Exam 70-294
Plan and Maintain a Microsoft Windows Server 2003 Active Directory Infrastructure

InsidersChoice to MCP / MCSE Certification: Exam 70-296
Planning, Implementing, and Maintaining a Microsoft Windows Server 2003
Environment for an MCSE Certified on Windows

InsidersChoice to MCP / MCSE Certification: Exam 70-297
Designing Microsoft Windows Server 2003 Active Directory and Network Infrastructure

InsidersChoice to MCP / MCSE Certification: Exam 70-298
Designing Security for a Microsoft Server 2003 Network

InsidersChoice to MCP / MCSE Certification: Exam 70-299
Implementing and Administering Security in a Microsoft Windows Server 2003 Network

ExamWise: TotalRecall IT Insight Certification Book Series:

ExamWise For MCP / MCSE Certification: **Exam 70-210**
Managing Microsoft Windows 2000 Professional

ExamWise For MCP / MCSE Certification: **Exam 70-216**
Implementing and Administering a Microsoft Windows 2000 Network Infrastructure

ExamWise For MCP / MCSE Certification: **Exam 70-217**
Managing a Microsoft Directory Services Infrastructure

ExamWise For MCP / MCSE Certification: **Exam 70-219**
Designing a Windows 2000 Directory Services Infrastructure

ExamWise For MCP / MCSE Certification: **Exam 70-220**
Designing Security for a Microsoft Windows 2000 Network

ExamWise For MCP / MCSE Certification: **Exam 70-221**
Designing a Microsoft Windows 2000 Network Infrastructure

ExamWise For MCP / MCSE Certification: **Exam 70-227**
Installing, Configuring, and Administering Microsoft Internet Security and Acceleration (ISA) Server 2000, Enterprise Edition

ExamWise For MCP / MCSE Certification: **Exam 70-270**
Installing, Configuring, and Administering Microsoft Windows XP Professional

ExamWise For MCP / MCSE Certification: **Exam 70-290**
Managing and Maintaining a Microsoft Windows Server 2003 Environment

ExamWise For MCP / MCSE Certification: **Exam 70-291**
Managing, and Maintaining a Microsoft Windows Server 2003 Network Infrastructure

ExamWise For MCP / MCSE Certification: **Exam 70-292**
Managing and Maintaining a Microsoft Windows Server 2003 Environment for an MCSA Certified on Windows 2000

ExamWise For MCP / MCSE Certification: **Exam 70-293**
Planning and Maintaining a Microsoft Windows Server 2003 Network Infrastructure

ExamWise For MCP / MCSE Certification: **Exam 70-294**
Plan and Maintain a Microsoft Windows Server 2003 Active Directory Infrastructure

ExamWise For MCP / MCSE Certification: **Exam 70-296**
Planning, Implementing, and Maintaining a Microsoft Windows Server 2003 Environment for an MCSE Certified on Windows

ExamWise For MCP / MCSE Certification: **Exam 70-297**
Designing Microsoft Windows Server 2003 Active Directory and Network Infrastructure

ExamWise For MCP / MCSE Certification: **Exam 70-298**
Designing Security for a Microsoft Server 2003 Network

ExamWise For MCP / MCSE Certification: **Exam 70-299**
Implementing and Administering Security in a Microsoft Windows Server 2003 Network

TotalRecall Certification Publications

CompTIA Titles

InsideScoop: TotalRecall's Complete Certification System Series:

InsideScoop to CompTIA A+ Hardware:	**Exam 220-301**
InsideScoop to CompTIA A+ OS:	**Exam 220-302**
InsideScoop to CompTIA Network+:	**Exam N10-001**
InsideScoop to CompTIA Security+ (Second Edition):	**Exam SY0-101**

InsidersChoice: TotalRecall IT Insight Certification Book Series:

InsidersChoice to CompTIA A+ Hardware:	**Exam 220-301**
InsidersChoice to CompTIA A+ OS:	**Exam 220-302**
InsidersChoice to CompTIA Network+:	**Exam N10-001**
InsidersChoice to CompTIA Security+: (Second Edition):	**Exam SY0-001**

ExamInsight: TotalRecall IT Insight Certification Book Series:

ExamInsight For CompTIA A+ Hardware:	**Exam 220-301**
ExamInsight For CompTIA A+ OS:	**Exam 220-302**
ExamInsight For CompTIA Network+:	**Exam N10-001**
ExamInsight For CompTIA Security+: (Second Edition):	**Exam SY0-001**

ExamWise: The TotalRecall Question Book Series:

ExamWise For CompTIA A+ Hardware:	**Exam 220-301**
ExamWise For CompTIA A+ OS:	**Exam 220-302**
ExamWise For CompTIA Network+:	**Exam N10-001**
ExamWise For CompTIA Security+ (Second Edition):	**Exam SY0-101**
ExamWise For CompTIA I-Net+ Certification:	**Exam IK0-002**
ExamWise For CompTIA Server+ Certification:	**Exam SK0-001**

Money Back Book Guarantee

This guarantee applies only to books published by TotalRecall Publications, Inc.! We are so confident in our products that we are prepared to offer the following guarantee to YOU, our valued customer: If you do not pass your certification exam after two attempts, we will give money back!

Visit http://www.totalrecallpress.com/

Select "Money Back Book Guarantee" for details.

Registered book purchasers who qualify will receive:

1. 50% cash refund of purchase price
2. free TotalRecall book of equal value

NOTE: You must pay for shipping and handling.

To qualify for this TotalRecall Guarantee

you must meet these requirements and perform the following tasks:

1. Register your purchase at the TotalRecall web site
   http://www.totalrecallpress.com/
2. Fail the corresponding exam twice (No time Limit)
3. Contact TotalRecall for the RMA # and to claim this guarantee
   Send email to **mailto:Guarantee@totalrecallpress.com**
   Subject must contain your Membership # or Registration #

Ship the following to claim your refund:

1. RMA # from returned email
2. Documents of exam scores for both failed attempts
3. Return the Book to the following address:

TotalRecall Publications, Inc.

Attn: Corby Tate

1103 Middlecreek

Friendswood, TX 77546

888-992-3131 **bfquiz@swbell.net**

281-992-3131

281-482-5390 Fax http://www.bfq.com/ or http://www.bfqd.com

It's a Passing day here at the BeachFront.

Thank you for using the TotalRecall Certification Success Program.

Bruce Moran, President

Total Recall

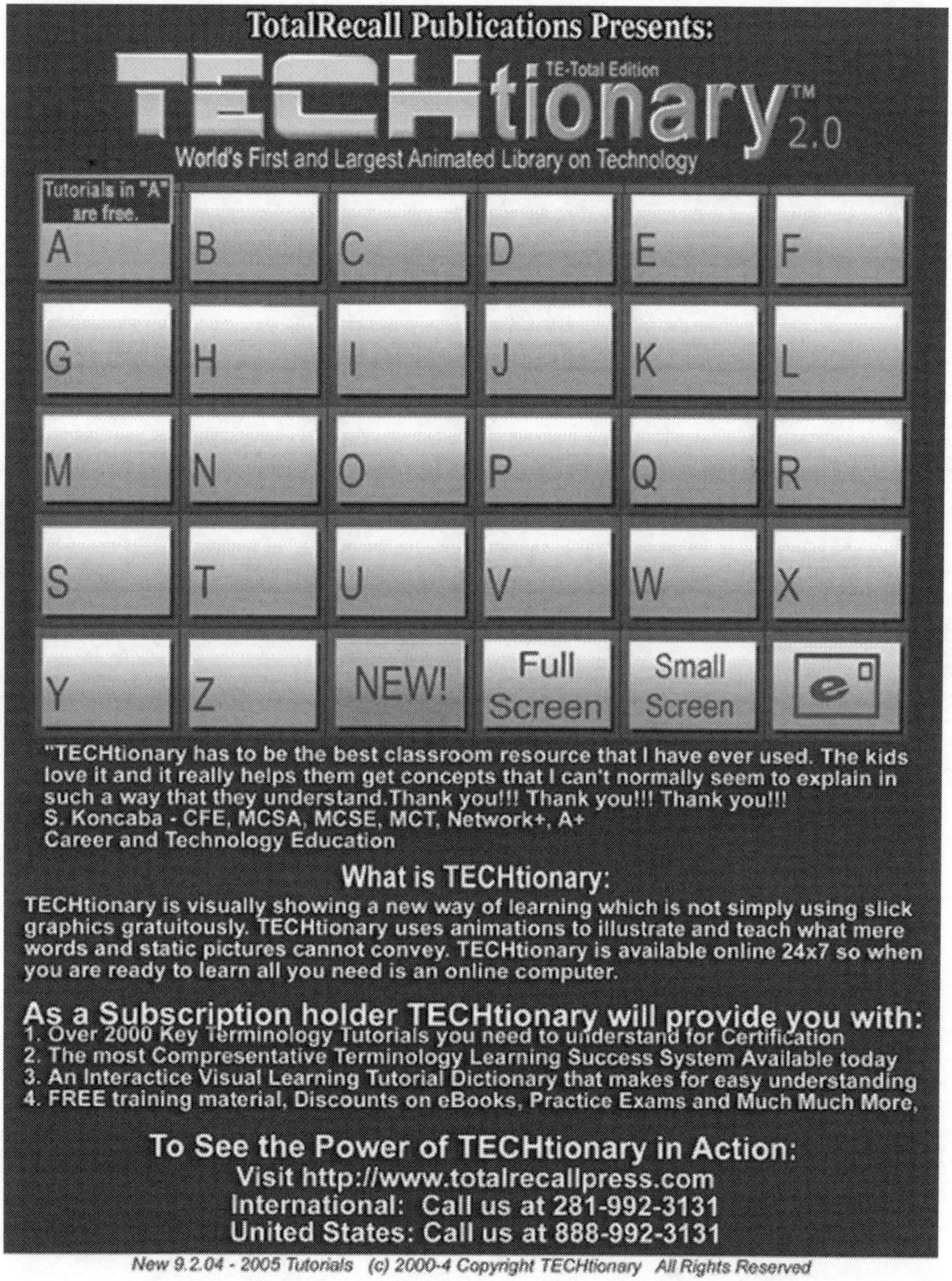
TotalRecall Publications Presents:
TECHtionary™ 2.0
TE-Total Edition
World's First and Largest Animated Library on Technology
Tutorials in "A" are free.
A B C D E F
G H I J K L
M N O P Q R
S T U V W X
Y Z NEW! Full Screen Small Screen
"TECHtionary has to be the best classroom resource that I have ever used. The kids love it and it really helps them get concepts that I can't normally seem to explain in such a way that they understand.Thank you!!! Thank you!!! Thank you!!!
S. Koncaba - CFE, MCSA, MCSE, MCT, Network+, A+
Career and Technology Education
What is TECHtionary:
TECHtionary is visually showing a new way of learning which is not simply using slick graphics gratuitously. TECHtionary uses animations to illustrate and teach what mere words and static pictures cannot convey. TECHtionary is available online 24x7 so when you are ready to learn all you need is an online computer.
As a Subscription holder TECHtionary will provide you with:
1. Over 2000 Key Terminology Tutorials you need to understand for Certification
2. The most Compresentative Terminology Learning Success System Available today
3. An Interactice Visual Learning Tutorial Dictionary that makes for easy understanding
4. FREE training material, Discounts on eBooks, Practice Exams and Much Much More,
To See the Power of TECHtionary in Action:
Visit http://www.totalrecallpress.com
International: Call us at 281-992-3131
United States: Call us at 888-992-3131

70-293 Download Instructions

BeachFront Quizzer (BFQ) version 4.0 Special Edition

System Requirements: Windows 95 & 98, Windows NT, XP Windows 2000 and Server 2003 with a minimum of 6 MB hard disk space and 16 MB RAM

The Center For Technology Certification, Inc. will help you accomplish your Microsoft Certifications. This state of art software program is designed to cut your study time in half, and get you to a passing level in the easiest and shortest amount of time possible. The program will adapt to you personally, and then lay out a prioritized study plan that will visually show you your progress on a day to day basis. When the software has recognized that you are at a passing level in each objective category, you're ready to sit for the exam! It's really that easy!!

Installation Instructions: 70-293 Practice Exam with eBook

1. Visit http://www.bfq.com/download.php Download and Install the latest version of the BFQ Engine: File Name Quiz32.exe

2. Visit to **http://snipurl.com/MS70293** and download the practice exam ZIP file to a folder on your hard drive.

This will install all software files:

3. Open the LicenseKey.txt file Copy and Insert the 12 digit number **License Key** when requested or type in the following License Key Numbers when requested.

TRP 70-293 Windows Server 2003 Environment = 383256707474

The software is very user friendly.

After you get the program installed Open Click on the Help button menu
Select contents for the on-screen manual. (You may want to print the Help File)
You will follow a six step process that will lead you through the program efficiently.
We are here to support you all the way. If you have any technical questions on the content, make sure you contact us. We are very proud of our pass rate, and we want you to contribute.

If you need additional assistance, visit our website www.totalrecallpress.com
Please let me know that the download and installation worked properly.
Thank you for purchasing our product and
Good Luck with your exam!

Sales:

877-654-2265

727-517-3694

Technical Support: info@bfq.com

888-992-3131 or 281-992-3131

Fax 281-482-5390

Made in the USA
Monee, IL
08 November 2026

68055339R00258